Oldenbarnevelt

VOLUME 1

Johan van Oldenbarnevelt, engraving by Hondius

Oldenbarnevelt

by Jan den Tex

1

1547–1606

CAMBRIDGE

At the University Press

1973

Published by the Syndics of the Cambridge University Press
Bentley House, 200 Euston Road, London NW1 2DB
American Branch: 32 East 57th Street, New York, N.Y.10022

This version and translation © Cambridge University Press 1973
Translated from the Dutch by R. B. Powell with the aid of a grant
from the Prince Bernhard Fund
Dutch Edition: *Oldenbarnevelt* vols. I–V published by H.D. Tjeenk Willink
& Zoon, Haarlem/Groningen, Holland (1960–1972)
In 1971 Tjeenk Willink & Zoon amalgamated with Wolters–Noordhoff, Groningen

Library of Congress Catalogue Card Number: 73-177937

ISBNS: vol 1 0 521 08427 X
vol 2 0 521 08428 8
set 0 521 08429 6

Printed in Great Britain
at the University Printing House, Cambridge
(Brooke Crutchley, University Printer)

Contents

Acknowledgments

Plate 1, vol. 1, is reproduced by gracious permission of Her Majesty the Queen of the Netherlands.

The author and publisher are also grateful to the following for granting permission to reproduce material in their possession:

to the Rijksprentenkabinet, Amsterdam, for the frontispieces to both volumes and for plate 4, vol. 1; to the Oudheidk. Vereniging, 'Flehite', Amersfoort, for plate 2, vol. 1; to the National Portrait Gallery, for plate 3, vol. 1 and for plates 2 and 11, vol. 2; to the Right Hon. the Lord Sackville for plates 5 and 6, vol. 1; to the Rijksmuseum, Amsterdam, for plate 7, vol. 1 and plates 1, 7 and 12, vol. 2; to The Trustees of the British Museum for plate 8, vol. 1; to Mr Hugh Paget and to the Dienst voor Schone Kunsten der Gemeente, The Hague, for plate 9, vol. 1; to the Konographisch Bureau, The Hague, for plate 10, vol. 1 and plate 8, vol. 2; to the Koninklijk Penning-kabinet, The Hague, for plate 4, vol. 2; to his Grace the Duke of Buccleuch for plate 5, vol. 2; to the Archives Générales du Royaume, Brussels, for plate 6, vol. 2; to the Mauritshuis, The Hague, for plate 9, vol. 2; and to the Remonstrantse Gemeente of Amsterdam and to the Rijksmuseum for plate 10, vol. 2.

Plates

PLATES

between pages 486 *and* 487 *(cont.)*

Old and New Style dating

Some letters from the early part of the period of this book were dated in accordance with the Paschal system: i.e. the dates between 1 January and Easter came under the previous calendar years. In such cases the date has been altered to that of the current year.

In October 1582, the Gregorian Calendar was introduced into the Catholic countries, and also into Holland and Zeeland. This was ten days ahead of the Julian Calendar, which was still used in England, Scotland, and the other provinces of the Northern Netherlands until 1700. In this book the Gregorian style has been used for events occurring, or letters dated, after 1582 in the former territories except in letters written by English ambassadors in The Hague. These were usually dated in the Julian style and therefore, in this book, they have been given both Old Style and New Style dating. Events in the other provinces of the Northern Netherlands have usually been dated according to the Gregorian Calendar: events in England and Scotland have generally been dated in the Julian style.

Glossary

Advocaat-fiscaal: Public Prosecutor

Alteratie: the local revolution which in 1578 replaced the Catholic town government in Amsterdam by a Protestant one

brandschat: a tax extorted under the threat of burning down property

capitulatie: (in this book) conditions under which sovereignty is vested in a prince

classis: in the reformed church, a body comprising several parishes, out of which a synod is chosen

Eerste Edele: Premier Nobleman (esp. in Zeeland)

fiscaal: abbreviation of *Advocaat-fiscaal*

Gasthuiskerk: one of the churches of The Hague attached to a hospital (*gasthuis*)

Gecommitteerde Raden: a relatively small committee chosen by the States to conduct current affairs during a recess

Hofkapel: Court Chapel; originally the private church of the Counts of Holland

Hof van Holland: the bi-provincial Court of Justice for Holland and Zeeland

Hoge Raad (lit. 'High Council'): a Court of Justice for Holland and Zeeland judging concurrently with, and sometimes hearing appeals from, the Hof van Holland

landvoogdes(sen): woman regent, women regents

licenten: documents allowing goods to be imported or exported; also the dues paid for obtaining these documents

lorrendraaier: smuggler

raadpensionaris (lit. 'Counsellor-pensionary'): the new name for Oldenbarnevelt's successors when the title of 'Advocate of Holland' had fallen into disrepute

Religionsfridt (German): religious peace allowing coexistence of two or more religions

Ridderzaal: the Knights' Hall of the old Castle of the Counts of Holland where the solemn opening of the States-General takes place every year in September

ruggespraak: consultation of principals by their deputies (expressly forbidden in the present Dutch constitution) *schout:* permanent head of the police and of the local judiciary appointed by the *stadtholder*

schepenen: sheriffs; yearly elected assessors sitting with the *schout* in local courts of justice

secreet besoigne: a small committee for foreign affairs

slijkgeuzen: 'Mud Beggars', a term of abuse for the staunch Calvinists ('Geuzen'), who waded through the mud on Sundays to attend an orthodox church service in a neighbouring village

straatvaart: passage to the Mediterranean through the Straits of Gibraltar

vroedschap: (approximately) town council

waardgelder: paid soldier in the service of a town or province

EAST
Emden
Leer(ort)
FRIESLAND

Delfzijl
GRONINGEN

Groningen

R. Ems

Leeuwarden
Franeker
FRIESLAND

DRENTE

Sneek

Texel
Steenwijk

Lingen

Koevorden

BENTHEIM

Vollenhove
Hasselt

Ootmarsum
Bentheim

Kampen
*Medemblik
Schagen   Zwolle
*Hoorn   *Enkhuizen   Raalte   Oldenzaal
Avenhorn   Hattem
*Alkmaar   ZUIDERZEE   Elburg   OVERIJSEL   Enschede
*Purmerend *Edam   Deventer
                                    Lochem
*Monnikendam   Harderwijk   Zutfen   Groenlo
Muiden   Nijkerk   Vorden
*Haarlem   Zelhem   Bredevoort
*Amsterdam Naarden   GELDERLAND Doesburg
Hilversum   Amersfoort   Doetinchem
        Gunterstein   Arnhem   Schenkenschans
HOLLAND Woerden Utrecht Wageningen
        Oudewater   UTRECHT Rhenen Nijmegen Emmerich
The Hague *Leiden   Vianen Opheusden Cleves
Rijswijk *Gouda R. Lek Schoonhoven R. Waal Mook CLEVES R. Rhine
*Delft Zoetermeer Bommel   Gelder(n)
Delfshaven *Gorinchem   R. Maas Grave Rheinberg
*Schiedam *Rotterdam St Andries
*Brill   *Dordrecht s-Hertogenbosch SPANISH
        Heusden   Venlo
                             GELDERLAND
        Geertruidenberg   JÜLICH
ZEELAND Willemstad Breda   Roermond
Zierikzee Steenbergen
        Tholen Wouw   Jülich
Walcheren Veere Bergen-op-Zoom Turnhout
Middelburg Goes Kruiningen
Flushing Rammekens Lillo
R. Scheldt Terneuzen Antwerp   Maastricht
        Hulst
Sluis IJzendijke Axel   Mechelen
Aardenburg Sas-van-Gent Rijmenam Tongeren LIMBURG
Blankenberghe Ghent R. Scheldt Vilvoorde
Bruges   Aalst Leuven   Liege
Ostend   Brussels
Nieuwpoort   Spa
FLANDERS   Huy
                    NAMUR
Ypres   Namur
Courtrai
Tournai   Mons
        HAINAULT

NORTH SEA
BRABANT
R. Lys

0   40 km
0   20 miles

Map of the Netherlands during the time of Oldenbarnevelt

CHAPTER 1

A statesman in the making

BY the middle of the sixteenth century seventeen Netherland provinces – all except Liége – had come into the possession of Charles V. He was Emperor of Germany by election, King of Spain by succession on his mother's side, on his father's side Lord of the Burgundian part of the Netherlands, that is to say present-day Belgium together with Holland and Zeeland to the north. In the course of his reign, begun in 1515, the remaining provinces of the North Netherlands were added by conquest to his possessions: Friesland and Groningen in 1524, Utrecht and Overijsel in 1528, and finally Gelderland in 1543.

In 1547, the future founder of the Netherlands Republic, Johan van Oldenbarnevelt, was born at Amersfoort, the second town of the former bishopric of Utrecht, frontier guard against enemies in Gelderland. He grew up there in a tradition of distrust towards the Burgundian and later the Austrian rulers. Amersfoort had been captured in 1543 by Gelderlanders, in a last convulsive military effort, in which the local authorities were suspected of having assisted. When it was recaptured in the same year the Austrian Stadtholder, Prince René of Orange, had curtailed the municipal privileges, including the town's right to elect its own town council. Little Johan was descended from families who had been sitting on the *vroedschap* for generations and were now turned out of it. His mother's family, the Weedes, had taken an active part in the struggle against the Utrecht bishops and their alliance with Burgundy. So the whole atmosphere in Amersfoort in general and in the Oldenbarnevelt home in particular was one of dubious loyalty to the Emperor Charles V and, when he abdicated in 1555, to his son, Philip II.

Nor was religious feeling as strictly Roman Catholic as the Emperor, and particularly Philip, could wish. The town in general was not indeed Protestant, but its Catholicism had a devotional and ethical rather than a dogmatic character.

Such were Oldenbarnevelt's surroundings until he was sixteen. He went to the Latin school at Amersfoort with the children of farmers, brewers and the rest of the middle class. Then he left for The Hague to be the pupil of a lawyer whose name is unknown.

It was not unusual in the sixteenth century for young men of fairly prosperous families, such as the Oldenbarnevelts, to leave home early on a tour of the universities at home and abroad. We can only surmise why Johan left home with another object in view, earning money. There are reasons to suppose that his father, who never took the family place on the Amersfoort council, was something of a psychopath. Perhaps the domestic atmosphere was one which the eldest son was glad to leave as soon as possible.

In The Hague he entered into quite different surroundings, almost another world. All his life Oldenbarnevelt felt himself to be primarily a 'Stichtenaar', a native of the 'sticht' or bishopric of Utrecht, and only gradually a Netherlander (*Nederlander*, a word that came into use during his lifetime) as well. In his youth people spoke of 'the country on this side', *les pays de par deçà*, as distinct from the Austrian dynasty's other hereditary lands. The spark of national feeling which did exist had a dynastic colouring, and, as we have seen, affection for the dynasty was not strong in Amersfoort. In The Hague, however, where he was to spend most of his life, a new provincial concept was growing: identified with Holland's interests, which he was called on to defend at assemblies, he felt himself to be a Hollander by adoption, and within Holland first a citizen of Delft, then of Rotterdam, finally of The Hague. In the centre of the Netherlands and in Brussels, French was spoken in government circles, as well as in the principal southern provinces: Artois, Hainault, Namur, Tournai: the Stichtenaar felt an absolute foreigner there and a partial one in Flanders and Brabant.

The Hague, though an unfortified village with a small population, was in some respects the most important place in Holland, as it was the seat of the government. In the absence of the sovereign, who had been in Spain for five years, of the Governor-General (or Regent), King Philip's half-sister, who lived in Brussels, and of the royal *stadtholder*, Prince William of Orange, who lived alternately in Brussels and Breda, the Hof van Holland formed the government, functioning at the same time as court of appeal in criminal and civil cases. Johan's employer was registered as a lawyer entitled to plead before this court. The young man thus associated mainly with councillors and their clerks, lawyers and their pupils, and this was to leave its mark on the future Advocate of Holland.

As a governing body, the Court dealt with any business not weighty enough to be referred to Brussels, and had the important right of summoning the States when it considered that necessary. Actually, this was an anachronism. At this time, before the revolt, the 'States' comprised the Estates of the Realm: the clergy having been eliminated early in Holland, these were the nobles and commons of the six large towns, Dordrecht, Haarlem, Delft, Leiden,

Amsterdam and Gouda, in that order of seniority. On special occasions the commons could be supplemented by 'convening' certain other towns at the court's discretion. The States in this sense could not meet but only send delegates, who in the following decades themselves assumed the name of 'States'. In the years of Spanish domination these meetings were convened only when the King needed money, as he could not impose, still less collect, taxes without the approval of the nobles and the towns. The nobles, who together had one vote, 'represented' the rural districts, the six large towns the lesser ones. In theory the King, in his capacity as Count of Holland, had absolute power in everything but financial matters. In practice the nobles and the towns had a great deal to say, since they could attach conditions to their consent to proposed taxation. Their position was especially strong with a sovereign like Charles V, who was constantly waging war and having to tap the States for money. For convenience the Governor often asked the States of the various provinces to send their delegates not to the provincial capital but to Brussels. This combined assembly was called the 'States-General', but had little or no influence, as it could do nothing except listen to the proposals of the Governor-General or her counsellors and, on coming back after a due interval, produce the written acquiescence (*consenten*) of the provinces they represented, and negotiate the conditions attached, while each also appeared in Brussels on its own behalf and bargained for advantages.

After Philip II had put an end to his war with France in 1559 he needed far less money than his father had, and was thus much less dependent on the provincial States, with the result that the States-General ceased to be summoned.

An important feature of the relations between sovereign and States was the royal privilege granted in exchange for services rendered. They might be of any kind: a charter for independent election of a town council, a trade monopoly or staple right, or a promise not to appoint any government servants born outside the country. One important privilege that nearly all provinces enjoyed was the *privilegium de non evocando*: the towns' right to bring their citizens to trial before their own sheriffs, except in cases of high treason.

At the time that Johan came to The Hague, this particular privilege was the subject of dispute between the Hof van Holland (supported by the Stadt-holder and public opinion) and the central government. The immediate point at issue was the prosecution of heretics which had been introduced under Charles V in the form of an episcopal inquisition. Philip II, surpassing his father in intolerance, had intensified this inquisition and thus, according to

3

many good Catholics, violated the *privilegium de non evocando*, since the suspects were removed from the jurisdiction of the local sheriffs and 'evoked' to the bishop's place of office. If found guilty they were handed over to the temporal power, again not that of sheriffs or the Hof van Holland, but a subservient royal court.

There was therefore loyalty to the King, and by and large to the faith in The Hague, but without enthusiasm; rather with typical Dutch hardheadedness. At the same time people were keen on their privileges and the financial advantages often assured by them.

Nevertheless there was something to be said for the King's point of view, apart from its repellent intolerance. However desirable respect for privileges might be in theory, in reality and in practice they did not all deserve it. The mere idea of variance in privileges among the different towns and provinces involved many seemingly needless complications, which impeded, not to say frustrated, the development of the Netherlands into the uniform state which should have been the aim of any progressive Burgundian statesman. The privileges hindered the development of the general Audit Office and the Grand Council at Malines, and prevented the implementation of the important reform of the penal code introduced by Charles V in Germany in 1532, and any advance in the efficiency and promptness in the administration of justice. With finance it was no different: the inequality of the collection of taxes and the lack of flexibility in the quota system made any fiscal equality or rapid levies impossible. The officials were constantly increasing in numbers but could only follow their careers in their own provinces; after years of passive resistance the Governor-General had been obliged to consent, in 1555, to a privilege against the appointment of 'foreigners', or people from provinces other than Holland, Zeeland and Utrecht, to office in one of these provinces.

This situation was intolerable for the lawyers at Brussels, trained in Roman law, and in Charles V's last years it was already predictable that this chronic dispute over the privileges would lead to an acute conflict in quieter times: just as from 1603 to 1609 it was the war abroad which prevented the explosion at home. And in both cases one's sympathies are divided. On the one hand, the advocates of the privileges were not merely – as some recent historians have held – greedy nobles and abbots opposing the enlightened progressiveness of Brussels and its court lawyers. On the other, the older theory that a few vile foreigners were trying to curtail the noble liberties of the Netherlands people, out of sheer lust for power and religious fanaticism, is no less strongly coloured. The truth is of course somewhere in between.

On both sides there were good Netherlanders who sincerely believed in loyalty to the King or in total resistance. On both sides, too, there were criminals. There was also 'progressiveness' on both sides. The government was moving towards absolutism, the term by which the following period of European history is usually known. The rebels were following a special Dutch form of progress, soon to be English too, of moving towards the constitutional state, polyarchy or divided responsibility. My aim is to explain Oldenbarnevelt's choice without praising or blaming him for it.

After the capture of Utrecht in 1528, the three provinces to which the 1555 privilege later applied, Holland, Zeeland and Utrecht, had been drawn into a closer relationship, confirmed by the Edict of Toledo in 1536. Among other things they had the same stadtholder, a circumstance which had certain political consequences in 1590 and again in 1617.

All Oldenbarnevelt has told us about this time is that 1564 was the year when he became an enemy of all 'constraint of conscience'. He may have remembered that well fifty-four years later. The whole of The Hague was in a commotion at the audacious behaviour of the young Stadtholder towards Cardinal Granvelle, prime minister to the Brussels government, and its almost incredible success in the departure of the hated Cardinal on 13 March. Little else can have been spoken of in The Hague for months. At the beginning of August the victor showed himself in Holland, probably trying to explain the true and, in reality, slight significance of an event which, to the ordinary citizen, must have seemed a total change in the system of government. In the eyes of the people the Cardinal personified the execution of heretics. The main subject of conversation at The Hague that summer and autumn was whether constraint of conscience was permissible. On New Year's Eve the Prince summarized the discussions in his famous speech in the Council of State; intolerance should be rejected, not because the Protestants were right – few people thought so at the time, though some supported Protestant criticism of church abuses – but for political reasons: it led to disruption and civil dissension without attaining the desired objective.

Oldenbarnevelt later became a typical thin-lipped man, always more apt to criticize than to enthuse. Let us hope that at sixteen he was different, and was moved to a not-too-calculating aversion from constraint of conscience and perhaps even to something like hero-worship for the Prince of Orange. In his later attitude towards the Prince are signs of what may have been youthful admiration. Furthermore Granvelle was regarded, rightly or wrongly, as the enemy of the nobles and the friend of the 'little man'. His aristocratic prejudice, later one of Oldenbarnevelt's chief characteristics, was in itself enough to set him heart and soul against the Cardinal.

The results of Granvelle's departure were, however, not as fortunate as his opponents hoped, and a state of near-anarchy ensued. Corruption was rife, hunger riots followed severe floods, the edicts against heretics were not with-drawn, though not enforced either. The nobles went into action at the end of 1565, and concluded a 'compromise' or league for relaxation of the edicts by organizing a large-scale demonstration in Brussels. The Prince of Orange, though welcoming support for measures he had recommended, was angry at the rebelliousness of the league and the commotion it would undoubtedly cause among the people. Oldenbarnevelt may have thought the same.

In 1566 Johan started the customary tour of the universities, which was to lead him in the course of four years to Louvain, Bourges, Cologne, Heidelberg and Italy successively. Except at Cologne, where he was enrolled in the arts faculty, he studied law at all these universities. He did not take a degree at any of them, but the title of *meester* (magister), accorded him later, shows that he must somewhere have obtained a degree in law.

He was at Louvain at the time of the image-breaking, when riotous young men destroyed the images in the churches throughout the Netherlands, to purify them for religious services freed from Roman abuses. The attempt failed in Louvain itself, as the students opposed it by force of arms. Johan can only have sympathized with this opposition, though he would have welcomed the attitude of the States of Holland and their 'Advocate', Johan van den Ende (a post he was to hold himself later): they wished to abate the disorders by more toleration of Protestant religious services rather than by severe repression. The Brussels government did not care for this attitude; two years later, when it had more means of enforcing power, Alva, the new Governor-General, had the impudent Advocate prosecuted in the Riots Court. Only his death in prison saved Van den Ende from the walk to the scaffold.

At Bourges Johan became acquainted with the new method of humanistic legal study, introduced by Cujas, inclining away from the medieval com-mentators and practice and towards classical sources and theory. He also went to lectures by two Protestant professors which increased his interest in the new faith. He was there only a short time, however, as the second war of religion broke out in France in the autumn of 1567 and it was no longer safe to study at Bourges. Johan set out to return via Basle and down the Rhine, but stopped at Cologne when he heard that a Spanish army under the Duke of Alva had arrived in the Netherlands and instituted a reign of terror.

Shortly afterwards he decided to go to Heidelberg – a brave decision, since Heidelberg was definitely a Calvinist university, and this could get him into difficulties on his return to Holland.

He did in fact join the prevalent church at Heidelberg, after character-istically making a detailed study of the basic ideas of the Calvinist faith. One

6

of them, later so stressed that it became its main dogma, was the doctrine of predestination: the Christian is not redeemed by his own efforts but by God's grace, granted or withheld according to His will, regardless of merit or sin. The young student, with his aversion from justification by works, may have felt drawn to the spirit of this teaching, but had some difficulty with pre-destination to hell, which from a human point of view makes God an unjust judge and in a certain sense an instigator of sin, since damnation presupposes sin in any case. But he wanted to conform to the Heidelberg church and remembered, as he wrote half a century later, a motto he had read on a card fixed inside the front door of his grandmother's house at Amersfoort. It had been put there by his great-grandfather and read: *Nil Scire Tutissima Fides* – to know nothing is the safest faith. In view of this he decided

not to torment himself any longer with the examination of these matters, but simply to believe that all faithful Christians and their children are chosen by God of His grace and created for salvation by the merit and satisfaction for our sins of our Saviour Jesus Christ.

These words bear the stamp of the period in which they were written. His decision in 1568 was one of inward apostasy from the Roman Church; and the idea of predestination, a point on which neither all Catholics nor all Pro-testants thought alike, was not one of the main differences between Roman and non-Roman. Nonetheless, the Calvinist doctrine of double election must have been a considerable impediment to his adherence to the Swiss form of Protestantism prevalent at Heidelberg. The anti-intellectual way in which this intellectual avoided that impediment is typical of the attitude to religion which prevented him from taking sides in most of the purely dogmatic dis-putes that divided the people of the Netherlands in his lifetime.

Even if Oldenbarnevelt deliberately opted for the Calvinist view of this question of dogma, his sympathies must have been more divided in a con-troversy between Calvinists and others more liberally inclined. Just at the time that Johan enrolled at Heidelberg a fierce conflict about church discipline broke out there, Thomas Erastus being the leader of the anti-disciplinarians. The question was whether the ecclesiastical, independently of the temporal authorities, had the right to bar a member from communion and ultimately to expel him from the church. Calvin himself had demanded this right, now rather taken for granted, for the church authorities. In a theocracy like Geneva this caused no difficulty – unless one wants to call burning the anti-Trinitarian, Michel Servet (1553) a difficulty. It was differ-ent in a state like the Palatinate, where the temporal authority, in this case the Elector, was indeed nicknamed the Pious, but desired to preserve a measure of independence where the church was concerned. This independence would be lost if the clergy gained the right not only publicly to rebuke him, his family and his trusted advisers – that could be borne if need be – but actually to excommunicate him, to the immeasurable detriment of his authority among the faithful. This involved the whole delicate relationship between church and state in Calvinist countries – in a Lutheran one the clergy ate out of the prince's hand. Erastus did not confine himself to the question of church discipline in his theses, developed and distributed among the students in the heat of the dispute. He produced the germ of a theory of general relations between church and state, advocating to a great extent the guardianship of the former by the latter. Under the name of Erastianism it was to influence men's minds for centuries both in England and the Netherlands.

This dispute and the pamphlets in which it was ventilated obviously were eagerly discussed by the students. The anti-Erastian party, who had the ear of the Elector Palatine and favoured a sharply anti-Spanish and pro-Orangist international policy, must have been sympathetic to Oldenbarnevelt for this reason. On the other hand the disciplinarians' fanatical tendencies cannot have attracted him. His religious feeling always showed a rationalistic and anticlerical streak which could be called 'Erasmianism' if that word were not sometimes used too loosely. In later life Oldenbarnevelt developed a great reverence for the supremacy of the temporal authorities, making him a definite, though not extreme, Erastian. But it was in Heidelberg that he began to think about this problem.

Practically all the Netherlands students and professors at Heidelberg were keen Calvinists and anti-Erastians. We shall meet many of them again as opponents of Oldenbarnevelt's religious policy. He cannot therefore have felt very much at home at Heidelberg. It was only among the Frenchmen studying there that he found two future friends: Du Plessis Mornay, who later on worked with Prince William of Orange, and Buzanval, some years younger, who when French envoy at The Hague from 1591 to 1607 was to be in almost daily contact with Oldenbarnevelt. The former left Heidelberg for Padua to go on studying, and Oldenbarnevelt either travelled with him or followed him shortly afterwards. In his autobiography, Oldenbarnevelt does not mention Padua among the universities where he studied, but he does say that he finished his tour in Italy, and Padua was the great attraction for lawyers in Italy.

Oldenbarnevelt only stayed there a short time but some features of his career can be explained by the atmosphere reigning in Padua. In Italy, centre and exemplary source of warmth for European civilization during the late Renaissance, one learned to regard European affairs from a lofty viewpoint, and the Netherlands' place in this perspective was small. During his stay at Padua, Walsingham, Oldenbarnevelt's great opposite number in the 1580s, is said by his biographer to have become, not indeed 'italianate' – meaning presumably 'Machiavellian' – but to have acquired a 'cosmopolitan spirit' and broad-minded view. The same applies to Oldenbarnevelt. Not that he was no patriot: he maintained the contrary on the scaffold and it was a true word. But his was not the untravelled general public's narrow-minded patriotism of temporary expediency.

So Padua too helped to prepare the way to his execution and according to an apposite legend this was foreseen by a fortune-teller. His violent death would be near, she said, when the mirror of prudence should be shattered. Later Oldenbarnevelt had a statue of Prudentia and another of Constantia on the top of his house in Kneuterdijk, and when the owner was put in prison the mirror in the hand of one of them fell.

Oldenbarnevelt returned to Alva's Netherlands in the spring of 1570 and conformed for two years to the religion prevailing at The Hague. That going to confession and communion involved a considerable amount of hypocrisy may not have worried him particularly, especially at first; not because, as his enemies were to allege, he was hypocritical by nature, but because he could salve his conscience by shifting the blame on to those who enforced the faith and should have made better use of their power. A devious argument which must eventually have led to a painful conflict. He found the solution two years later by joining the rebellion, in contrast to most of his colleagues.

Oldenbarnevelt had a lucrative practice. He was considered an expert on feudal law and the laws connected with dykes and drainage. In his auto-biography he says that 'nearly all the Nobles, Lords, many towns . . . and nearly all dyke-reeves and polder-board officials' were his clients in civil cases. The States of Holland also employed him, although not yet twenty-five in cases of this kind.

Then the rising began. In April 1572 the 'Sea Beggars' captured Brill for the Prince, who was still in Germany, and in May and June one town after another in Holland and Zeeland took the rebels' side, usually being forced to do so by the common people. The Hof van Holland, custodian of legality, fled to Utrecht, abandoning Holland to the anarchy of wild gangs of 'Beggars'. Oldenbarnevelt cannot have cared much for them, though he approved of their aim, the curtailment of Alva's tyranny. With like-minded libertarians[1]

---

[1] By 'libertarians' (Dutch: *libertijnen*) I mean those individualists who did not see their faith expressed by the tenets of one particular denomination, even though they might become members of one such church.

however, he considered it better to take the leadership of the rising out of the hands of the brutal soldiery than to take the part of the universally hated Spaniards and their Riots Court, opposed to all privileges. This succeeded. When the Prince, recognized by the rebels as Stadtholder of Holland, arrived in October he found the nobles and most of the towns – Amsterdam was the most important exception – prepared to maintain his authority, and in the towns it was not the militant Calvinists who were in control but the moderate Catholics, libertarians and Protestants, who had only seen a few loyalists leave for Utrecht or Amsterdam. The young lawyer played no special part in this but joined in the libertarian chorus. He helped collect 'voluntary' contributions at The Hague and make an inventory of the arms there. In some places in South Holland he also had to enquire into the damage done by the roving 'Beggars', for which the rebel authorities wished to grant partial compensation.

The Prince reached The Hague on 14 November, welcomed by a 'curious display': on this occasion Oldenbarnevelt must have seen him for the first time.

The Prince did not stay at The Hague, an unfortified place, and unsafe now that Spanish bands could be expected in Holland at any moment. The government was instead set up at Delft, a walled town, and Oldenbarnevelt moved there too. He subscribed forty-two pounds of forty (Dutch) groats (about £4 sterling) to a compulsory loan issued by the town, and was recruited for a military expedition that was to make a last desperate attempt to relieve Haarlem, under siege by the Spaniards. After the disastrous defeat at the Manpad, in which the leader was killed, Oldenbarnevelt escaped, unharmed. That was the last time the Prince was to sacrifice civilians, and the last time Oldenbarnevelt took up arms. Haarlem capitulated a few days later. An anxious summer followed. Sonoy, commander of the 'Beggars' in North Holland, lost heart and the Prince, with his usual psychological insight, consoled the keen Calvinist with the alliance that he had joined with the King of Kings: meanwhile he helped his cause by having great stretches of land inundated, in spite of the farmers whose cattle were deprived of food for the winter and who could not put in a claim for war damage.

Oldenbarnevelt watched and learned; questions concerning dykes and water-levels interested him and in the following year he was accounted an expert. In the meantime he had to deal with other claims by farmers. Some English auxiliary troops, who had helped to make the rising in Zeeland a success, were commanded by a certain Thomas Morgan. He and his troops, after liberating half of Zeeland, were encamped in Hoekse Waard. There were no Spaniards there, and the troops, without pay or food, had been plundering the farmers, as usually happened. This was one of the 'delights of the war', still unchanged in the time of Jacques Callot,[1] usually ending in distress for the farmers and here and there a soldier strung up by the roadside.

But the farmers in Hoekse Waard had a powerful protector in the background: Sabina van Egmont, widow of Count Lamoral, beheaded by Alva, and owner of the greater part of the island which her husband had had embanked. Oldenbarnevelt, the Countess's lawyer, was ordered by the States of Holland to hold an enquiry, an assignment not without danger, as Oldenbarnevelt said in a statement of the expenses incurred, handed in years later.

From Haarlem the Spaniards moved to Leiden which they besieged for nearly a year. Towards the end of the siege, in September 1574, the situation was so desperate that the Prince decided to take drastic measures; the fertile meadows round Leiden would have to be flooded to drive away the besiegers and allow the relief force to approach in their flat-bottomed boats. As an expert in this field Oldenbarnevelt was appointed one of the commissioners for breaching the dykes: his work was not supervision of the labourers, but rather land measurement, verification of ownership and calculation of damage to be compensated later.

In a later stage of the relief he accompanied the fleet, probably as an orderly or an interpreter for the French officers who took part in the expedition, but before the relief on 3 October 1574, a date which is still commemorated, he was taken ill and had to leave the fleet.

In the next few years he was twice given instructions by the Prince regarding criminal cases. The first concerned the defence of the burgomaster of Zierikzee, dismissed for defeatism, and accused of having advised surrender during the siege of the town. He was of distinguished birth, related to the most prominent families in Zeeland and certainly not pro-Spanish; the Prince desired his acquittal and was looking for a lawyer who was on the one hand a good patriot, on the other moderate enough to be willing to take on such a case. It is not known whether it was Oldenbarnevelt's eloquence or the Prince's obvious wishes that got the burgomaster acquitted.

Another proof of the Prince's confidence in him was his appointment in July 1576 as a supplementary member of the special court set up by the above-mentioned Sonoy in North Holland to try Catholic farmers and citizens in the district for their part in an alleged plot to deliver up the country to the Spaniards. This tribunal had obtained a number of false confessions by means of horrible torture and had one innocent farmer after another executed. When however it started work on the citizens of Hoorn

---

[1] French artist (1592–1635), whose grim etchings of the Thirty Years War depicted its horrors.

this town protested to the Prince, who arranged with Sonoy that cases should be stopped till the Prince had appointed two supplementary judges to decide what procedure should be followed. The cases were finally stopped without the cooperation of the judges appointed, partly as a result of the Pacification of Ghent, in November 1576, when the war with Spain came to a temporary halt. So Oldenbarnevelt did not act, in the event, and his appointment is only mentioned here to show the confidence the Prince evidently placed in him by wishing to use him no longer as a lawyer but as a judge.

The year before, in 1575, Oldenbarnevelt had found a wife at Delft.

Near his rooms on the Oude Delft lived the distinguished Van Utrecht family, owners of a number of manors and other property nearby. The family consisted of two bachelor brothers, for whom the illegitimate daughter of their deceased sister kept house. Oldenbarnevelt helped the two old gentlemen in the disposition of their estate, which they wished their niece to inherit after a third childless brother in Antwerp. To qualify for this Maria had to obtain a deed of legitimacy, which was particularly difficult as her mother was dead and she could not be legitimized by marriage. On the other hand this was a good thing, as her father was a barge-hand, and a *mésalliance* in the family was almost worse than illegitimacy. Oldenbarnevelt was able to solve this problem through his contacts in government circles, and once the girl by one means or another had become a rich heiress, Oldenbarnevelt overlooked her illegitimate birth and married her. He admitted later that the dowry she brought had decided him, but that he also had 'pleasure in her person'. The combination was good enough for a happy marriage. Not much was heard about Maria van Utrecht, who seems to have been a colourless person, but no storms were heard of in their forty-three years of married life; and Oldenbarnevelt's enemies, who eagerly collected everything that could be used against him, could not find a single scandal and have nothing to say against Maria except that she was illegitimate. This she could not help.

Towards the end of 1576 Alva's successor, Requesens, died; the Council of State with its Netherlands (Belgian) majority took over *ad interim*, the Spanish soldiers started to mutiny and plundered Antwerp, and the provinces loyal to the King, more afraid of the rabid Spaniards than of the more civilized rebels from Holland and Zeeland, resolved to come to terms with the latter. Thus was concluded the Pacification of Ghent which introduced a new period both in the history of the rebellion and the career of Oldenbarnevelt.

In December of that year the largest of the small towns of Holland, Rotterdam, needed a pensionary, and after some unsuccessful efforts appealed to the young Delft lawyer, Johan van Oldenbarnevelt.

Since the rebellion many more than the original six towns had been allowed to take part in the sessions of the States. The number, variable at first, was fixed at about this time at eighteen. They were represented in the States of Holland by one or more burgomasters, generally accompanied by the pensionary, a salaried official, primarily concerned with the town's 'foreign affairs'. This post had become much more important since the rebellion, because the States had in fact become a governing body, the orders of the central government not being obeyed any more. They no longer met only once or twice a year for a few days, as they used to, but four times a year for sessions of several weeks. During the recesses they left two committees elected from their number, one for South Holland and one for North Holland, north of Haarlem and Amsterdam (which belonged to South Holland), empowered to settle current business. These committees were called *Gecommitteerde Raden*, and in particular the one for South Holland, having its seat at The Hague and consisting of one nobleman and burgomasters of the chief towns, soon acquired experience of affairs of state and gained predominant influence. It was presided over by the official comparable at States level to the pensionary at town level: the Advocate of Holland, who, because of this and the lead that he took in the full sessions of the States as a sort of political secretary, was the most powerful man in the province after the stadtholder. And not only in the provinces: in the conglomeration of provinces together fighting the Spanish army he was also a man of great, almost paramount importance because, except in a short period after the Pacification of Ghent, Holland was the most powerful province in the association, as well as the strongest financially, and so usually able to impose its will on the others.

For the time then Oldenbarnevelt represented one of the nineteen members together forming the States of Holland. He did not sit in *Gecommitteerde Raden*, where Rotterdam was represented at the time by a burgomaster, so his influence on national policy was limited. Rotterdam, a herring-fishing town, restricted in its increasing overseas trade by the staple right of the nearby first town in Holland, Dordrecht, only took seventh place among the towns, especially after Haarlem and Amsterdam had joined the rest again after the Pacification. There were two other respects in which the unwritten constitution of Holland hampered the young pensionary in exerting influence. In the first place it was the custom for the most important resolutions, those concerning finance, war and peace, to be passed unanimously. Oldenbarnevelt was therefore unable to cooperate in these cases in forming a majority for any proposals by the nobility who voted first, made by the mouth of the Advocate. Then there was the binding mandate. Oldenbarnevelt had to attend the meeting of the States 'charged' by his town regarding the items of the agenda. If a resolution was tabled that had not been provided for he had to hold a 'consultation' (*ruggespraak*), that is he had to declare himself 'uncharged' and return to Rotterdam to hear his principals' 'good opinion'. This rule was not, of course, always strictly kept: for unimportant routine matters on the one hand, on the other for urgent decisions, a town deputy could break it at his own risk. As in course of time Rotterdam began to place more confidence in their pensionary his charge was framed in such loose terms that consultation was seldom necessary, especially when Oldenbarnevelt felt at liberty to join in the majority vote. Nevertheless, the demand for *ruggespraak* and the delay occasioned by this in dealing with affairs of state, for this requirement applied to meetings of the States-General as well, was the despair of all vigorous statesmen till the end of the Republic in 1795. The Netherlands of today is the only country in the world with a clause in its constitution instructing members of Parliament to vote 'without charge or *ruggespraak*'.

After the Pacification of Ghent, when the fifteen other provinces were invited by the Brussels Council of State on its own authority to a meeting of the States-General, and Holland and Zeeland after some hesitation sent their delegates, Oldenbarnevelt was twice chosen, in 1580 and 1582, to represent Holland. He did not come into the limelight but acquired an understanding of foreign policy and gained the confidence of Prince William.

On one occasion during his nine years of office Oldenbarnevelt incited his town to a strong line of opposition, a tax strike, or at least supported it in this. Taxes were not raised through payment by the citizens to collectors but via the municipal exchequers. When in 1578 the States refused to hand over to Rotterdam the office of dyke-reeve of Schieland, which the town had bought a year before, delivery was enforced by this drastic measure at a critical moment in the war with the new Spanish Governor-General, Don Juan.

The town's finances were the pensionary's chief concern. He afterwards took pride in the fact that he had introduced the distinction between capital and current expenditure in the municipal accounts and at the same time modernized their annual audit.

Rotterdam had advanced money to the States of Holland in former years on a mortgage basis. When it appeared that the still insolvent States could not meet this claim and Rotterdam had to foreclose, it was Oldenbarnevelt who with some others took over the land so that Rotterdam received some badly needed cash.

Finally Oldenbarnevelt succeeded in gaining from the States recognition of Rotterdam as the seventh of the so-called 'big towns'. This meant that in future no edicts were to be issued, no loans taken up, unless Rotterdam had attached its seal as the last town, after the nobles and the six older ones.

The town was therefore extremely satisfied with its pensionary. On his appointment as deputy to the States-General they would hardly allow him to go to Antwerp and fixed an early date for his return. Also when, in 1585, he was appointed ambassador to England they let him go with reluctance 'seeing how necessary the services of the said pensionary are to the town'. When he was elected Advocate of Holland he was discharged with effusive thanks for these his services, together with . . . his diligence, loyalty and all good offices, which he has done during the period of the said pensionaryship in the furtherance of the affairs of this town in general and its inhabitants in particular.

As his successor his brother Elias was appointed, fresh from the academy at Leiden, entirely on his recommendation. Later, when Elias was succeeded as pensionary by Hugo de Groot, relations with the town remained excellent. Now Oldenbarnevelt's statue has a position of honour among famous Rotterdammers, in a niche in the façade of Rotterdam Town Hall.

Meanwhile pensionary Oldenbarnevelt was twice in the limelight in national politics: in the conclusion of the Union of Utrecht (1578–9) and the repeal of the 'Satisfaction' of Amsterdam, as it was called, the treaty concluded by Amsterdam with the States when after its six years under Spain it rejoined the rest of Holland.

In Holland it had been hoped that the Pacification of Ghent would mean the end of the war. But the new Governor General, Don Juan, bastard brother of King Philip, was playing a cunning game and finding supporters in both North and South, though mainly in the Wallonian provinces, especially Hainault and Artois. So the war went on, but the front moved from Holland to Brabant, and with the front went Prince William's interest. In 1576 he left Holland, to pay it only three short visits up to 1583. His spirit was absent too, now the defence of the province was no longer of primary importance. He was beginning to see problems in the much more general context of the Netherlands, sometimes even in a European context. The general context of the Netherlands meant Brabant and Flanders in the first place; Europe meant the French and English courts; the arcana of the Escurial, where he had his spy; the squabbles of the German princes in the Rhineland. His spirit soared in the heights too, sometimes rather far from reality, the Hollanders complained, unable to follow either his religious or his French policy, despite their inclination to trust him. Committees had to see to it that contact was maintained in the increasing divergence. It was virtually the most important political work to be done in Holland and Oldenbarnevelt was often elected to the contact committees. Not always – Rotterdam would not have allowed it – nor was he the life and soul of his committee. There were others, older men who had the ear of the Prince and the confidence of the States to a greater degree than the cocksure young pensionary of a not very distinguished town.

Oldenbarnevelt's undeniable genius was not immediately obvious. There was something sour and dry about him that had to be penetrated before the underlying richness and indeed gentleness could be appreciated. He was altogether without the Prince's exceptional charm. He must often have envied him for it, perhaps despised it a bit, as excessive charm must sometimes appear insincere to a sceptical observer. We thus have the ambivalent relationship often typical of a great man and his great teacher. It is certain that Oldenbarnevelt learnt a lot from those many conferences. Later he referred a few times explicitly, many times implicitly to the Prince. Both his French policy and, in part, his policy of toleration were inspired by the Prince.

For his policy towards Don Juan and the Walloons the Prince needed some backing from the North. As early as 1577, when the poet Philip Sidney visited him at Dordrecht, representing Queen Elizabeth at the baptism of her god-child, Orange's second daughter, they discussed the desirability of a 'closer union' of those areas in favour of a policy of intransigence towards Don Juan. Then and later it was by no means intended to found a new state, least of all an independent one. The King of Spain was recognized for four more years, though no longer obeyed.

After the plan had been relegated to the background for a time it became acute again at the beginning of 1578 when the army of the States-General, led by Belgian Catholic nobles, suffered a heavy defeat at the hands of the newly arrived Prince of Parma, whose mother had been Governor-General in 1566. Sharp Protestant reaction in Flanders alarmed the Catholics of the South, among whom a group was formed calling themselves 'Malcontents', who might well go and make overtures towards Don Juan or Parma. Plans for a closer union were therefore again of current interest, and now that the most important provinces, Flanders and Brabant, were divided and weakened, it was clear that Holland would have to form its nucleus. There was indescribable confusion in the anti-Spanish camp. At one time there were no fewer than four mutually independent armies, each trying to fight the Spaniards on their own. A closer union would have to coordinate these efforts and undertake the leadership of the resistance. However, in the next few months differences of opinion about the basis of this closer union occurred between the Prince, residing in Antwerp, and the Hollanders, who had long since prohibited Roman services in their province and now in Amsterdam too. The former, accustomed to look at things in their European context, considered that resistance to Spanish 'tyranny' could succeed only if all Netherlanders from the north and the south, Catholic and Protestant, could be persuaded to join in, and if the Protestant Queen of England and the Catholic King of France supported them. The closer union would have to be acceptable to both the northern and the southern provinces and based on a *Religionsfridt* drawn up by the Prince and his French collaborators, obliging Catholics and Protestants in every province to live peaceably and freely side by side. The union would also have to be based on the Pacification of Ghent and not appear to be aimed against some of the participating provinces.

The Hollanders, among whom Oldenbarnevelt was gradually coming to the fore, thought differently. Libertarians and Calvinists, oligarchs and the politically active citizens, were agreed that the Catholics in the North Netherlands were not to be trusted, nor, probably, those in the South either. Holland and Zeeland had settled the religious question in their own provinces as they saw fit; they wanted no interference from other provinces in their internal affairs. In theory the largely libertarian oligarchs were in favour of something like Orange's *Religionsfridt*, but, as long as war was being waged against a Catholic monarch whose avowed aim was to protect the Netherlands Catholics and who had the full support of the Pope, they regarded it as utopian. They also considered the degree of centralization envisaged by the Prince and the powerless central government at Antwerp impracticable, in view of the particularism and divergent interests of the provinces to be united.

In the months that follow we see a constant tug of war between the Prince, unable to intervene in person because of the critical military situation in the south, and the realists among the leaders in Holland. The matter was complicated by the fact that the Prince was represented at the negotiations by his younger brother John; though ruling Count of Nassau-Dillenburg William had the States-General appoint him Stadtholder of Gelderland for the express purpose of bringing the negotiation of the closer union to a successful conclusion. In spite of his affection for his brilliant elder brother, however, he was in no way in agreement with his *Religionsfridt* or with his insistence on the inviolability of the Pacification: with the first, not because he was a realist like the Hollanders but because as a pious and fanatical Calvinist he wished the Catholics nothing but harm and indeed was attempting to establish Protestantism in Gelderland in a fairly forcible way. And he could not care less about the Pacification, since the opponents of the closer union were constantly using it to prove that such a special league within the larger Pacification league was unnecessary and dangerous.

When Count John approached the Hollanders in August 1578 with his proposal for closer union it came on to the agenda of the Rotterdam Council on the 16th. It was decided, at the instance of the pensionary, to vote for it in the States of Holland. Oldenbarnevelt did so a few days later and defended the idea so eloquently that he was chosen to be one of the five deputies to go to Arnhem, the seat of the Gelderland diet, to discuss it with them and the representatives of other provinces.

Although Oldenbarnevelt was only fourth in terms of precedence in this delegation, he usually acted as spokesman in the discussions. His task was delicate in two respects. He had to persuade the other provinces to join Holland in a union in which this province, economically far the most powerful, would inevitably rule the roost. To do this he needed to hold out a prospect of guarantees against misuse of power by Holland, but these guarantees were not to be substantial enough to impair his principals' interests. Furthermore one of his main arguments in favour of the union had to be the fact that it was desired by the greatly revered Prince of Orange. For the foregoing reasons he had, however, to oppose the draft submitted by the Prince based on *Religionsfridt* and Pacification. This opposition would make the negotiators doubtful whether the Prince would want the Union as proposed by Holland.

Oldenbarnevelt's proposal must have stuck in the throats of some other provinces, expecially in the field of religion. In consultation with John of Nassau he proposed that, contrary to the Prince's intentions, an explicit distinction should be made between Holland and Zeeland which were to deal with religion as they liked, and the other provinces, which were either to apply the religious truce or 'institute there such order in general and in particular as they shall find practicable for the peace and prosperity of the provinces'. The Maas was accepted as the frontier of the areas the closer union intended to embrace. This robbed the project of any attraction for the Prince. The proposed union of northern provinces, led by Holland and Zeeland, where the practice of Catholicism was prohibited, had now of necessity to assume a Calvinistic character. If Gelderland and Utrecht joined it no longer meant the building up of pressure to strengthen the anti-Spanish elements in the States-General but – as the Gelderland towns had seen – the defection of these provinces from the fifteen-province party to the two-province party.

The distinction seemed subtle. In the long run it was not enough to prevent the Prince signing the Union, but for the present it was enough to make him put spokes in the wheels.

It had been arranged to meet again at Gorcum on 6 October. The meeting did not take place, since the Prince's representatives could not come. He did not send any others and the meeting was cancelled. They were to meet again at Utrecht on 17 October. The same delegates were sent as to Arnhem. John of Nassau, still absent, was represented by a totally ignorant deputy, a German count, but now the Zeelanders and the Flemings were missing, while the delegates from Gelderland and Overijsel had not been instructed. Oldenbarnevelt had to report with disappointment that in the circumstances it had been found better to adjourn the discussions till the States of Holland met, to be convened at Gorcum again as soon as John was back from Germany. This time it is certain that at any rate the absence of the Zeeland delegation was due to the machinations of the Prince, who wanted to win time in which to get the religious truce generally accepted and regain the confidence of the Malcontents.

It may well cause surprise that the Holland delegation at Arnhem, so liberal in its sympathies, should have risked open conflict in the matter of the religious truce, as individually they were all as keen on toleration as the Prince and did not in the least intend to allow a Calvinistic monopoly in Holland. There were other reasons for this than distrust of Catholics in Holland and the impracticability of the religious truce which foreshadowed, as it were, the disputes during the Twelve Years Truce (1609–21).

The religious truce was not a final solution for the Prince either. It was intended as a temporary arrangement, applicable to all provinces, pending the final arrangement to be made later by the States-General, after the complete expulsion of the Spanish troops. It is not quite clear how the Prince envisaged a final arrangement which was acceptable to all parties: perhaps one should think of something like the German Interim of 1548, a comprehension with which Catholics and Protestants could be satisfied. That was left vague, but it was certain that both the temporary two-religion solution and the final arrangement would be inter-provincial. Oldenbarnevelt and the Dutch libertarians could never accept that, however. They wanted to decide their own religious life, in the Erastian way, *cuius regio illius religio*, as the other *Religionsfridt*, that of Augsburg in 1555, had proclaimed. The principle is not so immoral as it looks. For sixteenth-century people the Church was not primarily a means of establishing personal contact between God and man. That had been Luther's opinion, largely abandoned by his adherents and only followed to a strict conclusion by Calvin. What the others – Romans, Lutherans, Erasmians, 'politicals' of all colours – saw in it was a sort of spiritual police, an ordering of spiritual life from above. If the Church was that – and to a certain extent it still is – the responsibility for its ordering rested with the ruler. The Prince and the libertarians from Holland were united in this against the lively but at present still powerless Calvinist minority. But the latter had the libertarians on their side, against the Prince, on the question of who the ruler in Holland was.

'The Prince', the Hollander said quickly, 'advised by the States.'

'The King of Spain, whom I have always honoured,'[1] answered the Prince in some embarrassment, 'of course in the person of whomever we regard now or in the future as his representative.'

It was a somewhat unreal position. The States-General, who in the last resort should have wielded this sort of sovereignty, did nothing but quarrel amongst themselves and were as little esteemed at Mons and Arras, at Ghent and The Hague, as at Namur or Louvain. It could be said that they had become a local authority in Antwerp much as the Byzantine Emperors were eventually to become in Constantinople.

The Prince, fully occupied with troubles at Ghent and with the Malcontents, was not equal to the determination of the faithful Hollanders. The roles were, so to speak, reversed: whereas in August the Hollanders were prepared to cooperate in a union because the Prince seemed to wish it, now he was leaving them to their impatient urge towards a union which left him cold. In the middle of November the States of Holland met, again at Gorcum, as close as possible to the Gelderland border. John of Nassau represented the Prince, whom he had not seen for a long time: everyone knew that he disagreed with his brother on a number of points. At this meeting at Gorcum the Hollanders, as appears from Oldenbarnevelt's notes which have been preserved, managed to introduce nearly all their particularistic wishes into the final text of the Union. The Prince indeed undertook a great responsibility by not coming in person to impose his more centralistic views. He felt that his presence in the south was demanded by the troubles in Ghent and the activities of the new Governor-General Parma. He was wrong, one can say now, but the Prince could not then know that all his work in the south was to vanish into thin air within five years, or that what was being debated in that remote spot further north would serve for two centuries as the constitution of a still undreamed-of state.

Another article provided for the introduction of uniform taxation, by which excise duty was meant, to be levied uniformly in all provinces. It was never put into practice, the Prince realizing that the particularism of the poorer provinces would make the introduction of consumption taxes of equal incidence impossible. The Prince had wanted to incorporate the quota system, that by which each province was assessed at a percentage of the money required, in the Act of Union. This was not done, though in practice it was the procedure, and when Oldenbarnevelt came to power he became resigned

---

[1] An allusion to the end of the first verse of the Netherlands National Anthem, 'Wilhelmus', in which the Prince says:

> Den Coninck van Hispaengien
> hebb' ick altijdt gheeert.

to it without much difficulty, since Holland after all preferred to be master in its own house.

The Union, concluded at Utrecht on 23 January 1579, aroused little enthusiasm in the country. The Catholic provinces were afraid of domination by Holland, turned Protestant and generally avid for power; Holland could see no good in the Union unless it were guided by a firm hand, that of a Hollander. Oldenbarnevelt began to realize this ten years later, but at the time he saw no way out. Where was the firm hand to come from?

No organ of administration was named in the text of the Union. The only functionaries given a part to play, not so much in the leadership of the Union as in settling differences, were the three stadtholders.

The Prince held aloof from them, and Rennenburg, Stadtholder of Friesland and Groningen, a Catholic from Hainault, following in his footsteps was hardly more in favour of the Union, now turned anti-Catholic. The only stadtholder eligible for the leadership was therefore John of Nassau, and so he was pushed forward at once by Holland against the wishes of Zeeland. Oldenbarnevelt knew him and cannot possibly have been happy about his leadership. He was a foreigner, less than a year in the country and ignorant of the language. He did not understand conditions in Holland. His religious zeal was not in harmony with the Prince's tolerance or with the libertarian spirit of the dominant group in Holland. Furthermore his temperament and, as a ruling count, his habits of absolutism made him unsuitable for a post such as director of the Union, for which above all tact, patience and perseverance were needed.

His lack of the first two qualities was shown by the first joint military exploit undertaken by the new allies. It was directed not against the Spanish armies but against Oldenbarnevelt's home town, Amersfoort, which had remained Catholic and would not change over fast enough and sign the Union. After a five-day siege it was taken and Protestantism was forcibly established. The Prince was against this as contrary to his policy towards the Malcontents. Oldenbarnevelt, whose uncles and cousins were removed from the local government for good, cannot have been happy about it. His feelings for the Prince may have been strengthened by what occurred.

From Holland's point of view, however, the Prince ought to be persuaded to sign the Union. After a last attempt to create a general union of all seventeen provinces on the basis of the religious truce he gave in and signed the Union on 3 June, more than four months after it had been concluded. The State of the Seventeen Netherlands had become a chimera. The founders of the Union had overcome the man who inspired them.

Oldenbarnevelt was not directly concerned with this struggle or the victory

of the particularist-republicans. For the present it was still an older generation that made the important decisions. He had not matured early, like Johan
de Witt or William Pitt. At thirty-two he was still a learner, and had learnt a
lot from the launching of the Union: distrust of the great lords. John of
Nassau, Rennenburg, William of Orange, all three had disappointed him.
The latter had been beaten by the lesser lords. Oldenbarnevelt was never to
forget that in the Netherlands, at any rate in the north, power rests with the
patricians. But the Prince had taught him a lot too, so much that Oldenbarnevelt's respect for him had hardly diminished. The Prince had been flexible.
He had alternately advanced the Union and retarded it, but had never tied
himself down. And now his secret defeat was transformed into an apparent
victory. The public thought the Prince wanted to fight the King of Spain and
the Union was the instrument given by God for this purpose. Oldenbarnevelt
realized that the Prince had opposed this Union. He knew this because he
was a discerning observer and moved in the circle of the real victors. The
people of the Netherlands saw only the essentials: for them the Union was a
wonderful affair, the work of the Prince, whose prestige it did not lower but
raised. Something to make Oldenbarnevelt jealous.

Oldenbarnevelt was not employed much at this period for high-level
politics – relations with France and England and defence organization. This
was conducted in Antwerp by the Prince and his camarilla and by the States-
General, in which Holland only played a subordinate role. The Union set up
at Utrecht was inefficient and hardly involved: it seems that many people in
the country had forgotten its existence. It was not till the Spanish occupation
of Flanders and Brabant some years later, when Union and States-General
territory were identical that the agreement acquired the great significance –
that of the constitution of a state in the making – which it retained for more
than two centuries.

Oldenbarnevelt's services were all the more in demand for domestic affairs
in Holland, more and more independently conducted by the States. But this
did not apply to the most important domestic question to crop up during these
years: the integration of Amsterdam. The dispute could be decided only by
the Prince, and Oldenbarnevelt played a leading part in the fruitless efforts
to induce him to pronounce in the States' favour. These efforts throw light on
Oldenbarnevelt's character, both on his talents and its defects.

In February 1578, the Catholic *vroedschap* of Amsterdam had, as already
mentioned, submitted to the Prince and the States on certain conditions laid
down in the Satisfaction of Amsterdam, as it was called. Clause I of this
document settled religious matters entirely in accordance with Amsterdam's
wishes: all Protestant services were prohibited within its jurisdiction, though

liberty of conscience and honourable burial were allowed to Protestants. The town did not have to contribute to the debts previously incurred by the States in the Four Years War (1572–6).

Four months later, in May 1578, the Protestant and libertarian exiles who had returned, incited by emissaries from the Prince and the States, carried out a *coup d'état* by which Protestantism was established in the town and Clause I of the Satisfaction made invalid. Difference of opinion now arose as to whether this *Alteratie* made the whole Satisfaction invalid, including the provisions favourable to Amsterdam as to non-payment of former debts and the payment by the States for the town militia; or whether the now Protestant town could continue to invoke those parts of the Satisfaction not made meaningless by the enforcement of Protestantism. The States naturally held to the first opinion, and for years Oldenbarnevelt was the principal negotiator, who had to persuade the Prince, acting as arbitrator, of the reasonableness of this point of view. Amsterdam was prepared to relinquish the Satisfaction provided monetary compensation was granted for the loss or the advantages stipulated therein. Oldenbarnevelt agreed to compensation, much smaller than Amsterdam demanded, stating explicitly that this was not because the town had any right to it but '*omme alle eenicheyt vruntschap ende nagebuerschap tonderhouden*'.[1]

Here we can see an early example of a method used by Oldenbarnevelt in subsequent difficult dealings. He begins by taking the view that the other side has no legal claim at all. Then he says he will, without prejudice, concede part of what is asked. This shows how friendly and moderate he is – indeed one sometimes feels that he is beginning to believe it himself. The result is that if the other side does not agree to his concession he feigns injured innocence and becomes far more exasperated than he would have with less apparent noderation. Then his obduracy asserts itself: he returns to his first position and refuses to negotiate.

Sometimes of course he is right. But his contentions are often over-ingenious, as in this case. He alleged that Amsterdam had renounced the Satisfaction both in word and deed. The words must have been shouts of joy from some burgomaster at the first impact of the successful *Alteratie*. It could scarcely be maintained that such an utterance had legal force. And the contention that the whole Satisfaction had lapsed owing to the lapse of Clause I is not tenable, since this clause made no stipulation favourable to the States, who would then have been entitled in the absence of a quid pro quo – the consideration of the contract – to regard the rest of it as invalid. It was chicanery, that could only be practised on the legally inexpert, to allege that

[1] In order to maintain all harmony, friendship and neighbourliness.

the town was not entitled to renounce one favourable clause and retain the others.

Oldenbarnevelt did indeed make a feeble attempt to let it appear that Clause I was also favourable to the States – but this was skating on thin ice and was most damaging at his trial in 1618. For this assertion implied that he considered the *Alteratie* an act against Holland's interests, against the treaty concluded with Holland, which weighed heavily against him with the hostile judge Reynier Pauw, a son of one of the originators of the *Alteratie*.

Oldenbarnevelt's argument at first convinced the Prince, on one of his visits to the north. It was only when he had been ceremonially received in Amsterdam and had the position of the town explained to him by local Orangists, that he changed his decree – perhaps more for reasons of policy than of equity – and gave Amsterdam what it wanted on most scores. At the same time he was invested with supreme authority over Holland and Zeeland, not just for the duration of the war but permanently, and we can assume that Amsterdam's favourable vote was more or less explicitly made dependent on a change in their favour of the Prince's first pronouncement.

Oldenbarnevelt was furious. He did not realize, as an advocate should, the weakness of the cause he was defending and adapt his pleadings accordingly, only seeming to identify with his client. *Oratorem irasci minime decet, iram simulare non dedecet*,[1] but perhaps there is something attractive about a quick-tempered advocate who gets angry in a cause that is not his own. This was Oldenbarnevelt's temperament and it cost him much peace of mind. Regarded purely objectively, he should not have written that the Prince's pronouncement '*mit rechte ofte redelijckheit nyet gemeens en heeft*'.[2]

He impressed the States with this. For a year they refused to accept the Prince's second arbitration award, and when they finally decided to, under strong pressure from their new 'supreme authority', Oldenbarnevelt was not on the committee that signed the agreement with Amsterdam on behalf of the States.

He was beginning to acquire a reputation for obduracy. Though highly skilled at initiating negotiations, at stating his own opinions clearly and sharply and at creating moral authority by making supercilious concessions, he lacked the flexibility to meet the other side halfway, if they would not let themselves be intimidated. Sometimes he could see, intellectually, the need for this, but emotionally he found it difficult to make the necessary approaches. Later he was occasionally able to overcome his feelings, but usually

---

[1] It little becomes an orator to grow angry, but it is not unbecoming to simulate anger (Cicero, *Tusculanae Disputationes* IV, 25).
[2] Has nothing in common with right or reason.

the pattern remained the same: he took risks constantly, till in August 1618, he overreached himself.

Oldenbarnevelt voted on behalf of Rotterdam in favour of the agreement with Amsterdam. Fate decreed that throughout the history of the Republic this town should be in opposition, instead of playing the dominant role that would have been natural. In the chain of cause and effect leading to this sterility the bitter dispute over the renunciation of the Satisfaction plays an important part. It caused the seventeen-year-old Calvinist, Reynier Pauw, son of a returned exile brought into the government by the *Alteratie*, to cherish a burning hatred of Oldenbarnevelt, only extinguished in his blood. It caused the general 'dissatisfaction' which again and again made Amsterdam chafe against rule by The Hague: in 1584, 1609, 1617, 1650 and 1683. When we remember that this embitterment originated partly in the temperament of the Rotterdam pensionary – to which, on the other hand, the independence of the Netherlands is partly due – one may draw attention here to the implicit tragedy, although in history one does not think in strictly causal categories.

At the time when the dispute with Amsterdam was coming to an end, the States-General, purged of their 'trimmers', had taken the drastic step of abjuring King Philip (25 July 1581), still nominally recognized as sovereign. Obviously he had to be replaced by another sovereign. There was one to hand in the person of Francis of Anjou, brother and heir presumptive to the childless King Henry III of France. Holland was most displeased at this choice. Another Catholic sovereign, things going from bad to worse, and furthermore Anjou himself neither able nor attractive. He came from an autocratic royal family and would adapt with difficulty to the constitutional role intended for him in the Netherlands. The Prince refused, however, to take any further responsibility if Anjou were not accepted; he was not only the French King's brother but a likely candidate for the hand of the English Queen, and so seemed to offer a certain guarantee of French and English military support, without which William rightly supposed that he would not be able to stand up to the Spaniards.

But Orange was no more pro-French than was Oldenbarnevelt, whose French policy was attuned to William's. Oldenbarnevelt's contemporaries thought he was: Henry IV thought he had him in his pocket and both Robert Cecil and, in Holland, the diarist Anthonie Duyck, regarded him as being so. It depends, of course, on what one means by pro-French. The Prince and Oldenbarnevelt both thought they could use, in fact urgently needed, France in the struggle against Spain. In order to use somebody one must on occasion let oneself be used. But neither had a permanent preference.

25

The Prince emphatically denied such a preference to Davison, the English minister, and Oldenbarnevelt repeatedly opposed French interests and may even have had visions of cooperation with Spain against France, as indeed took place half a century after his death. They would not have deserved the name of statesman if they had thought differently. In this matter the Prince was certainly Oldenbarnevelt's instructor.

Master and pupil thought differently however about the acceptance of Anjou as sovereign. Oldenbarnevelt did not want to oppose it in view of Prince William's vehement advocacy, but he was highly sceptical. France had nothing at stake in the heir to the throne's Netherlands escapade. Because of this the Netherlands would not gain anything either by the acquisition of Anjou. The Prince did not realize this, being too long-sighted in his ideas. Eventually France would clash again with Spain and the Netherlands would have to try and profit by it. But the time was not yet ripe for this. Eight years were to elapse before the murder of the Guises led to the rupture from which Oldenbarnevelt, following in the Prince's footsteps, managed to profit in a masterly way.

During the rule of Anjou, who was not allowed to act as sovereign in Holland owing to a secret clause in which he acknowledged William as such, Oldenbarnevelt was entrusted with the drafting of instructions for the establishment of a new court, the Hoge Raad, to which in certain cases appeals would be possible from the verdicts of the Hof van Holland. According to law the stadtholder had to sign these instructions, after taking advice from the States, for them to be valid. But an attempt had been made to assassinate the Prince and he was dangerously ill at Antwerp when the document was ready for his signature. The States then decided – was it on Oldenbarnevelt's insistence? – to put it into effect without the Prince's approval. This was an important step towards a republican form of government for the province.

In the same year Oldenbarnevelt was appointed to a committee for drawing up ecclesiastical regulations. The year before a national synod at Middelburg had drawn up a polity according to which the power of the government with regard to the church had been reduced to a minimum. The States of Holland regarded this as an infringement of their lawful authority. They appointed and paid the ministers and maintained the church buildings and so it was for them to make church regulations. A committee solely of laymen, including several non-churchgoers and some crypto-Catholics, now drafted extremely Erastian regulations which were no more accepted by the church than the church's had been by the States. At Oldenbarnevelt's trial in 1618 the Calvinist section of the bench accused him of lending himself to this attack on the church. Oldenbarnevelt defended himself by feebly observing that he had been the youngest member of the commission and that the older members were each and every one good patriots and seasoned enemies of Spain.

Confronted with the opposition of all ecclesiastical elements, the States did not dare to promulgate the regulations proposed by the committee. Oldenbarnevelt learnt a lesson from this failure: when nine years later the States under his leadership made another attempt, they appointed a committee consisting of an equal number of ministers and laymen, all church members. But the lesson was insufficient: the draft regulations of 1591 were never accepted by the church.

Later in the year Oldenbarnevelt was deputed to the States-General, where Anjou was proposing the introduction of taxation as provided for in the Union of Utrecht: uniform excise collected by officials and paid into the exchequer of a collector-general. In opposing this the Prince and the States took the same line.

Not that the Prince was not a centralist: but he remained a realist. He understood that the system of general taxation was incompatible with the inflexible doctrine of provincial autonomy. Anyway at the first hint of trouble the provinces would impound the collectors' funds. Every possible provincial stratagem would be used to ensure the unequal incidence of taxation intended to be uniform. Any check would be more difficult and fraud would be rife if the provinces were no longer to be responsible for what was collected in their territory.

Oldenbarnevelt was well aware of the defects of the quota system. But it was too soon for this, solidarity was not strong enough, economic conditions varied too much in the different provinces. We can safely assume that the Prince and Oldenbarnevelt did the emerging state of the Netherlands a service by preventing the introduction into this federation of taxation that smelled of centralization – with the exception of convoys and *licenten* – at short notice and without psychological preparation.

Another thing that gave rise to lively debate was whether or not to permit trading with the enemy, a problem that was to vex Oldenbarnevelt for many years. This time the main concern was trade along the Rhine and the Maas. What went up the Maas could not fail to reach the enemy and what went up the Rhine often reached him too, by an indirect route. For a ruler who wanted to defeat his enemy (and who was being excessively short-sighted) it was an intolerable idea that Dutch traders should be provisioning the enemy. Over and over again, starting with the Prince during the Four Years War, we see the central authorities launching attempts to prohibit all trading with the enemy. The Dutch merchants gave way when pressure became too great, but soon started smuggling again with grim persistence, and then the edicts had to be altered to suit them. We shall see this occur with regrettable regularity, at this time with Anjou, at a later period with Leicester, then with Elizabeth. It was always Oldenbarnevelt who was to defend – not always enthusiastically – Holland's position against successive rulers.

Not always enthusiastically. Oldenbarnevelt was not a merchant. The defeat of the enemy was the main thing for him no less than for Orange or Anjou. He had something of Clemenceau's hardness with his 'Je fais la guerre'. Then there were considerations of foreign policy. It was very hard to explain to a foreign ally why the Hollanders insisted on supplying the enemy, not only in Belgium but also in Spain and Portugal, with all his needs and at the same time asked for support in fighting him. This was the case again now.

Holland's prosperity was after all based on trade, and in this trade Belgium was an indispensable link. If herring, for instance, could not be exported to Belgium and the Rhineland, a large part of the catch would be destroyed or the number of fishing boats putting out reduced.

Furthermore, it was not as if Holland were the only possible source of all the good things being transported to Belgium. There was the Hanseatic League, there were Denmark, England and the Upper Rhine area. Would not the only effect be to divert trade to these places, with results which in the long run might be even more disastrous for Holland than the immediate effects of an export embargo?

A third argument must have impressed the Prince strongly. High duties were charged on exports to the enemy. These *licenten* were the only taxes provided for at Utrecht still available to the States-General – in theory at any rate. They paid for the sea power of the Netherlands. If the Rhine and Maas were closed to outgoing traffic the merchants would suffer financially and clearly taxation would have to be raised just as the merchant class was stunned by the effects of the embargo.

It was a dilemma equally felt by the enemy. Until the end of the war trade embargoes were to alternate with periods of free trade. Often trifles, small questions of power, tipped the scales. This time they were tipped to retain the embargo for the Maas and to raise the duty on the Rhine, which after all did not lead '*directelijck naar svijants gebied*'.[1]

On his return Oldenbarnevelt was in trouble for his weak attitude. Anjou had stated, he explained, that with the embargo he could win the war in a short time; without it he would not guarantee anything. The States resigned themselves to this . . . for the time being.

[1] Direct to the enemy's territory.

A few months later the constitutional rule of Anjou ended abruptly in the French Fury, as it was called (17 January 1583), when the Duke attempted to seize Antwerp and the Prince, but was forced to retreat by the vigilance of the loyal citizens and soldiers. Nevertheless the Prince's prestige in Antwerp had been seriously affected by this episode, especially when it was learnt that he was again going to open negotiations with this treasonous ruler, under the pretext that the Netherlands could not dispense with French help in the war against Spain, even if it took the form of a tyrannical princeling. In Antwerp a storm of abuse broke out against the Prince, who had just married for the fourth time, and it had to be to a Frenchwoman, a member of that treacherous nation. That she was a Huguenot and a daughter of Admiral de Coligny, a victim of St Bartholomew's Night, instigated by Anjou's brothers, counted for nothing with the embittered and mistrustful people. The result of all this was that Holland got its Stadtholder back. On 22 July the Prince left Antwerp for good and settled after a time at Delft, where Oldenbarnevelt was to meet him constantly, until he was assassinated there on 10 July 1584 by Balthasar Gerard.

The principal concern all that year of both the Prince and Oldenbarnevelt was the elevation of the former to the rank of Count of Holland. Once that had been done, and if other provinces undertook a similar elevation, it was much less dangerous to accept the French duke again as a ruler – treacherous Florentine (his mother was a Medici) though he was. His power would then be completely neutralized by the ostensibly lesser power of the Prince.

Oldenbarnevelt, as pro-Orange at this time as he was to become anti-Orange over the years, did all he could in support of the Prince's elevation, and came within a hair's breadth of success. Only Amsterdam, with its strongly republican ideas, caused the installation to be delayed, so that it was to have taken place a few days after the murder. Hollanders in general did not like walking on thin ice. The opinions of most of the towns and of the adjacent provinces of Zeeland and Utrecht had first to be sounded. Then a sort of constitution had to be set up, a *capitulatie*, a series of conditions curtailing the Count's power, for nobody intended making him an absolute ruler. In fact they wanted to have their cake and eat it: to have on the one hand an eminent leader capable of waging war vigorously and cancelling Anjou's power; and on the other an executive authority completely dependent on the States and in particular not strong enough to do anything to their sacred privileges.

The Prince gave full cooperation. He knew that the vigour and charm of his personality were enough to ensure him much more power than the *capitulatie* seemed to accord him. His relations with Oldenbarnevelt, whom we may regard as part-author of this *capitulatie*, were therefore continuously good in this last year of his life.

At one of their meetings the Prince introduced him to his new wife, Louise de Coligny. She immediately felt drawn towards the Rotterdam pensionary and this led to an understanding, a friendship almost, which did not flag in the ensuing thirty-five years.

At the end of 1583 Oldenbarnevelt was again deputed to the States-General, who had now removed to Holland and transacted all their business in Dutch. The Prince, unconcerned at fiercely anti-French public opinion, suggested serious resumption of the negotiations with Anjou. As the Governor-General Parma was now occupying all the rural area of Flanders and the fall of Bruges and Ghent seemed only a question of weeks, French help was the only thing that could keep prosperous Flanders within the fold.

The delegation from Holland was faced with a difficult dilemma. If they voted for Anjou and the Prince it might cost them their popularity with the community and also affect unfavourably the chances of English support. A strong party in Holland, led by the Grand Pensionary Paulus Buys, expected more help from this direction than from a France on the verge of yet another civil war. On the other hand it would be a serious responsibility if the chief towns in Flanders were to fall into Spanish hands after the remedy recommended by the Prince had been disdained. Apart from the possibility of immediate military help there was the reinforcement of the prestige in France itself of the anti-Spanish heir to the throne; by means of this prestige he might checkmate the Guises and involve his brother the king against Spain.

Oldenbarnevelt, with his well-known indifference to the ordinary citizen and growing tendency to see things in their wider international context, did not hesitate about the Hollanders' vote. Anjou would have to be tried again. In February 1584 a mission left for France to discuss a reacceptance of the conditions. The naturally somewhat laborious negotiations had not shown any result when Anjou died in June. According to the stipulations of the draft agreement Henry III was to succeed his brother. Here again Oldenbarnevelt followed the Prince's urgent advice, although opposition to the new candidate, a leading instigator of the St Bartholomew's Day massacres, was perhaps even stronger than that to the man responsible for the French Fury.

This session of the States-General at Delft, in the presence of the Prince, was of great importance to Oldenbarnevelt for the rest of his life. His whole position in the assembly had grown much more important than in 1580 or 1582. This was because Holland had meanwhile become the focal point of the United Provinces, both geographically and morally. Flanders could be considered a write-off, Brussels had long been a lost outpost and Parma's troops were appearing alarmingly close to the gates of Antwerp. Brabant was indeed still assessed for a quota of $28\frac{1}{2}\%$ as against Holland and Zeeland with $43\frac{1}{2}\%$ together, but this was almost a nominal quota, largely or entirely absorbed by the preparations for the defence of Antwerp. In practice Holland and Zeeland yielded more than all the other provinces together. Holland thus paid the piper and was supposed to call the tune. The quality of Holland's statesmen, however, had not increased as much as the importance of its quota. Most members of the rising oligarch class at that time were nine-tenths merchant with little political sense. There were no longer any great nobles. Nine-tenths of the lesser nobility were landowners with more knowledge of the produce of a field than of the potentials of a diplomatic manoeuvre. In the ensuing period therefore a great many of the prominent politicians in Holland were not Hollanders. Buys and Oldenbarnevelt were from the Sticht, the pensionary of Dordrecht, Menijn, and later that of Haarlem, De Haen, were Flemings, as was the ambassador to England, Caron. The pensionaries of Amsterdam, Gouda and Alkmaar were from Brabant. So too was the clerk to the States-General, Cornelis van Aerssen.

We can therefore see why, apart from his exceptional talents, Oldenbarnevelt had to take a prominent part in the Delft session of the States-General. He was near the centre of things and was involved for the first time in all sorts of foreign affairs. This can sometimes be seen from the committees to which he was appointed and sometimes rests merely on assumptions. He was not officially concerned with the Prince's French policy. It was the centre of the latter's preoccupations and he seldom wrote a longer letter than the apologia for this policy sent to his brother Johann.[1]

Oldenbarnevelt never saw this letter but its principles were his for thirty-five years. The Prince certainly did not express these ideas only in writing. They must have been the main theme of his conversation in February and March. Oldenbarnevelt must have hung on his lips, and the rather haughty aversion from know-all political theologians to be found in the letter was also his: in the disputes with Leicester, in those about the Truce, in the French civil wars under Louis XIII. It was his temporal undoing and his eternal honour. It was the Prince who led him to that undoing and that honour.

Nor did William of Orange neglect policy towards England, always inextricably entangled with that towards France. Again it cannot be proved but may be assumed that Oldenbarnevelt was familiar with that policy and learnt its lessons. It concerned John Norris, general over the English auxiliaries.

[1] *Archives de la Maison d'Orange-Nassau*, première série, Leiden, 1841–7, VIII, 339–63 (8 March 1584, O.S.).

John Norris had rendered outstanding service to the States-General for six years. For a time at first jointly with La Noue, then with Hohenlohe, he had been commander-in-chief of the States' armies. According to Van Meteren[1] he was '*cloeck ende dapper maar veel te hoochmoedich*'[2] and quarrelled with all his fellow-officers. The Prince respected him and Oldenbarnevelt was always able to get on with him even in his most anti-English periods. His troops and he himself were badly paid. In 1583 they had been stationed at Alost and depended for their pay on the tender mercies of the people of Ghent. Some of Norris's subordinates had had enough of this and sold Alost to the Prince of Parma. The result was the first wave of hatred for the English. Norris was innocent, but his position had become impossible and he was honourably dismissed. The Prince arranged for a gratuity for him so that he could pay his creditors and gave him an official letter to the Queen. If Oldenbarnevelt knew its contents he learnt less from it than from the Prince's French policy. The latter had never met Elizabeth, and only knew of her through her envoys. He seems to have understood from them, Walsingham in particular, that Elizabeth was devout and regarded the Pope as antichrist. The document is therefore a rather unpleasing mixture of flattery and hypocrisy and cannot have impressed Elizabeth greatly. He asks for support in general terms without suggesting any definite plan. Later on Oldenbarnevelt was to tackle this quite differently. The Prince did seem to be aware of Elizabeth's understandable anxiety about Ostend and the Flemish coast in general. He informed her that his attitude towards France was entirely in agreement with her advice conveyed by Walsingham. Oldenbarnevelt will have noted this for future reference: constant coordination of his French and English policies, harnessing France and England to Holland's cart, were to be his tactics just as they had been those of the Prince.

Oldenbarnevelt was still not in the centre of the web of international politics, but his interest and the confidence of the Prince had been engaged. The latter was about to break with Paulus Buys, Marnix was no longer close to him since becoming burgomaster of Antwerp. There was, so to speak, a situation vacant at Delft: that of (unofficial) adviser on foreign affairs. At a subsequent session of the States-General Oldenbarnevelt could hope for this position.

Balthasar Gerard's bullets, on 10 July 1584, dashed this hope but a still fairer one rose on the horizon.

Four days before the assassination, on Friday, 6 July, two deputies of the nobility had come to Delft, where the States of Holland met too at this time,

---

[1] Emanuel van Meteren, *Historien der Nederlanden*, 1697 edition.
[2] 'Manly and brave but much too arrogant'.

to report on their mission to Amsterdam, that would still not agree to the immediate recognition of the Prince as Count. Under the influence of the Orangist ex-burgomaster Cant they were still not totally against it as another ex-burgomaster, Cornelis Pietersz Hooft had wished, but they kept the affair dragging on till Zeeland on the one hand and the Amsterdam citizenry on the other would agree to the elevation. Gouda was hanging back too. Should they now go on against the wishes of these two towns? It was discussed on Friday and again on Saturday, but no resolution was passed. To utter threats is one thing, to carry them out another. No doubt Oldenbarnevelt was fuming: in his most cutting tone he must have criticized the weakness inherent in further delay. But the States were cautious. Majority voting in matters of government was forbidden from of old. On that Saturday, the decision was postponed in the hope that Zeeland would give its consent and Amsterdam withdraw its objections. The States met again on Sunday after church. There was no meeting in the afternoon, but on Monday morning, the 9th, a subject was dealt with in which Oldenbarnevelt had a personal interest. A fortnight before a delegation had left for France to offer sovereignty to the King. They had to bring troops at once for the relief of Antwerp, for which purpose they had been given 52,000 guilders. There was not much money in the exchequer, of course, and Oldenbarnevelt and seven others had advanced it – proof that he was already well off financially. The envoys now promised in writing from Dieppe that they would not pay out the money unless Henry III did indeed undertake the protection of the Netherlands.

The next morning Oldenbarnevelt was not present, the first occasion for a long time. If he was in Rotterdam he was riding along the Schie when the Prince was shot between 1 and 2 p.m. He was told of it when he arrived in Delft just before three and was one of the seventeen men who met at the town hall to decide what had to be done first. It was to write letters to the towns whose representatives were absent, telling them to send deputations to Delft immediately, and to the commanders of military units to promise them money at short notice – the States were on the rocks for the present – and to assure them that the States would look after their interests and those of their soldiers as assiduously as the Prince could have done. Oldenbarnevelt was specially charged with the letter to Hohenlohe, the Prince's military deputy, then engaged in besieging Zutfen. He knew the touchy count well and understood how to deal with him.

When the letters were ready the States requested the deputies present to go home and return as soon as possible with extensive powers to pass resolutions concerning government and taxation without having to go for further instructions. The Council met in Rotterdam and appointed a delegation of six men with a twofold authorization: one to a mayor and the pensionary to decide on 'all matters occurring, with whatever depends on them', one to the same men plus four members of the council 'to help advise and make resolutions in the definitive and provisional governments of the country, with whatever depends on them, without any report'. The last three words are the important feature here, in which the Council showed an unusual degree of self-denial. In effect *ruggespraak*, the backbone of Netherland political practice, was put out of action on account of the exceptional circumstances.

This resolution was of course not only passed in Rotterdam. All the other towns did the same as a result of a resolution of desirability on principle passed at the small meeting on Tuesday afternoon. Oldenbarnevelt was certainly not against it. The resolution could be regarded as posthumous homage to the Prince, who in recent years had repeatedly urged the abolition of *ruggespraak*.

Another basic principle, heroically defended only three days before, was also departed from without ceremony in this essential resolution: the prohibition of majority voting on the reserved subjects: government, peace, taxes. To establish a new government this principle was expressly departed from in the resolution of 10 July just mentioned. It soon proved necessary to take similar measures for taxation. The situation was critical. The death of the Prince necessitated restoring the soldiers' lost confidence by prompt payment. Everything that was available, and much that was not, was needed for the relief of Antwerp. The *licenten* yielded little or nothing since the Prince, to help Antwerp, had once again brusquely forbidden the export of food to the enemy. It was not possible to delay the collection of taxes till some recalcitrant *vroedschap* chose to give its consent. The nobles therefore suggested that in all matters that arose the minority should be bound by the majority. The opposition to this measure was much stronger than to the abolition of *ruggespraak*. Again it was Amsterdam which, as a large town, did not want to be outvoted by a coalition of small towns; Oldenbarnevelt supported a compromise proposed by Leiden: a majority must consist of two-thirds. Amsterdam was instructed to vote against this and maintained the principle, though promising in practice to be amenable. This was not binding and in fact Amsterdam again frustrated these efforts, to Oldenbarnevelt's great annoyance.

Three days later Oldenbarnevelt received his first assignment of crucial importance: the compilation of an 'estimate of war' for the province of Holland, a survey of all troops and civilian officials and of their expenses, a sort of budget, the only occasion in Oldenbarnevelt's time that the need of such a document was felt, though it seems indispensable to us now.

A little later, on Sunday 22nd, Oldenbarnevelt was appointed to a committee of ten for planning a closer union with Zeeland, and soon after with other provinces, as since the Prince's death all central executive authority had been lacking. The committee worked out instructions for a Council of State to be set up anew, to which a great majority in the States of Holland had wished Oldenbarnevelt to be appointed. It was not a felicitous idea. With his high estimation of Holland's sovereignty he was not suited to an interprovincial body with mainly administrative duties. There are indications that he did not desire this appointment and was glad to drop out, when at a later stage it was decided to reduce the Council's numbers.

He appeared as a champion of that sovereignty at the beginning of August, when Prince William's long-delayed funeral had to be arranged. Oldenbarnevelt took the view that the Prince was count-designate of Holland and that the States of Holland must lead the procession. He had to make excuses for this attitude, however, when the States-General claimed precedence 'as being at present the highest authority in the country'.[1] A remarkable foreshadowing of the events of 1617–18, though then Oldenbarnevelt was not able to retreat under cover of excuses.

In 1584 he tried to get his own back by supporting a rather obvious idea of the Grand Pensionary's, Paulus Buys: to elevate to the rank of Count of Holland the young Count Maurice, second son of the late Prince – the elder, Philip William, was a prisoner in Spain. This would have been a considerable strengthening of Holland's position with regard to the expected French ruler. The States would have none of this, however, before it could be shown that the sixteen-year-old Maurice had inherited some of his father's talents.

Though Oldenbarnevelt joined forces with Buys here, he opposed him with regard to the offer of sovereignty to Henry III. A French envoy reported that the offer appealed to the King, provided it were extended to include Holland and Zeeland. The States decided to send a new delegation with extensive powers, notwithstanding advice to the contrary from Paulus Buys, who saw that this delegation was a mere waste of time and that only a resolute appeal to England might still raise the siege of Antwerp. For since Anjou's death, the Protestant King of Navarre had become heir to the throne according to the Salic law. Three-quarters of France's population would not recognize him as such. King Henry III himself, pious though he was, expected more from the conversion of Navarre, if he were given time, than from a change in the laws of succession, so seriously harmful to the prestige of the monarchy. The extremists under Henri de Guise opposed these delaying tactics. Guise was known to be negotiating with Spain to put pressure on

[1] '*als wesende nu ter tyt de hoochste overicheyt van den lande*'.

the King, whose reputation for piety and the prestige of the crown gave him a certain advantage. In these circumstances it would have been madness for Henry III to embark on open war with the King of Spain to defend a heretical community of rebels. Henry III may have been abnormal but he was not mad. The Hollanders should have thought of this. They cannot be greatly blamed though. The Prince had always kept them out of foreign politics till shortly before his death. No Hollander had ever been in France except as a student. They did not possess a foreign information service, even in the most elementary form.

So Oldenbarnevelt made one of his few serious mistakes. At the end of August he, together with a majority of the States of Holland, took the French line and abandoned Buys. That Buys 'drew his conclusions' from this and departed has a curiously modern flavour, like a twentieth-century minister resigning when his policy no longer commands a majority. Sixteenth-century – and also much later – public servants used calmly to help carry out policies they disagreed with.

Relations between Buys and the States, had, however, been bad for a long time. The States thought that they could well do without a pensionary. The pensionary of the oldest town, Dordrecht, could do the job as a sideline, they thought. So for a year and a half they did not appoint a successor to Buys.

Oldenbarnevelt was appointed with another pensionary to draw up instructions for the new delegation. Till Henry III's answer arrived all measures taken were of a temporary nature. People held their breath, so to speak, awaiting the unknown French prince who, master of formidable troops but servant of the Dutch cheesemongers, was to relieve Brussels and Antwerp – Ghent had fallen meanwhile. This was a curiously naive expectation, pitifully betraying the small knowledge of the world possessed by the orphaned patriots. Three years muddling with Leicester were to follow before they learnt their lesson: heaven helps those that help themselves. Oldenbarnevelt was to be the embodiment of this lesson learned.

For the present he was regarded as a specialist in foreign affairs. Thus the States of Holland entrusted to him the correspondence with an envoy from King Henry of Navarre, travelling round Europe in search of support from Protestant powers against threats by the Guises. It shows that at this time the States-General had no monopoly of relations with foreign countries. The agent in England too, Ortel, with whom Oldenbarnevelt was soon to establish closer relations, was an agent of Holland and Zeeland, not of the parent body.

In the early spring of 1585, when it began to look as if Henry III would refuse the sovereignty offered, and when Elizabeth sent William Davison to the Netherlands to discuss possible support for Antwerp and Ostend, it was once again the States of Holland that made contact with him and again Oldenbarnevelt who was delegated with two others to conduct the discussions. During them the delegates came to the conclusion that an embassy consisting of plenipotentiaries from all the provinces should be sent to England as soon as possible. Elizabeth demanded guarantees for her help, not only financial ones but also in the form of cautionary towns, only to be evacuated on repayment of the debt incurred by the States-General. Henry III's refusal arrived just at this time and Oldenbarnevelt hastened as much as possible the departure of the delegation with unlimited powers. In the first place they were to offer Elizabeth sovereignty, alternatively a formal protectorate, or again they had to ask for an auxiliary army under an eminent nobleman who would be given ample authority to intervene in government matters.

Holland completed the instructions on 4 May and appointed three envoys from the province, of whom Oldenbarnevelt was the youngest. As such, and also because of his limited familiarity with the French language, he was the least important one in the eyes of the English, but perhaps within the delegation had the most influence.

Fortunately for the success of the delegation the other provinces were not nearly ready. Elizabeth, after sending Davison to Holland in March, had cooled off rapidly. A temperamental woman, she was easily affected by passing events and could genuinely forget a decision taken in different circumstances. This time it was the Péronne manifesto that made her hesitate. This constitution of the newly founded Ligue sounded like a trumpet of Jericho to make the unsteady walls of the decadent house of Valois collapse. A united Catholic France would make an alliance with the Spanish king, and woe betide the queen caught collaborating with rebellious subjects of Spain. She wanted in no circumstances to hear any more about sovereignty. Davison was sharply rebuked for having influenced the States-General in that direction. If the envoys had come over then they would have had a rough reception. When, however, after a long delay, caused especially by pro-French Zeeland, they at last arrived in England on 5 July (N.S., 25 June O.S.), Elizabeth was already in a better mood. On the one hand the Péronne manifesto had not had the crushing effect that she had feared, on the other the danger of Antwerp had been greatly increased by encirclement.

The delegates succeeded, after laborious negotiations, in extorting two agreements from Elizabeth, in which she promised the Netherlands military and financial help. As an earnest of this help the first English troops under the Earl of Oxford had landed at Flushing. At the darkest hour dawn seemed to be approaching. Nobody was to know that both Parma's offensive and

Leicester's defence would turn out less efficient than they appeared. For the present Oldenbarnevelt and his fellow-envoys could consider themselves saviours of the Netherlands.

The spokesman of this delegation was the Dordrecht pensionary, Menijn. But the envoy who made most contacts in England and used them for his personal political future was the ex-Advocate of Holland, Paulus Buys, not representing this province but his native Utrecht. He soon observed that Burghley was close-fisted and contested every shilling of subsidy; that Walsingham was the leader of the anti-Spanish faction and therefore distrusted by Elizabeth; and that Leicester, closely connected with Walsingham, was the man he needed. A few days after the delegates arrived in London he managed to obtain an invitation to dinner with Leicester together with Menijn and the Zeeland envoy Valcke, the two most important figures among the others. On this occasion the Netherlanders must have promised to support Leicester's ambition of becoming governor-general and to buttress his authority with their own – a promise which the two others kept scrupulously. Leicester no doubt promised to get the treaty through provided the delegates had enough to offer, and to Buys in particular he may have given the undertaking to include him in the Council of State. The first of the two treaties dealt only with the sending of a small force under John Norris, which, though intended to relieve Antwerp, did not arrive in Zeeland till Antwerp had capitulated. The second treaty, concluded on 22 August (N.S., 12 August O.S.) at the royal residence of Nonsuch, was for the next thirteen years to remain the basis of relations between England and the Netherlands and a source of much anxiety for Oldenbarnevelt.

The Queen promised to send an army of 4,000 infantry and 400 cavalry to the Netherlands and to pay them herself. This pay was to be refunded by the States after the war. The troops were to be under the command of a 'Governor-General' who, besides his military duties, would be charged with the maintenance of unity among the provinces, without, however, there being any question of a form of protectorate. The towns of Brill in Holland and Flushing in Zeeland, as well as the fortress of Rammekens, were to be occupied by English garrisons as a pledge for the repayment stipulated. As governing body of the rebellious provinces the treaty envisaged a Council of State to which the Queen would be able to appoint two members. The relationship thus created was not to be called a protectorate, though in effect it bore all the marks of one.

It can be said that the Hollanders had obtained both more and less than they had hoped for by this treaty. Less, in so far as the Governor-General in Elizabeth's view was not to be called Viceroy – two ideas which were synonymous in the Netherlands till far into the twentieth century. To the outside world, and formally within the country, he was not to act as the successor of Alva, Matthias or Anjou, as the Netherlanders hoped and assumed. But they also got more, because this Governor-General, according to Elizabeth's intention, was in fact to exercise the highest authority, not bound by oligarchic restrictions such as had become second nature to the Hollanders in only a few years. It will be seen how in the ensuing months the nature of this double misunderstanding was gradually brought home to Oldenbarnevelt.

CHAPTER 2

Leicester opposed

THE return of the envoys was eagerly awaited in Holland. The implementation of the treaty with England involved a great deal of work. One after the other the captains, followed by the colonels and the generals, came streaming into the country. They had to be mustered and paid and their minds set at rest about the most un-English behaviour of Dutch officials. This was just the job for Oldenbarnevelt, long a specialist in dealing with troublesome soldiers. He could twist Hohenlohe round his little finger and this was needed, as Hohenlohe was in an awkward position: after being commander-in-chief he would soon be number two under a fellow from overseas. This fellow's subordinates, sent on in advance, were already unwilling to obey Hohenlohe's orders. The first of them had just been mustered in The Hague when Oldenbarnevelt arrived there from England. The Binnenhof and the Buitenhof were cordoned off, the soldiers were sleeping everywhere in the galleries, the citizens of The Hague were horrified at the thought that a few might slip past the Dutch guard at the Gevangenpoort, the members of the States had difficulty in picking their way through the encampments. A few days later John Norris arrived there. He was an old acquaintance of the States and of Oldenbarnevelt, no less troublesome than Hohenlohe but a much more capable commander, from long service on the continent less insular than the Englishmen who came after him. Money troubles cropped up at once: about the day when the troops were to become a charge on Elizabeth, about the cost of their transport and supply of arms, about the 'service moneys', as they were called, the money advanced by the garrison town for such things as bedding, candles and beer: about loans and ammunition, *mortepayes*, sick men and deserters. On his return from his English embassy Oldenbarnevelt was at once entrusted by the States-General with the negotiations on all these points and in the coming months it was one of his chief occupations. He always worked jointly with someone else, though doubtless almost always as the chief.

It might be supposed this constant bickering must ruin his relationship with the English general. The opposite was true and this perhaps explains many of Oldenbarnevelt's successes in later years. He could get excited and hurl angry accusations and unforgivably wounding reproaches about, if he thought that right was on his side and when he was imputing bad faith to his opponents. But if it was not certain where the right lay he allowed the other person quietly to speak up for his own interests and they parted friends. So mutual respect, not easily shaken, resulted from his disputes with John Norris: this was to smooth the road towards the independence of the Netherlands; especially as Norris was a cousin of Walsingham, Oldenbarnevelt's counterpart after Leicester's departure.

There were other difficulties. Morale had been weakened by the fall of Antwerp. The cause of the rebellion was considered lost by many people, especially in Holland and Zeeland. The 'common man' in particular inclined towards submission to the King. A Spanish invasion of the Betuwe aroused a kind of panic among the public. The first duty of the envoys on their return was to extol the wonders to be expected from Elizabeth's auxiliaries and her irresistible favourite. The Rotterdam *vroedschap* took heart on 4 September; at the first meeting attended by their pensionary after his return they passed a resolution that the defeatists should be removed from the council. Stringent measures were proposed and taken by Holland against Marnix, with some justification regarded as the leading defeatist. Oldenbarnevelt may well have had a hand in this; he had found out in England what a grudge the statesmen had against Marnix, whom they blamed more than was reasonable – and more than Oldenbarnevelt himself must have thought reasonable – for the fall of Antwerp.

It was in these months, just when forceful leadership seemed needed more than ever, that it was lacking. Holland possessed neither a stadtholder nor an advocate. The latter could more easily be dispensed with. His functions at the meetings of the States were fulfilled, according to tradition, by Menijn. The rest of the work was done by the secretary to the States. Neither received any extra emoluments for this, so that the prolonged vacancy represented a considerable economy. But penny-wisdom has always been a familiar Dutch trait.

In September efforts were made to put an end to this provisional state of affairs. Oldenbarnevelt was one of the four candidates. But none was able to secure an absolute majority and it was decided to defer discussion, especially as there was a party that wanted to appoint two advocates; this may well have been a sign of mistrust of Oldenbarnevelt, the most likely candidate, whose domineering character had made him unpopular with some people.

It seemed to be harder to do without a stadtholder than without an advocate. Young Count Maurice, appointed 'Head of the Council of State' in August of the previous year, became eighteen in the autumn of 1585. When

the delegation in England had had to state the names of the provincial stadtholders, they had been told to declare that the States of Holland 'regarded'
Maurice as stadtholder of Holland and Zeeland. He was not yet appointed,
however. Now Leicester was on the way and something was needed to
counterbalance the great power which was to be conferred on him; it was
resolved, on the suggestion of Zeeland, to hold a formal election in the two
provinces. Oldenbarnevelt prided himself in 1618 on having organized
Maurice's elevation to the office of stadtholder. It is one of the many in-
accuracies, generally redounding to his own credit, occurring in his Remonstrance. His actual role, important enough, seems to have been to help the
proposal of the Zeeland Orangist Valcke prevail against strong opposition in
Holland. This came on the one hand from towns with republican leanings,
such as Amsterdam and Gouda; on the other from the pro-English, who
thought it rather discourteous, just before Leicester's arrival, to appoint a
stadtholder over the two principal provinces without letting him know.
Oldenbarnevelt was not a republican – at any rate not as long as he could
count on being the *éminence grise* behind the 'throne'. And courtesies must
not be paid at the expense of the supremacy of the States of Holland, which
he defended all his life and at the cost of his life.

Another stratagem of Oldenbarnevelt's was to give Count Maurice a higher
title, 'Prince of Orange by birth', by which he would take precedence over
Leicester. Leicester did not recognize the title, so the plan failed. The only
result was that the States began to speak of His Excellency instead of His
Grace. And as they also granted Leicester the title of Excellency – to the annoyance of Elizabeth, who thought it made him 'excel' too much – confusion
might occur. Perhaps this was just what was intended.

On the same occasion Maurice was recognized as Marquis of Bergen-op-
Zoom, but his power was restricted in his seigneury of Flushing, as this had
become a cautionary town. Oldenbarnevelt's task was to persuade Maurice to
give his consent to the occupation of his town by an English garrison. He
soon reached agreement with the young count and his advisers on the terms
of the act of indemnity to guarantee Maurice the return of Flushing intact
when the occupation should end, for whatever reason. It is the first personal
contact that is known of between the two and boded well for the future. On
7 October the English troops under the temporary governor, Edward Norris,
entered Flushing quietly and in good order. This delicate matter, the cause of
great opposition in Zeeland as well, was brought to a satisfactory conclusion
with much 'politeness'.

There was nothing to prevent Leicester arriving soon and he was awaited
impatiently. No doubt Oldenbarnevelt shared this impatience.

Anarchy had mounted to the highest pitch. Every few weeks the Council of State threatened to resign if money was not forthcoming. While a large-scale attack by Parma could be expected at any moment the States-General had to disband troops for lack of money. This disbanding was always troublesome, as arrears of pay had to be settled first and therefore cash was needed in order to economize. There was no money in the States-General's exchequer, so that the States of Holland were landed with the thankless task of dismissal. The only bright spot was the capture by John Norris of some entrenchments in Gelderland which had made Arnhem virtually a besieged town. But his troops had not been paid either, so that he could not touch Nijmegen. Fortunately Parma had the same financial difficulties: he also had a food shortage, for the Scheldt was closed and export via the other rivers forbidden. Here was another reason for Leicester to come quickly, since not all the provinces were taking the prohibition equally seriously. Public opinion wanted a measure applicable to all the provinces, but this had to wait for Leicester's arrival. There was sharp disagreement on this point between the Utrecht militia captains, who did no trade, and the Amsterdam merchants, who did a lot: the States of Holland entrusted the matter to Oldenbarnevelt, who tried in vain to make the enraged parties see reason.

Here too Leicester must provide the solution. But October became November, and November December and still Leicester could not leave, thwarted by the caprices of his Queen and the thriftiness of her ministers. Seldom has such a failure been awaited with such high hopes. When on 20 December he was at last within sight of Flushing there was no end to the demonstrations. Oldenbarnevelt had his part in them when the great man passed through Rotterdam on 3 January and he had to 'congratulate' him. The speech has not been preserved but it can be imagined. What was going on in the speaker's mind? Oldenbarnevelt's attitude in the next two years was one of almost constant hostility and this may have dated from before the Governor-General's arrival. Oldenbarnevelt's congratulation would then be pure hypocrisy. But this is an oversimplification of the matter. Oldenbarnevelt never denied the necessity for a strong central authority in time of war. On the very day of Leicester's arrival at Flushing he could see from his negotiations with the angry men from Amsterdam and Utrecht that an arbitrator placed above the parties was indispensable. Furthermore Leicester brought money and soldiers with him. He was the great Queen's favourite, he guaranteed her friendship and help. His presence alone made the defeatists and peace-seekers climb down. This was enough to enable Oldenbarnevelt to greet his future opponent with a great measure of sincere sympathy.

There was another thing. Leicester was of necessity largely dependent on his Dutch advisers and Oldenbarnevelt saw him arrive surrounded by Buys, Leoninus and Thin, by Valcke and Menijn, all figures who had been great in the Prince's time, aristocratic, anti-Calvinist, but also reliably anti-Spanish. They did not belong to the oligarchs' party now being formed in Holland, with its strong tendency to autonomy, but at that time the difference was only a nuance. It is true that Leicester's chief adviser, Paulus Buys, was not persona grata with the States of Holland. His ambition caused alarm, his honesty was not above suspicion. But the team as such was calculated to inspire confidence. Leicester was a vain man, as Oldenbarnevelt knew from his stay in England. This was confirmed when he saw how the man's head was turned by the effusive flattery he met with at Middelburg and Dordrecht. Vain people are easily captured and led.

So far all was well, but there were danger signals of which the realistic pensionary was well aware.

Leicester had gained an unfavourable impression of Count Maurice in Zeeland. He made no effort to conceal his opinion that he did not appreciate the attempt to set up that young man as a counterpoise to himself. The Earl seems never to have known that Oldenbarnevelt was the man behind Maurice's promotion in Holland, but here was a hidden element of danger. Furthermore he was constantly inveighing against merchants in politics. Oldenbarnevelt was not a merchant either and could feel some sympathy, but he had been in the politics of Holland long enough to know that merchants were indispensable. Some had always been in the Council of State and Leicester's idea of forming a Council in which the merchants were not represented at all was as anti-Holland as could be. There is a great likelihood that Buys, his right-hand man in recent months in England, had insinuated the idea out of resentment against his former employers. With this high nobleman little insinuation was needed to create much prejudice.

Since his arrival in Flushing this prejudice had greatly increased. The Zeelanders had had different interests from the Hollanders with regard to trade with the enemy. They had complained to Leicester about the Council of State consisting mainly of Hollanders and merchants or their friends. Dordrecht too, with little foreign trade and traditionally at loggerheads with Amsterdam, joined loudly in this chorus. The anxiety this caused was not allayed by the personalities of his English and Belgian advisers. John Norris, with whom Oldenbarnevelt got on so well, was not among the former. Leicester, himself without military experience, was jealous of his strategic gifts and was soon on bad terms with him. His chief English favourite was his nephew Philip Sidney, who had hoped to become stadtholder of Zeeland and was now trying to steer his function as governor of Flushing, in which he succeeded Edward Norris, as far as possible in that direction. There was a danger in this, not reduced by Sidney's intelligence and charm.

However, it was not North-Netherlanders and Englishmen who were to affect Leicester's political actions above all, but rather Belgians: South-Netherlanders driven from Flanders and Brabant because of their faith. Netherlanders, then, but Netherlanders without an economic background and thus entirely dependent on the Governor-General, who in his turn was to a large extent dependent on them, owing to his lack of languages (he knew little French and less Latin and conversed mainly in Italian) and slight knowledge of their country. His Netherlands secretary, Borchgrave, was a Fleming of this kind. He had been attorney-general of Flanders and in the previous year had been returned by the 'rump' States of Flanders to the States-General. Of his two fellow-deputies at that time, Caron and Meetkerken, the former was Leicester's supporter but not his favourite. To the other, Adolf van Meetkerken, Leicester listened gladly. He appointed him to the Council of State, where for a year he was Leicester's principal spokesman, after the latter had fallen out with Buys.

All his life, Oldenbarnevelt felt a deep-seated distrust of Flemish refugees. In the interrogatories during his trial in 1618–19 he was still constantly attacking the 'Flanderizers', meaning the supporters of the Ghent Calvinist fanatics of 1578–84. His antipathy was not always justified but it was understandable. There is always something grim about refugees, extreme in their opposition to the authorities in their old country, discontented with those in their new one. For the last two years, since the fall of Ypres, Bruges and Ghent, they had been flooding into Zeeland and Holland – both Middelburg and Amsterdam owed some expansion to this – and they were no less numerous in Leiden, owing to the textile industry. Excluded from municipal government they naturally joined the resident manual workers, always opposed to the oligarchs, and the Calvinists, to whom they usually belonged already. They were not alive to Holland's interests, had no respect for its traditions. Neither had Leicester. From Oldenbarnevelt's point of view – and from the point of view of a reasonable Dutch policy – these refugees were a dangerous entourage for the Governor-General. But there was hope of neutralizing their influence once Leicester had arrived in The Hague, in daily contact with the leaders of the States of Holland.

In the Print Room at Amsterdam there is a picture representing the ceremonious entry of the Earl of Leicester into The Hague on 7 January 1586. It shows Leicester at the moment when the deputies of the States of Holland are being introduced to him. The Latin prayer at the top has a rather doubtful sound: addressed to God it seems, both by the wording and the figure below, more or less to equate Leicester with God, which indeed corresponded to the spirit in which the Netherlanders received him and of which the evidence they were to give some days later would arouse Elizabeth's anger.

For Oldenbarnevelt this moment was one on which a lot depended and that might be the start of a wholesome process: the winning over of the new god by his acolytes.

The meeting did not have the results that Oldenbarnevelt probably hoped for. The relationship between the men bowing to each other in the print remained cordial for only a few days.

They were in agreement as to the first step to be taken: Leicester's powers could not be kept within the limits of the Treaty of Nonsuch. Here it was stated that the governor-general to be appointed should in the first place be commander-in-chief of the English auxiliary troops. After his rights as such had been described in detail, a second part of the treaty, beginning at clause 17, defined his competence in civil affairs held jointly with the Council of State. He was to have 'power and authority', says clause 17, 'to remedy the abuses in the matter of imposts and collections and to cut down the excessive number of officers' – this meant tax officials. In clause 18 a similar right is granted him, still in agreement with the Council of State, regarding the currency; in clause 19, more vaguely set out than the rest, this is extended to reformation of the government in general; while finally clause 20 is a sort of master-key, with which anything or nothing could be done.

These clauses put the States in a quandary. The authority described in them amounted to sovereign power. A governor-general exercising that, even jointly with a Council of State, can only do so in the name of another who is sovereign. But Elizabeth had expressly refused sovereignty. She cannot have meant it, the Netherlanders thought, hers having been a gesture for the outside world, and no notice should be taken of it. The English tendency to allow contradictions to exist in constitutional provisions and wide differences between theory and practice in constitutional law was unfamiliar to the Netherlanders. They liked and needed to speak in plain terms: in the minds of his 'subjects' Leicester could only obtain the authority Elizabeth desired for him as the consequence of an official title, officially conferred upon him by the representatives of the provinces united in the States-General. This involved further definition of the power conferred on him, and in particular his relationship to the States-General and the Council of State, in a document comparable to the conditions on which sovereignty had been offered to Henry III. But in this construction who was to be the sovereign? Leicester would obtain the powers of the *landvoogdessen* under Charles V, but who would obtain those of Charles V himself? The ingenious-looking solution was: the States-General who, after all, appointed the viceroy. Theoretically this was a decisive step on the road towards independence. There might even be some reason for regarding 4 February 1586 (N.S.), the day on which Leicester accepted the 'government of the country' from the States-General in the Hall of Rolls of the Hof van Holland in the Binnenhof, as the day on which the independent state was born. The unfortunate thing was that the theoretical construction – it is not known whose idea it was – was not practicable. For the relationship between viceroy and sovereign it is essential that the sovereign should be absent and that the viceroy should derive his authority from that of the absent sovereign. In this case, however, the sovereign was present and the viceroy in reality derived his authority not from him but from a foreign sovereign and the troops and assistance she provided. Here can be seen an inherent contradiction which would have brought about the collapse of Leicester's rule, even if other causes had been lacking.

Oldenbarnevelt was not appointed to the committee to negotiate with Leicester about the *capitulatie*. This was perhaps not wise, as Oldenbarnevelt was much better versed in constitutional law than Menijn or Maelson who were appointed to the committee by Holland. But it was understandable. The divine honours paid to Leicester wherever he went had given him a great idea of his own indispensability. His briefing told him in actual fact, though not in so many words, to aim for absolute power. It was obvious he would make far-reaching demands. Great flexibility was required to keep him in a good humour, and as soon as flexibility was needed, as we have seen already, Oldenbarnevelt was not called upon.

The hope that Leicester would allow himself to be used for realizing Holland's aims regarding the other provinces faded during the negotiations about the *capitulatie*. When the Governor-General published the names of those he had chosen for the Council of State the anti-Hollanders proved to be in the majority not only in numbers but in influence: the resentments of men like Meetkerken and Buys would dominate the Council and Leicester himself. His entourage was strengthened in January by Burghley's brother-in-law, little Hal Killigrew, a sharp-witted lawyer with Padua and Heidelberg as background, a strict Calvinist and absolutist. Ringault came over from England with him, full of alarming ideas about financial manipulations to strengthen Leicester's dictatorship by making him independent of the purse-strings of Holland.

The States of Holland could see that it would end in a fight and for that a champion was needed. At last they resolved to appoint an Advocate and elected Oldenbarnevelt unanimously. A committee was sent to Rotterdam to tell him of his appointment, and at the same time to ask the Rotterdam authorities, who had been absent from the meeting of the States, to release their pensionary. Contracts of employment could not be terminated by giving notice in the sixteenth and seventeenth centuries. People were engaged for life or a stated number of years. In this case it seems to have been ten years, at any rate the Rotterdam *vroedschap* considered that Oldenbarnevelt was under contract to them for another year, up to the beginning of 1587, just ten years after his assumption of office.

The *vroedschap*'s first reaction, when the burgomasters had reported on the request by Van Zuylen van Nyevelt and Ruychaver, was to offer the pensionary an increased salary and thus engage him for another period of ten years or more. Some councillors thought Oldenbarnevelt desired the new post mainly for financial reasons. His value to Rotterdam had increased considerably as his influence in the States had grown, and it must have been worth an exceptional sacrifice to Rotterdam to keep such an exceptional man in their service. Other councillors could see further: ambition spurred on their pensionary more than cupidity, and even from this point of view Rotterdam could not have offered him financial rewards to balance not only the higher salary, but also the many indirect benefits the office of Advocate could provide. There was no point in keeping him against his will. He had to be released with good grace and the second part of the *vroedschap*'s resolution attempted to do this. Oldenbarnevelt however felt himself too much bound by the clause that 'should he excuse himself in any way from the said service and office of advocateship of this country . . . he shall be held to continue his service within this town where he is still bound'. He asked for unconditional release, which was granted 'absolutely'. Before assuming office as Advocate he made rather stringent demands, which appear to have been discussed in private for some weeks. The States then set up a committee of three men who, in consultation with Oldenbarnevelt, drew up his letter of appointment. It differed in three points from that given to Buys, as the post of Advocate of Holland was beginning to change its character as a result of the rebellion.

It was a job with prospects. Originally, at the beginning of the sixteenth century, Oldenbarnevelt's predecessor had indeed been an advocate, namely the legal adviser to the nobles, the first component of the States. He was to the nobles what the pensionary was to the towns. He had various tasks to fulfil, at first only during the States' sporadic meetings, later outside the meetings as well, as a sort of executive. At the meetings the function is somewhat hard to define, as there is nothing to show whether there was a president or not, and if so, who he was and how he was appointed. Probably the eldest noble present presided by right, but not knowing much about the matters, largely financial, that came up for discussion, relied greatly on the advocate. The latter therefore naturally had the job of drawing up the agenda and seeing that it was followed; ensuring that the member appointed teller by rota recorded the votes; noting the result of the voting and working it up into a resolution in all cases where it did not agree with a previous draft, often too the advocate's own work. In effect this made him president of the meeting. Oldenbarnevelt enhanced this still further by having the recording of the votes entrusted to the advocate in his letter of appointment. He now had still less the character of a secretary to the States, a post that in fact had been separated from his shortly after the revolt. The Advocate was thus relieved of a lot of writing work, a good thing, as apart from the sessions of the States his work had increased enormously since they had become a governing rather than a supervisory body. The Advocate's oldest duty in this field was to defend the States' interests, particularly in their privileges, and to maintain their authority against everyone, first of all the ruler of the country. It was therefore important that he should not hold any other post – in the service of others than the States, of course; the Advocates always had other provincial functions – and that he should be quite neutral with regard to the separate towns. Logically he should not have been in the service of the nobility, but obviously no one thought a conflict of interests possible between the nobles and the general public, so not only was there no tampering with this historically developed relationship, but the Advocate was even expressly told in his letter of appointment to act as pensionary for the nobility.

Furthermore, the Advocate was usually the spokesman of the States in their relations with the outside world. In Buys' time this had already led to a conflict of duties. The States had been in the habit of sending their Advocate with increasing frequency on missions – to the Prince, to various authorities, to army officers. But he could not at the same time personally draw up the resolutions – *extenderen*, as it was called – and have them given their second reading – *resumeren* – an important basis of his power, write letters and keep minutes, not to mention making copies of the resolutions for all the towns and sending out these copies and summonses and agendas, all matters with which he was charged by his letter of appointment. Buys neglected all these duties, letting the secretary take his place. The States of Holland criticized this, because the drawing up of resolutions in particular was a political task to which a mere civil servant like the secretary was not so suited. Buys answered that he would do this work in future provided he was no longer put on committees. Oldenbarnevelt, undoubtedly more energetic than his predecessor, did not object to this combination of functions. He only made one condition: that he was not to be sent on foreign missions against his will. The reason he gives stamps the man: 'so as to be able to have continuity in matters and to prevent the order made by me being interrupted in my absence'.

It is clear that Oldenbarnevelt had the ambition of making the post of Advocate into something it had not been under Buys. He did not care to be understudied for long periods by the pensionary of Dordrecht, the oldest town, especially when that was Menijn, a weak man and devoted to Leicester. This stipulation was kept for twelve years: in 1598 and again in 1603 he was sent on missions against his will, but by then the 'order' he had 'made' was firmly enough established for his absence to cause no danger.

Oldenbarnevelt's stipulation did not apply to journeys within the country. They were such an essential part of the Advocate's work that he could hardly have avoided them. Usually they only lasted a few days, at most a few weeks, if the destination was Zeeland or Groningen. Oldenbarnevelt did, however, have a change made in the clause in his letter of appointment about travelling allowances. At Buys' request this clause had been included in the letter of 1581. It allowed the Advocate compensation of three guilders per day for travelling inside Holland and four guilders outside it, not counting boat and waggon fares which he might claim. This seems to show that the Advocate was not expected to travel on horseback, as must often have happened in actual fact. The cost of a servant but not of a clerk was included in the three or four guilders. Oldenbarnevelt was determined not to stop his correspondence on affairs of state during journeys. His own handwriting was so illegible that he preferred not to write fair copies of his letters himself. He therefore stipulated that with the approval of the States he should be allowed to take a clerk with him and charge an extra guilder per day.

Oldenbarnevelt did not ask for a higher salary. Buys had had 300 guilders per quarter and he wanted to make do with that too, though it was notorious that Buys could not have lived on this salary and only made ends meet by the stamp duty granted him by the Prince, not at present held by the new Advocate.

What he did ask for was a removal allowance of a lump sum of 200 guilders, since clause 18 of his letter of appointment, just as in that of Buys, insisted categorically on his living in The Hague. Buys had taken no notice of this regulation and stayed in Leiden for the whole of his term of office. Perhaps when Oldenbarnevelt asked for the allowance, he intended to follow his instructions more 'precisely', the more so as it was in his own interest: he had to keep close to his base to play the important role for which he had cast himself. However, there are reasons for supposing that he, or at any rate his family, stayed another three years in Rotterdam. There was a housing shortage in The Hague, especially of the type of mansion suitable for a rich landowner. The return of the Hof van Holland and the States, of the pro-Spanish party after the Pacification, the establishment of the Hoge Raad and the States-General had changed The Hague in a few years from a sleepy, half-ruined provincial town into the political centre of the Northern Netherlands. Leicester and his henchmen had on their arrival naturally requisitioned the best accommodation. Not till 1589 did Oldenbarnevelt succeed in buying a house in Spuistraat, soon followed by two neighbouring houses, which he occupied together for more than twenty years. A year after his appointment, in the spring of 1587, he managed to obtain dispensation from the obligation to live in The Hague. In December of that year he is described in a report by an English agent as 'a dweller in Rotterdam'. The conclusion therefore does not seem too bold that during the whole Leicester period and for a year afterwards Oldenbarnevelt exercised his office without taking up residence in The Hague. This throws a surprising light on the small amount of work to be done in this office at first.

So the 200 guilders removal money was not used for removing. It was not, however, obtained under false pretences, as staying in The Hague cost money too. Oldenbarnevelt did not gain by this, nor was his official salary increased. But there was another condition to Buys' letter of appointment which he had changed for financial reasons.

Clause 21 of Buys' letter of appointment forbade the Advocate to receive any gifts, large or small, 'or any *esculenta* (food) or *poculenta* (drink) that may be consumed in a few days'. This clause was certainly never observed, though transgression was punishable by 'infamy and deprivation of office'. Making presents to government officials to oil the machinery of state was a way of life whose spirit was too strong to be suppressed by the letter of the law. Oldenbarnevelt feared the weapons that breaking the rules could put into his enemies' hands. Only the gifts 'forbidden by law' should not be allowed him: in other words, he must not take bribes but he could take tips. It came out at his trial that tips could mount up considerably without anyone taking much notice. In his interrogation it was revealed that he had accepted a present of 90,000 guilders from Henry IV at the time of the negotiations over the Twelve Years Truce. It was one of the charges against him and he was found guilty on it, but only because the amount was so excessively high and he had not informed his masters, the States. No investigation was required of the many other presents he was given as Advocate, some of which are known about from his correspondence. Even his enemies did not take exception to his gains. One must therefore regard the change desired in his letter of appointment not as avariciousness but rather as the scruples of a legal mind. If he had meant to change what was done in Buys' time to his own advantage, not only would the committee that drew up his instructions not have agreed to the alteration so readily, but it would have been cancelled on the appointment of Duyck as Grand Pensionary in 1620. Many of the conditions were indeed altered to the disadvantage of Oldenbarnevelt's successor, but this clause was left word for word as Oldenbarnevelt drafted it.

He did not want any more alterations, or, if he did, he dropped them in view of objections by the committee. He did, however, make two other conditions in addition to the terms of the letter of appointment, which were accepted. A present-day minister – and the comparison with Oldenbarnevelt's new office is permissible – would not need to make them as he is not bound to his portfolio and can relinquish it at any time, both in theory and in practice. In 1585 this was different, at any rate in theory: to dissolve a contract of employment the same agreement between the parties was necessary as for entering into it. If an official wished to reserve the right to resign in certain circumstances it had to be explicitly stipulated. Oldenbarnevelt foresaw two such circumstances, of which only one is mentioned in the Resolutions. One of them was: 'Provided that . . . if he finds by experience that he cannot serve the said State in such a way and to the satisfaction of the Lords, Nobles and Towns, he may leave them at his discretion.'

Here was a plain annulment of the rule against unilateral termination of contract. Oldenbarnevelt on his part recognized the right of the States to dismiss him without notice.

According to the Remonstrance he also asked in advance for release in the event of negotiations aimed at 'handing over the country to the Spaniards'. We shall see that he had reasons for such misgivings, as negotiations were already proceeding on this basis. Such negotiations, if Holland entered into them, would naturally be entrusted in the first place to the Advocate. Quite apart from the possibility of actually going as far as submission, Oldenbarnevelt regarded even negotiations on this basis as fatal for Holland, and himself therefore as the wrong man to conduct them. Following Buys' resignation in 1584 this was another sign that the Advocate of Holland had begun to develop from a servant of the state in the direction of a responsible nineteenth-century minister.

When agreement had been reached on the letter and conditions of appointment Oldenbarnevelt had to attend the afternoon session on 6 March. He was 'exhorted and requested' to take up the appointment and answered with a speech that at his express request was minuted in detail. He stressed his unsuitability for the office of Advocate owing to his 'indisposition', his lack of experience, his youth and the fact that he was pensionary of a town of such low rank, and furthermore born outside Holland. This last point did not weigh heavily with the States: the Advocate of Utrecht was a Hollander, so there was reciprocity – which was not the case in Brabant. Moreover, Oldenbarnevelt had lived for twenty years and more in Holland, had married there and identified himself completely with Holland's interests and prejudices. Oldenbarnevelt was asked to withdraw and after a short discussion it was decided not to accept his excuses. Probably he was not taken seriously. It was not in his nature to underestimate his own capabilities. On the other hand it might be useful, in the event of subsequent opposition, to be able to refer to his unaccepted excuses.

Two days later, when the letter of appointment and the form of oath had been drawn up, Oldenbarnevelt was sworn in before Joost de Menijn, pensionary of Dordrecht. The States had an Advocate again. This was bound to have consequences.

The first consequence was intensified opposition to Leicester. In the view of many people – especially of Leicester and his satellites but also of many Netherlanders who had pinned their faith to him – it seemed that the States of Holland under their new leader wanted to make it impossible for Leicester to govern. This was an exaggeration. The States certainly wished to keep the Viceroy on the narrow path, all that the privileges allowed the central authority. As far as Holland was concerned this amounted in practice to Holland's interests and views having to form the unshakeable basis of that central authority's rule. Oldenbarnevelt was appointed in order to achieve and maintain this state of affairs; this struggle was the alpha and omega of his activity. The omega was the clash in 1618 leading to his fall; the alpha was the imminent dispute with Leicester.

The day before Oldenbarnevelt became Advocate he had been elected to a committee formed to protest to Leicester against the use of his right of appointment. He had made a certain Dirck van Sijpesteijn bailiff and sheriff of The Hague. This bailiwick, however, was regarded as one of the 'principal offices' which Leicester, according to his *capitulatie*, could only grant by selection from a short list of three names submitted by the States. Oldenbarnevelt was sent with Schagen, Menijn – as lubricant – and Maelson to the Council of State. He proposed that since Sijpesteijn had already been appointed and had taken up office, the States would still make out a nomination, including Sijpesteijn's name, so as to 'preserve the authority of his Excellency (on which the entire prosperity of the country rests)'. The English members of the Council asked for a definition of 'principal office'.

Oldenbarnevelt gave a vague answer referring to the time of Maria of Hungary and the compromise proposed by the States was accepted with compliments on both sides. It was in reality a victory for the States and displeased Leicester greatly: 'I am threatened to be used as the Prince of Orange was,' he wrote on 9 March (O.S., 19 March N.S.) to Walsingham, 'yet . . . if it be found that Her Majesty will go thorow with all . . . they will leave those practices.' The comparison with the Prince referred not to his assassination but to his lack of power, which Leicester, not altogether unjustly, considered the principal cause of the decline in the Prince's fortunes in the last few years of his life.

The day after Leicester had written this letter we find him for the first time in conference with his new opponent, who, with the same three members of the States, came to complain about the activities of a certain Hans Vlaminck, appointed master of the mint in Amsterdam by Leicester. This time it was not a question of a 'principal office', but there were two other objections. In the first place Dordrecht had the privilege of being the only town in Holland allowed to possess a mint. However, it did not suit Leicester at all to have the coins he wanted struck by Vlaminck minted at Dordrecht, as the mint there was traditionally under a certain amount of supervision by the town authorities. Leicester wanted to mint coinage without any supervision. One of his advisers was the Belgian Jacques de Ringault, come over from the south, a financial wizard who had recommended to him a means of getting money into his exchequer and thus being less dependent on the States-General. This was to mint a large number of English rose nobles with which to pay the soldiers. The intrinsic value of the rose noble was fifteen guilders, but they were to be issued at an imposed rate of seventeen guilders, to the benefit of the exchequer but to the great disadvantage of business life in Holland. It was the technique called coin clipping in the Middle Ages and in modern times inflation. Oldenbarnevelt's protest, however, was not in the first place against financial juggling but against the violation of an ancient privilege. According to the ideas of the time legislative power was wholly vested in the viceroy, whom one could only endeavour to mollify with humble requests. If he violated the privileges, however, he was exceeding his authority and obedience could be withdrawn.

Leicester's reaction during and after the interview with the four men was just as characteristic as Oldenbarnevelt's choice of subject matter. He professed to be shocked at the violation of the privilege, of which he had not known, and promised to make Hans Vlaminck stop. In actual fact the latter calmly went on minting rose nobles. The untrustworthy behaviour of Leicester and his advisers in matters like this was the chief cause of his

54

unpopularity in the coming years. The double-dealing was of course a result of weakness and the weakness a result of distrust: a vicious circle only to be broken by Leicester's eventual departure.

Another decision based on the privileges was taken on the day after Oldenbarnevelt's appointment. Here too we may recognize his influence and perhaps his defective knowledge of French. No documents were to be accepted, let alone issued, in any language other than Dutch. This resolution was another handicap for the Viceroy and his English advisers. No doubt it was made with just this intention. Of course it was not always adhered to. In 1588 the resolution was renewed and in 1590 Elizabeth protested against the impoliteness of speaking Dutch in the presence of her representatives, as if it were something new.

These little conflicts naturally detracted from Leicester's authority. Much more serious damage was done to his prestige in the same month of March 1586 by an outburst of rage from Queen Elizabeth, who wrote to Leicester on 10 February 1586 (O.S., 20 February N.S.), telling him to resign immediately from his post. Three days later she vehemently reproached the States-General on the subject. She had at first been left in ignorance of the position accorded to Leicester in the Netherlands, for her ministers knew that in that respect her views were diametrically opposed to those of the States-General. In the Netherlands the intention was to involve the Queen as deeply as possible in the war with Spain. Mainly with this in view Leicester had been given an almost sovereign position, at any rate in theory, while the States meant to retain the real power, gained by holding the purse-strings, as far as possible themselves. Elizabeth, on the other hand, had expressly forbidden Leicester to accept a higher title than Governor-General in the English sense, that described in the treaty: general of the auxiliary troops and adviser to the States-General. By this description she hoped to avoid war *à outrance* with Spain, in contrast to her minister Walsingham's anti-Spanish and fanatically Protestant party, of which Leicester was 'the incongruous figure-head'.[1] She even wished to avoid the undeclared war as much as possible. Neither the state of her finances, her peace-loving nature nor her interpretation of the divine right of kings permitted her to wage war on a large scale for the liberation of the Netherlands and the triumph of Protestantism. As sometimes happens among allies, her war aims were completely different from those of the Netherlanders. From the very beginning of the Treaty of Nonsuch she had been engaged in peace negotiations, at first without the knowledge of Walsingham and the ultra-Protestant party, and of course

[1] Sir George Clark, 'The Birth of the Dutch Republic', *Proceedings of the British Academy* (1946), p. 190.

entirely without the knowledge of her new allies or protégés. The negotiations were always on the basis of the recognition of the King of Spain's nominal sovereignty over the North and South Netherlands. They were hampered and thwarted by Leicester's appointment as Governor-General with 'absolute' power. Elizabeth's irritation was increased by the fact that she had to keep its real reason secret. The States-General were genuinely amazed at her scant appreciation of their good intentions. Their letter of 25 March gives evidence of their amazement and at the same time shows the utter absence of political grasp of foreign affairs prevalent in the Netherlands since the Prince's death.

The question was whether Elizabeth was in earnest or only pretending to be. If she was in earnest did Leicester still have her support? He was getting no money for the troops' pay. Could Elizabeth be going to wash her hands of him? His authority in the Netherlands was severely shaken. The whole purpose for which he had been reluctantly invested with so much power was defeated by Elizabeth's attitude. The Hollanders had never wanted to give him any real power, only prestige with the outside world, as a symbol of unity in the conduct of the war, a sort of modern constitutional monarch. This prestige was just what he had now lost. The Queen demanded at first that he should resign at a solemn session of the States-General with the same ceremonial as at his inauguration. Fortunately the ministers were able to make it clear to Elizabeth that unless she wanted anarchy in the Netherlands she would have to accept the *fait accompli*, for the same reasons that the States of Holland had accepted the *fait accompli* of Sijpesteijn's appointment. It took about five months to convince Elizabeth of this, however, and meanwhile a strategically valuable spring had passed, Leicester's prestige was irreparably damaged, his dispute with the States of Holland intensified by the embargo on trade with the enemy, while he himself, stamping with rage at the opposition of the Holland oligarchs, had shaken the dust of Holland off his feet and thrown himself, to his detriment, into the arms of the Utrecht democrats.

With the trade embargo the position was as follows. The champions of a general prohibition of trade with Belgium had been greatly strengthened in their position by the fall of Antwerp. This large town had always been dependent for its food supply on trade with the North. Without this trade famine would be fairly certain. Parma's expected advance northwards would then become difficult if not impossible, and the Netherlands troops, supported by the English, would have a chance to counterattack. At the insistence of Zeeland the States-General therefore issued a general prohibition of the export of food on 28 August 1585. In England too the envoys had had to listen to a good deal in that month about the flourishing trade with the enemy, thus being supplied with war material – at a moment when the Netherlanders were appearing at the English court as petitioners. The English, like the French in 1582, found this very difficult to understand. In England itself trade with Spain was forbidden after the Treaty of Nonsuch. Smuggling began to flourish at once and could not be effectively prevented unless the Netherlanders issued a similar prohibition. In addition, in the summer of 1585 Philip II placed an embargo on Netherlands ships in Spanish and Portuguese harbours, so that whoever ventured to do business in this hell burned more than his sails.

The prohibition of exports of 28 August was therefore justified from three angles. Nevertheless it was, as Charles Maurras wrote about the Treaty of Versailles, 'trop mou pour ce qu'il avait de dur'. The Hollanders, especially the Amsterdammers, flouted it on a large scale, as their living depended on the grain trade. Supervision was not strict enough, the penalties for infringement did not deter. Furthermore Holland, absent from the States-General on 28 August, had weakened the embargo on its own authority. Holland and the other provinces were thus sharply divided. Already on 3 October Oldenbarnevelt, with four other members of the States, two of them Amsterdammers, was sent to the Council of State to try and find a compromise, consisting of a considerable increase in the *licenten* for dry goods. Meanwhile Holland carried on as usual and in spite of the edict permitted the export of a large consignment of grain to the Sound.

When Leicester landed in Zeeland he was bombarded with complaints from all the Zeelanders, South Netherlanders and Calvinists about the wicked *lorrendraaiers* in Amsterdam, profiteers in general and particularly the over-powerful Hollanders. An embargo on trade with the enemy was one of the principal points in Leicester's briefing and he needed only one prompting where a thousand were given him. However, he did not issue his edict immediately after his inauguration. He had heard a number of counter-arguments in Holland during January and realized that he had to formulate the regulations and penalties with great care for Amsterdam's resistance to be broken and his embargo to be effective. After Ringault's arrival from England he did indeed speak threateningly about his intentions. In Holland at any rate considerable alarm was felt and Amsterdam and North Holland submitted a remonstrance to Leicester, which he forwarded to the States of Holland for their advice. Their answer was conveyed by Oldenbarnevelt in the form of a memorandum, a procedure which sounds remarkably modern, though Leicester had not the slightest intention of taking any unwelcome advice.

Utrecht was fiercely Calvinist at this time, and, having no interest in foreign trade, just as fiercely enthusiastic for a strict export embargo. Leicester's chief adviser from the Northern Netherlands, Buys, originated from Amersfoort in that province and managed to persuade Leicester that he would find a more congenial climate there than in The Hague with its tiresome members of the States of Holland. Leicester therefore settled in the town of Utrecht early in April and in the middle of the month the States of Holland sent him a committee of five men to present him with the memorandum composed by Oldenbarnevelt. It is a good example of Oldenbarnevelt's method, discussed already, of giving an opponent plenty of rope so that he can hang himself later. It is therefore worthwhile going into the memorandum more closely, especially as it was his first important document since being appointed Advocate.

He begins characteristically by paying a tribute to Roman law and to the 'usage of all Potentates and Republics', which both prohibit trading with the enemy. Therefore great exception will be taken to our toleration of this trade by 'foreign potentates and princes' (meaning Elizabeth?), since it appears that private profit is preferred to the public interest. Furthermore it is not only the ships' cargoes that are delivered to the enemy, but the ships themselves, which, with their guns and ammunition, and thousands of sailors may fall into his hands. The previous year showed how dangerous that was, when only the lax execution of the embargo by lesser Spanish officials prevented the loss of the 'principal riches'. The prohibition would have to last only a short time and experience had shown that a town like Amsterdam could if necessary refrain from all maritime trade for five years, 1572 to 1577, and survive. The provisioning of enemy armies was an argument particularly applicable to the export of food. Oldenbarnevelt mentions it at once but without stressing that in this respect the embargo on trade with Belgium had already had important results. Great shortages and famine had occurred in the Southern Netherlands in the winter after the capture of Antwerp, accompanied by mutinies among Parma's troops that prevented him from following up his victory. The Spanish troops had not appeared in the field in the seven months since the fall of Antwerp. Now, in April, they marched on Grave, wasting two months on this small town. The Spaniards' lack of success, although partly due to the English auxiliaries, was also certainly to a considerable extent a result of the famine in Belgium. The champions of an embargo on the export of food were in a stronger position than Oldenbarnevelt would admit.

But this is the only point on which Oldenbarnevelt is not fair. At the end of his disquisition in favour of the embargo he underlines the argument of its champions: the morale of the people is ruined by the suspicion that merchants who are profiting from the war send food to the enemy, and so prevent it ending, for this very reason. This argument sounds very twentieth-century. Its strength was to be felt later in the truce negotiations.

At the end of this first part of the memorandum the uninitiated reader is thoroughly convinced that trading with the enemy is most objectionable and greatly wonders whatever counter-arguments can be brought forward in the other half. Exciting curiosity in this way is just a lawyer's trick, together with his apparent impartiality. The arguments against are much more convincing, indeed this must have been done deliberately. We know them already: trade is the chief occupation in these parts; all taxation, not only the vital *licenten*, depends in the long run on commercial prosperity. The government has to provide the revenue for the upkeep of the state in the way least harmful to the inhabitants 'without him (i.e. the sovereign) having to follow any rights, customs or examples, or to heed what is well or evilly interpreted'. The Danes' and the Hanseatic League's trade with Spain and Germany's with Belgium cannot be prevented, so that the enemy eventually obtains his requirements from our competitors. The danger of a new embargo can be guarded against by a 'good middle course' or by sailing in convoy. To cripple the trade of a mercantile nation was the best way to help the enemy: even the late Prince would not have been able to hold out so long if he had not 'by means of navigation . . . kept the public . . . in good devotion and office and drawn the taxes from them: special attention should be paid to this.' It is striking to see how Oldenbarnevelt, usually so formal, lets himself go about the Prince – quoted, incidentally, by the supporters of the embargo as well. The enemy can manage without the importation of Netherlands food.

This last is thus a flat contradiction of the contentions of those advocating the embargo. The fact was that both were right, one party from a short term, the other from a long term view. The sudden cutting off of food supplies could without doubt do the enemy great harm, but this weapon would eventually be blunted by the switching over of the trade routes. The difference, obvious to us, between the long run and the short run appears at that time to have escaped everyone's notice. In theory at any rate. In practice things went on until the Truce more or less as theory ought to have laid down: as a rule trading with the enemy was permitted with certain restrictions. From time to time it was suddenly prohibited. Both the ship of state and the country's ships benefited.

The memorandum was never submitted, for as the delegates were preparing to leave for Utrecht news came that on 14 April Leicester had issued an embargo on trade in the sharpest possible form.

Leicester wrote later that he had not realized the importance of the edict, but calls the members of the Council of State to witness that during the consultations of that body he was the only one to raise objections. This is not as impossible as it seems. On his first visit to Amsterdam he may well have been impressed by the objections expressed there. In Utrecht, however, the atmosphere was quite different. Paulus Buys, regarded in his own province as a somewhat Hollandized libertarian, urged a strict embargo, the stricter the better. Instead of the *licenten* and convoys it abolished, it would provide new and much richer sources of income, probably making Leicester largely independent of the troublesome States-General.

It was this financial side of the plan, rather than the prohibition itself, that made Oldenbarnevelt the implacable opponent of the Governor-General. Ringault's idea, originally supported by Buys, was this: trade was such a deep-seated instinct of the Hollanders that they would be sure to continue carrying it on after the publication of the embargo. They would then become *lorrendraaiers* and their ships, with their cargoes, could be declared forfeit. Better still: if illicit trade were made a capital offence the merchants could be allowed to buy themselves off for an unlimited sum, enough to cover the cost of the war even after deduction of the percentage that the inventors of the trick, Ringault and his partner Perret, had stipulated for themselves.

This financial lunacy, kept secret for a time even from the Council of State, was probably Leicester's chief motive for having the edict issued in such an impossibly strict form. The States-General were meeting at Utrecht just at that time, but the Viceroy did not see fit to consult them. According to the *capitulaties*, which gave him unlimited legislative power, he was not obliged to. However, he was maladroit and thoughtless enough to have the standard formula included in the edict that it was issued 'according to the will and opinion of the States-General'. They promptly protested; they requested Leicester to postpone publication till the meeting was better attended and they could give their judgment calmly. Leicester, strong in the popularity the edict had won him, would not agree and at once began hanging a few smugglers here and there to spread terror among the great merchants. The hangings took place on the authority of the old regulations. The new edict would not come into force till it was published and owing to the federal constitution of the United Provinces Leicester had neither the competence nor even the material means to effect publications independently of the provinces.

Amsterdam and the North Holland hinterland tried to make use of this to prevent publication in Holland. This would have been a departure from legality and Oldenbarnevelt would not lend himself to it. On 23 April the States, under his calm and determined leadership, resolved to submit his memorandum to Leicester even after the event, without doing anything by which, as the resolution has it, 'His Excellency's legal authority would be encroached upon'.

The prohibition was not, in any case, being thoroughly applied. Almost every day infractions were permitted those with access to Leicester or his advisers. Moreover, supervision was wholly inadequate now that big export harbours like Amsterdam, Rotterdam and Enkhuizen would not cooperate. The officials responsible for collecting the *licenten* and convoy-money in each harbour were nominally responsible to the central authorities, but in practice could not work without the consent of the towns where they resided. The result, now that abolition of the *licenten* had so greatly increased profits, while prices in Belgium were still rising, was that smuggling was most favourably affected by the edict. The severe penalties worked in the same direction: people were prepared now and then to report a smuggler if he had to pay with a heavy fine but not if he had to do so with his life. Stricter control was clearly needed if Ringault and Perret were to fulfil their golden promises. So they conceived a new plan: smuggling must be uncovered by the inspection not of outgoing shipping but of merchants' accounts. A special corps of officials must be appointed, independent of the provinces. It was not to be in charge of the Council of State, for three of the members were far too sub-servient to their provinces, but of a body dependent solely on Leicester, in control of the proceeds of fines and confiscations, and empowered to try offenders. Leicester's Belgian advisers now joined Ringault in working out a project for a Chamber of Finance with the principal task of soaking the merchants of Holland. The main participants were to be a German, an Englishman and a fiercely anti-Holland Utrecht nobleman. The moving spirit was to be Ringault as treasurer supported by Leicester's Belgian secretary, Borchgrave, as auditor. Three members of the Council of State were appointed to it, only because the *capitulaties* prescribed that all orders for payment had to be signed by three such persons.

It shows how completely lacking in realism were both Leicester and his Belgian and Utrecht counsellors that they should have thought for a moment that they could enforce this fantastic plan in the face of opposition from Holland. The first consequence was that all the moderate politicians from Holland and Zeeland broke with Leicester. Paulus Buys, by his contemptuous refusal to take office under Ringault, was the first to challenge him. Olden-barnevelt now appears beside him for the first time in the front rank of Leicester's opponents, and that in consequence of an act we may well regard as of dubious legality. Three members sat on the Council of State who were supposed to represent Holland. Where the dispute with Holland over trading with the enemy arose, Leicester got into the habit of sending the members from Holland off somewhere at critical moments so that the Council could pass questionable resolutions unanimously. Not that he needed to: according to the *capitulaties* he could if necessary make a decision against the advice of the whole council, but it looked better and lent more authority to the resolutions taken. Thus one of them, Bardes, burgomaster of Amsterdam, was sent to Friesland before the edict of 14 April came before the Council. Oldenbarnevelt proposed to the States of Holland that they should write to the three members, warning them against accepting commissions likely to keep them away from Council meetings for more than a few days. The letter was sent on 8 June, before Leicester's plans for fleecing the merchants became public. Its opening shows that Oldenbarnevelt had, or pretended to have, an inaccurate idea of the position of the Council of State in the constitution of the United Provinces. He tells them:

You are thus commissioned to the Council of State, beside His Excellency, on account of the lands of Holland, to have good regard to the state of the lands in general, and of the land of Holland in particular . . .

But the members of the Council were not commissioned by the provinces but by the Governor-General. They were under oath to him and attention to the special interests of the provinces was just what they were not supposed to give. It is typical of Oldenbarnevelt's way of thinking that it had no time for a body not dependent on the provinces. It explains both his later conflict with the Council and its total nullification after its recognition as supraprovincial. Oldenbarnevelt would only have one thing or the other: either the Council was a powerful central body, but entirely dependent on the provinces; or it was an independent body, but then with an exclusively administrative function.

There was more to come from this letter. Though its recipients acquiesced in the content, two of them were somewhat displeased by the form. Bardes felt he had been tricked when he learnt in Friesland what had been going on in the Council during his absence. He determined not to let himself be used any longer, if this were possible, but he could stand up to Leicester for his views the better with the solidarity of the two others. It is therefore not impossible that Bardes, mentioned in the next few years among Leicester's chief opponents, urged Oldebarnevelt to send the letter of 8 June. The two others, however, did not care for receiving unconstitutional orders from the States. They were the first of the long line of enemies made by Oldenbarnevelt during his term of office. They were not greatly to be feared. With one, Brederode, he was afterwards reconciled; the other, Loozen, was not a strong character.

The States of Holland had still not made any official stand against the edict of 14 April. We may assume that it was Oldenbarnevelt who prevented this despite the growing insistence of Amsterdam and the district to the north of it. The edict was undeniably popular. Several inland towns were entirely in favour of it. It did not seem desirable at this point to force a rupture with Leicester which could easily lead to a rupture within the States themselves. Perhaps too Oldenbarnevelt was counting on the ill effects of the edict soon becoming so obvious, especially through the loss of the *licenten* money and the increase in smuggling, that Leicester would come to relax it of his own accord. It was not till 24 June, two days before Leicester produced his Chamber of Finance, that the States of Holland resolved to protest to him at the ruinous edict. Oldenbarnevelt had taken all the fences down, most likely because Leicester's plan had leaked out. It was not only that it would ruin many Holland merchants, who, as it were, formed the raft on which Holland and the United Provinces were keeping afloat: to Oldenbarnevelt it may well have seemed worse that an infringement of provincial sovereignty was about to be attempted far beyond anything ever tried by Alva. The central authority's religious inquisition had been bad enough: Calvinists and oligarchs had buried the hatchet in order to revolt against it together. But this was an inquisition into account books by a supraprovincial authority, which thus acquired revenue compared with which Alva's ten per cent sales tax was child's play. Small-time smugglers were already dangling from the gibbets: half the States deputies imagined themselves hanging beside them, or being ruined to buy off the frightful Ringault; the most vigorous resistance was justified. Not only Oldenbarnevelt thought so, but also the Menijns and the Loozens, the people of Leiden and Haarlem, who would otherwise have had a grudge against Amsterdam. Valcke and the Zeelanders thought the same. Any rivalry between the seaboard provinces was gone. Instead of 'divide and rule', Leicester was forced to read the motto on the reverse of the medal: unite and become powerless.

The Viceroy and circumstances had between them achieved more than Oldenbarnevelt could ever have dared to hope on taking office. Within four months they had made the pensionary of a herring-fishing town into the undisputed leader of the Netherlands people in their struggle against anti-national trade policy. At any rate, he could feel that he was this and his adherents, the oligarchs, felt so too. They meant – and not without justification – by 'the people' only that articulate and organized part of the population that kept them in office. The lower classes, those excluded from political influence, believed and continued to believe in Leicester, the hero sent by God, who drove the money-changers from the temple. Leicester was visibly turning into a democrat since living in Utrecht. Of course, it was a highly qualified democracy and tempered by a strong theocratic inclination. But it was after all democracy. In Leicester's entourage they were working out a theory of it. It was a good bridle on the egotism of the oligarchs, later on in the absence of this bridle to become ungovernable. But it was no more than a bridle. Democracy in the sense of government in accordance with public opinion is only possible when public opinion is more or less well-informed and the various prejudices keep one another well balanced. If this is not the case the sovereignty of the people leads almost inevitably to the tyranny of an individual. This anyway was how people understood the matter in the sixteenth century, partly relying, like good Renaissance men, on the classical writers, and partly on recent history, especially that of the Italian republics. Oldenbarnevelt hated both democracy and tyranny, but, in contrast to Plato, he always preferred the latter to the former: '*beter verheerd dan verknecht*'.[1] The reason he gives is revealing: 'masters always using discretion, slaves none'. Discretion: it reminds one of Francesco Guicciardini, whose ideal of the good republic coincided in many ways with Oldenbarnevelt's and who made *discrezione* – the Platonic σωφροσύνη – moderation, an essential prerequisite for a statesman. This does not mean that Oldenbarnevelt did not attach any importance to the continuance of the oligarchy, for he certainly did. He could cling with a clear conscience to the conviction that its continued existence was in the interest of the republic. Guicciardini regards it as a lucky chance if the world can be persuaded that what we are doing in our own interests is really being done for the general good. Both at this time and later Oldenbarnevelt had a great deal of this luck. One must guard, however, against the cynical, superficial view that self-interest always comes first and concern with the general good is just a fig-leaf to cover it.

Oldenbarnevelt had therefore become the leader in the struggle against democracy and tyranny. His only rival for this position was at this time taken out of circulation by Leicester. Paulus Buys, Leicester's chief adviser when he arrived, had turned against him when it appeared that the Flemings had more influence and when the viceroy joined the Calvinist, democratic and absolutist camp. Buys was connected with the aristocratic party in Utrecht of St James community and Floris Thin. The enforcement by Leicester of the amalgamation of this libertarian community with that of the consistory made him an irreconcilable adversary. Leicester, nervous at the sudden fierce opposition in Holland, left on 19 July with the Council of State for The Hague. Pretending with clumsy Machiavellianism to know nothing about it,

---

[1] Better enslaved by a master than tyrannized over by a mob.

he had Buys fetched from his bed and imprisoned by the citizen militia of Utrecht.

Oldenbarnevelt did not react at once. On the one hand he was delighted at the fall of his hated predecessor. On the other, his feeling for justice was offended by the totally illegal arrest of a member of the government by un-authorized representatives of the people. When it was soon found out that Leicester must have had a hand in the matter, it was a question of tyranny, which made things worse. Here was the second Advocate of Holland in succession to be imprisoned on the orders of the central authority and threa-tened with death. It must not be allowed to become a habit. Here again self-interest was interacting with a sense of justice. Protest was not easy as Leicester strenuously denied all responsibility, and the States of Utrecht, entirely dominated by the democrats, took no notice of the States of Holland or the States-General. Oldenbarnevelt took the safest way of saving Buys' life, via London. Ortel, the province's agent in London, was told to acquaint Wal-singham with Buys' point of view. Walsingham at once recognized the unjustness of Leicester's action and got the Queen to intervene. Buys was in prison for six months, no doubt to Oldenbarnevelt's secret enjoyment. By then Leicester was in England and Buys forgotten and without influence. His imprisonment had played a part in the agitation against Leicester, there was no point in prolonging it. We shall see how Oldenbarnevelt succeeded in obtaining his release.

On the evening after Buys' arrest Leicester arrived in The Hague, where he found the leading figures of the united Holland–Zeeland opposition assem-bled. On 17 July delegates of the States of Holland and of Zeeland met to draw up a joint remonstrance against the export embargo. This long-winded document, largely a repetition of the memorandum of April, is fairly non-committal, probably because agreement with Zeeland was after all not so complete. It is therefore not likely that Leicester yielded to the force of the arguments in the new remonstrance. What he yielded to was Holland's closed purse-strings. Within a fortnight of arriving at The Hague, where he had learnt to fear Oldenbarnevelt's somewhat prolix eloquence, he gave his consent to a new list of *licenten* and on 4 August published a new and modified edict, permitting trade with neutrals again. The edict was drafted by a commission headed by Oldenbarnevelt and was approved by the States of Holland, despite the objections still raised by Amsterdam.

The first round in the disputes about the trade embargo was thus a qualified victory for Oldenbarnevelt's policy of mediation. He was able to profit from the Viceroy's lack of money in other respects too, according to the old and well-tried system from Emperor Charles's time. A second remonstrance, full of detailed complaints, was submitted to Leicester and discussed with him in 'the Emperor's Chapel', that is to say the Court Chapel, adjoining Leicester's quarters in the Binnenhof.

We must pity Leicester as we read the apostils he made on the multitudinous complaints, notes which admit almost everything, or at the very least promise an investigation; they are the written translation of the many forced smiles which must have concealed his inner rage on hearing Oldenbarnevelt's speech, translated by Menijn into Italian. He could have wept at his dependence on these tradesmen in such a sacred cause as the war against Spain. He felt that he was not made for such humiliations and began to insist on his recall. Till this came about he departed for the front, where he felt more at ease than at the conference table.

Oldenbarnevelt remained as victor in The Hague, but it was a victory that could cause anxiety. It had been gained at the expense of something that even in the spring it had still been hoped to preserve: Leicester's prestige. His prestige had had an important function in the régime: it filled the vacuum in authority that since the Prince's death had had a paralysing effect. Though not destroyed it was damaged. It was Oldenbarnevelt's task to replace this dwindling authority by another, more lasting one, in accordance with the traditions of Holland and yet without causing offence to the Queen.

For the present the dispute with Leicester was still in full progress. It had to be conducted with extreme caution. Leicester was not obliging enough to promote a united front among his opponents on all points. For instance, there was the question of religion. Leicester's motto was *Beatus qui facit opus Domini fideliter*: so it was not only policy but certainly conviction as well that caused him, after the fusion of the two congregations at Utrecht, to accede to the proposal of the Utrecht clergy and call a national synod.

The controversy over the calling of a national synod was later to cost Oldenbarnevelt his liberty and his life. It is therefore interesting to see how Oldenbarnevelt, or the States of Holland under his leadership, reacted to Leicester's initiative. The summons took the form of a letter to the three stadtholders, containing the request to have the synod convened by the several provincial courts in The Hague by 20 June. Maurice did not hesitate for a moment to carry out this order. He – or the court in his name – immediately wrote to the *classes* telling them to send delegates. They in their turn agreed to hold a preparatory synod in Rotterdam for their appointment. The States raised no objection to this either and one cannot even read anywhere that they sent political commissioners. Only one town was against it: at Leiden the clergy were brusquely forbidden to attend. Leiden though had always been extremely anticlerical. The States of Holland, on the other hand,

66

behaved as meekly as lambs, and even voted an allowance of 240 pounds for the four South Holland clerics who had been away from home for seven weeks to attend the synod. There is not a word, either in the remonstrance of the end of July or the later one of 12 November, about this synod, to be called by Oldenbarnevelt in 1618 'an allegedly national synod'. It is clear that he and his supporters did not regard 'Leicester's synod' as illegal when it was held, and it is also clear why not. It was very popular with the Calvinists in the country. The strongly anti-Erastian church regulations complied with their wishes, as did the instructions to Marnix to translate the Bible and action against the Gouda heretic Herman Herbertsz. It was of importance not to turn the existing sympathy between the Calvinist element and the viceroy into a firm alliance against the States by an untimely frontal attack on their beloved synod. If one thinks one has to fight a powerful opposition on important issues it is good policy to let them have their own way in minor ones. The relations between church and state were not yet considered important by Oldenbarnevelt.

It was another matter to prevent this Presbyterian system, denying the authorities practically any right of intervention, from acquiring legal force. To do this it was not necessary to swim straight against the current. Passive obstruction was sufficient. The régime was splendidly equipped for practising passive obstruction. When Leicester requested the States-General to 'explain' their 'advice' on the church regulations they answered that they would have to consult their principals. Leicester was still so little conversant with the cumbrousness of procedure in the Netherlands that this answer was a disagreeable surprise to him. At any rate, two days afterwards he ratified the regulations of his own accord, thus putting the churches in an awkward situation. They had church regulations sanctioned by the highest authority and drawn up by their own people: but they could not be sustained against the States of their provinces as long as the States – whose approval Leicester had not asked for – had not attached their seal to them.

The States were in a difficult position too. They did not want to reject the church regulations for the political reason indicated, but they did not want to accept them either, since the relationship between church and state was altered entirely in favour of the former. Moreover the disciplinary provisions, modelled entirely on Geneva and Heidelberg, might form a great danger for libertarian oligarchs. At the same time the States of Holland were not averse to Leicester's church regulations being put into practice. The only thing they could never do was to give them legal recognition. Adriaen van der Mijle expressed this well on 15 May the following year. He was spokesman for the States of Holland at a conference with delegates of the South Holland synod, who had come to complain about the attitude of the States towards the church, especially about the fact that the Hague church regulations had not been ratified. Van der Mijle was the president of the Hof van Holland that had convened the synod in Holland. He was also one of the three men who on 2 August had asked the States-General for their advice in Leicester's name. On the other hand he was a good friend of Oldenbarnevelt's and just as wholeheartedly Erastian. In his words we can sense the spirit of his friend, whom he had no doubt consulted beforehand. Ratification of your church regulations, he said more or less, is unnecessary. Leicester has ratified, let that suffice. In practice you have gained what is laid down in them, particularly the appointment of ministers by the church councils, that you were so keen on. But if the matter were to be brought up officially in the States it would not pass without *ruggespraak*. The matter would then have to be tabled in every *vroedschap* and many of them would not consent to the confirmation. He added that these bodies, as the clerics had said themselves, consisted mostly of papists, 'who would suspect the regulations, since they aimed at imposing strict discipline, fettered the conscience, and were a second Inquisition, of which the very recollection was hateful to them'.

This is no doubt Van der Mijle speaking, or his friend and instructor the Advocate, in the disguise of a member of the 'papist' (for this read 'libertarian') majority in the *vroedschappen*.

The clergy had indeed some grounds for complaint. The States of Holland had approved these church regulations in general terms and with a number of equally general restrictions on 26 November 1586. But the clerics found out, to their detriment, that the States could hide behind these restrictions so as to treat the recognition as a matter of no importance, when political circumstances had changed and tension between Leicester and the States became more acute.

Regarding the control of the navy, Leicester's policy ran exactly counter to the ideas and interests of the States of Holland. Maritime affairs had up to this time been nominally conducted by the Council of State, but in actual fact by the provinces. Maurice was appointed admiral of Holland, under Leicester, it is true, but as the latter had to give all his commands through Maurice, and thus in practice through the States of Holland, his influence was very slight. One of his advisers, we do not know which, now had the bright idea of appointing three admiralties under the Council of State, of which only that at Veere in Zeeland was to extend over a whole province. Holland was to be divided between two admiralties, each with some other provinces under them. The body for North Holland and West Friesland (its eastern part with the towns of Enkhuizen, Hoorn and Medemblik) was set up not in

Amsterdam but at Hoorn, at the same time a good means of promoting enmity between Amsterdam and West Friesland. Maurice would have to see how he got on with these three admiralties, of which only that at Veere was entirely within his territory. The plan was cunningly thought out, especially as no formal objection could be made to it. From a practical point of view it was an improvement. The admiralties naturally worked more harmoniously together than the provincial governments had done, and this was not only in Leicester's but also the country's interest. The principle of this arrangement was preserved for more than two hundred years, in spite of all fine but unrealistic theories about provincial sovereignty. Oldenbarnevelt understood that he must resign himself to this. When on 17 July three Hollanders, appointed by Leicester, politely came to ask the States' permission to sit on the admiralties which were to be established, leave was granted, with the votes of Amsterdam, Hoorn and Enkhuizen against the motion. The condition was made, however, that the instructions should not conflict with provincial or municipal privileges. The door was thus left open for future action. The Holland deputies to the States-General were charged by the *Gecommitteerde Raden* – i.e. by Oldenbarnevelt – to mention Holland's objections to Leicester's admiralties, but only in the most discreet way. In practice this meant that these grievances were kept quiet till an opportunity should arise for a thorough overhaul of the entire admiralty plan.

The more Oldenbarnevelt is seen in action after less than six months in office, the more he is to be admired for what he did, and in particular for what he did not do. A sense of opportunity is an important intuition, perhaps the most important one in forming a statesman. To know when one can strike one's blow, when one has to wait and when one must accept a defeat, if possible with a friendly smile. It is a question of ability indeed, but also one of character. It is not a statesman's objectives that make him great. Oldenbarnevelt's, the maintenance of Holland's rights as he saw them, were no better than his opponents'. But they were not to be despised. They formed, as it were, the ship of state in which Holland was to sail for centuries. Another vessel could have been chosen but the ship constructed by Oldenbarnevelt with dogged perseverance and the materials that came to hand became the trusty vessel, the Seven Provinces,[1] which was able to withstand the storms of history.

After this exemplary self-control, in August Oldenbarnevelt was able to indulge himself in one of his greatest pleasures: the pursuit and elimination of a hated opponent. A nobler pastime for a statesman could be thought of, but if the *bête* is really *noire* we must give it its due. Jacques Ringault was

De *Zeven Provincien*: name of Admiral de Ruyter's flagship in the Second Dutch War, 1665-7.

much too black to be allowed to act in Utrecht as a sort of secret prime minister to the Viceroy. He had that knack of discovering unexpected sources of income which has always impressed absolute rulers of little perspicacity. The financial wizards of later generations, John Law, Casanova, Calonne, were of the same type. Their object was always to make a percentage themselves on their discoveries. This was a bad thing in itself, though Oldenbarnevelt might not have grudged Ringault a little profit, had his tricks not meant the ruin of trade. Such profits were too normal in those days to trip anyone up with. Nor was Ringault's past as Requesens' faithful Roman Catholic clerk, involved in unsavoury trials, enough to deprive him of Leicester's hearing. Something else had to be found and on 16 August one of Ringault's henchmen, Steven Perret from Rotterdam – another Belgian in the north – irresponsibly provided the material for the cheerful campaign which soon led to the desired result. On that Saturday he was drinking at Gouda with a large company that included the astute young pensionary of that town, François Francken, one of the ablest members of Oldenbarnevelt's party in the States. In this (for him) dangerous company, Perret was heard boasting about the deputies of Holland and Zeeland, saying that they were mostly *lorrendraaiers* and hostile to His Excellency, whom they tried 'to deprive of land and people'. But he, Perret, and his friend Ringault would take care that these evildoers were laid by the heels. And so on. Francken reported the matter, perhaps to Oldenbarnevelt, perhaps to the Attorney-General of the Hof van Holland. A few days later the unsuspecting Perret was arrested on his return to Rotterdam. Pensionary Elias van Oldenbarnevelt may well have had a hand in it, though the responsibility was not his but the sheriff's. On interrogation Perret had the impertinence to repeat his threats. He must have greatly overestimated Leicester's power in Holland and the future of the Chamber of Finance. The States-General had already conferred on this Chamber of Finance and gone into recess. As long as the delegates had not returned with complete instructions on the matter, the States-General regarded the Chamber of Finance as not yet established. The States of Holland, of course, took this position *a fortiori*. In these circumstances there was not the slightest chance of the sixteen commissioners, of whom Perret was one, being able to start on their revenge tactics successfully. When his house was searched, letters by Ringault were found, full of abuse not only of the States deputies but also of the Council of State and of the young Count Maurice. There were also minutes of Leicester's orders, drawn up by Ringault, and a formal contract by which he and Perret agreed to divide, in various proportions, the profit made on the application of their joint financial 'inventions'. Ringault had tried to bargain for as much as five per cent on some of them, but Leicester had haggled and settled for three and one-third per cent.

Here indeed were grounds for some sensational legal action. It was hoped that the Hof van Holland would find sufficient reason for pronouncing the death sentence. Treason was mentioned in the indictment. However, the first priority was not a trial but the suppression of Ringault. At the end of August it was shown that this was indeed necessary. On the 28th Leicester promulgated a new general export embargo, intensified in its effect by some of his subordinates – perhaps the inland provincial governments. He had invited Oldenbarnevelt to Utrecht the day before, allegedly to discuss the army's financial requirements before his departure for the front – which was always being postponed. In reality he probably had no other intention. His reputation, in England too, which he always had one eye on, was involved in the result of the approaching autumn campaign, in which Parma must be prevented, whatever the cost, from crowning his Rhine campaign with the capture of Rheinberg. There was the most appalling shortage of money. Wilkes was not to return till the end of October from England with 20,000 pounds sterling; till then Holland was the only possible source of supplies and even Leicester would not have wanted to block this source by doing anything to the first servant of the States. But Oldenbarnevelt, thinking of Paulus Buys, smelled a rat. Though the altercation in The Hague had been most decorously conducted and Leicester had as yet no idea of what Oldenbarnevelt was planning, obviously the latter had a bad conscience and no desire to venture into the English lion's den. Leicester now sent Bardes to The Hague to speak to Oldenbarnevelt on his behalf and none the less to repeat his invitation to Utrecht in reassuring phraseology. The only result was that Oldenbarnevelt became still more nervous, *comme ce chien d'Jean de Nivelle, qui s'enfuit lorsqu'on l'appelle*. From this moment Oldenbarnevelt was convinced that Leicester was after his liberty, if not his life. He resolved never to put himself in Leicester's power. For the present the preparations for Ringault's fall were proceeding in the deepest secrecy. Shortly after 12 September a resolution was taken that had to serve as a cover against Leicester's revenge in two respects. It was resolved that 'anyone's proposition, advice or resolution' concerning 'the State of the said Country, and also the orders and despatches issued in the name of his Excellency' should be kept strictly secret. This secrecy was promised on the oath taken on admission as deputy, and in every town a special oath of secrecy had to be taken by all members of the *vroedschap* before the deputy began his report on the States meeting. It is clear that this resolution was taken mainly for the protection of Oldenbarnevelt, just as the second half, promising protection if anyone of the Nobles or Towns or other, frequenting the meeting of the States, by cause of the Proposition . . . etc. . . . without or within the Country of Holland in fact or by right be at any time molested, disquieted or injured in Body or Property, that the same shall be compensated to the common charge of the Country of Holland.

This is the first time that we find such a safeguarding clause in the Resolutions of Holland. It was an expedient often employed by Oldenbarnevelt later on, probably without many illusions as to the practical value of a resolution of this kind. Nevertheless, his lawyer's nature made him provide it with all the guarantees and saving clauses that he could think of.

Immediately afterwards it was decided to send a deputation to Utrecht to get hold of Ringault's papers in the first place, and in the second place the man himself, if possible. The deputation arrived at Utrecht on 14 September.

Leicester had captured Doesburg two days before. He was resting there on his laurels and in his absence the delegates applied to the Council of State and the English envoy Wilkes, who worked in the Council every day. But before they had passed their resolution Ringault took to his heels. A new deputation, this time to Leicester in person, succeeded in browbeating the viceroy to such an extent that he agreed to the arrest of Ringault, without, however, handing him over to the vengeful States: Leicester's own provost would guard him. The Governor-General reserved the right to decide later on jurisdiction.

Thomas Wilkes had been sent to the Netherlands by Queen Elizabeth at Leicester's special request; he needed someone to support his authority after the blow dealt to his prestige in the spring, and to convince the States-General of Elizabeth's continuing favour. He trusted Wilkes, whom he knew as a good lawyer and a creature of Walsingham's. Elizabeth had appointed him on 29 July and he arrived at the beginning of August in Holland, where he was instantly besieged by the opposition and also felt critical of Leicester's régime on his own behalf. He observed that the great and powerful Earl did not rule but was ruled, and at that by elements who greatly complicated his task and aimed at making a fiasco of the Treaty of Nonsuch. It was not pleasant news to take back to England but it had become obvious to poor Wilkes while working with the Council of State at Utrecht that there was nothing else he could say. He seems to have gained a particularly poor impression of Ringault, confirmed when he was in The Hague at the end of September, and had a conference every day with Oldenbarnevelt. The two lawyers seem to have got on well together; Wilkes had a candid way of speaking, was not overawed by the nobility and appreciated outspokenness in others.

This good relationship was of great importance for the future. It helped to prevent the sometimes sharply anti-English slant of Oldenbarnevelt's policy permanently impairing the harmony between the allies. For the present the result was that Wilkes, on his return to court, was able to convince the Queen and ministers that Leicester was wrong on almost all counts which Oldenbarnevelt held against him: the export embargo, Buys' imprisonment without trial, the expulsion of Utrecht libertarians and Catholics, the setting-up of the Chamber of Finance, and the confidence placed in Ringault and his associates. All these points were in the letters of instruction given when Elizabeth sent him back to the Netherlands almost at once. On 5 November he arrived, quaking, at Utrecht, where Leicester gave him an unmerciful dressing-down, as he had expected.

He had arrived at an unfortunate moment as well. So far the Viceroy had consoled himself for his political setbacks with the joyful expectation of military triumphs. He realized, rightly, that his popularity, the basis of his authority, would be boosted more by the spectacular capture of towns than it would be harmed by the complaints of rich libertarians. But now military matters were going wrong too, or at any rate not well. Leicester's first campaign had ended with the loss of Grave and Venlo; the second had, it is true, saved Rheinberg – though who in Holland cared about those Germans at Rheinberg? – but produced no greater compensation for the June losses than the tiny town of Doesburg, which, however, did not open the IJsel to commerce as long as Tassis, the Spanish colonel, remained in Zutfen. During a feeble attempt to starve out this town a catastrophe occurred, not serious from the military point of view but totally discouraging to Leicester personally: his beloved nephew and right-hand man Philip Sidney was wounded and, on 26 October, died of his wounds. It was the last straw for Leicester. Immediately afterwards he decided to prepare to leave for England.

He informed the Council of State of his decision on the last day of the month. Wilkes heard later that the members had made 'but slender intreatie' to induce him to stay. No wonder, they were relieved. With all respect for Leicester's intentions they must have found him most difficult to advise: like all weak despots he was capricious, stubborn and prejudiced, a bad judge of character and situations.

Perhaps Oldenbarnevelt, however strange this may sound, was one of the few who genuinely regretted Leicester's decision. He would lose what he needed most: a sparring partner. Just before, in September, he had given the impetus to the drawing-up of a remonstrance in fifteen clauses, to be handed to the Viceroy as soon as he should condescend to come to The Hague. All the grievances, even those only discussed in July behind closed doors, were neatly displayed. Leicester's prestige had sunk so low in the last few months that it could no longer do any harm. Only the complaint about the synod was kept back, a sign that Oldenbarnevelt cannot have considered this grievance, though it did exist, to be so painful as he suggested in 1618.

From the typically Oldenbarneveltian preamble – probably not read to Leicester – we can easily see that the draft must date from the time before Ringault's arrest.

It thus being found [so it reads] that some restless minds are attempting and working by all means to abuse his Excellency and to the disservice of his Excellency and the ruin of the Country to bring the State of the Country of Holland and Zeeland into the utmost confusion, that furthermore the resolution taken by his Excellency with complete deliberation and knowledge of the matter, to the appetite of some, not born or having property in the Country of Holland and Zeeland, but apparently come here from Brabant and Flanders to trouble the State of these Countries in the service of the common enemies, and to bring them into equal calamities and misery as was done in Brabant and Flanders.

Such language is purely demagogic. The suggestion that Ringault, Meetkerken and Burchgrave were concerned with making Holland as unhappy as Brabant and Flanders is malicious slander. Oldenbarnevelt was not aware of that however at such a moment. He only realized that to make yourself heard you had to shout as loud as possible, something like the Prince when he had similar libels printed in his Apologia. It was the polemical style of the day, a style that made it more or less obligatory to behead your opponents if you could catch them.

The preamble actually referred only to the eleventh clause in the remonstrance, where arguments against a general export embargo are again briefly and vigorously summarized, and the alteration of 28 August is attributed to 'restless minds', without the further invective in the preamble. The States asked for a simple withdrawal of the alteration and restitution of the resolution of 4 August, which they had drawn up themselves. Oldenbarnevelt was certain that he would get his way on this point. But for him, unlike the Amsterdam merchants, it was not just a question of the matter itself, but even more of Leicester's personal defeat, consisting of openly having to swallow what Ringault had made him spit out. This plan was now frustrated by Leicester's decision to go to England.

On 13 November 1586 a committee under Oldenbarnevelt had a meeting with Leicester and his advisers. He seemed very accommodating on various points, but in such a vague way that his promises did not commit him to anything. He said that he well knew that 'this country existed by navigation' and would charge the Council of State during his absence, which he explained by the imminence of the trial of Mary Queen of Scots, 'to take steps to preserve the traffic'. Oldenbarnevelt must have had a feeling that he had been beating empty air. He had little confidence in the Council of State.

The only possibility would be that the States-General, without recalcitrant Utrecht, should themselves use Leicester's half-promise to settle the question of trade with the enemy according to their own ideas. This is what indeed happened.

The ninth clause of Oldenbarnevelt's remonstrance referred to this recalcitrance of Utrecht. The province was in fact trying to withdraw from the union. It is in a rather cryptic style, often affected by Oldenbarnevelt when he touched on a delicate point and did not wish to be pinned down to a written text. He complained, without mentioning any facts, that in that province the 'public authority' was diminished, almost removed, and requested Leicester to reinforce the Utrecht authority with his own. In his answer Leicester feigned ignorance: what was meant by flouted authority? Oldenbarnevelt hereupon delivered a long speech showing that the civil militia of Utrecht had usurped the authority of the States, among other things by presenting Leicester with an 'act' in which they again offered Elizabeth the sovereignty she had already refused, this time without any restriction of privileges and such like.

Leicester's answer to the first clause was short and weak: he had not quite understood the militia's request, which was drawn up in the 'Flemish language', but he had made it clear to them that Elizabeth's refusal of sovereignty of last summer had not been brought about by Paulus Buys. In reality everyone knew that the request proceeded from Leicester himself or from his immediate entourage. All the letters from these circles written to England at this time show that the success of the expedition was despaired of by English officials in the Netherlands, unless Elizabeth had second thoughts and accepted sovereignty after all. This blatant untruth cannot have raised Leicester's prestige, especially as he answered Oldenbarnevelt's second complaint with an equally weak lie.

The second complaint was about Buys' arrest by the same militia. Again Leicester denied all knowledge of it, though everyone knew better. Buys was not set free only because 'they could not agree to it' – 'they' being the militia – as if they would dare do anything to which their idol objected!

The third complaint was the exile of about forty important citizens of Utrecht on 31 July, only a few days after Buys' arrest. Here again the militia had acted without any formal decree of the States of Utrecht. The English garrison commandant had told these citizens in Leicester's name that they had to leave the town before sundown. Among them, branded as papists, but for the most part members of the dissolved St James community, were the leading members of the aristocratic anti-Leicester party, all good patriots, some of them personal friends of Oldenbarnevelt's, who had represented Utrecht in the States-General for a long time. Leicester stuck to his guns here more than with the first two complaints. He admitted ordering the banishment, saying that his spies had been told that Parma had contacts inside Utrecht, again an obvious excuse and certainly not calculated to add to the respect felt for the Governor-General.

The last clause of the remonstrance was the most virulent, according to Oldenbarnevelt's tried formula. Owing to the expulsion of the forty prominent citizens there were a number of vacant posts in Utrecht. The victors were dividing the spoils. A man from Brabant became attorney-general at the Court of Utrecht, a man from Brussels *schout*. At the usual reappointments on 1st October Leicester appointed Gerard Prouninck, also called Deventer, burgomaster. He had fled from his native town, 's Hertogenbosch when it was seized by the Catholics in 1579, and was indemnified in the north with the post of military receiver. Three Belgians in three high positions were a thorn in the side of Oldenbarnevelt and his friends, who in their imagination saw the northern Netherlands flooded and dominated by a crowd of rootless and insatiable refugees from the south, ready to wreck the country on the rock of their adamantine principles. Oldenbarnevelt could not prevent Prouninck's election at Utrecht. He could, however, hinder his return as Utrecht's deputy to the States-General. When he arrived in The Hague on 10 November with clear credentials, the States of Holland, at the proposal of their Advocate, threatened not to send any deputies to the States-General 'before it appears that Gerard Prouninck van Deventer is legally appointed and chosen burgomaster of Utrecht according to the Privileges and Rights of the Country'.

It can be seen here that the idea of the States-General as a representative body had hardly yet come to be accepted. Majority voting in important matters was prohibited by the Union of Utrecht. In less important matters, such as the admission of a deputy, Holland simply refused to be outvoted and usually got its way, as a meeting of the States-General without Holland would have been a farce.

In this case too. When the resolution was passed in the States of Holland, the four deputies for Holland were attending a meeting of the States-General. In the evening they may well have received oral instructions from Oldenbarnevelt as to the attitude they were to adopt the next day. A short interview with one of the three Zeeland delegates, with the Frisian delegates and with the friendly Utrecht nobleman, Moersbergen, completed the arrangement which was to defeat the hated Belgians.

Oldenbarnevelt, lover of dramatic scenes as he was, must have been sorry to be unable to witness in person the disappointment of the angry burgo-master. But the meeting of the States of Holland that day was too important to miss. The remonstrance in fifteen clauses had to be handed to Leicester. For this the text had to be finalized and signed, a procession arranged, two delegates from the nobility and one from each of the eighteen towns plus the five from Zeeland and Friesland; other delegates had to be appointed to instruct Leicester about the Ringault affair; and finally a resolution had to be passed as to the exercise of the highest authority during Leicester's absence. This was all too important for him to allow himself the pleasure of watching Brabant's humiliation.

It took place, without Oldenbarnevelt's presence, entirely in accordance with the programme drawn up by him. At the beginning of the meeting Prouninck came in and handed over his credentials. He was requested to go outside till the States had deliberated on them. One of the Hollanders recited his lesson, one of the Zeelanders, 'although not charged to do so', supported him. The Utrecht delegation was divided; the delegates from the town said sharply that they could not continue to attend the States-General if Prouninck were not admitted; but Moersbergen, delegate of the nobility, said that for his part he accepted the resolution of the majority, although he did not agree with it. Friesland joined Holland and Zeeland in a few words, whereupon Prouninck was called in to hear the majority resolution. His Flemish reaction must have aroused amazement and annoyance among the cool northerners listening to him. It was a series of threats in flowery language which his fellow-countryman and political opponent, Cornelis van Aerssen, noted down with obvious relish. He protested that he 'wished to be excused for all the inconveniences which will arise therefrom, so great that they cannot be endured, and if the gentlemen present had as much wisdom as hair on their heads, they still would not be able to understand the misery, inconvenience and difficulties which would be caused to the country'. And later on, when the assembly confirmed its resolution, 'that this day and hour is the one that the country will bewail and bemoan'.

What did all these fine words mean? Did they point to the outbreak of a civil war with the help of the English garrison at Utrecht, which as a farewell gesture to the ungrateful Netherlands was to occupy The Hague and institute the democratic tyranny? Probably the angry man did not know himself what he meant at that moment. Oldenbarnevelt however assumed that this was in his mind; he would not rest till, after Ringault and Perret, he had rendered this third impudent southerner innocuous as well.

When Prouninck was invited by the States-General to put his protest into writing he expressed himself much more moderately and not without an underlying plausibility. The refusal to admit me, he argued more or less, was a demonstration against the Earl of Leicester, already returning in a bad mood to England. It was to be feared that, having once shaken the dust of the Netherlands off his boots, 'he will recommend our cause to Her Majesty too little', so that the Queen could drop us altogether.

This view was shared by many in the country, even among critics of Leicester's methods of government. Without English help we are at Parma's mercy; this was the major premise of the syllogism. The minor premise, which could be disputed though at first it seemed self-evident, was that without Leicester's goodwill we should not get that help. Conclusion: let Leicester have his way in everything.

It was Oldenbarnevelt's great achievement that he detected the flaw in the minor premise and so saved the independence of the Netherlands. Again and again in the following years he frustrated Leicester and his successor in everything, without any real fear of the country being left in the lurch by Elizabeth – though in view of her well-known capriciousness he must have had some anxious moments. Elizabeth did not give her support out of friendship, and still less for Leicester's *beaux yeux*, which had long ceased to charm her. Her aim was to compel respect from the King of Spain and force him to make an honourable peace, which, leaving Mary Queen of Scots to her fate and recognizing the Protestant régime in England, would in effect leave the Netherlands divided. Until she could enforce such a peace Elizabeth intended to continue her support, however much her general in The Hague was bullied. At any rate, as long as her finances permitted. Peace and Elizabeth's empty purse were the two chief dangers that Oldenbarnevelt discerned. Leicester's twists and turns, his intrigues with clerics, democrats, Belgians and officers with a grievance were in his opinion just clowning, ludicrous and irritating but essentially harmless. Oldenbarnevelt could already see in his mind's eye the new government that must replace him: it would not be the Council of State but the States of Holland, dominated by their Advocate, in their turn dominating the States-General on the upper floor, as on this memorable 11th November.

This had to develop slowly. At first it seemed necessary to curtail the influence of the Belgians in Leicester's entourage. Prouninck's attitude had given new force to the fifteenth clause of the remonstrance, in which the three provinces requested that 'no hearing or credence should be given to persons who have been in the government in the provinces of Brabant, Flanders and others now disunited',[1] but that everything concerning the three provinces should be done with the advice of the States of those provinces, after the

---

[1] I.e. no longer forming part of the United (Northern) Netherlands.

example of the late Prince, who in this constitutional manner had succeeded in such a masterly way in defending Holland and Zeeland, whereas the Brabanders and the Flemings with their 'factions' had reduced their provinces to the desolate state in which they now found themselves.

Leicester defended his advisers and referred among other things to the Christian duty of providing a new existence for refugees from the south. All very well, Oldenbarnevelt answered, but that did not imply that one had to be dominated by them. This concluded the interview, after Leicester had promised to give his favourable answers in the form of an apostil and that Ringault should be 'brought to justice'; an equivocal promise, as was shown when the States tried to put it to the test. For Leicester regarded it as a matter of honour to save Ringault's life. He was in the same sort of position with him as Charles I was to be later with Strafford: a minister who had advised him satisfactorily and whom he trusted was threatened by his subjects with a trial which, though legal, was conducted by highly prejudiced judges, determined on his death. Leicester could not hand him over in such circumstances. Wilkes, whose instructions implied that the man must be removed, agreed with Leicester on this point. The result was a remarkable scene in the High Street at The Hague, the first time physical force was used in the dispute between Viceroy and advocate, and the only time that Leicester was the victor.

Ringault, captured on 20 September in the camp near Doesburg, was now under arrest in The Hague, under the responsibility of Leicester's provost. But there were no warders and Oldenbarnevelt told the Attorney-General to post four court messengers there for the time being as warders and then ask the provost, who was with Leicester in the Binnenhof, whether Ringault was still his prisoner and, if so, why he was not guarded. The provost said yes in answer to the first question and in answer to the second told him rudely to mind his own business: as for the messengers placed there he hoped to chop their heads off good and quickly. While saying this he left hastily for the High Street. The Attorney-General followed him to protect his messengers and soon came to blows with the enraged Englishman, who encouraged soldiers to taunt him. The Attorney-General was attacked by the provost, his beard was pulled and further violence used. The misused man made a complaint to the States, the messengers gave evidence, but Ringault remained in English custody, guarded this time not to prevent him escaping but from falling into Oldenbarnevelt's clutches.

He never fell into them. It was the first strain on Oldenbarnevelt's normally good relations with Wilkes. On the eve of his departure for Zeeland on 25 November, Leicester again promised to have Ringault brought to trial.

But when he had left it appeared that Ringault had gone too. He was said to have been transported under military escort to Brill, without Leicester's previous knowledge (again!), evidently with the intention of taking him over to England. Oldenbarnevelt succeeded in preventing that and induced Wilkes to have him taken into the interior again, informing the Dordrecht authorities that Ringault and his guards would be passing through, so as to seize him and 'under colour of justice to bereave him of his life' (the phrase used by Wilkes in the conversation to be reported below). Wilkes found out, however, that Dordrecht was not safe for his prisoner and had him taken to Utrecht by another route. Some days later he spoke to Oldenbarnevelt in The Hague and excused his breach of Leicester's promise with his fear of a judicial murder. Oldenbarnevelt was furious but did not wish to incur Wilkes' displeasure. He took refuge behind the States of Holland, who would be *fort altérés* at Ringault's escaping them. Unfortunately this might well express itself in a change of mood towards Leicester, which Oldenbarnevelt would of course deeply regret – for which reason he requested Wilkes 'not be be overhasty to deal with the States therein until he (Oldenbarnevelt) should upon better occasion advise me thereunto'.[1] Some days later the States-General again came to the Council of State to claim Ringault. Wilkes, under attack, nevertheless remained steadfast, whereupon Oldenbarnevelt delivered an impassioned speech. All the old grievances against Leicester were brought up once more and he was made responsible for nothing less than the dissolution of the Union of Utrecht. It was obvious that Oldenbarnevelt was in just the right mood for a judicial murder. Wilkes chose the wisest part and after a time let Ringault escape to the Southern Netherlands, where he was reconciled to Mother Church and the Spaniards.

These days before Leicester's departure were a time of nervous tension for Oldenbarnevelt. He had to pick his way through a maze of complications, always on the look-out for any advantages to be gained from the situation for Holland and Holland's leadership of the central government.

The Utrecht militia had made the Utrecht town authorities resolve to offer unconditional sovereignty to Elizabeth.[2] They then went to The Hague to demand that the States of Holland should join them in this offer. Holland and Zeeland had indeed co-operated in sending a delegation to England, but were not in favour of giving it such far-reaching powers. They had no such high expectations with regard to English help resulting from the offer, whether accepted or not, and did not wish to give up their precious

---

[1] Wilkes in a letter to Leicester of 13 December (O.S., 23 December N.S.), 1586, Calendar of State Papers, foreign series, XXI, ii, 253.
[2] See p. 75.

privileges for it. Oldenbarnevelt thought it most unbecoming that the militia once again presumed to come and lecture the States in a way smacking of intimidation. He had the States of Holland resolve that they should not be admitted. They would have to submit their remonstrance in writing.

Not only did the States object to Leicester, Leicester objected to the States. He summed up seven objections in a memorandum that he handed to the States-General on 21 November, to be answered in a short time. Most of this work fell on Oldenbarnevelt, and while he was engaged on it Leicester invited him to a discussion in the Council of State, together with five other delegates of the States-General. He began with the Prouninck affair. Why would they not admit this man to the States-General, knowing that he, the Viceroy, liked him? With typical caution the delegates began to explain that they had not been charged on this point. Oldenbarnevelt, though, was not a man to shy at responsibility and wished to say something about it. He gave a neat résumé of four different reasons, three of which had not been used at the States-General meeting of 11 November. That the real reason was to do Leicester some harm Oldenbarnevelt was naturally not going to tell him. A man like Wilkes cannot have been in doubt about it.

The first and chief reason was that Prouninck was from Brabant, where inhabitants of Utrecht were not admitted to office; there must be reciprocity in this matter, therefore the appointment as burgomaster was illegal, being also contrary to the privilege of 7 May 1555. The second reason was that Prouninck was not a citizen of Utrecht, the third that he was in debt to the military authorities, having never finally settled accounts as receiver. The fourth reason was that he owned no property in Utrecht. Oldenbarnevelt did not quote any law for this: it was a generally acknowledged fact that a member of a *vroedschap*, thus *a fortiori* a burgomaster, must be one of the richest residents. Democrats and oligarchs were in full agreement about this. As a fifth point he produced a statement said to have been made by Prouninck in the States of Utrecht and communicated to him by one of his supporters in those States, Moersbergen or Buth: 'some wished to support the privileges so much that there would be bloody heads'.

Prouninck was called and denied most of these points; he also gave another version of the bloody heads. The main result of the conference seems to have been an intensification of the mutual hatred felt by its two main participants. Leicester did recommend moderation to Prouninck, particularly in not making the appearance of Utrecht in the States-General dependent on his own admittance, but in general he was on Prouninck's side and his dissatisfaction with the States was correspondingly increased. One of the delegates gave a honeyed address, imploring Leicester not to leave in anger: neither in their respectful submission of the remonstrance in fifteen clauses nor in any other respect had the opponents intended to be unpleasant to the Viceroy. The opposite would certainly be put about by the clerics with whom Leicester had had 'familiarity', and they had heard from English officers that they were not satisfied with their treatment by the States. When Leicester left there would certainly be disputes among the officers, especially as there were too many soldiers in service, more than the States and the Queen together could pay.

The tone, one could see, was greatly changed since the meeting on 12 November. Then Leicester had been conciliatory, since he could not afford to go back to England with the reputation of having set all Holland up in arms against himself. But now the conciliation was on the other side, for neither could Oldenbarnevelt afford Leicester reporting in England that the States and their leaders undermined his authority, starved his officers and men, sabotaged the execution of his instructions, suspected his advisers and made the conduct of the war impossible, all against the will of the population. That the latter point was true must have been realized by Oldenbarnevelt during that November. The interview on 22 or 23 November was preceded by a private conversation between Leicester and Oldenbarnevelt. Leicester complained of many things done to him by the States. In particular they had complained behind his back to the Queen about the export embargo and his relations with Ringault. This should not have been done without his previous knowledge. The channel for these complaints was of course Ortel, who at this time was engaged in a lively correspondence with Oldenbarnevelt; Leicester had long been aware of it and repeatedly asked Walsingham not to receive the man any more and to send him away if possible. However, Oldenbarnevelt had satisfied him in this respect, he explained to the six delegates. He did not say how and we do not know. Leicester also stated that he was 'piqued' at the remonstrance and would not fail to let Elizabeth know it, although on the other hand it was not owing to this pique that he was leaving the country. The next day he had this supplemented by Wilkes at a session of the States-General which Oldenbarnevelt also took the trouble to attend. It is quite entertaining to see how Leicester took courage in proportion as Oldenbarnevelt retreated. This time the former presumed to demand the punishment of 'some of the States who work to show his actions in the worst light and cause misunderstanding between him and the States'. Oldenbarnevelt answered: 'that he (i.e. Leicester) should not believe all these reports and that there was no one in the States but knew well that this country was only to be preserved by favour of Her Majesty and His Excellency under God'.

The best way of doing this was to create and maintain 'good understanding between Viceroy and States-General, after the example of the late Prince, who by this means was able to resist a more powerful enemy for so many years, so that such would not be found in histories to have been done by any Prince for his subjects'.

The Prince was no doubt brought into the picture here to make Leicester look ridiculous and odious in comparison. But the tribute sounds as if it were cordially meant. Oldenbarnevelt may have had outbursts of anger against the Prince when he was alive: his opposition was never systematic, his admiration was unconcealed and the Prince was his example in everything where their difference in character did not prevent him from following it.

The Governor-General swallowed the admonition in silence. He knew that there were even many in his immediate circle who did not consider it undeserved. His seven grievances were answered the following day with the syrupy platitudes which Oldenbarnevelt was always good at. There was only one point that was answered sharply and that was one that Leicester, in duty bound but against his own judgment, had raised himself: whether the States-General would cooperate in peace negotiations.

Leicester, like Walsingham and the whole of the Puritan party, was strongly opposed to peace negotiations as long as no decisive advantage had been gained in the military campaign. Oldenbarnevelt's answer, of impeccable logic, must have pleased him; it completely explains why its composer did not believe in peace negotiations for the following twenty years, and after that did believe in them. It was a question of sovereignty. Till the negotiations at Cologne in 1579 it had been endeavoured to reach agreement with the King on the basis of restoration of his sovereignty with guarantees for his subjects in the matter of self-government and religious freedom. The negotiations broke down owing to the demand for religious freedom. Since then the situation had changed radically. From a religious hodge-podge with strong loyalist currents and a set of temporary rebel leaders, the insurgents had both shrunk and grown in seven years into a state in the making under the leadership of one province-plus-assistant. Some of the loyalists had returned to 'Father Philip', some, deprived of all power, had gone underground against an established régime. Three times another sovereign had been elected; the Prince's blood had been shed: these were things of the past that could not be altered. Reconciliation with the King would now be possible only at the cost of a revolution. The States urgently requested Leicester to see that such negotiations did not take place.

There was still one thing to be settled before the Viceroy took his leave: the interim government. For the chief command Leicester chose for some obscure reason his confirmed enemy John Norris. Civil interim government was conferred on the Council of State, which as a Netherlands body naturally had no authority over its English senior officers. Then, in accordance with his weak personality, Leicester had recourse to a secret Act of Restriction, forbidding the Council to act in matters which Leicester reserved for himself. Thus in his own devious way he destroyed all the benefits that might have been obtained from his ostentatious confidence in the Council and Norris.

Although the game was played with velvet gloves, mutual mistrust had by no means vanished. A typical piece of trouble demonstrated that almost on the gangplank. Leicester had invited Maurice to go with him to England, presumably without any evil intentions beyond having him grow up under his influence (*Tandem fit surculus arbor*: At length the sapling becomes a tree, was Maurice's motto). Oldenbarnevelt thought there was more to it than that. Vehement argument was necessary to dissuade the States of Holland from their original intention to agree. Did Oldenbarnevelt really consider his opponent so lacking in imagination as to attempt anything like poisoning or imprisonment against Maurice in England, thus inviting the most deplorable comparisons with Philip and Philip William?[1] We may assume the opposite. His alarm was feigned and his real motive was the same as Leicester's: he wanted to grow a useful hothouse plant which, left to itself or others, might become dangerous instead. Both results were obtained. Maurice was first useful and then highly dangerous to his mentor. But the useful period lasted thirty years – quite a time.

Leicester had left too soon for Oldenbarnevelt, but sometimes it is better early than never. Oldenbarnevelt's task was to profit from his departure to establish Holland's preponderance without alarming the Queen. It was difficult but made considerably easier by the ill-advised Act of Restriction and its indirect result: the betrayal of Deventer and Zutfen.

[1] William of Orange's eldest son, abducted by Philip II to Spain and kept prisoner there for twenty-eight years.

CHAPTER 3

Leicester frozen out

LEICESTER had gone, but he might come back. It did not seem likely that he would put his hand into the wasps' nest again, but he had said in as many words that he would. He had retained the governorship and, entrenched in their powerful positions, his adherents continued their policy of anti-Holland centralism, opposed with all his strength by Oldenbarnevelt. A medal which Leicester issued on his first departure reflects the objections of a man like Prouninck to the Holland States Party: one side shows a she-ape with her young in her arms and the inscription round the edge: *Libertas ne ita chara ut simiae catuli* (Let liberty be not so dear (to you) as to the she-ape her young); the reverse shows a man who, trying to escape from the smoke, falls into the fire: *Fugiens fumum incidit in ignem.* Could one, like the ape on the medal, cherish liberty – safeguarding it from Leicester at the risk of allowing it to be suffocated – by depriving him of the means to fight Parma? Was not English smoke always more bearable than Spanish fire? We can hear the Utrecht burgomaster speaking through the gauze of allegory. For thousands in the country these questions were purely rhetorical. Oldenbarnevelt alone did not regard them as rhetorical and answered them with complete conviction. Liberty for him was indivisible. The war, undertaken in defence of the privileges – *Haec libertatis ergo!* – had no point if these privileges were to be sacrificed, as Prouninck would have liked, to another tyrant. Also he was less afraid of the Spanish fire than his opponents: his opposition to Leicester was a calculated risk. The result proved him right.

The first question of importance after Leicester had left was the disbanding, now become necessary, of the soldiers taken on by him above the war estimate. The money needed for that was not available, whereupon the soldiers, mostly Catholic Irishmen, started to mutiny. By a cunning mixture of bribery and vague promises Oldenbarnevelt, who not without danger went to see the mutineers, induced them to let themselves be disbanded without cash payment.

While this matter was being dealt with, the hitherto secret Act of Restriction became known. The Council of State had based its refusal to cooperate in the disbanding of troops on the Act, which stated that Leicester's consent from England was necessary. After powerful urging from Oldenbarnevelt the Council finally agreed to give its consent, thus setting aside the Act of Restriction in an important matter of principle. The effect of the Act was not yet exhausted, however, as the States were soon to notice to their detriment.

It was not practicable to wait for Leicester's personal decisions. Communication with England was always difficult during the winter; moreover everyone's attention there was gripped by the last act but one in the tragedy of Mary Stuart.

In January there were almost daily onslaughts on the absent Viceroy's authority and that of his Council of State. A sharp financial resolution full of criticism of the waste of public funds was unofficially changed by Oldenbarnevelt. The strengthening of Maurice's position, first by increasing his bodyguard to more than the number fixed by Leicester, and then his high-handed promotion to captain-general of Holland and Zeeland served the same purpose; slowly to haul Leicester down from the pedestal on to which popular idolatry had raised him.

The cunning liberation of Paulus Buys managed by Oldenbarnevelt at this time was another blow to Leicester's prestige and infuriated the hated Prouninck. In this case too the Hollanders were unable to attain their ends through the Council of State, and the States-General acted as executive body, just as in the disbanding of the superfluous troops, because the Council of States' 'hand was closed'. Oldenbarnevelt persuaded the assembly to send a direct order for Buys' release, not to the Utrecht town authorities or to the militia, who officially held him prisoner, but to the under-sheriff of Utrecht, Gerrit van Remundt, who was more specially responsible for his custody.

This was all strictly illegal; the under-sheriff was dismissed on the spot and threatened with more drastic measures, which he evaded by flight. On the other hand Buys' arrest had also been illegal and he had been in prison for six months without a charge being made. We can, however, regard Van Remundt to a certain extent as a victim of Oldenbarnevelt's persuasiveness.

This episode is important, showing that Oldenbarnevelt, good lawyer though he was, would transgress the rules of formal justice if it was necessary for his policy. This policy was founded on the interests of the Holland merchants, vital indeed for the Netherlands. To satisfy them Leicester's stature had to be reduced.

The last months of 1586 and the first of 1587 were of decisive significance for the development of the republic in the making. It was made clear in and by the struggle against Leicester and the hangers-on he had left behind, that neither a foreign monarch, nor her representative in the Netherlands, nor the tight-fisted Council of State, nor the various provinces, always at odds with one another, were to determine the fate of the Netherlands, but the Hollander who was leader of the States-General. It was the only possible exercise of power in the Netherlands after the fall of Antwerp, and it is to Oldenbarnevelt's lasting credit that he grasped and persisted in it in spite of the serious risks involved.

Oldenbarnevelt took these risks. They were not precisely calculated but neither were they accepted blindly, as the price of the establishment of Holland's hegemony. He let Elizabeth's friendship cool off and made help from her side doubtful. Without it, as he admitted himself, Spain could not be held back. No wonder that Prouninck and his clique considered Oldenbarnevelt soft in the head and probably a traitor as well.

The first blow was the betrayal by Stanley and York on 29 January of Deventer and the fortifications near Zutfen to the Spaniards: both were cash transactions, though in Stanley's case his Roman Catholic solidarity may have been a more honourable motive. More fundamental causes were: the disagreement between Leicester and the States-General, on politics; bad military administration that encouraged the captains' dishonesty; lack of coordination between the English and Netherlands administrative bodies; and, probably, the economic crisis and the inability of the rich Holland territory to pay. The crisis was due to various factors but was ascribed by the Holland merchants entirely to the edict of 14 April causing paralysis of trade. These circumstances had two results: Leicester greatly overspent his budget, and neither the States-General nor Queen Elizabeth was forthcoming with supplementary grants. The sufferers were the soldiers and sailors. As early as December a large body of English horse made a direct attack on Holland, reaching Zoetermeer and threatening The Hague. The English councillor Wilkes was able to raise a small loan on his personal credit and thus induce a retreat. This retreat did not proceed smoothly and a number of cavalrymen, harassed by the outraged citizens of Hilversum, paid for it with their lives.

Wilkes's loan was of course a mere palliative: for one trooper who got paid there were certainly ten others and fifty infantry who were not. A raid on The Hague was for trustworthy commanders a way of getting money; the untrustworthy ones had another. It was known who these commanders were: every day the Council of State received reports on suspicious relations with the Spaniards. First it was Willoughby, the commander of Bergen-op-Zoom, whose steward was received much too cordially at negotiations over prisoners of war in Antwerp. Then there were similar rumours from Ostend, Flushing, Arnhem and Zwolle. Most persistent were the rumours concerning Rowland York, in the redoubt on the IJsel opposite Zutfen, and concerning Leicester's special favourite, Sir William Stanley, at Deventer. Both had been in Spanish service: the latter was a Roman Catholic, and the former had wanted, in similar conditions of non-payment in 1583, to hand Ghent over to the Spaniards, and was condemned to death though not executed for it. Leicester, who was short of capable officers – and Stanley was certainly capable – had made no bones about promoting him to high office; indeed, Stanley was one of the three candidates he had put forward to the States as commander-in-chief during his absence. He had not been affected by the warnings by Ortel from England, and it was certainly in the first place for the benefit of these two that the Act of Restriction expressly prohibited the replacement of high-ranking officers. Fresh complaints from Deventer led to serious pleading in the Council of State for their removal, but as has repeatedly been seen, the Council was acting in a spineless manner. Oldenbarnevelt could not intervene through the States-General in this case, as he had in the disbandment and in the release of Paulus Buys, since the soldiers in question would not have allowed themselves to be dismissed by the States-General. A very rude letter from York and some officers to the Council of State, dated 10 December, made it quite clear that they would accept orders from Leicester and from no one else. Furthermore Leicester had given his own life as surety for the loyalty of Stanley and York. That may have aroused some suspicion against the suspicious.

While the courier was riding to The Hague with this alarming news, Oldenbarnevelt was quietly engaged there on his next step in diminishing Leicester's prestige, bringing money into the treasury and satisfying the merchants. It was, of course, concerned with trade with the enemy. Leicester's mitigations of the April edict at the beginning of August had been of little avail and had been partially invalidated by Ringault's actions at the end of that month. The result was that the tax-collectors' cash-boxes were empty and the merchants had suffered considerable losses, while it could not be said that the Spanish war effort had been seriously impeded. The price of food had certainly risen in the southern part of the Netherlands, but there was no question of famine among Parma's troops and some months later Oldenbarnevelt was remarking scornfully about

the opinion of those who for some consideration (best known to themselves) think that they can starve out whole provinces (which enjoy the greatest and most fertile land in all Europe) and so to bring the war to an end.

On 26 January the States-General resolved to withdraw the April edict, as altered in August, and to replace it by another, in which

both residents and foreigners were to be allowed to export goods imported into these regions from foreign places, against payment of tax, to neighbouring countries 'not under obedience to the . . . King of Spain'.

It appeared later that the intention was to permit trade with Spain as well.

When the Council of State objected to announcing this resolution, with its character of 'advice', Oldenbarnevelt threatened to issue the edict in the name of the States-General, whereupon the Council, not unaccustomed to giving in, did so once again. The day after the betrayal of Deventer, 30 January, the Council of State signed 'under protest': only Wilkes had sufficient warlike spirit to refuse his signature.

Amsterdam had achieved almost total victory by securing the Advocate of Holland as its ally. An almost unanimous vote in the States of Holland had empowered Oldenbarnevelt to take his action in the States-General: only Dordrecht sounded a warning note against this disregard of the central authority. Oldenbarnevelt did not care for being warned and never forgave the Dordrecht pensionary Menijn, the leading spirit of the pro-Leicester party. Eight years later Oldenbarnevelt had his revenge.

The day after the Council of State's concession the 'sad tidings and announcement that the English Governor, Sir William Stanley, appointed to Deventer by his Excellency has betrayed the said town' arrived early in the morning.

Note how it was formulated. The dismay aroused in the country – unequalled till 1672 – was not primarily due to the loss of Deventer, although it was counted as the third mercantile town of the Netherlands after Amsterdam and Antwerp. It was the fact that treachery had been committed by an English governor, a confidant of Leicester's, and appointed governor by him, that incited an indescribable rage against everything English, in accordance with the familiar line of thought: one scoundrel, two scoundrels, all scoundrels. Historical sources provide more than ample evidence that the English were suddenly regarded as enemies, that an Englishman dared not show himself in the streets, that isolated English soldiers were molested and that English detachments, going through the country with perfectly legal passes, were refused all facilities of passage. Leicester had made his life Stanley's security. This was nonsense; not even a Shylock would have ventured to demand his pound of flesh now the guarantee had not been honoured. It would have been more realistic if he had staked his popularity, for this had been reduced by the blazing hatred of the people to an insignificant fragment.

Oldenbarnevelt struck while this iron was hot. Did he himself believe all the evil circulated by himself and others about the English? It is difficult to say. There is something ambivalent in his character on this subject. He no doubt practised a certain Machiavellism. He may well be thought capable of striking the chords of popular indignation like a cool virtuoso to achieve a desired result. On the other hand there were moments in his life when, under the influence of his emotions, he gives the impression of not thinking purely logically. The days and weeks after the betrayal of Deventer may have been such a period. Now and again his anger seems to be genuine. But that Leicester had appointed the two commanders with the object of treachery, and that it should have taken place with the knowledge and approval of the Queen, were rumours believed, for a time, by the public, but too irrational for Oldenbarnevelt.

There were also adherents of Leicester who remained cool-headed and did not place the responsibility for these two acts of treachery solely upon the English. Prouninck wrote an impassioned and readable plea to this effect. The brochure did not affect the course of events at the time, but eventually it harmed Oldenbarnevelt immensely, since for the first time the imputation of bribery by Spanish *pistoles* can be read between the lines. The accusation was untrue but sounded plausible. One must beware of regarding Prouninck as a villain for putting it into words without mentioning any names. As has been seen, Oldenbarnevelt's policy was an expensive one, with short-term advantages for Parma. It was known that Parma was lavish with *pistoles*, when he had any. Oldenbarnevelt was obviously growing rich. Two years later he was to buy a mansion in The Hague and have it restored at great expense. Moreover he had a reputation for money-grubbing and certainly tolerated corruption, at any rate in his own circle. Only those who could discern well beyond the expediencies of the moment could realize that he was anything but pro-Spanish. Only a psychologist or good friends appreciated that his money-making instincts were limited and that his corrupt inclinations could never compete with his patriotism. It was known only in Delft that his riches had less murky sources than Prouninck supposed. It is a remarkable and moving paradox that the very moment when Oldenbarnevelt was in harmony with popular feeling saw the foundation laid of the bitter public hatred that was to be his downfall. The populace (*varium et mutabile semper femina*) is always a fickle and changeable thing.

The States-General's first reaction to the loss of Deventer was a military measure, directed against the Council of State, distrusted on account of its weak attitude towards Leicester. In Leicester's absence this body possessed the sole right to move troops by means of letters patent to the commanders of military units, instructing them to move from place to place along a certain route, the authorities in towns and villages along these routes being ordered to help them in their march. Understandably, though quite illegally, Oldenbarnevelt wished in the circumstances to keep the issue of letters patent under his own control, formally under that of Maurice. As soon as the betrayal became known he had himself sent at the head of a commission of the States of

Holland to the Council of State to 'notify them that they should no longer take cognizance of the changes of garrisons within the land of Holland'. An unpleasant message, equivalent to a declaration of civil war. Without awaiting the Council's reaction the States wrote to the towns of Holland forbidding them to allow changes in their garrisons without the new letters patent from Maurice and furthermore 'take all care that these towns should be kept in good defence and security' and 'to indict and take suitable proceedings' against all the too vocal critics of these measures. At the same time all the towns earlier given the right of raising *waardgelders* were now instructed to do so, to cover themselves against the expected English troop movements. The States of Holland thought that this was enough for one day to foil any English surprise attack. In fact Holland was not in the least danger. The English in general showed no inclination to follow the example of Stanley's and York's troops; Norris, the commander-in-chief, did all he could to regain Deventer and kept the remaining troops under control. The majority of the English army, Protestant in contrast to Stanley's wild Irishmen, were hungry but loyal. Oldenbarnevelt, who was on good terms with Norris, must have known all this. One cannot therefore help suspecting that the measures taken that Saturday, however efficient in themselves, had the main object of exciting public feeling in Holland and of profiting by Leicester's departure, which could only serve Holland's interests.

After the meeting of the States of Holland, held as usual in the town hall of The Hague, Oldenbarnevelt proceeded with an unusually strong 'retinue' to the Binnenhof to induce the States-General to follow his line of action. We can imagine how they looked: secretly triumphant rather than afraid, but with anxious glances at the many citizens who stopped them to hear the latest news from the IJsel line. In the assembly room of the States-General they found a mood wavering between depression and determination, not unlike that of July 1584: then the Prince was dead; his successor was morally dead and no one expected that after this scandal he would ever set foot in Holland again. In both cases the central government had virtually disappeared; the States-General had to ensure the country's safety and improvise a new temporary government, vested with authority.

That morning it was too late to pass any resolutions, but they went together to the Council of State, which was in dire need of money and asked the States-General to provide some as soon as possible. In the afternoon session Oldenbarnevelt proposed that a part of Leicester's powers should be transferred to Maurice – in effect to the States of Holland with their Advocate. It was a question of control of the fleet, in which was involved the authority to raise or lower *licenten* and to allow or prohibit sailing to certain ports. The resolution, approved by the Zeelanders only on the condition that those they represented would consent to it, was not carried out, owing to the particularism of this province which did not want to lose its own admiralty. But it showed how the wind was blowing, as did the other decision taken that afternoon: to submit a number of questions to the Council of State with regard to their military administration. The real significance of these questions was that the Council, in theory the highest authority in the country, was degraded to a body of officials in the service of the sovereign States-General. Oldenbarnevelt had envisaged this state of affairs since Leicester's departure and it was a reality as long as the Republic existed. There were some disputes after this 31 January and the English members Wilkes, and later Bodley, defended themselves stoutly, but the matter was largely decided by the fall of Deventer. No wonder Oldenbarnevelt spoke cheerfully about the Deventer disaster.

The next morning, a Sunday, there was another joint meeting with the Council of State. Oldenbarnevelt was the only speaker for the 'opposition', against four members of the Council as representatives of the 'government'. One of these, the English secretary to the Council, George Gilpin, drew up a lively report of this meeting in French. Oldenbarnevelt took a sharp tone from the start. In defence of the revolutionary resolution concerning the admiralty he alleged that the affairs of state had come into great disorder as a result of bad conduct and mistakes in government. After this a heated debate produced accusations on one side, excuses on the other, Oldenbarnevelt exclaiming: 'Est-ce la servir le pays?' One of the Dutch members of the Council answered that they always had to listen to harsh words, as if they were subjects and slaves. So he had well understood what was meant! They could seek others to serve them, and be subjected to their continual calumnies and protests.

The threat of resignation was then and in the future the Council's only weapon against mordant criticism. It was an effective one, for membership was a thankless task for which people had to neglect their affairs for years and bear responsibility without real power. The States-General constantly yielded to this threat. In this case too Oldenbarnevelt at once stopped his attack on the Council of State and turned to his real target, the English nation:

... whereupon the said Barnevelt, as though impassioned by spirit and anger, said loudly that it was the Cabinet Council, and that various things were done, of which none knew but those in the said Cabinet . . . and so the Council was here, and the authority in England, or that it seemed that His Excellency was consulting a kind of secret Council over there which the States in no way intended to be so.[1]

The accumulation of English troops under English officers would also be

[1] Gilpin's report.

against the Treaty of Nonsuch, it was an intolerable situation 'being mal-treated and thoroughly deceived by the English Nation'.

This was clearly going too far. Such expressions might be used in private but were unsuitable in the highest governing body, in the presence of Wilkes and Gilpin, who reported everything that was said to the English ministers. Gilpin was doubtless referring to these and similar strongly anti-English out-bursts at this session when he wrote a few days later to Walsingham:

There were of late in open assembly used speaches by one, proceeding of abound-ance of passion, that were afterwards wished unspoken and would have made a cullor over them;[1] but I both answered thereto, noted them well and so bear them in memory as, yf need requyre, can sett the same in wrytinge.

Indeed Oldenbarnevelt soon had to draw in his horns, at any rate with regard to his general imputations against the English nation. When a Nether-lands councillor cited the French Fury to demonstrate that French deceit had been far worse in any case and that the Prince himself had on that occasion been the victim, Oldenbarnevelt retorted: 'We were never so deceived by the French as now by these English. Their behaviour is in no way comparable.'[2] Gilpin, who as secretary was not really allowed to take part in the debates tried in vain to calm the vociferous speaker, who then abandoned the subject of the dishonesty of the English to concentrate for the rest of the morning on the responsibility for the Act of Restriction. Oldenbarnevelt's position was stronger here. Apart from the deeper grounds for the disaffection of higher British officers, the Act of Restriction was without doubt the direct reason for the betrayal, which had been anticipated for a long time. Oldenbarnevelt claimed that he did not believe Leicester capable of committing this stupidity himself, thus making a subtle distinction between the impeccable Viceroy and his wicked subordinates.

Who was responsible then? The rest of that Sunday morning was spent in deciding this. Gilpin was found to have signed the Act, but excused himself by saying that it was the practice for the secretary to sign below and at the same time as his master. There was then an investigation into who had written the document, the clerks were called in and asked who had handed it to them. After some twisting and turning it appeared that it was a member of the Council of State, not recognized by the States-General, Reinhard van Aes-wijne, Lord of Brakel. He was absent on state business, as indeed were most of the members of the Council, who at that time were very sparse. All Olden-barnevelt's wrath was now directed against this absentee, whose life would certainly have been in danger if he had been in The Hague. The meeting

---

[1] i.e. put another complexion on. [2] Gilpin's report.

adjourned at midday with feeling running high. Oldenbarnevelt had acquired a new bugbear: Brakel. He would not rest till he had brought about the political downfall of the Utrecht nobleman and ruined him by besieging his castle. Remarkably enough, however, his esteem for Wilkes and Gilpin had risen. They were English and had done their duty as such. When Wilkes intervened in the discussions it was in a calm manner. He had not so much denied the justification for Oldenbarnevelt's accusations as pointed out that Elizabeth's help was needed and that it was therefore important not to irritate her. Oldenbarnevelt knew this quite well and was grateful to the English lawyer for restraining him.

Oldenbarnevelt composed a long letter to Leicester, to be sent by the States-General, in which all the familiar complaints were recapitulated and he and his advisers – for form's sake – held responsible for the betrayal of Deventer. The whole letter was sharply worded. Menijn was later to apologize for the letter as being written *in amaritudine cordis*.

There was not much news in it for Leicester; all that was new, the complaint concerning the Act of Restriction and the defence of the release of Buys, was moderate by Oldenbarnevelt's standards and does not explain the storm raised by the letter in England and apparently unexpected by anyone in the States-General. The text was settled without alteration, though not without discussion, and none of the deputies felt the need for any *ruggespraak*. Oldenbarnevelt was not only a man of steel himself, he also knew how to steel the nerves of others. It was decided to read the letter to the Council of State before despatch. They made no objection either, in spite of Wilkes's warning on the explosive effect of sending a copy to the Queen, who would not take it kindly. He made an attempt to prevent the letter being sent. He called on the young Stadtholder Maurice, among others, but the young Prince, who knew how to simulate incomprehension, gave little comfort, no more than did Van der Mijle, who, as the most prominent of Leicester's men present in Holland, was also consulted. It was a wasted effort: no power in the world could prevent the sending of a letter approved in full session, and which, as Oldenbarnevelt hoped, would once and for all put a stop to the return of the hated viceroy.

The letter was dated 4 February. On the same day the year expired for which the Council of State had been appointed in 1586. Then it had been done by Leicester, but now, at Oldenbarnevelt's instigation, the States-General, who had formerly always chosen the Council of State, once more took this appointment upon themselves and removed a number of Leicester's adherents from that body, so that for months it numbered instead of eleven members from seven provinces, six members from three provinces, far too small a number to function properly, as the members often left for the front, and only two or three met at The Hague. But these were good Hollanders and this was Oldenbarnevelt's intention. The party politician should not be condemned too hastily. In his opinion the interests of the country could only be fostered if his party was in power. The future vindicated him.

Leicester's power had to be still further cut down, if the Hollanders were to feel safe. Now that the central authority was no longer to be trusted, particularism was in its heyday. On the Friday after the memorable Wednesday which saw the explosive letter and the renewal of the Council of State, the States of Holland passed an Act of Authority, intended to make effective the appointment made in January of Maurice as Captain-General. This Act invested him with practically unlimited authority over the troops for the repartition of Holland and Zeeland, which had also signed the Act. It was certainly illegal. Dordrecht and Gorinchem voted against it. The tables of the law were broken of necessity and Maurice did in fact become commander of the troops in Holland and Zeeland and thus in effect of the United Provinces. The foundation was laid for the victorious campaigns of 1591-7 at the end of this winter. Here again the present, not without wise intuition, was sacrificed to the future.

Holland submitted its grants for the current year. The conditions were so strongly worded that they conferred almost complete autonomy on the province. Thus Holland could mortgage its common property, exercise authority over the troops it paid for and also conduct courts martial; on the other hand Leicester was expressly denied the right to pass sentence through deputy judges, the *privilegium de non evocando* was invoked against him, while letters patent were to be given only by 'His Excellency of Nassau or the Lieutenant-General of Holland and Zeeland . . . on the advice of the States or those commissioned by them'. The immediate result was a kind of anarchy in the issue of patents: 'everyone gives letters patent as he pleases' the Council of State complained on 4 August. But Oldenbarnevelt knew what he was doing.

He must have been working like a Trojan at this time. He was of course not alone. A list of party chiefs is given by Cartwright, an English official in Flushing, and those hostile 'to His Excellency and our whole nation' are named. First of all 'all Dutch counts and barons' (by 'Dutch' he probably meant 'German'). He was referring both to the two Nassau Stadtholders and the Count of Nieuwenaar and to the commanding officers Hohenlohe and Hohensachsen. Neither of them played a leading part in the opposition. All that is heard of them is that they did nothing but drink and dance and that Hohenlohe was drunk for a fortnight on end. Then 'Barnevelt' is mentioned as leader. In the same letter we hear that the States dance to his tune and certainly do nothing without his advice. Immediately after Oldenbarnevelt we find in Cartwright's list of hostile statesmen two with whom Oldenbarnevelt soon afterwards came into conflict. They were François Maelson, dreaming of West Friesland as a seventh province, and Carel Roorda, who did not want either Englishmen or Hollanders to have a say in Frisian affairs. The former had spread a rumour that Leicester had spent 4,600,000 guilders.[1] He meant of course that grants had been given for a total of $4\frac{1}{2}$ million guilders and that they had not produced much result. But it was said in a way implying that the Englishman and his cronies had squandered the money themselves. Vile slander, which was of course readily believed and was soon to be made subject to heavy penalties by the Council of State. The fourth on Cartwright's list, a fat man called Brasser from Delft, had openly expressed pleasure that Leicester's period of office was over. Wilkes also names the same four people as opponents, not of Leicester personally but of the policy he had followed up till then. He thought that they were all mortally afraid of Leicester's revenge but he considered that Leicester would not be able to govern without them: if he returned to the Netherlands he would have to win them back.[2] Wilkes must have been rather ingenuous to think this. If there was one thing on which the State party was firmly determined it was to stick to its guns and get rid of Leicester.

The party had also penetrated the Council of State. According to both Cartwright and Wilkes[3] the councillor Willem Bardes from Amsterdam was a keen party man, in spite of his pretended moderation. He and Buys – no longer regarded by the experts as a great man – were very unpopular with their colleagues owing to their well-known partisanship; on the other hand the general hatred of Leicester also reflected on the Council of State. Bardes and Buys did not care for this and after a month of the new period of office could not be persuaded to remain. As one member was ill and another in England the number of effective members of the Council dwindled to three, quite inadequate for the preparation of the summer campaign.

Military measures were the first requisite for assuring the position created by the actions on 31 January and 1 February, both against the English and against the Spaniards. It is therefore no wonder that Hohenlohe's house at Delft was the place where the members of the States party used to meet. Ringault, still working at Utrecht for Leicester's interests, sent a spy there, who saw Oldenbarnevelt, Buys and Brasser go in, but could not find out what was discussed, even by bribing the kitchen staff.[4]

---

[1] Calendar of State Papers, foreign series, XXI, ii, 395: Ringault calls him there 'pretty well known for his extraordinary and rude behaviour'.
[2] Correspondentie van Robert Dudley, uitg. H. Brugmans, Utrecht, 1931, II, 404.
[3] ibid. II, 165: 'very cunning and nothing affected to our party'.
[4] Calendar of State Papers, XXI, ii, 396.

The result of these discussions was that the idea began for the first time to take root that Holland could perhaps be defended against Parma without foreign help. At about the same time we find the idea expressed by Oldenbarnevelt in the States of Holland and by Buys in conversation with an anonymous Briton.[1] If this were true, Holland was in a much stronger position with regard to its English ally. But it remained a speculation. In the meantime it was important to know how the Queen and Leicester would take the news of the events following on the fall of Deventer.

At this time, there was a Netherlands Embassy in England. It had to allay the shock these measures must cause there, a difficult task to which the envoys were not altogether equal. The States-General still had no permanent ambassador in England. The States of Holland and Zeeland had an agent there, Joachim Ortel, but he did not enjoy diplomatic status. The States-General were only represented on particular occasions by a special embassy, consisting of a large number of members. Numbers made for distinction, and dullness for importance. They were chosen by old custom either from the Courts of Justice, or, as was becoming more and more usual, from the deputies of the States-General. The respective provinces elected them and their mutual jealousy prevented one man being appointed leader. These envoys usually quarrelled and conducted unsuitable correspondence with their provinces. Buys, seeing how inefficient this system was, had already suggested the appointment of a permanent ambassador of the States-General in England. Oldenbarnevelt had been against it, because in 1586, when the proposal was tabled in the States of Holland, such an ambassador would have been appointed by Leicester and corresponded with him or with the Council of State. Ortel sent Oldenbarnevelt valuable news during the whole Leicester period. It did not occur to him to pay a salary to a diplomat in the service of 'the enemy'. The States generously gave permission to the other provinces to maintain an envoy in London as well as Ortel. This would have indeed been a retrograde step in the formation of the State, but Oldenbarnevelt was not serious with his half-hearted proposal. Zeeland also used Ortel and Utrecht and Friesland could not afford an envoy. It was part of his political armoury to make impracticable suggestions in a friendly way. As soon as Leicester had left Oldenbarnevelt acted quite differently. Professional diplomats were appointed to France and England, corresponding officially only with the States-General, unofficially with Oldenbarnevelt. 'L'Etat c'est moi.'

The reason for sending an embassy that winter was Leicester's conviction that the financial straits in which he found himself could only be put right if

---

[1] Calendar of State Papers, XXI, iii, 43–4. Cartwright even speaks of a 'generall maxim and speeche in the mouthes of the principall men of this Countrey'.

Elizabeth withdrew her refusal to accept sovereignty. So it had to be offered her again, wrapped up in as few restrictions as possible. It would naturally be accompanied by a considerable increase in the subsidy. Everyone was in favour of the latter. If the former was the condition, very well, although Holland did not expect much of it and feared rather than hoped for it. Because of Leicester's departure and the violent discord among the provinces themselves it was months before an embassy was finally appointed. Obviously the provinces mainly sent people who were persona grata with Leicester. Zeeland sent Valcke and Holland Menijn, an advantage for Oldenbarnevelt, as these gentlemen could not now witness what he was preparing against the English. It was difficult for them when they had to defend measures with which they were not in agreement before Elizabeth. Their instructions were carefully restricted, Oldenbarnevelt had taken care of this himself. When they arrived in England the barometer stood at stormy, owing to Elizabeth's personal crisis over the execution of Mary Stuart. There was nothing to be done with her, the ministers complained.

The first audience on 5 February, just after the arrival of the bad news about Deventer, was not encouraging. Elizabeth considered herself insulted in the person of Leicester. She blamed the States for the betrayal of Deventer; they had starved the brave English soldiers, even made them beg at people's houses. And as if she had heard Oldenbarnevelt speaking in his private circle: 'although some say that the Queen of England must do what she does for her own safety, no, no, you are mistaken. That is nothing but false persuasions.' *Protestatio actui contraria!* In fact the state of affairs was exactly what she said it was not. That applied on 5 February and still more on 18 February, when Mary Stuart's head had fallen and Philip began to prepare the Armada. Oldenbarnevelt had seen it all coming: the safety of England was incompatible with leaving the Netherlands in the lurch. Elizabeth admitted it in substance in her fulminations. She said that in spite of their discourtesy and stupidity she would not let the States down, so as not to break her royal promise, as she said. Perhaps Menijn was impressed by this; the other envoys, and Oldenbarnevelt, hearing of it at home, laughed scornfully.

When the letter of 4 February arrived it made matters worse. The envoys did not know where to put themselves and cursed Oldenbarnevelt's forcefulness.

Elizabeth asked at once if Leicester was wanted back in Holland or not. When the envoys answered timidly that they were not instructed on this point the Queen postponed her decision on the aid to be granted and Leicester's possible return till after the report by a special envoy entrusted with the task of examining the grievances of Leicester against the States-

General and vice versa and to find out if the breach could be mended. Thomas Sackville, Lord Buckhurst, a distinguished nobleman and high court functionary, was chosen as the most suitable. He was experienced and belonged to Lord Burghley's peace party. He could therefore be counted on enthusiastically to follow the secret clause in his instructions on sounding out the Netherlanders about the current peace negotiations.

When Oldenbarnevelt heard from the envoys of Buckhurst's impending arrival he was probably not displeased. The present envoys had failed where he had hoped they would fail. For the present they had succeeded in the only important point: Elizabeth would not abandon the Netherlands.

The unfortunate Wilkes found himself amid all this excitement in a difficult position. He was convinced of the mistakes made by Leicester. He knew that Elizabeth wanted to make peace and that she was not in the least inclined to accept the new offer of sovereignty inspired by Leicester. But how much influence had Leicester still at the English court? Was it safe to dissociate himself from him altogether? Had he stressed Leicester's errors too strongly in his letters to England? He tried to make this good by continual protests against the almost daily encroachments on Leicester's authority which The Hague indulged in. They behaved as if they were sovereign, but were they that in fact? Was it not rather the people itself, the 'community', upon whom the sovereignty had relapsed since the abjuration of Philip and the deposition of Anjou?

When Wilkes made one of his many protests against the States-General, who had appeared in the Council of State, Oldenbarnevelt asked him 'openly and roundly' to state what 'discontentment' he had with the actions of the States, for Oldenbarnevelt had heard that Wilkes and others 'spoke variously of them'.

Hereupon there was a long altercation between Oldenbarnevelt and Wilkes, over the rather theoretical point put forward by Oldenbarnevelt, about the increase in Maurice's power, and about the concrete matter for which the States had come, the disbandment of a large number of English soldiers without Leicester's previous knowledge. Wilkes set to work in the first place to give a summary of everything done since the end of January against Leicester's authority and the English in general, and secondly to put forward a theoretical argument on the basis of Prouninck's democratic doctrine. Oldenbarnevelt began to think too about the theoretical basis of the exercise of power by the States. He consulted his supporter François Francken, pensionary of Gouda, more of a lawyer than himself. The statement about democracy was nonsense, Francken thought, a fantasy of the Calvinists that Calvin himself would never have approved. Thus fortified,

Oldenbarnevelt appeared in the Council of State on 20 March, four days after the above discussion. He stated boldly that the States-General were now sovereign. Wilkes had not yet got his counter-argument ready. He addressed it to the States-General and to the States of Holland and handed it to the latter a few days later.

Oldenbarnevelt thought that a written answer was necessary. Of course Francken was entrusted with it. Oldenbarnevelt had no time for such things, and really no interest in them. The document would serve, however, as a defence against dangerous English influence and to make dangerous influence on the English harmless. When it was finished, Oldenbarnevelt must have been pleased with it. It really said everything that was relevant, rather long-windedly, but completely and convincingly. There were various references in it to the six or seven hundred years that the government had been as Francken and Oldenbarnevelt would now have it. No one could check on this and it sounded extraordinarily well. But when the document came before the States of Holland on 16 April, the arrival of Lord Buckhurst had introduced a warm spring wind into the cold war against Leicester. It was decided to keep Francken's memorandum on the files for a later date. Oldenbarnevelt had suffered a reverse – the first since becoming Advocate thirteen months before – which he could only consider intolerable. The Council of State had recently scored a slight success by threatening to resign. Paulus Buys had often used the same method with good results. Oldenbarnevelt too would cut the States down to size. On 20 April he sent in his resignation, naturally not giving this reason. In fact he did have others. But his first offer of resignation four days after his first defeat is too much of a coincidence. Oldenbarnevelt was a bad loser and would suffer for it.

The reasons he gave for his resignation are pretexts:

... that notwithstanding he had done all his duty during his said office and that his zest and energy were not diminished, and that he hoped to remain unchanged in this, he cannot do enough for his conscience, as some qualities are lacking in the execution of the said office, and that he therefore, and for various other reasons, had disposed of his affairs so as to quit the said office ...

Oldenbarnevelt may have been overworked after the great tension of recent months. When the States of Holland were in full session he had to attend their meeting as well as that of the States-General from beginning to end; though the hours of the meetings were arranged so that this was possible, they took so long, including the short midday break, that nothing could come of 'extending' the minutes and official correspondence till the evening. During the weeks that the States were not meeting, about half the time, the remaining body of *Gecommitteerde Raden* had to take small decisions, mostly in personal affairs, or in connection with dykes and canals. In times of tension over big-time politics it took up too much time and attention.

So when the States requested him to withdraw his resignation he made it a condition that every assistance should be given him at the meetings. Other conditions included not being strictly bound by his instructions, a dispensation from the restriction to living in The Hague and the right to quit his service if the States decided to enter into peace negotiations without preservation of religion and privileges.

He had made this last condition because meanwhile Elizabeth's delegate, Buckhurst, had arrived in the country, and it was presumed that he would have been given orders, among others, to urge the Netherlanders to take part in peace negotiations. One of the envoys sent to England, the Zeelander Valcke, had had an interview with Lord Burghley shortly before his return. He had been asked whether the States-General could produce more money for the maintenance of troops and go over to the offensive. If not, whether it was not better to conclude a peace, since nothing more was to be expected from Elizabeth. Valcke denied both: the States could not pay more money because of the economic situation and could not make peace or even start negotiations, because the Spaniards were untrustworthy and defeatism was too strong in the Netherlands.

'Your affairs are in a wretched state then' (said the Treasurer), 'if they are not capable of sustaining either war or peace.'

'The war', Valcke said, 'was undertaken of necessity and not for pleasure. We must use all our strength to repel the enemy and commend the outcome to God.'

Valcke was thus speaking as he had to speak to an English statesman on behalf of the Netherlanders. The envoys, however, when they made their report in the States-General at the end of March, would have stressed Burghley's opinion in their private conversations with Dutch leaders. Defeatism, as so often in world history, had some logic. English support had proved insufficient in the past year to prevent fresh conquests by Parma. There was no chance of Elizabeth increasing her support, in spite of Leicester's and Walsingham's efforts in this direction, unless it became clear that the Spanish peace terms were unacceptable or unjust. If the States now refused even to listen to the terms, would not the Queen leave the Netherlands to their fate – the fate of Antwerp, Nijmegen and Deventer?

Oldenbarnevelt did not believe in Elizabeth's defection. Nor did he consider it impossible to continue the war without increased English help. He was never willing, therefore, in the next ten years, to make important sacrifices in order to win Elizabeth's favour. When she withdrew part of her troops he complained but did not despair. It was not till 1598, in entirely changed circumstances, that he made a handsome offer of money to retain Elizabeth as an ally.

This optimism about the power of the rising republic was rationally justifiable. It was a question of belief and faith. It was a risk, such as is taken only by a statesman with foresight who does not shrink from a formidable burden of responsibility. Great statesmen are few and far between, however. The opposition to his hazardous policy naturally increased. His offer of resignation was the countermove that confirmed him in power for a long time.

Furthermore Buckhurst's peace mission turned out quite well. He arrived on 3 April 1587 at Flushing. Here in Zeeland he could already perceive that both the pro-English and the state party were against making peace. Zeeland had strong interests in privateering and was, if possible, even less peacefully inclined than the merchants of Holland. Buckhurst realized at once that he would lose prestige if he began talking about peace, and must keep quiet about it for the present if he was to carry out his instructions as to the preparation of a reconciliation with Leicester. Even if he had not noticed it in Zeeland, Wilkes, whom he at once contacted at The Hague, could tell him. Indeed a letter from the States-General composed by Oldenbarnevelt had reached the Queen before Buckhurst left, emphasizing the arguments against the opening of peace negotiations. And the reconciliation with Leicester? Wilkes had a recipe for this which Buckhurst, a long-standing enemy of Leicester's, had no trouble in accepting. Both sides must forget the past and in future Leicester must not rule with his Utrecht friends but with the real leaders of the Netherlands' resistance to Spain, the oligarchs of Holland. Wilkes had rapidly abandoned his democratic notions. He had probably only displayed them to cover himself against Leicester, who might have accused him of not supporting his interest adequately. Now, however, the Queen had proved by sending Buckhurst that she was once again not supporting Leicester. It seemed safe to throw away the mask of a Leicester adherent.

On Wilkes' advice Buckhurst soon consorted with the heads of the anti-Leicester party: Buys, Roorda and Thin. He then asked the States of Holland to give their deputies in the States-General full powers, so that Buckhurst could negotiate with the latter without being constantly delayed by the need for *ruggespraak*. Oldenbarnevelt made the States give an evasive answer to this request: that it did not accord with the Netherlands constitution based as it was on custom. The moderately pro-English Adriaen van der Mijle was deputed to explain this to Buckhurst, also how the difficulties with Leicester had arisen and how the writing of the notorious letter of 4 February had come about.

Now there was a surprise: Buckhurst seemed to be quite uninterested in the carefully prepared arguments by the president of the court. He would scarcely listen to them. What he had was a fine list of grievances in Latin. He had them read to the States-General in a solemn meeting on 14 April, with a Holland delegation numbering eleven, as well as the entire Council of State, headed by Prince Maurice. There were forty-two grievances, enough for a week's discussion. The document was undoubtedly drawn up in Leicester's entourage, perhaps by Borchgrave,[1] who must have imagined that its recital and the accompanying threats would be a great salve to his amour-propre. Leicester had sent his secretary Athy with Buckhurst to join in the enjoyment.

Things turned out quite otherwise. Buckhurst had no intention of starting a quarrel. He had the document read out because Elizabeth had expressly ordered it. But he refused to give the States a copy when they asked for one, so as to be able to answer his complaints one by one. The Queen had forbidden that, he said, to guard against all bitterness and misunderstanding. If the Resolutions are to be believed, Menijn, chosen for the same reason as Van der Mijle a few days before, nevertheless managed to answer all the points one by one. Then there followed the anticlimax at which Athy must have turned pale. The ambassador let it be announced that he had received 'complete satisfaction, in respect of Her Majesty, His Excellency and the English nation'.

He also requested that all that had been written on both sides about the letter of 4 February should be burnt and that the matter should be forgotten.

Gelderland had been disturbed about the possible effect of the letter of 4 February, of which a copy had been obtained by Prouninck, who had sent it with malicious comments to the States of that province. They had not been aware of it; their deputies in the States-General had kept them in ignorance and voted for it without instructions or *ruggespraak*. The States decided to send other delegates to The Hague, in the first place to Oldenbarnevelt himself, for information as to the possible adverse effects of this letter. They called on Oldenbarnevelt on the very day that Buckhurst had made his conciliatory declaration. Oldenbarnevelt could therefore confidently explain that Prouninck's insinuations were baseless. It was not true that the letter had prevented Parliament from passing a pro-Netherlands resolution – meaning the acceptance of the protectorate offered.

The Advocate defended the letter being kept secret from the States on the grounds of saving Leicester's reputation: 'So that they were not sorry that it had been written, and they made it up together. The Ambassador had declared

---

[1] The English text (Calendar of State Papers XXI, iii, 6) says: 'presented by one of that country'.

himself...perfectly satisfied.' One can feel the triumph in the tone of the victor, who had taken a serious risk and brought it off.

After this Oldenbarnevelt gave some information of the extraordinary aid to be expected from England: if the States could raise a million guilders to set up a field army, Buckhurst had promised that the Queen would add another half-million. He ended with the assurance that the Hollanders, contrary to current rumours,[1] would not desert Gelderland and the other inland provinces.

It may be assumed that Oldenbarnevelt was sincere in this last respect. Those around him may well have made plans for concentrating inside the fortress of Holland, as in 1572–6. Now that Gelderland and Overijsel made no payments, Utrecht was recalcitrant and Friesland could hardly afford its own defence, there was a certain amount of logic in Holland and Zeeland withdrawing into their shells. But this would have been a counsel of despair and Oldenbarnevelt was not at all in a desperate mood. Maurice and Oldenbarnevelt had become masters of the war as a result of Buckhurst's attitude, by which he implicitly recognized the military and financial resolutions of February. Things were easier now that the prohibition of exports had been brushed aside. Elizabeth had showed signs of continuing her help. There was no more talk of peace on unfavourable terms, either by the English or the Dutch defeatists, whom Oldenbarnevelt had muzzled. In the circumstances, the best possible in the best possible world, Holland could afford to vote a million for an army in the field and to provide the tamed Council of State with the money enabling it to peiform its function again.

There were still some clouds, but Buckhurst tried to dispel them. In the first place there was a quarrel in the highest ranks of the army between Hohenlohe and Edward Norris. Both were enemies of Leicester. Quite apart from the interests of the service that two high-ranking officers should not be on such bad terms – Norris had challenged Hohenlohe to a duel – Oldenbarnevelt's policy required Leicester's enemies, whether German or English, to toe the same line. Buckhurst managed to bring about a reconciliation. Hohenlohe and the Norris brothers were friends again but John Norris refused to drink Leicester's health at a banquet.

That was one small cloud gone. Two other larger ones were still casting a shadow over Oldenbarnevelt's triumph. Two of Leicester's adherents, the objects of Oldenbarnevelt's lasting hatred, were still in positions of power, one in North Holland, the other at Utrecht: Dirck Sonoy and Gerard Prouninck van Deventer. Eventually Oldenbarnevelt engineered the down-

---

[1] See a memorandum by Wilkes after his return to England, *Correspondence of Robert Dudley*, II, 403.

fall of both of them, but the time was not yet ripe for it, his own power was not yet sufficiently consolidated to strike. Buckhurst's support was of no avail either.

There is no doubt that his hatred of Sonoy was of long standing. He was the only one in Holland to oppose a system of government on which Oldenbarnevelt had set his heart – rightly as the future was to show.

Sonoy's system was essentially one of military dictatorship. An obvious method in the mortal struggle with a superior enemy and in view of the cheeseparing habits of some town governments. Prince William had also had similar inclinations but had managed to suppress them. He had found out that waging war in the Netherlands on its own resources was only possible if the burgher was in command of the general. Parma acted differently, but he got soldiers and money from Spain. If Leicester had been as generously supported by the Queen as he had hoped it might have been possible for him to introduce Sonoy's system. In any case lively sympathy had arisen between the two foreign noblemen, both full of pride of rank, Calvinist and anti-mercantile. It must have been Sonoy who gave Leicester the idea of paralysing Maurice's military command and stadtholdership in Holland by appointing governors of the towns and districts, under oath to Leicester and directly responsible to him. Thus Sonoy had become governor of North Holland north of the IJ. Maurice had from the first regarded this as an encroachment on his authority. After the revolutionary measures taken in February it was quite intolerable that there should be military commanders in Holland who would have nothing to do with Maurice. Sonoy refused to take the oath to Maurice as long as he was not released from his oath to Leicester. An attempt was made to replace his garrison by a trick, but it failed. Then Oldenbarnevelt sent Maurice himself, with Hohenlohe, which was a mistake. Hohenlohe and Sonoy were sworn enemies and now the latter could be justifiably afraid that some harsh steps were intended against him. In his alarm he resorted to the extremity of refusing admittance, when Maurice arrived with his plumed retinue at the gate of Medemblik. Troops were summoned by both sides and there was a clash at Hoorn on Easter day. If Oldenbarnevelt had been present a strong line might have been taken. But it was once more the peace-loving Adriaen van der Mijle who used a moderating influence and caused Maurice to withdraw with nothing achieved, after Sonoy had agreed to delay till news came from England.

It came soon both from Leicester and the Queen.[1] It said nothing, except that it was overflowing with sympathy and gratitude for Sonoy's loyalty. There was nothing in it about taking an oath or not. Sonoy could interpret it

---

[1] Calendar of State Papers, xxx, iii, 46; *Correspondence of Robert Dudley*, II, 184.

as he liked. It was not difficult for him: so long as he was not explicitly released from his oath to Leicester he would keep it. This may have been chivalrous honour or self-interest, as the profitable power he had exercised for fifteen years would be reduced if he were subordinated, instead of to the friendly Prince William, to his youthful son, wholly influenced by Sonoy's greatest enemies, Hohenlohe and Oldenbarnevelt.

Thus although Buckhurst did not attempt to settle the trouble at Medemblik, he went into action at Utrecht. The opposition to the States-General, now entirely inspired by Oldenbarnevelt, had grown more acute there. Prouninck had succeeded on 9 February in having both the Utrecht deputies, Buth and Moersbergen, recalled. Since then Utrecht had not recognized the States-General in The Hague and attempted to set up a sort of opposition States-General at Utrecht. Letters and pamphlets kept on appearing in which the States of Holland and the States-General were accused of everything evil. Oldenbarnevelt had wasted a lot of time on answers that were only fuel to the flames. In the town itself party strife was violent too; Norris wrote to the Council of State that he dared not leave Utrecht in case one of the parties let the Spaniards in. Wilkes, whose difficulties with Leicester were not generally known, had as an Englishman more influence than Oldenbarnevelt's letters and envoys. He persuaded Prouninck to dispense with his counter-assembly and let Utrecht be represented in The Hague again, this time by three of his own party members. The situation was still difficult, however. The States-General had acquired the character of a government and were practically permanent, though no formal resolution to this effect had been taken. The hated merchants of Holland were thus predominant. Utrecht and Prouninck therefore demanded a much greater measure of *ruggespraak* and a strict limitation of the competence of the central governing body. They were centralistic enough when it was a question of Leicester or his creatures. But now that Leicester was absent and his creatures powerless, Utrecht became as particularist as ever Holland had been. Just the opposite was the case with Oldenbarnevelt. The fact that he had defended provincial sovereignty against Leicester and later against the counter-remonstrant majority in the States-General must not tempt one to see in him a consistent theoretical champion of such sovereignty. Zeeland and Groningen were to find that out later. Utrecht was finding it out now.

Buckhurst cooperated fully with Oldenbarnevelt. England needed a strong central government in the Netherlands as its ally, both for war and peace. Such strong authority could be exercised only by Holland. So Buckhurst supported Oldenbarnevelt through thick and thin, perhaps in the hope of making him more amenable to the peace proposals which he had not yet revealed. He left for Utrecht to try to bring the province back into the fold. On behalf of the Queen, with whose name he was hoping to do miracles in Utrecht, he made four demands on the province, which however were all rejected by Prouninck. Utrecht would not recognize the Council of State, re-formed in February, as legal, nor allow the return of the eighty-six people exiled in August. For this refusal they pleaded their privileges. The answers seemed fairly rough, but Buckhurst had received various letters from England entirely disavowing his attitude.[1] His easy-going acceptance of the States' explanations of the letter of 4 February met with a particularly bad reception. Since the contents of such letters naturally became known in the Netherlands this disavowal suddenly lowered his prestige greatly. Wilkes at once lost his self-confidence[2] and Oldenbarnevelt did not pay much more attention to matters brought up by Buckhurst.

The latter had still not said anything about peace. Oldenbarnevelt decided to sound him. Should he be forced to admit that the preparation of peace negotiations was included in his instructions, Leicester, whose precursor he must be, would lose all support from his Calvinist adherents on his return. Buckhurst, without any suspicion of Oldenbarnevelt, candidly admitted his peace mission, at first in private. It was necessary that he should repeat his statements before witnesses. For the second conversation Oldenbarnevelt took Brederode, Van der Mijle and Menijn with him, Leicester's three chief adherents in Holland. Buckhurst, who seems to have been somewhat gullible, was persuaded to repeat his message in detail. An hour later the four had gone again and were spreading the news, each in his own circle, Menijn and Oldenbarnevelt in the States of Holland, which had just assembled. The Advocate told them what Buckhurst had said and called his opponent Menijn as witness. The latter's confirmation caused a great depression in the assembly. In the afternoon the ambassador informed the Advocate that the matter should be kept secret.

By then it was too late. The Leicester faction had been sidetracked, the peace party in Holland were the lukewarm, the half- or crypto-Catholics, all of course opposed to Leicester and his Calvinists. The defeatism of April, that had led to Oldenbarnevelt offering his resignation, had disappeared now that English help was continuing and Parma did not stir. And the Calvinists, from whom Leicester obtained his main support, were as anti-Spanish as could be. Buckhurst's injudicious utterance had deprived Leicester of almost

---

[1] The first hundred pages of The Calendar of State Papers, XXI, iii, are full of such letters. Some from the Queen are definitely insulting. Elizabeth had not the knack of giving her employees a free hand.

[2] Calendar of State Papers, XXI, iii.

all his following. Elizabeth afterwards chided him for this indiscretion;[1] here was a case, she considered, in which he should have used his own judgment to depart from his instructions.

Oldenbarnevelt, with his characteristic energy, at once made use of Buckhurst's revelations to influence the Calvinist ministers against Leicester. He invited thirteen to the Binnenhof, and let the president of the Court, Adriaen van der Mijle, address them. At this time he and the Advocate were rather like figures in a weather-house: the latter came out in time of conflict and Van der Mijle to placate.

The States had been attacked on two sides from the pulpit, the president began. On the one hand the suspicion had been voiced that they were arranging underhand peace negotiations, to the detriment of the reformed church. From other pulpits they had been accused of trampling on Christian principles because they would not hear of peace. Van der Mijle was able to convince the preachers without much difficulty that the States were indeed peace-loving, as Christian doctrine demanded, but nevertheless in practice opposed to any peace negotiations. That was just what the preachers wanted. About Leicester they were only told that the States still continued to maintain His Excellency in government, provided he left the provinces and lower offices their authority.

The preachers' answer showed that they, naturally generalizing about all the English, thought that Buckhurst's arrival and friendliness foreshadowed the same friendly attitude in Leicester himself, by which all popular anxiety would be removed.

Nearly four months after Stanley's and York's treason Oldenbarnevelt could be satisfied with the result of the two-day conference. Naturally the churchpeople had not suddenly given up their love and trust in the second David, whom they had awaited and ecstatically welcomed eighteen months before. But their love had rather tepid and dependent on the two conditions that he should be as wise as the States with regard to peace and also as friendly as Buckhurst. Oldenbarnevelt knew very well that neither condition would be fulfilled.

If Leicester came back. It seemed unlikely. Buckhurst had only been sent to reconnoitre and could not fail to notice that Leicester was deeply hated by the Holland faction without which the Netherlands could not be governed. Moreover, Elizabeth wanted peace and Leicester's arrival would mean a vigorous resumption of military activity. Though the people might think the viceroy's speedy return desirable and probable – after all the preachers had said so – government circles in The Hague were not worrying about it. They had enough other troubles.

---

[1] Calendar of State Papers, XXI, iii, 95.

Parma had not taken advantage of Stanley's and York's treachery to go over to the offensive till May. This was a disturbing mystery for the Hollanders. It was more than a year before it appeared that Philip II was concentrating his attention on the conquest of England. Money and soldiers were sent to Parma but neither were to be used for any other purpose, such as a push across the Veluwe, than the support of the coming Armada. So when he went into the field in May it was only to besiege Sluis as a useful port on the North Sea coast, now that Antwerp was blockaded and Ostend seemed impregnable.

Oldenbarnevelt was not much worried about Sluis. There was a brave garrison under a brave commander. The defence of the town was greatly in the interest of the English, as in Parma's hands it would have been like a pistol to their heads. Oldenbarnevelt was dreaming of a field army and an offensive, the top class in Maurice's training school. That cost money. He managed to get two extra grants from the States-General as an instalment of the million they had voted in March. Buckhurst, who had first consented to half a million, now came down to 150,000. It was stingy, but it would do. In June they had reached the point of setting up an army in the field; Maurice was appointed commander; under him, in a relationship still to be settled, were Hohenlohe, and the two other stadtholders, Nieuwenaar and William Louis, John Norris and Colonel Schenck.

On the same day the news arrived like a thunderbolt that Leicester was coming. Norris was transferred to Ireland. Wilkes was recalled at his urgent request – he dared not face Leicester of course. Buckhurst's mission automatically came to an end with the arrival of Leicester. The whole leading English group was replaced in one day, a last attempt to persist in the anti-Holland policy against all the odds.

It is a mystery why the Queen decided to send Leicester back again. Buckhurst had been instructed to ask for guarantees that his authority would not be infringed as it had been during his first stay. He had not been given such guarantees. On the contrary, the longer he stayed in the country, the more he must have realized that Leicester's arrival could only harm the good cause of the alliance. Leicester himself felt no desire to put his hand into the wasps' nest again. Elizabeth finally had to bribe him by paying some of his debts. It was mainly Walsingham who spurred him on, perhaps not altogether from friendship. Walsingham is a mysterious figure, whose letters more often hide than reveal his real thoughts. Perhaps he thought it possible at this time to overthrow the States party by force and rule the Netherlands from London. A figment of the imagination, unworthy of Walsingham's usual perspicacity. But he was a keen Protestant. A lukewarm Protestant seemed to him half a traitor. If he regarded the leaders of the States party as lukewarm Protestants – and there was some reason for this – it may explain Leicester's ill-fated second mission.

Buckhurst and Oldenbarnevelt tried to stop Leicester at the last moment. Why else would Oldenbarnevelt have reacted by writing an even sharper letter than that of 4 February and Buckhurst have taken and promised to send it?

Oldenbarnevelt seldom wrote so unrestrainedly. Compared with the letter of 4 February the invective is heightened. Three complaints are added, not made in the earlier letter. The summoning of the synod of The Hague is represented as a mortifying proof of mistrust of the States, as though they were the enemies of religion. An interesting addition. It shows that since the conference with the ministers it was felt that there was less need to propitiate the churchgoers. Then for the first time there was a complaint that there had been no review of the troops, to the great harm of the English and ultimately also of the Netherlands treasury. Finally he discussed the controversy over the sovereignty with the greatest bitterness and passion.

On 18 June the money came in that was to be used for the setting up of an army, and particularly for recruiting cavalry in Germany, which inexplicably had been a failure the year before. Leicester was suspected of being responsible for this failure, perhaps because he did not want any German cavalry and wished to use the money voted for the relief of Sluis – more an English than a Netherlands interest, the Hollanders thought. But there could be no army in the field without cavalry. It was decided to take no risks this time and to send three prominent members of the States to Bremen with money in their pockets.[1] Oldenbarnevelt went to see them off at Amsterdam himself, it is not known why. He must have had other things to do but does not say anything about them in a letter written on 29 June from Amsterdam to the Netherlands envoys engaged on a mission to Denmark. If he is to be believed, his chief concern at this time was not the arrival of Leicester, in which he said he did not really believe, but the vacillation of Buckhurst in respect of peace negotiations. He gave his version of the interview with Buckhurst, who had first wanted to speak about peace in the States of Holland, but after going to the town hall had changed his mind owing to the news of Drake's success at Cadiz, as a result of which Elizabeth would have some cash in the till and Philip would most likely vindictively break off the negotiations. Oldenbarnevelt did not believe in this motive but did not know what to believe.

It is the first instance of a letter from Oldenbarnevelt to an embassy from

[1] Calendar of State Papers, XXI, iii, 121.

the States-General. Officially he had no competence to write them. In practice his words already held an overriding authority with all envoys.

A week after this letter had been written Leicester arrived at Flushing. Oldenbarnevelt rolled up his sleeves cautiously.

For a time the battle was to be waged at a distance. Before going to Holland Leicester wanted to occupy himself with the relief of Sluis. Perhaps this was the chief reason for his crossing the North Sea, despite contrary advice from Buckhurst and Wilkes and without getting any satisfaction from the States-General. From England he had invited the States-General to hold a meeting with him in Zeeland but they did not go. They said that they were afraid to suffer the fate of Paulus Buys.[1] There may have been something in this. In Walcheren the Viceroy had the English garrison of Flushing at his disposal and had also brought some five thousand recruits with him. That might be a temptation to use force in a dispute with the States-General.

Such a conflict could not long be postponed by money. The States had voted a million, as they had made known, without adding two things: first, that the money granted only came to hand piecemeal, and secondly that all the available cash had put off to sea at Amsterdam under Oldenbarnevelt's watchful eye in the direction of Bremen.

Leicester would find this out soon enough and be angry, so that there was reason to be afraid. But it should not be exaggerated. Leicester could expect some money and some help for Sluis from the States-General and particularly from Holland and he would think twice about starting a civil war in such a desperate state. He was not well placed to do so. For such a wild *coup d'état* he had to be near the centre of government in person. So the States sent young Maurice to Flushing to welcome Leicester without too much mistrust. They even went as far as Dordrecht to meet him, where the moderates did everything possible to create a *modus vivendi*. Two anonymous letters which reached Leicester at this time, one from Brederode, the other from Wilkes, advised him radically to change his system of government. He should aim at good relations with the leaders of the States faction. True, some of them were too anti-English ever to give up their opposition to an English viceroy. Brederode said that Oldenbarnevelt and Roorda were such. He should not, however, use force or quarrel with them, but try to neutralize them by appointing them to the Council of State or sending them on prolonged missions. Furthermore he must behave in everything like the late Prince of Orange: deal familiarly with the municipal oligarchs, who, as 'gens de basse qualité' would greatly appreciate it, carefully observe the competence of the various bodies, not make too many promises but keep those he did make, use patience

[1] Calendar of State Papers, XXI, iii, 125.

and impartiality, give many public audiences and never propose anything in the Council of State or the States-General without previous advice from trusted counsellors. They might as well have advised a squirrel to behave like a stag. Apart from Leicester's impatience and duplicity, such a line of conduct can only be based on deep mutual trust, on the almost passionate devotion shown by the States to the Prince.

Leicester had not the least intention of following this well-meant utopianism. Something had just occurred to arouse his extreme displeasure. He had sent his secretary Junius ahead of him with instructions which came to Oldenbarnevelt's knowledge and were calculated to anger him. Junius was to go round the towns of Holland and try to form a pro-Leicester party, consisting of the 'affectionnez que cognoissez' and those who 'ont charge sur le peuple et y penserez pouvoir servir' – not the *vroedschappen* but the preachers and the civil militia.

Oldenbarnevelt felt his authority threatened. In the States of Holland he suggested getting hold of the original of the instructions. This could only be done by arresting Junius and taking them from him by force. His movements were followed and while he was working with the letter at Delft he was summoned to the town hall, where the councillors (Oldenbarnevelt was waiting in a back room) forcibly took the letter from him. Leicester was seized by a paroxysm of indignation[1] and the moderates despaired of a reconciliation.

The situation favoured Oldenbarnevelt. It was in his interest that there should be no reconciliation but also that public opinion should not blame the States party, even if only to keep the moderates, the Menijns and Valckes and in particular the influential president of the Court, Van der Mijle, within the fold.

The States-General, no doubt on Oldenbarnevelt's advice, chose as delegates to treat with Leicester only deputies who were in favour of reconciliation, headed by the Dordrecht pensionary, Menijn. They made excuses for the fact that Holland had achieved so little and promised improvement in this respect. Leicester calmed down sooner than Oldenbarnevelt can have expected. He was at once all for the relief of Sluis, feeling that his prestige as governor-general depended on it. So when his efforts failed and Sluis capitulated on 5 August 1587 it was popularly regarded as a disaster, but from Oldenbarnevelt's point of view as a blessing in disguise, increasing the possibility of soon getting rid of this tiresome and dangerous dictator.

Leicester promptly excused his failure by accusing the States of lack of cooperation. He may well have been largely right here, but it was not much help to him. It was generally expected that Parma would exploit his success

---

[1] Calendar of State Papers, XXI, iii, 149.

by an attack on Ostend or Bergen-op-Zoom. If one of these places were lost, through the fault either of the States or Leicester, it was always the latter who would be held responsible in England. We must not forget that all through his residence in the Netherlands Leicester kept his weather eye on England. His three greatest enemies were there to stir up trouble against him, all of them better acquainted with Netherlands affairs than himself: Buckhurst, Norris and Wilkes. It is true that the first two were banished from court on their arrival in England and the third was even imprisoned, but Elizabeth's moods could not be relied upon and the powerful ministers Burghley and Walsingham would certainly not support him any longer than their interests required. So Leicester began to feel that he must not suffer any more defeats. The States would have to help him and he assumed a conciliatory mood, saving up his vengeance for a more suitable moment. Not that he forgot it. The officers from Sluis took care of that: Meetkerken's son Nicolaas, Nicolas de Maulde, Charles de Héraugière. They did not blame their misfortunes on Leicester but on the Zeeland naval authorities and especially on the members of the States of Holland, by whom they felt they had been sold down the river. Leicester should throw them out. They would help him form a military government.

Leicester wanted nothing of the kind just then. He had to dissemble. Nor could Oldenbarnevelt indulge in sincerity: he too was blamed for the loss of Sluis, for the relief of which the States had voted the necessary *matériel* only a week before. The two hypocrites were brought together by one honest man. Menijn set to work. An 'Act of Satisfaction' was drawn up and handed to Leicester with some solemnity on 16 August. He said that he was satisfied by it. A letter of the same content to the Queen would show whether it would have the same effect on her. It was a triumph for Menijn and those around him. The States-General expressed their regret that the tone of the letter of 4 February had made a bad impression on the Viceroy. They protested 'sacredly before God and the world' that they bore him a 'true and sincere love' and further:

that it may please him to unite your Excellency with the said States-General and to keep them in mutual love and unbreakable concord, to his honour and glory, to the service of her Majesty, the welfare of this state, the preservation of the true Christian religion, the authority of your Excellency and the confusion of our enemies.

This could lead in any direction. Oldenbarnevelt knew well which way he wanted to go.

Leicester did not. His secret instructions[1] produced an inner conflict which

---

[1] Calendar of State Papers, XXI, iii, 121.

made him uncertain and not much to be feared by Oldenbarnevelt as an opponent.

According to his instructions he had first to insist on greater power, especially in financial matters, and to reintroduce the edict against trade with the enemy. This was a delicate task, in view of the opposition of the great majority of the States of Holland and Zeeland, but it was not inconceivable that it could be carried out with a judicious mixture of force and gentle pressure; use could also be made of the popularity still enjoyed by Leicester with the democrats and Calvinists in and outside Holland, diminished though it was, who expected an offensive from him and from the English help and were willing to give up certain privileges for it. The loss of Sluis and of military prestige was an obstacle to this policy, but in the hands of a second William of Orange need not have been an insuperable one. Either persuasion could be used – the policy of Buckhurst and Wilkes, Brederode and Menijn – or resort to the English troops and the discontented soldiers from Sluis.

But now both a policy of trust and one of power were made impossible by the second part of the instructions, in which Leicester was told to induce the States-General to take part in the long-prepared peace negotiations with Spain. Perhaps even this was not an entirely impossible task. In Holland, but even more in the inland provinces, there was a not inconsiderable party who wanted to treat with the King, in the hope that fifteen years of bloody war had taught him a lesson. In Holland the town of Gouda, in this respect not in agreement with its pensionary Francken, wished to follow this path. A powerful, rich nobleman such as Arend van Dorp could serve as leader of the party.[1] A non-sectarian town and a Catholic noble were much less congenial company for Leicester than his trusted Calvinists and Flemish exiles, or his brawling officers. He could not lean on the former and the latter at the same time. There were some people, pro-English on principle, who would support Leicester if he spoke of peace, probably in the hope that the Escurial's conditions would prove so unacceptable that Elizabeth could be induced to wage war more vigorously by the failure of the negotiations. Valcke and Menijn would have thought so; Leicester himself, and Walsingham in England must have cherished this hope. It was easy for Oldenbarnevelt to demonstrate that this was a dangerous and illogical policy. He had no need to fear that it would find much adherence in Holland, outside Dordrecht, swayed by Menijn. The danger lay elsewhere: a combination of Leicester, the officers and the Calvinist faction to overthrow the States by force. The easiest way to prevent this was to sow discord between Leicester and his followers. The instructions provided an excellent opportunity for this, as we have seen.

[1] According to Wilkes, Calendar of State Papers, XXI, iii, 18.

Oldenbarnevelt knew about them, thanks to Ortel. Good statesmen always have good intelligence services. Through a connection at the English court, Ortel managed to get a look at a copy of the instructions, a translation of which he sent to Oldenbarnevelt. Parma also took care that copies of his official peace correspondence with Elizabeth were distributed in the Northern Netherlands.[1] Leicester himself saw that an untimely discussion of the second part of his instructions would do his cause great harm and confined himself for the time to warnings such as: take care what you do, the Queen might abandon you.[2] It would look – and Oldenbarnevelt was prompt to present the appearance as reality – as though Leicester's plans for a *coup d'état* were not aimed at conducting the war more efficiently, but on the contrary, at handing over the Netherlands, bound hand and foot, to Spain.

It is difficult to make out whether Oldenbarnevelt was being sincere or not here. Probability suggests that he was not. Everyone knew that Leicester was a fierce opponent of the Queen's peace policy. The loss of Sluis, a reason for Elizabeth to take the negotiations more seriously,[3] only made her governor-general more vengeful against the Spaniards. Oldenbarnevelt must have known him well enough to realize that he was not able to take the serious risk of a civil war to promote a plan that he himself detested. On the other hand, it may have been difficult for a man with a set purpose in his policy to imagine that his opponent could intertwine three different themes into a wonderful discord.

In any case he need be spared no longer. When he met the States-General again at Dordrecht in August he was confronted, not by Oldenbarnevelt in person, but by a nine-point remonstrance drawn up by him, entirely on the lines of the letters of 4 February and 17 June and without a trace of Menijn's half-heartedness.

Leicester was in an awkward spot. He had just been given Elizabeth's peremptory order to bring the question of peace up for discussion and was preparing to make this bad news sound as attractive as possible. So it was important for him to bottle up his anger. Once more, and for the last time, he fell into line with the patient policy of his Dutch adherents. The reflections on theoretical constitutional law, as an effect of the controversy with Wilkes early in the year, were set out in more detail than was Oldenbarnevelt's habit. They covered six of the nine points complained of. Leicester passed them over somewhat impatiently in his apostils: he was not aiming at more

---

[1] Calendar of State Papers, XXI, iii, 246. A curious parallelism but not based on collusion.
[2] Calendar of State Papers, XXI, iii, 222 and 246.
[3] See Elizabeth's letter of 19 August (O.S., 29 August N.S.) to Leicester, expressly charging him to inform the States-General that negotiations would be entered into. Calendar of State Papers, XXI, iii, 227.

power than was allowed him by treaty and viceregal appointment, and particularly not at sovereignty; so there was no difference of opinion between him and the States of Holland here. The seventh point concerned the oath to be taken by the forces, a formality of the utmost importance at a time when the constitution was in the balance. It also played a great part in the 1618 trial. Both parties agreed that the soldiers should swear loyalty to 'the country' and to Leicester as governor-general. Oldenbarnevelt, however, wanted them to take a further oath to the provinces and towns where they were to be used. The oath had been introduced in substance during the February crisis. From the military point of view it was a monstrosity, unacceptable to a commander with any political sense, and certainly not at a time when relations between central government and provinces were bad. Oldenbarnevelt knew that quite well. He was not a theoretical federalist in the sense of trying to fight Spain with half a dozen loosely connected little armies. He was a practical statesman and he had Maurice in his hands. For this reason, and only for this reason, the troops in Holland had to take the oath to Maurice. Oldenbarnevelt could not yield on this point, nor could Leicester. The crisis was thus approaching rapidly. Only the smooth wording of Leicester's apostil could conceal this from optimistic go-betweens.

On 2 September, one day after the apostils had been signed, Menijn and Valcke, the leaders of the moderate pro-Leicester party, appeared in the States of Holland and delivered an unpalatable message from the viceroy. Leicester asked the States of Holland whether they possessed the means to continue the war. He thought not. He had not seen much produced by Holland for Sluis, for Bergen-op-Zoom or for other military purposes. There was no question of his being able to take the field this year. Waging war without money was a farce. Elizabeth would not grant any further subsidy. Would it not then be better if the States began to think seriously about peace? Elizabeth would be glad to help them, but they could also negotiate without her, if they thought that in this way they could obtain better terms. A prompt reply was desired.

Now Oldenbarnevelt had the Viceroy where he wanted him. He asked the two delegates to put their proposals in writing, which they did after some hesitation. Many copies were made at once and in a few days the whole of the Netherlands knew that the hero from England, the defender of the faith, did not mean to wage war or protect religion, but on the contrary to hand over the whole country to the wicked King and his papists. This was the only way in which in the Netherlands peace was assumed to be possible.

At the same time Leicester ordered some suspicious troop movements. With his usual inconsistency he wanted to win absolute power, just when this made no sense after his peace message. He sent troops into Dordrecht, from which all Holland and Zeeland deputies instantly fled. He also occupied Delfshaven, Schoonhoven and Gouda with weak forces. The States were alarmed, Oldenbarnevelt was not. He sent his two most trustworthy followers to the Viceroy to demand explanations. Their report typifies Leicester's mentality; he was not as formidable an opponent as his lofty tone suggested. Notwithstanding all humble requests from the two deputies Leicester had answered angrily that the English nation was badly treated in this country, that no plundering by the English had been heard of, that he would notify Her Majesty of everything; that he would know how to address himself to the real sovereign of this country, of which the States were nothing but deputies.

Insubstantial threats of this sort were a foolish weapon. It was not possible in Holland to play off the sovereign *vroedschappen* against their deputies in the States assemblies, and still less to make the sovereign people reject their *vroedschappen*. Nor could ten companies here or two companies there achieve anything against well-walled towns and Hohenlohe's troops, in firm possession of Geertruidenberg, Vianen, Naarden and Lillo and making threatening movements towards Delfshaven.

The day after the interview with the two deputies Leicester's 'remonstrance' was available to everyone in print. It was rather tamely worded for someone who was on the brink of a *coup d'état*. Only in one passage was there a menacing undertone. If the States-General, he wrote, were not willing to allow him the authority he had hitherto held, and if they did not agree to unmodified consent,

I shall need, to preserve the honour of her Majesty and myself, again to protest, if any loss or hardship occurs, that the blame and shame should not be given to her Majesty nor to me, but to those who are showing such dishonour and discourtesy to her Majesty.

Oldenbarnevelt was not inactive. He showed copies of Leicester's secret instructions everywhere; he seems to have known through Ortel about Leicester's confidential letters to Elizabeth.[1] With a little ill-will the texts, in combination with the unfortunate letter to Junius, could be taken to mean that Leicester was striving for unlimited power for the express purpose of selling the country to Spain. The Viceroy came to hear of this talk. It instigated his first direct attack upon Oldenbarnevelt, whom he only now seems to have recognized as his foremost opponent. The attack took the form of a letter to the three bodies, the Hof van Holland, the Hoge Raad and the Audit Office. Van der Mijle, the president of the Court, once more attempted to mediate. He left for Dordrecht with a deputation from the three

---

[1] *Correspondence of Robert Dudley*, III, 96.

bodies. But Leicester was too embittered by this slander in which there was a basis of truth. His language was so menacing that the deputies could see that Oldenbarnevelt was in danger. On returning from Dordrecht late in the evening of 11 September two of them went to warn the Advocate of Leicester's intended arrival in The Hague. Oldenbarnevelt, mindful of the fate of his two predecessors,[1] did not need telling twice, and left in the night for Delft. From there he led the opposition to Leicester during the following weeks. The States of Holland granted him an Act of Indemnity and requested him to return to The Hague on the basis of this Act 'for the direction of the united country's affairs, of which the Advocate has thorough knowledge'.

Oldenbarnevelt did not trust in pieces of paper and stayed behind safe walls. He heard that in Zeeland the rumour was being spread that Maurice, himself and some others were to be arrested and sent to England. He therefore suggested to Maurice that he should flee, with an honest pretext: that he was going to prepare an attack on Antwerp in Zeeland, which Leicester, after initial indignation, was forced to accept.

There is something mysterious in Leicester's behaviour at this time. When he entered The Hague with a strong military escort he probably intended to capture, if not to kill, Maurice and Oldenbarnevelt. When this did not succeed he had no plan for seizing power. In his letters to England he shows himself completely demoralized and does nothing but ask for recall. The peace negotiations had made his position impossible, he complained. He would certainly win the States and public opinion over to a reasonable peace, but he must be allowed time. There were a few bad people who worked against it, especially merchants who were enriching themselves by the war, and 'the two counts', Maurice and Hohenlohe, whom peace would cost their jobs. The peace proposals had been made at the wrong time: Menijn and Valcke were only charged with an oral message and in their written proposals had concealed the essentials: that the Queen was bound to nothing, that she remained the ally of the States and would only conclude a peace that was advantageous to them. This was what Leicester said in his letters to England: the latter part was a libel on his delegates; when they had their proposals translated and shown to Leicester they proved to contain it and he had to withdraw his accusation.

The nobles and all except two of the towns of Holland now composed a joint answer to Leicester's complaints, showing a spirit of determination and not yielding a single point, nor wishing to know anything of peace. Leicester, acquainted by secret informers of everything that took place in the most secret meetings of the States, and still hesitating between force and flattery,

---

[1] Van den Ende, imprisoned by Alva in 1569, and Buys (see above, pp. 64, 65).

was half-intimidated by it. He had no effective forces for a civil war in *optima forma*, nor had he the strength of mind. Some attacks, undertaken with inadequate means, failed before they had properly started. When his last hope, the faithful Colonel Sonoy, was unable to achieve anything for him in North Holland, he gave up and retired defeated to Zeeland on the pretext of putting the province into a state of defence.

Only one of the assaults had cost blood. It was Oldenbarnevelt who caused it to be shed. He was for a long time reproached for his attitude in this matter. There are some who regard his own trial in 1618 as a nemesis for the intransigence shown in October 1587.

Two companies from Sluis were at or near Leiden at the beginning of October, full of resentment at the indifference shown by the States of Holland during the siege. The commander of one of them was an Italian, Pescarengis, devoted to Leicester, who had appointed him colonel. Leicester had sent him to Leiden to try and secure the town. Though the Viceroy afterwards repeatedly denied under oath knowing anything of the attack, it must have been a white lie; the circumstantial confessions of the conspirators make a more trustworthy impression than these cheap oaths. Pescarengis obtained the blessing of a professor of theology and the active cooperation of an elder of Flemish origin, and of the other company commander from Sluis, Nicolas de Maulde, also a Fleming, who promised to use his company to depose the magistracy. The plot was uncovered before it could be put into effect. Pescarengis and the elder were arrested, other conspirators fled, the young and attractive Maulde was allowed by the magistrates to leave for Utrecht, where Leicester was thought to be. He would have to see what to do with him. Actually he had already left for Naarden, the first stage of his miserable progress through North Holland. But that was not known in Leiden, nor in Delft, where Oldenbarnevelt expected the conspiracy to be one of many, and that Leicester would appear in person to reap the rewards, as a properly Machiavellian statesman would have done. Leicester was perhaps Machiavellian, but not properly: his policy was uncoordinated and incoherent.

The States of Holland had been meeting since the beginning of the month at Delft to have their Advocate at hand and also to be guarded against any desperate acts by the convulsive Viceroy. Their first idea was to keep Leicester out of Leiden. The *vroedschap* was sent a request to write to Leicester saying that at present he would not be welcome there. Other towns might receive him, but with an escort of 150 at the most. Oldenbarnevelt was not at all in agreement with letting Maulde go free. Through family connections he was by far the best-known of the conspirators and, if the plot had been carried out, he would have been at its head: however *sympathique* and heroic, he was just the one to make an example of to discourage others. Three deputies from the States of Holland were sent to Woerden, where it had been learnt that Maulde was resting on his way to Utrecht, to arrest him at the head of his company. A delicate procedure, which went according to plan. Another proof that Maulde was not of the stuff of which rebels are made.

The trial of the imprisoned conspirators could now begin. The sheriff and magistrates of Leiden were competent to conduct it, for four different reasons, all determining competence and giving rise to striking juridical disputes. The crime was committed in Leiden, one of the ringleaders was a burgher of Leiden, all but one of the accused had been arrested in Leiden, and, above all, their action was aimed at the safety of the town. In modern times only the first reason would apply, but in the spirit of those times the fourth outweighed all the rest. But there was a complication: it was not only Leiden's safety that was threatened but that of the whole of Holland. This automatically resulted in the States of Holland, already responsible for Maulde's arrest, going two steps further and demanding to take part in the judicial investigation and the trial. For the prosecution the States sent two extremely anti-Leicester politicians, a choice that offends our sense of justice. There were some at that time too who, considering this unfair, would have thought the Hof van Holland more suitable to assist the Leiden justices. Public opinion did not take so juridical a view. It was hardly a matter of lawyers, it was argued; a confession had been obtained from the chief accused and more could be obtained with a little torture. There was therefore no difficulty in the way of proof and one need not be concerned with qualification of the crime or interpretation of the law. The only point that had to be decided at the beginning of the trial was the penalty. As the security of the state was closely involved with the penalty its determination was rightly considered a matter for politicians.

Oldenbarnevelt, anxious to give the verdict the widest publicity, took care that those appointed to the bench consisted of the most prominent members of the States, presided over by Maurice himself. Maurice did not care about having his old comrade-in-arms' head cut off, but Oldenbarnevelt persuaded him. Other judges were Oldenbarnevelt himself and his brother Elias. There was a judge from almost every town, only Dordrecht and Gouda holding aloof. A curious detail is that the son of the Leiden sheriff Foy van Brouckhoven, prosecutor at the trials, was later a judge at the trial of Oldenbarnevelt. This explains why, at a trial where so many old sores were opened, Oldenbarnevelt was never accused of having taken part in this display, regarded by many in the country as judicial murder. The moderate Calvinists, allied in

1587 with the non-sectarians, had gone over to the extremists by 1609 and had to be spared by their new allies.

The heads of the three conspirators fell at Leiden on 26 October. On the same day Oldenbarnevelt returned after an absence of six weeks to The Hague where the States resumed their meetings. It was safe there again. Leicester gave the game up; checkmate could no longer be avoided. After a short farewell visit to his supporters in Utrecht and Dordrecht he slipped off to Flushing to await his recall. It soon came. Now that he could neither induce the Netherlanders to wage war vigorously nor to take part in peace negotiations, he had become a useless instrument for Elizabeth's policy. As military leader he was replaced by Willoughby, as peace advocate by John Herbert, who arrived at Flushing on 16 November. He was accompanied by Ortel, the agent, who was to make it clear to the States that Elizabeth was in earnest about the peace negotiations and would be very angry if the States did not cooperate.

The States were no longer afraid of her anger. In a series of rearguard actions Oldenbarnevelt had succeeded in consolidating their position and stopping the breach in the united front.

Previously, on 2 October, the day when the States of Holland moved to Delft, some preachers had appeared among them to express anxiety about the hostile policy followed against Leicester. Oldenbarnevelt gave them a most discourteous rebuke:

That the States knew what they had said in their remonstrance and more yet: that the States had the welfare of the country as much at heart as they and would provide for it without them. The remonstrants could go home and let the States deal with the matter.

Oldenbarnevelt can only have spoken thus if his irritation at pedantic meddlesomeness overcame his political good sense. It was dangerous to humiliate the preachers, who were quite well-disposed at this time. They were incensed at such attacks, especially when a few days later the States made it worse by sending an unpleasant written answer to this remonstrance to the magistrates of all towns with the order:

that the same Magistrates shall summon the Preachers within the Towns of each and present to them the contents of the said answers, giving the same a Copy, with serious admonitions that they shall henceforth behave and acquit themselves accordingly, without involving themselves in the Policy or Government of the Country or concerning themselves therewith, but let it be as the same is commanded of God, else shall the States be constrained to proceed against the Contraveners as is fitting.

The threat helped for a time. The black-coated gentry refrained from any action to protect the departing Leicester. Perhaps that was all Oldenbarnevelt intended.

When it was made known in the middle of October that Leicester was to go, the answer to his letter of 9 September, not yet sent off, had to be made milder than originally planned. A harsh tone was no longer needed to remove the undesirable Viceroy and the accent had shifted: the thing was now to persuade the Queen, in spite of the States' adverse attitude towards treating for peace, not to stop or decrease her military aid. At the same time it must and could be endeavoured to accommodate the pro-Leicester minority in the States. While standing firm on all important points – protestation that the treaty had been adhered to in every respect, rejection of any responsibility for the loss of Sluis and defence of the remonstrance of 30 August – its mood was more temperate than was usual for Oldenbarnevelt. The letter of 4 February was partly retracted; there were abundant expressions of thanks to Her Majesty and the Governor-General and full support for next year's campaign was promised. The States were not in such financial straits, it went on, that peace had to be concluded. If only the war estimate agreed on with Buckhurst in the summer were continued, and no additional troops taken on, things would indeed be all right.

The document is to be regarded as the programme on which the majority and the minority in the States were agreed. From the point of view of the majority there was the risk that the friendly tone would tempt Leicester still to continue his practices, but the danger was not great. Two other documents were intended to reduce it still more. One, the 'Further Declaration' was a reply to Leicester's apostils on the remonstrance of 30 August. It was a kind of lecture on constitutional law, but given by a prejudiced and easy-going professor. Oldenbarnevelt had not much interest in constitutional law as such. When he entered this field it was only to give his political views a respectable basis. Here it was a matter of sovereignty and the military oath. Sovereignty was vested in the States, it was argued: if that was not the case both the abjuration and the conferment of the viceroyalty on Leicester were illegal: *nemo plus juris conferre potest quam ipse habet*,[1] a maxim of Roman law. This was in itself correct, but was disputing a view that Leicester had never made his own. He did indeed recognize the States-General as formally sovereign: in the letter to Junius, quoted in the Further Declaration, he had only wished to show that the States-General, by granting him the exercise of sovereignty, had denied themselves this exercise so long as the appointment lasted. In this way the discussion did not make much progress, nor did the

[1] No one can confer more rights than he himself possesses.

dispute about the oath. Here too Oldenbarnevelt was guilty of intellectual dishonesty. Leicester had protested against the formulation of the oath in that officers and soldiers had to swear loyalty not only to the viceroy but to the stadtholders of the provinces and even to the towns where they were garrisoned. Clearly this would cause difficulties as soon as the governors, the provincial stadtholders and the towns were not following the same course. Oldenbarnevelt did not understand that, or pretended not to. The stadtholders were the commanders of the troops in their districts. How could they then exercise their authority, if the soldiers did not obey them? He was confusing two separate issues, presumably on purpose: obedience and the oath. Every soldier must obey his superior, not only the stadtholder but also his captain and his sergeant. But obedience applies only in so far as they in their turn obey their highest superior, in this case the Viceroy. On these two points, the sovereignty of the provinces and their representative body, the States-General, and the oath to the stadtholders and the towns, Oldenbarnevelt easily obtained the agreement of every oligarch. So he achieved his object with this document: the united front and the departure of the pestered, powerless English earl.

The third document was of the same tenor. It was a second, somewhat modified edition of the declaration compiled by Francken in the spring and shelved so as not to upset Buckhurst's joyous welcome. Various things had happened since then. Wilkes and even Buckhurst himself had become convinced of the idea that the Netherlands had an aristocratic form of government. Leicester had stated the contrary in his letter to Junius, but obviously not all the Queen's advisers were behind him. Everyone really was now convinced that the setting up of monarchical government under English leadership had proved a failure. The States must take over the authority that Leicester had long abandoned. To lay the foundations of this authority without the support of a German prince, a French duke or an English earl a theory was needed. Francken produced it, very concisely, in a way unexcelled till the time of Johan de Witt. True, he went wide of the mark historically, but the 'Short Presentation' (*Corte Verthoning*) as the document was called henceforward, provided what was needed: the creed of the victorious oligarchical faction. Beside the Union of Utrecht it became the Magna Carta of the mercantile republic now being formed.

For Leicester the Short Presentation sounded like a knell. He had still thought he could be of service in Zeeland by repulsing an attack by Parma, expected in that quarter. The immense military preparations seemed to indicate an attack, but Parma did nothing, to the surprise of those who had not guessed the secret of the Armada.[1] Leicester was still hoping that the States-General,

---

[1] See a letter from an English officer, Calendar of State Papers, XXI, iii, 322.

when informed of his departure, would come to Flushing for a solemn leave-taking. They had no such intention. So nothing remained for Leicester but to write a farewell letter, the most sensible document to leave his chancery during these two years. It is the sad story of a series of failures. Naturally he ascribes them to the States and in particular to Oldenbarnevelt, whom he does not mention by name but constantly hints at. There is no trace of the bitterness he cannot but have felt: it is written more in sorrow than in anger. His checkmate, like those of his predecessors, seems to have shown him that there was too much particularism for long-term defence against centralized leadership in the south. He particularly noticed the narrow-minded niggardliness of the Hollanders that made them neglect Sluis 'as if it were S. Domingo or Hispaniola'![1] He could no longer serve them as governor-general now they had withdrawn his authority. Perhaps his last service could be good advice: solidarity, reconciliation between the parties and not to depend on a defensive war that could only end in disaster. If there was no money for an offensive war it was better to seize the opportunity for a good peace. He himself loved the country and would continue to champion their interests in England in spite of their unreasonableness and stupidity.

Oldenbarnevelt could smile when the letter was read out in the States-General on 22 December. He was sitting among the triumphant party bosses, all deputed by Holland to the States-General. They shrugged off Leicester's reproaches somewhat casually, not being people much given to heart-searching. The programme at the end, of solidarity, a truce to party strife and offensive warfare, was, on the other hand, their own, only they had other means of effecting it. Leicester's departure would give them the opportunity to prove that their methods were better than his.

[1] Cuba.

CHAPTER 4

Independence

'*BIEN taillé, mon fils! Et maintenant il faut recoudre.*'[1] It would not be an easy task. The new clothes Oldenbarnevelt intended for the government of the country had to be designed carefully. In the first place the cut would be quite different from that provided by the Treaty of Nonsuch. The power both of the governor-general and of the Council of State would have to be curtailed, but the treaty itself must be preserved. Leicester's following must be cut off, without Parma profiting from a civil war. The provinces must be placed under the yoke of rich Holland, which they hated so much, without their breaking loose and making overtures to Parma. The danger of a sudden peace, depriving the Holland oligarchs of all their advantages, must be warded off. The contrary danger, that of a tremendous Spanish offensive, towards which Parma's extensive preparations seemed to point, had to be minimized, even if only to show Leicester's adherents and the English that the *farà da se*[2] policy was justified and would not lead to the disasters forecast by Prouninck and Leicester himself.

So about New Year 1588 the problems were numerous. When New Year came again they were all solved or as good as solved. It was not due to Oldenbarnevelt alone: he had taken risks, serious ones, but circumstances had been favourable and fortune had been kind to him. He had colleagues who were not to be looked down on. Yet he was never so great as in the year in which he laid the foundations of Netherlands independence.

The first thing to be done was to refuse Elizabeth's peace proposals in such a way that on the one hand the Queen would not take offence and on the other that the Netherlands should not fall into 'tyranny and slavery'. This is how Oldenbarnevelt expressed it in the States of Holland, where there were three parties with regard to this question. Two towns wanted to accept Elizabeth's invitation, in the hope that she would succeed in obtaining tolerable conditions from the Spanish king for the Netherlands, particularly religious freedom, or else would be convinced of the necessity of continuing the war. The majority in the States thought this too dangerous, as possible differences

---

[1] Alleged to have been said by Catherine de Medici to her son Henry III after the murder of the Guises, December 1588.
[2] The term used by Hinds, Calendar of State Papers, XXI, iv, xi.

of opinion with the English would have to be disputed before a forum of Spaniards, and in the country itself premature hopes of peace might cause discord, carelessness and disaffection. So they wanted to reject the proposals. Oldenbarnevelt thought, however, that such a brusque rejection of Elizabeth's offer might ruin relations with England, and would strengthen the suspicion held by the English in the Netherlands that the latter meant to make a separate peace with Spain behind the backs of the English. Oldenbarnevelt therefore insisted on a middle course: neither to accept nor to reject the offer but to send envoys to England to explain the States' objections by word of mouth. He managed to get his way as usual and in January the embassy of two partly pro-Leicester men, supported by the agent of Holland and Zeeland in England, Ortel, and accompanied by their English colleague, Herbert, put to sea. Just before their departure a courier arrived from England and handed Herbert a large packet of letters. The envoy had no time to deal with them all. He put the letters in his pocket, a piece of negligence which was to have unfortunate results for the Netherlands in general and Oldenbarnevelt in particular.

The latter had meanwhile been occupied with the second problem, that of Willoughby. He was a brave soldier and a cultured man, straightforward and without cunning, in short quite unfit to represent England in the hotbed of intrigue that was the Netherlands of that time. He seems also to have had little prestige with his officers, partly perhaps because of his youth. He was only thirty-two and had no grasp whatever of Dutch mentality and circumstances. He was also of disarming modesty and quite convinced of his own unsuitability.[1] Elizabeth thought that she could counter this unsuitability by expressly forbidding him to have anything to do with Netherlands politics.[2] An understandable but impracticable, indeed unworkable, decision. The general in charge of an army of occupation cannot be indifferent to the politics of the country where he is in command.

One of Willoughby's first problems was what he was to do with the badly paid troops, with their grudge against the States, put under oath to Leicester before he left, and still regarding him as their commander-in-chief. It was acute in Veere and Arnemuiden, two garrison towns on the island of Walcheren, which, together with the English garrison at Flushing were liable to clash with the Netherlands troops in the capital of the island, Middelburg. In other parts of the country garrisons were also following the example of Veere and were willing only to obey the English Queen. The reason was of

---

[1] 'Let this cup pass me', he wrote pathetically to Walsingham, when his appointment was still being considered (Calendar of State Papers, XXI, iii, 418).
[2] Calendar of State Papers, XXI, iii, 452.

course not pure loyalty to their commander Leicester, but a financial one based on a naive idea of royal munificence. At Naarden, Medemblik, Heusden, Woudrichem and Geertruidenberg the badly paid garrisons were watching eagerly for financial support from London. Willoughby and Russell, the commandant of Flushing, wanted to take advantage of this by bringing all these garrisons under English administration, not so much in order virtually to annex the Netherlands to England, as because they did not trust the leaders in Holland and thought that they were on the point of betraying the Netherlands to Spain. Willoughby soon realized, however, that he could not expect any cooperation from Elizabeth in a policy that would cost her money and increase her commitments. She was flattered by the protestations of devotion received from all sides, encouraged her devoted subjects in their admirable sentiments, promised support in vague terms, but that was all.

Oldenbarnevelt did not for a moment think that there was any danger in Elizabeth's anger. Again we see here the optimism which is the keynote of the great statesman and easily leads to irresponsibility in lesser ones. Only this optimism can explain his attitude to the mutinies and in particular to the chief mutineer at Medemblik, Diederik Sonoy. The latter had never been willing to take the oath to the young Count Maurice, in spite of his overall command of all troops stationed in Holland. He refused to take a new oath till Leicester had released him from the first. When he saw that Oldenbarnevelt and Maurice intended to compel him to do so he reinforced the garrison of Medemblik to the formidable number of six hundred and bought a large amount of gunpowder in Amsterdam. Oldenbarnevelt travelled to Alkmaar and tried from there to bribe the soldiers, whose pay was six years in arrears, to hand over Sonoy to the States. His offer was not high enough, however, and when Oldenbarnevelt reached Hoorn the soldiers had formed a united front with their colonel.

Maurice and Oldenbarnevelt, with their fellow deputies, were in an awkward situation at Hoorn. The town was divided into two sharply opposed parties. The town government were moderate state supporters and tried to restrain their own adherents who infuriated the opposition party by shouting 'English Beggars'. A company of Sonoy's regiment was quartered in the town. Maurice browbeat the Utrecht squire in command of them into taking the oath to him personally. When this was done, Maurice and his officers had dinner as guests of the town authorities. Oldenbarnevelt and two other deputies were sent to the principal church, where the company was assembled, to take the oath from the other ranks.

Maurice would have done better to listen to the advice of the local officials, who knew their men, and leave well alone: or, if he insisted on an oath, to send someone else. Oldenbarnevelt, with his dry and somewhat masterful nature, was not exactly the person to calm down a church full of excited soldiers. When he saw that things were going wrong he sent a courier to the town hall for help. Maurice sent two representatives in succession, each with new offers (of a month's pay) but, to quote a contemporary historian:

having been previously incited by some . . . they would in no way listen, so that at last Barneveld dismissed them. On this dismissal they rushed like mad people out of the Church and ran to the Square, where they could easily have taken the Town Hall, but for the prudence of a certain burgher, who happened to be walking in the Square and, to his surprise seeing them coming, hastily ran up the stairs and closed the gate of the Town Hall.

The unrest continued throughout the evening and the night, the delegation more than once finding itself among armed and threatening soldiers. Only the moderate conduct of the town government and the military measures taken by Maurice's bodyguard prevented bloodshed. Oldenbarnevelt left the same evening in great haste for The Hague. The next day, 18 February, he was in his place at the meeting of the States to impel them to take strong measures.

Maurice now began to besiege Medemblik, though in a fairly peaceful way, leaving his artillery behind on the advice of the Council of State, which was anxious for Elizabeth's favour. At this time the fear that the English would use force was great. When Maurice, leaving the siege of Medemblik to his commanders, went to Zeeland to make Veere and Arnemuiden see reason, Admiral Howard, not yet famous, appeared at Flushing at the head of an English squadron. Maurice fled at once to the state fleet at Lillo. Oldenbarnevelt waited apprehensively to see what Howard would do: attack Walcheren or sail on to Medemblik. He did neither; he had only come to bring 220,000 guilders for the English auxiliaries. Such payments were made at that time through admirals, just as Oldenbarnevelt had used statesmen to take money to Bremen. His intervention on behalf of Sonoy was confined to a friendly message to Maurice to use moderation in his measures against Sonoy for the Queen's sake.

Willoughby was in Utrecht when he heard of the siege of Medemblik. After much insistence on his part Elizabeth had restored his political authority,[1] but not at all for the use that Leicester had made of it. English soldiers were not to be used as an argument in his political activities. He was to mediate and mediate again, encourage supporters, but not intimidate opponents: that was the weak and equivocal policy on which the capricious Queen had decided for the moment. Sighing at the waste of his military talents,

[1] On 23 February (O.S., 5 March N.S.). Calendar of State Papers, XXI, iii, 86.

1 Miniature of Oldenbarnevelt

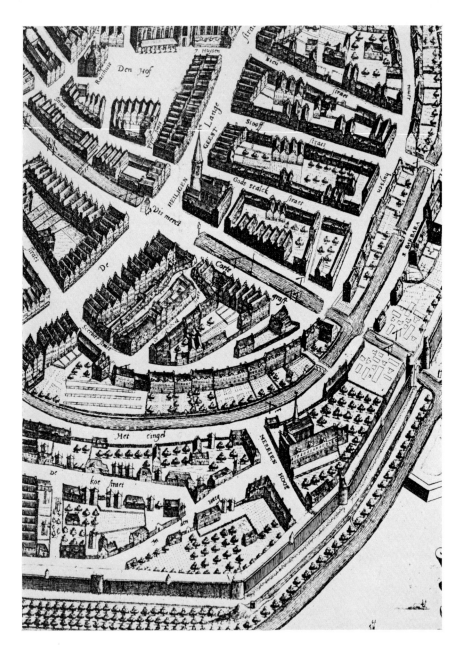

2 View of Amersfoort in the sixteenth century

3 Queen Elizabeth I (1533–1603)

Deus optime maxime,
tibi
Vota precesq;
ore et corde
nuncupantes,
Vt propitius placabiliq;
legas respicias:
nobis regnum, per illam
nos patriamq; fruens,
longum sanat aeterne deus,
audi, exaudi.

Ordines Hol:

ROB: Dudlei: Co: Lyc:

Elector: Colo:

Co: Hohenlo,

Co: Mauriti:

4 Leicester's arrival at The Hague (*see* pp. 45–6)

5 Sir John Norris (1547?–1597), probably by Jan van Belkamp

6 Thomas Sackville, Lord Buckhurst, 1st Earl of Dorset (1536–1608),
attributed to Marcus Gheeraerts the younger

7 Robert Dudley, Earl of Leicester (1531–1588), by J. van Ravensteyn

8 Sir Thomas Bodley (1544-1613), engraving by M. Burghers

9 Sir William Cecil, 1st Lord Burghley (1520–1598), attributed to
Marcus Gheeraerts the younger

10 Pieter van der Meer (1534-1616), Pensionary of Delft, engraving by Willem Jacobsz Delfft after a lost painting by Mierevelt

Willoughby set to work at Utrecht, still seething with rivalry between Prouninck and his noble opponents. He achieved nothing and left for The Hague to try out the unsatisfactory policy of the clenched fist on Oldenbarnevelt too.

He was lucky in that Oldenbarnevelt also had a request to make of him. There was a captain at Naarden who, like Sonoy, had refused to take the oath to Maurice. Would Willoughby write to him and ask him to give up his opposition? On 14 March some deputies from the States of Holland went to Willoughby's lodgings in The Hague to discuss Medemblik and Naarden. Owing to carefully taken minutes[1] in English and in Dutch we can follow the conversation almost verbatim. Oldenbarnevelt began with Naarden. Willoughby coupled it with Medemblik: if the States withdrew their troops from the walls of Medemblik he would write his letter to the recalcitrant captain. The conversation continued in this vein and ended in a sort of rift; Willoughby, on the one hand, saying that the Queen's wishes were not respected, Oldenbarnevelt replying that neither she nor Leicester had anything to do with the matters in question and that 'We must take our own measures then'. Willoughby protested that for his part he would not be to blame if he were forced to do his duty by the Queen with the means at his disposal.

Oldenbarnevelt's colleagues were trembling in their shoes. What risks the man was taking! Did not Willoughby's final words mean that he would relieve Medemblik by force? Oldenbarnevelt cannot have been without apprehension either, though he had reasons for greater calm, because contrary to what might be thought, at that moment Elizabeth had more need of the States than they had of her.

In the first place because of the peace negotiations. It was necessary for the Netherlanders to take part, but Elizabeth needed them not only for peace but for war. Parma's military preparations, taken in conjunction with those reported from Spain, could hardly leave any doubt of a large-scale attack on England itself in the near future. Dutch help at sea was imperative. The States were only able and willing to give this help if some of their troops were not hampered by pro-Leicester mutinies. Now that Oldenbarnevelt was not going to capitulate to the mutineers, as the Queen was still able to hope in February, she had to capitulate to Oldenbarnevelt. She therefore did so with, for her, unusual graciousness and without too much loss of prestige. She instructed Willoughby to instruct Sonoy to yield on the two main matters: the acceptance of a new commission or an honourable discharge, and the despatch of troops to Zeeland.

The agreement was facilitated by the announcement at this time to the States-General of Leicester's resignation as Viceroy and commander-in-chief

---

[1] Calendar of State Papers, XXI, iv, 176.

in the Netherlands. It was this resignation that Herbert had taken back unread to England, and which now, after more misunderstandings and detours, arrived at Dordrecht.

For the first time in their history the Netherlands were without a supreme authority and without plans for seeking one. The mutinous officers no longer had any pretext for resisting the authority of the Council of State and Maurice. The way lay open for a rapid reconciliation. When Maurice and Oldenbarnevelt, accompanied by Willoughby and a deputation from the States, went northwards, peace was soon signed. Sonoy was not discharged, as Oldenbarnevelt had hoped, but he made both the concessions demanded by Willoughby. This satisfied Oldenbarnevelt for the moment. Now that Sonoy retained only 150 men and was militarily dependent on the States it would soon be possible to make things too hot for him. Indeed this was done as soon as Willoughby's attention was engaged elsewhere, and the harassed colonel handed in his own resignation. Oldenbarnevelt had the satisfaction of accepting it personally.

Another rival to Oldenbarnevelt for the highest power in the new republic was also tamed in this early spring of Netherlands independence: the Council of State. This was at once easier and more difficult than the defeat of Sonoy. More difficult, because the Council of State could not be eliminated. In the absence of a personal sovereign a body was needed in which the executive authority of the Union was concentrated, a body with a coordinating function in military affairs and an administrative one with regard to the war fund. Furthermore the Council of State was mentioned in the Treaty of Nonsuch. It was considered in that treaty as the essential government of the country, in which the Queen was to be represented by two councillors and a Governor-General, and by means of which she might hope to exercise an effective protectorate, although she had refused the title. In theory this body was most suited to directing the conduct of the war. The members had to swear 'that without respect to the provinces or towns in which they were born or elected . . . they would only have regard to the honour of God and the welfare and preservation of the said Country and the common cause'.

In practice things were different. As long as the provinces did not renounce their right of free consent – and we have seen that this right was firmly fixed in popular consciousness – the Council of State was financially entirely dependent on the States of the provinces or their congress, the States-General. This dependence was enhanced by the fact that they were elected and deposed by the same provinces and States-General. Membership of the Council of State was an onerous office, a full-time job and well paid, not one to be taken on temporarily or lightly given up. This inevitably produced a civil service mentality in the Council, industrious and capable but loath to take responsibility and with little aptitude for the wide vision that marks the statesman. Such vision was most decidedly what the emergent state needed in full measure.

There was more to it than this. The King's Governor, whose former position was intended for the Council of State, had had a natural prestige which largely counterbalanced his embarrassing financial dependence. Leicester had still retained some of that prestige, the Council did not. Its whole history during the previous thirty years as an advisory and a governing body was one of helpless futility. Its role under Leicester's governorship had only strengthened this impression. Even if they had protested more than once among themselves at his stupidities, they had shown to the world solidarity with him. His hopeless unpopularity reflected on them. Nor was the fact that three English members sat in it calculated to increase its usefulness as a governing body. It had become more than clear – and the difficulties in Walcheren and North Holland as well as the peace negotiations substantiated this – that no necessary community of interest existed between England and the United Provinces.

When Leicester had gone the problem was therefore to make the Council of State a body giving the external impression of governing, whereas it was in fact to be like wax in the hands of the States-General. The instructions must be changed for this. They had to be in any case: the existing ones assumed Leicester's supreme power in every clause. A start was now made on carefully whittling them down.

The Council of State and Willoughby, whose prestige was impaired by the new instructions as conceived by Oldenbarnevelt, were intractable for months. There was even an interregnum when the Council resigned *en bloc* as a protest against the powerlessness intended for them. Oldenbarnevelt was determined never again to tolerate unlimited power from a central authority which would not be controlled by him.

Here again Oldenbarnevelt won, and once more for the same reason as in the Sonoy affair: Elizabeth needed the goodwill of the Netherlands and ordered Willoughby to withdraw his opposition. Without English support the Council was powerless and resigned itself meekly to having its competence restricted to matters concerning the Union, defence and the Treaty of Nonsuch, and to the States-General reserving the right in a special clause to take measures even regarding the matters entrusted to the Council in the instructions.

Obviously the difficulties with England and the consequent two months' interregnum had increased the opposition to Oldenbarnevelt's conduct of affairs. To Menijn, the pensionary of Dordrecht, and those of his persuasion, it must have seemed that Oldenbarnevelt, by alienating the English, was heading straight for the ruin of the country. In their view every victory gained by Oldenbarnevelt over England foreboded an eventual defeat at the hands of the Spaniards. In March they took a stand and tried for the last time to change the political trend.

Killigrew, the English member of the Council of State who after Leicester's departure filled the office of ambassador, induced the Dordrecht *vroedschap* to send two of its members as an extra embassy to the States of Holland to make serious representations about participation in peace negotiations; not that there was any hope that such negotiations would lead to peace, but rather as observers and so as not to displease the Queen. Oldenbarnevelt saw great danger in this, especially from the point of view of domestic politics. He could see, what was perhaps not so apparent in Dordrecht, that there was a great deal of defeatism in Holland, particularly in rural areas and in some small towns. All through his life Oldenbarnevelt never feared anything as much as popular movements, which would endanger the achievements of the oligarchic revolution of 1572. For this reason, though it may seem surprising, the question of whether or not to treat for peace was of vital importance for Oldenbarnevelt. He mobilized all the opponents of peace by subjection, in any case the only possible peace at that time. The leading opponents were, obviously, the ministers of religion. Strangely enough then, the ministers were called to witness by the lifelong anticlerical. The way in which it was done is typical of Oldenbarnevelt's political methods.

The majority of the States of Holland were anticlerical. This had been proved time and again, most recently in October 1587, when Oldenbarnevelt, in the name of the States, had treated the petitioning preachers so churlishly.[1] It would therefore have been rather implausible if the States had now suddenly shown themselves anxious to hear these gentlemen's opinions. Maurice, however, was still to a certain extent an unknown quantity. It looked well if a young man of twenty, who had to give his opinion on the question of participation, modestly sought advice from the ministers as his spiritual guides. So Maurice was put foward and things went just as Oldenbarnevelt had hoped. There was only one thing he did not foresee: that this contact formed a tie between Maurice and the clergy which thirty years later was to be used to fatal effect against himself.

For the moment the ministers allowed themselves to be led by the hated Advocate, though with many protestations of devotion to the pious Queen Elizabeth and without committing themselves on the tactical question of

[1] See p. 121f.

whether or not it was better to take part in negotiations. But peace could not result from them, certainly not if the King consented only to freedom of conscience, and not even if freedom of worship could be obtained, as this would involve freedom for the Catholics as well. A few days later there was a large meeting of the States of Holland. About forty members appeared and the small towns were summoned too. The parties balanced each other evenly. It was decided to appoint a commission and nine members were named, four being opponents of participation, five in favour of it, so that feelings could calm down. Oldenbarnevelt would have been more likely to exacerbate them and he was not elected to the reconciliation committee. It was clear that the majority of the States were in favour of participation. Oldenbarnevelt again had recourse to the ultimate sanction that had served him so well a year before: he resigned.

The records are silent about this action. Two days later Oldenbarnevelt left for Hoorn to help Maurice and Willoughby wind up matters with Sonoy. One can only guess what happened. Adriaen van der Mijle, the president of the Court, sat on the committee as a representative of the anti-participation party. Owing to his office he was the natural chairman. He may have pointed out what indeed had been expressed in public session, that there could be no majority vote in matters of war and peace. The nobles were divided; most of the large towns were against participation. A majority resolution to urge the States-General to send delegates would hardly be the right tactics in the circumstances. The whole question of whether or not to send delegates was one of statesmanship. Surely it was agreed that peace must not be concluded on the available terms? Oldenbarnevelt had shown himself to be a master of statecraft. Must he be allowed to go for the sake of an intrinsically unimportant question that evidently embittered him so much? And was it really true that Oldenbarnevelt was gambling with England's friendship? This accusation was always being made. He himself, Van der Mijle, had sometimes thought on these lines. But Elizabeth had always come round. She would do so again this time.

Van der Mijle was right. Elizabeth had every reason to come round again this time. The reason became obvious in the afternoon of the day when Oldenbarnevelt offered his resignation.

It had become more and more apparent during February and March that King Philip was preparing an attack on England. Eventually Parma made no secret of it to the English negotiators.[1] Elizabeth could hardly believe this as it would mean bad faith on the part of the chivalrous Duke of Parma. However, she abandoned her carefree attitude to a certain extent and decided to

---

[1] Calendar of State Papers, XXI, iv, 193, 195.

prepare for defence at sea. The English fleet was weak and badly equipped. It desperately needed help from the Hollanders and Zeelanders. On 8 April the Queen ordered Willoughby to ask the States officially for the naval assistance promised in the treaty.[1]

The States-General, seven men strong, all called upon Willoughby, who was unwell, at his house. He informed them that the Queen 'had received definite warning that the King of Spain purposed to use the Armada equipped by him against England, making the same Armada seaworthy, to put to sea at the beginning of next May'.

It is amusing to see how the whole political situation took on another aspect from this moment. Under the menace of a common danger internal difficulties lost their importance. Within a few days of the conversation at Willoughby's sick-bed the siege of Medemblik was ended, the interregnum was over and the Council of State submissively returned to office.

It was a reconciliation after Oldenbarnevelt's own heart. The other party gave in and he himself acted generously by supporting them vigorously in their time of need – on terms and without sparing them reproaches. By 16 April the States of Holland had passed the resolution to oblige the Queen in everything she asked 'notwithstanding the present difficult situation in this country, partly caused by the actions of Her Majesty's ministers'.[2]

As well as Oldenbarnevelt's gibe, the States attached two conditions to their agreement to maritime assistance: namely that Willoughby should 'proceed roundly and sincerely', and that Medemblik and Geertruidenberg should be 'reduced' to obedience to His Excellency (Prince Maurice).

When Medemblik submitted, through Willoughby's mediation, and affairs seemed to be heading in the right direction at Geertruidenberg, all at once everything in the garden was lovely.

These men [Killigrew wrote[3]] have changed their copy. Now very obsequious to her Majesty . . . The ships demanded they have agreed and more; the 1,000 mariners also; but yet have they not resolved to send any to join with her Majesty's commissioners [Killigrew means for participation in the peace negotiations] . . . Count Maurice . . . now agrees very well with Lord Wyllughby, who so carries himself that he has credit with them all; for such they like of, both to governor and assist (but so) as they may rule and not stand in awe of, as they did of my lord of Leicester, without cause . . .

Oldenbarnevelt was the sort of person who liked people only when they did as he wished: Killigrew did not need much knowledge of character to

[1] Calendar of State Papers, XXI, iv, 230.
[2] By 'ministers' they meant Willoughby in the first place, and Leicester and Killigrew to a lesser extent, not Burghley and Walsingham, who were Elizabeth's ministers in the present-day sense. But this meaning only came into use in the course of the seventeenth century.
[3] Calendar of State Papers, XXI, iv, 326 (6 May O.S.; 16 May N.S.).

realize this. Since Elizabeth's capitulation in March the English had on principle and for good given up encouraging dissident towns and discontented soldiers; Walsingham was constantly issuing instructions of this tenor, both to English officers and Netherlands supporters of Leicester.[1]

Oldenbarnevelt is seen at his best during these months. For the first time we see him dedicatedly and almost exclusively engaged on constructive work, thus showing himself worthy of the power he had acquired by so much intrigue and wrangling. While Maurice went to Zeeland to fit out the Zeeland fleet and coordinate the joint action with the English,[2] Oldenbarnevelt saw to it that he obtained the necessary powers from the provinces. Oldenbarnevelt was in the States of Holland or their *Gecommitteerde Raden* daily, and on most days in the States-General as well. He often appeared in the Council of State to activate or direct its work. His continual intervention must have irritated the members. To sugar the pill they were authorized by the States-General to take up a maximum of 100,000 guilders in cash without a previous resolution, a right which they had had under the instruction of 1586, but of which the new ones made no mention. They were also told that they need not adhere 'exactly' to this instruction. Here is an example of the way in which Oldenbarnevelt managed to combine a certain flexibility in practice with strict adherence to the book when it favoured his legal position: it is also a warning that one must not interpret the texts of the edicts, resolutions and instructions of this time too 'exactly' either; Oldenbarnevelt, as can be seen, was not tied to his instruction 'exactly'.

The agreement with the English consisted of sending a squadron under Cornelis Lonck van Roosendaal to reinforce Admiral Seymour's North Sea fleet; all the remaining sea power was to be used to prevent Parma's flat-bottomed barges from putting to sea and thus to stop his landing-troops joining the Armada. This unspectacular task, under the command of Justin of Nassau, was performed so well by the Holland–Zeeland fleet that Parma did not venture on any attempt to leave Dunkirk or Sluis. But the greater part of the fleet took no part in the famous defeat of the Armada in the Channel. Lonck's ships arrived later than the English expected. At the beginning of July Elizabeth told Ortel how dissatisfied she was that the help requested and promised in April according to the treaty had not appeared; when at last the ships arrived off Dover on 7 July both tonnage and crews were smaller than at one time promised by Prince William to the English agent Dyer.[3] Oldenbarnevelt thus only achieved part of his objective:

---

[1] Calendar of State Papers, xxi, iv, 317.

[2] Calendar of State Papers, xxi, iv, 358, 390, 421.

[3] Admiral Howard was still angry about this fourteen years later: Calendar of Salisbury Papers, xxi, 9[11].

to erase the impression of anti-English action in the two preceding years by energetic support in time of need – and in a matter in which the independence of the Netherlands was not threatened by English requirements. Seymour's squadron did not take part in the battle with the Armada till it had almost been put to flight. It does not appear that Lonck and his men had a significant share in these last engagements. The defeat of the Armada was an English one, and not an Anglo–Dutch one as Oldenbarnevelt had hoped.

There were indeed excuses for the inadequate performance on the part of the Netherlands, and Oldenbarnevelt made them more than once. In the first place it was not certain till the last moment that the attack was not aimed at Holland. From a military point of view the whole operation against England without proper naval bases on the Continent did not make sense, as Parma knew. He had repeatedly urged that he should gain possession of Walcheren before the attack on England was made. The King had not shared his view, but Oldenbarnevelt could not be certain that the Spaniards would commit such a blunder, especially as Parma was assembling large numbers of landing-troops not only at Dunkirk but also at Sluis.

In the second place peace negotiations were continuing undisturbed till late in July, and it gave a strange impression in the Netherlands at the same time to be asked to give help to their ally in dire need and urged to make far-reaching concessions to the enemy.[1] Oldenbarnevelt knew what to do but he was not alone. The useless conference certainly hampered him in his work. There was simply no money to be had from the suspicious States.

When at last some was produced it had largely to be used for other purposes. The garrison of the important town of Geertruidenberg, Dordrecht's last protection, was blackmailing him. They threatened to go over to the enemy unless a large amount was paid out at once in cash. In fact it was a sum no larger than was owing to them. At the almost hysterical insistence of the Dordrecht authorities, no longer as pro-English, almost all the available cash had to be paid to the mutineers, 200,000 guilders; the States protested explicitly that 'if the raising of ships promised to her Majesty for assistance falls short, the same must not be laid to their charge'.

It was a dramatic moment. Only the day before, 26 June 1588, the news had come that the Armada had set sail from Lisbon at the end of May. Thereupon orders had been given to remove the tar barrels and trust was placed in God,

seeing that during the war such an enemy force has never put to sea . . . and though it is to be hoped that God the Lord will assist in preventing and breaking the

---

[1] Calendar of State Papers, XXI, iv, Preface xxxvii.

enemies' intention and attacks, as He has done many times, yet shall all duty and diligence be used against it . . .

The Secretary of the States of Holland, De Regtere, represented his masters' feelings in these plain words. Those of Oldenbarnevelt too may be surmised. And now Oldenbarnevelt, with his two colleagues on the committee of secret naval affairs, Johan Pauli and Berkenrode, had to make the onerous journey to Geertruidenberg to pay out the money, so badly needed for Maurice and the fleet, to mutinous soldiers.

How differently things can turn out from what is expected! The mutineers, on the one hand, were not drawn into the fold by the 200,000 guilders. The Armada, on the other, was easily defeated without them. On 11 August in The Hague a touching spectacle was enacted at a joint meeting of the States-General, the States of Holland, the three bodies, Hof van Holland, Hoge Raad and Audit Office, and the *vroedschap* of The Hague. When this large assembly had gathered, presumably in the town hall, Prince Maurice appeared at the head of the Council of State. Van der Mijle, on behalf of Maurice, asked the meeting in emotional terms, according to the praise-worthy custom of the late Prince

first to have recourse to the Lord and afterwards promptly to consent to the sum of twice hundred thousand guilders extraordinary, above all previous consents, so as to bring all war ships to sea, provided with sailors, men of war, victuals and ammunition needed . . . advancing many good reasons as inducement and per-suasion . . .

The proposal had certainly been discussed previously with Oldenbarne-velt, if not inspired by him. But his talents were not suited to that sort of moving speech which is sometimes necessary. Van der Mijle did it much better, having learnt from Prince William, a master of such addresses. Oldenbarnevelt, on the other hand, was in his element when the States had returned to the Binnenhof and resolved in the enthusiasm of the moment 'that as much should be done in this matter as ever had been done before'.

Unfortunately this fine enthusiasm had evaporated by the next day. Holland's share of the sum required would amount to 130,000 guilders, and that was not an amount to be agreed on lightly.

'And the Nobles and the Towns could not agree to the grant nor to the means for covering it', the secretary wrote laconically.

By that time, though, the danger had already passed. Two days earlier the sea battle of Grevelingen (Gravelines) had chased the panic-stricken Armada into the North Sea, far from Parma's waiting troops. For a time there was fear of an attack on the Frisian Islands. On 9 September a partial demobilization of the expensive fleet was started and on the 20th it was learnt that the

Armada had rounded the Orkneys and no longer represented any danger. The main problem now was the prisoners from the Spanish ships driven on to the Flemish coast, for whom all the towns of Holland hardly had enough prison space. The senior in rank among the prisoners, Don Diego de Pimentel, commander of the galleon *S. Matteo*, was kept prisoner for a short time at The Hague, probably in one of the rooms above the Hall of Rolls which were later to house Oldenbarnevelt and those accused with him. While in The Hague he was interrogated by a joint civilian and military committee under Oldenbarnevelt. During this examination nothing important came to light – although the prisoner was, as usual, most communicative – except perhaps the amazing foolishness shown in the arduous preparation of the expedition. This may have given Oldenbarnevelt encouragement for the future. Pimentel's exchange, however, caused talk about Oldenbarnevelt in a sphere in which slander was later to flourish abundantly.

The allegation was that Pimentel, at Oldenbarnevelt's instigation, had been set free for a small ransom. The latter was said to have received a monetary reward for this through the intermediary of a mysterious personage referred to as 'Precursor'. The accusation is unfounded and probably based on nothing but the fact that Maurice's entourage considered the ransom fixed for Pimentel, and later for the Almirante of Aragon, to be low and could only explain it by corruption on the part of the Advocate, said not always to be very particular in money matters. In their interrogation in 1618 the judges, although the accusation was known to them, did not touch on the point. Corruption was possible but not probable.

The result of the loss of the Armada was that friendship between England and the Netherlands became firmer than ever. On 26 October, a day of public thanksgiving and prayer was ordered both in England and the Netherlands. In the same months envoys were exchanged for mutual congratulation and those from England solemnly expressed the Queen's thanks for the help provided.[1]

All this was an occasion of twofold joy for Oldenbarnevelt. Not only was he, as a good patriot, delighted at the veritably shattering victory over Spanish world power, but his own prestige rose to unprecedented heights. His opponents had always complained of his endangering the English alliance. At the beginning of 1588 it still seemed as though his policy regarding Sonoy, the Council of State and the peace negotiations was doing everything to estrange Elizabeth from the Netherlands. And now, long before the year was over, everything had turned out for the best. In spite, indeed in a sense because of Oldenbarnevelt's policy, the alliance was cemented, and not at the

---

[1] *Instructions for John Norris on going to Holland 16/10*: Calendar of State Papers, XXII.

price of humiliating dependence. In fact, foundations were laid in 1588 for the independence of the emerging Netherlands state. Building on these foundations would of necessity give rise to difficulties, but it was to continue without interruption and eight years later the new state was given de jure recognition by England and France.

The death of Leicester on 14 September set the seal on the unity that had been regained. There was no longer any pro-English party of importance to support such intervention, except for two remnants. Oldenbarnevelt's first task was to eliminate them. It was accomplished in the next seven months, in one case with complete success, in the other at the cost of something like a national disaster. The period of destruction was over; Oldenbarnevelt could show that he also knew how to handle reconstruction.

The first remnant was Utrecht. Prouninck, since Ringault's downfall Oldenbarnevelt's *bête noire*, was still precariously in power there. As burgomaster of Utrecht he also controlled the States. He could see that after Leicester's death and Elizabeth's capitulation his power would soon be over, especially now that he had lost the support of the stadtholder Nieuwenaar. The German count, also stadtholder of Gelderland, had long followed Leicester but now went over to Oldenbarnevelt, probably in exchange for his promise to support the count in Germany. As stadtholder he had the right to appoint the Utrecht magistracy on their annual re-election on 10 October. Prouninck sent a plea for help to England but only got a non-committal expression of sympathy from the Queen he had hoped to see sovereign of the Netherlands.

During the election campaigns in Utrecht disturbances broke out on each side, probably provoked by Nieuwenaar on the advice of his master in The Hague. Prouninck and some of his supporters were arrested in the course of them, and a few days later a set of pro-Oldenbarnevelt burgomasters was peacefully elected. Henceforward, except for a quickly suppressed uprising in 1610, Oldenbarnevelt could count on both the town and province of Utrecht as loyal allies. The first thing done was to recall the exiles of 1586, who had taken refuge in Holland, and restore them to their prominent positions. Floris Thin, who became the principal leader in the States, had great obligations to Oldenbarnevelt. After Thin's death in 1590 his protégé, Gillis van Ledenberg, inherited both his position and his relationship with Oldenbarnevelt, thus becoming the real beneficiary of Nieuwenaar's coup.

As in the case of Medemblik, there was only one respect in which Oldenbarnevelt could not achieve his aim: his revenge on Prouninck could not be completed. After a long trial comparable in many ways to Oldenbarnevelt's own thirty years later, Prouninck was condemned in a sentence of twenty lines to perpetual banishment. Elizabeth's intervention, which could not prevent his fall, had at any rate saved his life.

In October 1588 Parma brought the troops assembled for the abortive crossing to England up to Bergen-op-Zoom. It could scarcely be hoped that the town would be held. The Council of State had been without means for a long time and the States-General were also penniless because of the defence measures against the Armada and the expense of quelling the mutinies at Medemblik and Geertruidenberg. As usual, only Holland had money available and Oldenbarnevelt with three other members of the States took it to Zeeland on 19 October. Their first objective was the States' army headquarters on the island of Tholen, where Parma had initiated the siege of Bergen-op-Zoom by an invasion. The deputies' job was entirely a military one. Maurice, in command of Tholen, was only twenty-one and inexperienced. The States evidently had little confidence in his judgment. Oldenbarnevelt therefore became accustomed at Tholen in concerning himself with military detail. He wrote in the report he sent to the States of Holland:

that they had gathered information as to what the number, order and courage of the troops might be, all of which was found strong, between six and seven thousand foot, and four and five hundred horse, in good order and courage, but that payments and loans[1] would have to be arranged, as was done with knowledge and advice of his Excellency and the Council of State ... report was also made of the necessary fortifications.

Clearly, such behaviour by the cheesemongers from Holland would not in the long run add to the prestige of the titled officers and Maurice himself. The proverb about paying the piper and calling the tune, later a clause in the creed of Oldenbarnevelt's party, was not supported by the oath or the regulations, but was inherent in the repartition system (to which we shall return later). It explains many of the later difficulties between Maurice and Oldenbarnevelt.

One detail that the deputies from Holland had to see to was Maurice's habit of going into the danger zone. Not because the States liked him personally, but because they could not do without him politically: he was the embodiment of the spirit of Prince William. Oldenbarnevelt therefore issued instructions

on behalf of the States seriously to ask, request and admonish (the young Prince) not to bring or keep his person in any dangerous places, ... and shall steadfastly continue to, so that his Excellency ... shall be pleased to leave the island of ter Tholen for Walcheren, ter Goes or Zirkzee.

[1] Advances of pay, sometimes made much later, intended for the upkeep of the soldiers, who at this time were not provisioned by the commissariat.

Maurice rightly paid little attention to these and subsequent recommendations of the same sort. It was not mere bravado – he was more cautious than daring – but just that he would have lost all his prestige with his soldiers if he had directed their movements from the rear, which, indeed, he could not have done efficiently. This is so obvious that one cannot help suspecting that Oldenbarnevelt was actually trying to prevent the Prince gaining too much military popularity and authority. It was possibly not his chief aim, nor even a conscious one, but the typically oligarchic mistrust of the victorious general was almost certainly latent in Oldenbarnevelt.

Maurice moved a day or two after the arrival of the deputation from Holland, not back but forward. He entered the besieged town of Bergen-op-Zoom, where two British commanders were endangering its defence by their rivalry. It was obviously Maurice's task to iron this out. Oldenbarnevelt, fully experienced in dealing with troublesome commanding officers, went with him. He was indeed charged with the inspection of the fortifications and to find out how matters stood on the spot.

The episode that follows does more credit to Maurice than to Oldenbarnevelt. The former succeeded in finding a *modus vivendi* for the quarrelling Britons. Oldenbarnevelt, on the other hand, started a furious row with Willoughby – the only time that it is insinuated that Oldenbarnevelt committed an indiscretion under the influence of alcohol.

Willoughby was living at the Markiezenhof and on 22 October invited Maurice and the States deputies to a festive lunch. There was evidently no hardship in the hard-pressed town. Towards the end of the meal Oldenbarnevelt began to complain to his host about the position at Geertruidenberg.

Mutiny had been raging there for almost a year, not quelled like the others by the news of Leicester's resignation. Hohenlohe, quartered there for some months, had not behaved tactfully. Then the mutineers had wanted nothing more to do with him or with the Holland oligarchs who were behind him. They had regarded the English Queen as their mainstay and said that they would only obey her and her representative in the Netherlands, Willoughby. The mistrust of Willoughby felt by the States had of course been accentuated: would he not follow in Leicester's footsteps and set up a military dictatorship in the Netherlands? To overcome this lack of confidence Willoughby, with typical lack of political acumen, had made a promise.[1] He would use his authority over the garrison so as to bring them under Maurice's authority again. This idea seems to have originated in Dordrecht, particularly with Menijn: Oldenbarnevelt and Hohenlohe are said to have agreed to it. The

---

[1] Calendar of State Papers, XXIII, 173.

Dordrecht magistracy was firmly convinced that if Geertruidenberg let the Spaniards in, as it continually threatened, the former town could not be defended against the Spaniards. It was a remarkable misconception, taking no account of the control by Holland of the river estuaries. It was, however, not only held in Dordrecht. Exaggerated pessimism was followed by exaggerated optimism with regard to averting the danger. If all means were used to make the garrison see reason, if all their demands were granted, the mutiny would be settled. Oldenbarnevelt was less hopeful; rightly, but for the wrong reasons. He was led astray by his rooted distrust of the English. He thought that Willoughby need do nothing but use the power, recognized by the garrison, for giving a single command: to obey Maurice as they would himself. It is hard to see how Oldenbarnevelt became possessed of such a naive argument. He had, after all, some experience of the ways of extortionate mutineers. In any case Oldenbarnevelt and those with him seem to have believed that the subjection of Geertruidenberg depended entirely on Willoughby's good faith.[1] The first step taken by the latter had aroused new suspicions. Since Hohenlohe had been rejected Geertruidenberg had been without a commandant. Willoughby had now put forward a candidate for the post: his own brother-in-law John Wingfield would be a good instrument for carrying out the great plan. The garrison had found him acceptable as a preliminary to formal incorporation in the British army, which they still hoped for and Oldenbarnevelt still feared. His nomination was therefore an unfortunate move, raising the soldiers' hopes and arousing Oldenbarnevelt's fears for the sake of a fantasy. The results were unpleasant for Wingfield himself: he became a hostage in the hands of the mutineers, and was thought a traitor by the States of Holland, and for a time by his own Queen, when he could not fulfil Willoughby's promise and was used to present the mutineers' far-reaching demands.[2]

Willoughby had negotiated with the mutinous troops from May till July 1588, first on his own, then more as an intermediary between them and the States. Oldenbarnevelt had been sent on 27 July to Dordrecht to finalize the negotiations. But the strange thing was – and it is surprising to see Oldenbarnevelt involved in it – that the garrison committed themselves to nothing, except to recognizing Sir John Wingfield as governor and for the time not handing the town over to the Spaniards. There was, for instance, no question of obeying Maurice's orders or submitting to his jurisdiction. Willoughby had certainly not fulfilled his promise.

The rebels had then begun systematically to bring into Geertruidenberg

[1] See p. 146.
[2] See p. 149.

ships and vehicles bound for the enemy territory of Brabant, as trading with the enemy seemed a direct invitation to attack them. They had taken no notice of the *licenten* issued by the Netherlands admiralties and rejected their criticisms. It is therefore natural that when he met Willoughby at Bergen-op-Zoom Oldenbarnevelt should have wanted to see if anything could be achieved through Willoughby and Wingfield. Willoughby described in a pamphlet he later issued in his own defence how things must have gone at the boisterous lunch at the Markiezenhof. Oldenbarnevelt complained of what was quoted and demanded that those responsible should be reprimanded and punished.

which, he said, could not easily be done unless the town were again placed under obedience to the States. To this end he requested Banneret Willugby to be mindful of his promise and accordingly to place the same town again in the hands of the Count . . . it being preferable that the same town should fall into the hands of the enemy than that it should remain in such a state.

Oldenbarnevelt clearly got excited while speaking and now began shouting

with a loud voice and with great bitterness and anger; as soon as this came to the ears of soldiers from Geertruydenberge (for there were still a hundred in Bergen-op-Zoom) they did not stop till they were again in their garrison at Geertruydenberghe, seeing that the said Barnevelt had made him lose all his credit by these speeches.

Here Willoughby is deceiving himself – his credit with the soldiers at Geertruidenberg cannot have been so great. The fact that the soldiers had heard the harsh voice of the Advocate demanding their punishment, must indeed have made them warn their comrades at Geertruidenberg never to place themselves in the despot's power. To this extent Willoughby may have been right in what he went on to state: 'That the said Barnevelt, by these arrogant words, was the cause of all the harm that followed . . .', namely the loss of Geertruidenberg six months later. It must be understood that this conversation was not the sole, not even the decisive factor in the betrayal of the town. Cause and effect are not usually so neatly arranged in history. It can, however, be assumed that Oldenbarnevelt's aggressive and acid words – spoken of course not only at Bergen-op-Zoom – contributed to the increasingly anti-Holland mood among the Geertruidenberg garrison.

Another result was that he had made a mortal enemy of Willoughby, even though Maurice may have settled the quarrel for the time being. That was dangerous, as Willoughby had the Queen's ear. He is certain to have influenced Elizabeth against Oldenbarnevelt, thus delaying their eventual reconciliation perhaps for some years. Some malice followed immediately in the pamphlet just quoted. Willoughby says that he had heard that Oldenbarnevelt

had written and promised to Richardot, President of the Council of State of the Duke of Parma, that he could so govern the affairs of the united Netherlands that the same should again fall into the hands of the King of Spain.

Here we find the first of a series of malicious and absurd accusations still denied by Oldenbarnevelt a few minutes before his death. It is therefore worth considering for a moment why these accusations are ridiculous. It is not because Oldenbarnevelt was too good and honest to commit treason. It is not possible to infer from someone's only half-known character that he would in no circumstances commit a certain crime. We do not even know what we ourselves might be capable of. The absurdity is of an intellectual and psychological, not of a moral nature.

Oldenbarnevelt had achieved a unique position in Holland and the United Provinces in the seventeen years since the beginning of the war. It was a position that might almost be called unshakeable, as long as the war in which he was pulling the strings in such a masterly and masterful way continued. At the period of which we are speaking he had just begun his life's work: the foundation and extension of a new state in the European polity. A state of which he was to be the leader. A task like this is not cast aside for money. In fact, the position of leader of the Netherlands commonwealth was itself lucrative, though it is impossible to assess to what extent. To sum up: we should not consider Oldenbarnevelt a traitor, not only because it was contrary to his character, not only because it was against his interests, but because it conflicted with the core of his personality, of which character and interests are only facets.

Bergen-op-Zoom was relieved, chiefly by vigorous and unusually prompt military help from Elizabeth. The last of the Spanish troops left on 13 November 1588. Just before that a new English envoy had arrived at Middelburg, where Oldenbarnevelt contacted him. It was Sir John Norris, with whom Oldenbarnevelt had worked pleasantly in the time of, and against, Leicester. He was a man who was sure to make a report to the Queen that would please the Advocate. Besides bringing 1,500 men from England to break the Spanish siege at Bergen-op-Zoom he also brought official expression of thanks for the help against the Armada and, as counterpart, complaints about certain details which Oldenbarnevelt was easily able to satisfy. The main part of his commission, however, was an invitation to the States-General to take part in a naval expedition with landing troops against Portugal, intended as revenge for the Armada. Francis Drake was to be the admiral,

Norris himself the general of the landing troops; his journey to the Nether-lands was for the purpose of fetching troops for this expedition to form the nucleus of the landing force. As this would bring the number of English troops in the Netherlands far below the figure named in the Treaty of Non-such, the agreement of the States-General was needed for their transfer.

Both in England and the Netherlands feelings were divided as to the use of the expedition. In England the Lord Treasurer, Burghley, was not one to pursue two birds in the bush if it meant releasing one in the hand. The expedition was entirely the work of Walsingham and his following.

Oldenbarnevelt championed the idea enthusiastically and Norris wrote to Walsingham that he was greatly satisfied with his cooperation, much more than with Willoughby, who was offering passive resistance.

The resistance one can understand; Oldenbarnevelt's cooperation, on the other hand, is at first sight somewhat surprising. The English troops in the Netherlands were not numerous, in spite of the reinforcements brought by Norris. Arms had to be provided, and this could only be done with difficulty in the Netherlands. Ostend, manned entirely by English troops, was seriously threatened; a renewed attack on Bergen-op-Zoom could be expected at any moment. In the circumstances it might seem almost madness to withdraw 1,600 English veterans as well as the requisite number of Netherlanders and Germans from the war in the Netherlands. None the less Oldenbarnevelt persuaded the States-General to permit the withdrawal of 2,000 Englishmen. Although probably not more than half of this number did in fact leave, one may well wonder why Oldenbarnevelt let the country be bled like this.

His motives compounded military, foreign and internal policy. The military ones cannot have been decisive. It was almost as foolish to believe that this counter-Armada would seriously harm Spain as it had been to expect Medina Sidonia's Armada to conquer England. However, Oldenbarnevelt may have had some military expectations of a limited kind, such as the possible destruc-tion of a new Armada in preparation. But his main reasons were undoubtedly political. To make the English alliance strong and lasting Elizabeth must be kept in a good mood. There were always difficulties of all kinds with England. Oldenbarnevelt could not and would not grant a number of English wishes. He was determined to reject the continued claims to a protectorate. He did not want to go into the thorny and chronic complaints about Netherlands trade with the enemy. So if Elizabeth required something to which there was no objection in principle she must be obliged as far as possible. Moreover, Oldenbarnevelt was not likely to take a very serious view of the dangers threatened from Parma's side. He must have known that Parma was ill, dis-couraged and partially disgraced. The demoralization of the Spaniards and their followers after the Armada disaster was great and not yet over, especially when followed by the failure at Bergen-op-Zoom. In France new developments were impending that might oblige the King to divert Parma's troops in that direction. Indeed, even before Norris had reported to the Queen, the news arrived of the murder of the Guises at Blois[1] which at once had this result.

Even if the expedition to Portugal was only a moderate success Philip would have to withdraw troops from the Netherlands and the sacrifices made would be justified. If, on the other hand, the expedition was a failure – Oldenbarnevelt must have taken this possibility into serious account – the adventurous policy of long-distance expeditions would stand condemned and Elizabeth would be more ready than before to take part in an offensive in the Netherlands.

Before the end of November Norris made his proposal in the Council of State – one of the last occasions on which that body was to be seen conferring with a foreign envoy. Norris understood, however, that the decision would not be taken there but in the States of Holland, where he appeared on 29 November, hat in hand, to ask for a favourable pronouncement on Portugal. Oldenbarnevelt made cunning[2] use of this mood in his speech, making thirteen demands, mainly concerned with the military clauses of the treaty. Only when Norris had promised to give the States their way in all respects did Oldenbarnevelt come down to fundamentals and promise to obtain help for Portugal through the States-General. This was promptly done when that body reassembled on 10 December.

Among the troops allotted to the expedition was the Geertruidenberg garrison, which Oldenbarnevelt hoped to get rid of in this way. They refused to leave in spite of Willoughby's promises and were still most mutinous, although nominally under Willoughby's command. They seem to have established good relations with his brother-in-law Wingfield, despite the difference of nationality. Receiving no pay from the national treasury the soldiers began to plunder friend and foe alike and interfered with the trade of Dordrecht, which was becoming nervous of a possible *coup de main*. At the same time well-founded rumours were circulated about their negotiations with Parma to hand over the town against payment of arrears.

But Willoughby had promised to see that the garrison obeyed Maurice. Was he hand in glove with his brother-in-law and were they being dishonest? It is questionable whether Oldenbarnevelt thought so. His passionate,

---

[1] See Chapter 5.

[2] This cunning is stressed by Edward P. Cheyney, *A History of England from the Defeat of the Armada to the Death of Elizabeth*, London, 1926, I, 208.

mistrustful and cynical nature may have led him to, but his political sense must have told him the opposite. It is certain that he loudly voiced his suspicion after the unfortunate dispute at Bergen-op-Zoom.[1] It may have been political Machiavellianism. Willoughby became more and more inclined to appeal to the less agreeable clauses in the Treaty of Nonsuch, in which considerable political power was granted to the governor-general. It was time to let him follow Leicester and be followed by a less high and mighty general. It would serve this purpose to cast suspicion on him, without of course accusing him in so many words.

Willoughby, about to sail for England on indefinite leave, again offered to mediate. Oldenbarnevelt had the offer rejected. When Willoughby came to take leave of the States-General a few days later, Oldenbarnevelt was not present. As in the case of Leicester, Willoughby's stay ended in rupture. As matters had developed in Geertruidenberg, Oldenbarnevelt cannot be blamed for letting things come to a head in these circumstances. He is sure to have found some agreement from Maurice and those around him for the idea of making the garrison see reason by force. Neither the Council of State nor the States-General could be made aware of the plan. There were English members of the former who could not be trusted. The States-General could not be told, first because the plan would certainly have leaked out prematurely, and secondly because its execution involved two risks which the deputies of the other provinces would certainly not have been willing to run without *ruggespraak* with those they represented: the risk of Geertruidenberg falling into Spanish hands and the risk of a break with England.

Those who shared the secret were a few trusted friends of Oldenbarnevelt's, commissioned by the States of Holland to accompany Maurice on an unspecified military expedition. The States of Holland, already entirely under Oldenbarnevelt's thumb, resigned themselves to all this. It is characteristic of his *sans-gêne* that he tried to treat the Council of State with the same haughty mistrust. He had Maurice tell this body that he had an 'exploit' in view, on which some deputies from the Council must accompany him. The answer was that he must first disclose the nature of the 'exploit'.[2] Some days later Maurice again wrote to the Council, from the fleet facing Geertruidenberg, asking them to send two of their members; he then naturally revealed

---

[1] An early example from November 1588: Calendar of State Papers, XXII, 312, where he calls Willoughby 'an interested party' with regard to Bergen-op-Zoom. In the letter from the States-General to Elizabeth of 24 April 1589 (N.S.) accompanying the edict of 20 April the passage is underlined in which the States declare that they dealt with Willoughby's actions 'avec toute modération et discrétion possibles'.

[2] The indignation of Bodley and Gilpin, the two English members of the Council is apparent in letters by both of them to England dated 19 March (O.S., 29 March N.S.): Calendar of State Papers, XXIII, 155.

the purpose of the expedition, the fact of which had now become known, and gave reasons for it scornfully described by Bodley as 'excuses' and not taken seriously by those present.[1] Oldenbarnevelt kept an accurate diary of what happened in the fleet at Geertruidenberg. It shows how the deputies from Holland had their fingers in every pie, not only in the negotiations preceding the opening of hostilities or the collection and distribution of the money voted for the expedition, but also in all kinds of military decisions.

The members set out on 12 March by ship for Delft, and a clerk was left there with instructions to travel on to Geertruidenberg with the town's contribution, as soon as it came in. A storekeeper confirmed that he had already sent off all the military requirements ordered from him, apart from a number of hammers for building defence works: these were loaded on to the ship the deputies were travelling in. In the afternoon they arrived at Rotterdam, where they met one of Maurice's couriers from Willemstad, also carrying letters from Geertruidenberg. They conferred there too with a burgomaster and substitute sheriff of Geertruidenberg, attempting mediation for the last time, with a delegate from Norris, with two admirals whom they 'summoned', as well as with the treasurer-general of the Union, De Bye, who on this occasion seems to have behaved as the subordinate of the States of Holland. They also spoke with the mayors of Rotterdam about the sending of carpenters to Geertruidenberg: evidently nails were more important than bullets in this siege.

After this well-spent Sunday, on which nothing is shown of later ideas of Sabbath calm, they boarded ship at ten in the evening for the next stage to Dordrecht. On Monday evening, after an almost uninterrupted voyage of forty hours, they arrived at Maurice's headquarters at Willemstad. The same evening, after consultation with Maurice, they sent a messenger to Ooltgensplaat to have a ship, which had been taking in ammunition there, sent on at once. This was an obvious omission on Maurice's part, only remedied by the arrival of his mentor.

The next morning the plan of campaign was formed in the presence of Maurice, his cousin Philip of Nassau, Solms, Villiers and Balfour, a Scottish colonel who, being anti-English, had been let into the secret early. Not till that meeting, at which mainly the disposal of the troops was discussed, was it decided to inform the Netherlands colonels Dorp and Lokeren. The next part of the report, comprising the actual siege, is full of military details, on which the States deputies were evidently consulted. Sometimes it was the fetching of reeds and straw, then again the distribution of the available gunpowder, also spruces and pines, as well as 900 shovels and spades and some

---

[1] 'Scorned by all': Calendar of State Papers, XXIII, 155.

axes, among the various units. The choice of a place for the redoubt, the interviews with the orderlies sent by the colonels, the ordering of 2,300 loaves and 1,900 cheeses, all came under the authority of the deputies, who also decided which of the 140 ships bringing the troops might go home after the landing. The deputies were not always at command headquarters: on 17 March they made a tour of inspection of the defences and took the opportunity of summoning to a council of war on Maurice's ship the three chief officers they had called on, as well as Field-Marshal Villiers. All pure staff work, so that the oversimplification attributing the successes of the coming years to the cooperation of Maurice as commander in the field and Oldenbarnevelt as statesman must be avoided. Maurice may have paid little attention to politics and let himself be used mainly as Oldenbarnevelt's instrument: but the opposite is certainly not the case. In the next few years Oldenbarnevelt was active not only as a statesman but also to a great extent as minister of war, indeed as co-commander.

At the walls of Geertruidenberg he was unsuccessful in both functions. Torrential rain and flooding interfered with the siege. Haughty letters from Maurice, inspired by Oldenbarnevelt, tried the garrison too far: Wingfield felt that his honour had been impugned and challenged Maurice to a rapier duel. The desperate authorities in Dordrecht tried in vain to mollify Oldenbarnevelt: after the town's pro-Leicester attitude and the failure of the agreement they had urged the previous summer he had no reason to sacrifice his principles to their alleged interests.

Oldenbarnevelt's intransigence in this difference of opinion as to how to deal with Geertruidenberg undoubtedly led to the subsequent hostility of the town of Dordrecht, which contributed so much to the Advocate's fall. The first sign of it appeared when Maurice, with good reason, raised the siege of the town after the garrison had sold it for a substantial sum of money to Parma. When Maurice's retreating troops appeared in front of Dordrecht on the Merwede,

the mob came out of the town to the ships, saying that they had been ordered to bring all the ordinance inside Dordrecht and using unsuitable words about the authorities. There was shouting and screaming about the conduct of affairs at Geertruidenberg that was instigated, it is to be presumed, by some enemies.[1]

For the last time English, inhabitants of Dordrecht, and other opponents of the Advocate protested with one voice against his apparently anti-English policy. Members of the Council of State told Bodley that Oldenbarnevelt 'taketh a direct course . . . to ruin himself and the state'.[2]

[1] In a letter from one of Maurice's party.
[2] Calendar of State Papers, XXIII, 116, Bodley to Walsingham.

Oldenbarnevelt reacted to this criticism in a typical way, with a counter-attack. He had an edict issued by the States-General declaring the garrison troops, one and all, traitors, without any form of trial, and threatening them with the gallows if and wherever they were caught. The edict was illegal as being a death sentence without possibility of defence. Still worse was that the preamble, in Oldenbarnevelt's choleric style, contained unproven accusations against Wingfield, Willoughby and the English in general. Willoughby exploded with rage. He would not be brought to see reason by Burghley's attempts at mediation,[1] but had his secretary write a defence, accusing Oldenbarnevelt in his turn of treason.

Both Oldenbarnevelt, who threatened to expose the English to the world, and the English indulged in a slanging match for the last time.[2] Then it was over, almost suddenly. Hatred and aversion between Oldenbarnevelt and the English made way for friendship and respect, despite recurrent difficulties. Nine years later, in the spring of 1598, when Oldenbarnevelt went to England for the second time as envoy, it was not at all as the mistrusted head of an anti-English faction, but as the personally trusted leader of the policy of a valued ally, with whom Elizabeth was glad to discuss the consequences of the Peace of Vervins. Things were now developing towards this zenith. Geertruidenberg had been the nadir.

After the fall of Geertruidenberg the rhythm of Oldenbarnevelt's life changed. He bought a house in Spuistraat at The Hague, only a few hundred yards from where he worked in the Binnenhof. It provided him with peace and security in his life. In politics the pace slackened. The almost unbearable tensions marking the first three years of his office gave way to the daily irritations inseparable from a position of power. Once he had dismissed any idea of foreign protectorate or sovereignty, the great dangers represented by Leicester, the Armada and Willoughby encouraged him to think in terms of a state structured according to his own wishes. Based on the Union of Utrecht, this structure became quite different from that envisaged by the makers of the Union, including Oldenbarnevelt himself. The Union may have remained formally the constitution of the embryo state, even up to 1795, but in actual fact the life of the state was governed by conventions, grown up and established, largely under Oldenbarnevelt's influence, long after 1579.

The Council of State, four years before regarded as the government of the country, had since declined to the status of a powerless body of officials. The States-General, on the other hand, was in fact becoming the supreme autho-

---

[1] Calendar of State Papers, XXIII, 333, 344; in a letter of 12 May (O.S., 22 May N.S.) 1589, to Burghley he threatened to murder Oldenbarnevelt: ibid. 252.
[2] Calendar of State Papers, XXIII, 311.

rity instead of being occasionally assembled to vote financial grants, as had been intended at the time of the Treaty of Nonsuch.

The Union of Utrecht had allowed the stadtholders fairly wide powers, owing to the enormous prestige of one of them, Prince William. Now that one of the stadtholders was twenty-one, without as yet having shown any special capability, and the two others were Germans without much popularity, the power assigned to them was not compatible with actual conditions. Oldenbarnevelt saw to it that the letter of this part of the Union was disregarded without doing violence to its spirit.

Control of the fleet, of finance and of any States-General territory gained by conquest was either not, or not practicably, regulated by the Union: it was Oldenbarnevelt who managed to bring about a tolerable settlement of these three points, though in the first he did not have his own way, owing to the obstinate opposition of Zeeland.

Finally there was the federal character of the Netherlands state. The Union, comprising as it did only a part of the rebellious Netherlands, had been intended as a temporary defensive alliance among provinces retaining their own sovereignty, even in military matters. War could not be waged efficiently with such an alliance. The Prince had already been urging a wider range of power for the central authority, nominally attained for the first time under Leicester. In this respect Oldenbarnevelt followed in Leicester's footsteps, but with much more practical effect, because he entirely renounced the name and by this means obtained the essence, that of a militarily formidable federal state, which could only be based on the inchoate but real predominance of Holland. It was this federal state that won the victorious truce in the next twenty years, due to unshaken trust in the leadership of Holland; though sometimes self-interested it never lost sight of the subordinate allies' interests. When the basis of this trust was undermined by religious animosities, in the period of the truce, the federal state fell apart and the letter of the Union was reinstated, implemented mainly by the same Holland and its Advocate who had at first calmly shelved it. Without war and with Holland's preeminence threatened, the province was no longer interested in the federal state and began, supported by the letter of the law, to fight against the spirit of the unified state it had forged itself.

We have just climbed the crest of a dune to see what is lying ahead. Now we must return to the hollows and trudge through the somewhat arid though rewarding sand of political description.

The Council of State did not accept its degradation without resistance. It was still called 'the government', but a genuine governing function, in place of that of the rejected Viceroy, was incompatible with the system of representation in force since 1579, ranging from municipal *vroedschappen* to the body of ministers, the States-General. The Council, owing no responsibility to those nominating it, thus lacked the moral authority to exercise its constitutional power. Nor, of course, could it boast the divine right to power of the Burgundians and the Habsburgs, born to rule, which had enabled them to carry out their thankless task.

This course of events was furthered and accelerated by three factors. The first was the repartition system, with its counterpart at sea, control of the fleet by their own governing bodies. By the repartition system almost all expenditure on the land forces came under the province concerned. Most of the companies were allotted to a province, more or less in proportion to the quota payable by the province to the States-General. Only the surplus of the quota granted after payment of the companies was remitted to the receiver-general in The Hague – mostly very little, sometimes nothing. The same sort of thing happened with the revenue from *licenten* levied by the admiralties, it being used primarily by the admiralties for the equipment of ships. The Council of State was therefore practically without money and so without power,[1] although numbering a treasurer-general and a receiver-general among its members. The latter had nothing to receive and the former, to his great regret, very little to keep in his coffers.

The second factor, which should not be underestimated, was the ideal set himself by the leader of the state, Johan van Oldenbarnevelt: a federal state directed by the richest and most powerful province, Holland. Oldenbarnevelt was able largely, though not entirely, to realize this ideal as long as the war continued. It was not compatible with government by a Council of State. One may wonder why. In the States-General Holland had one vote out of six, till Groningen was reduced in 1594; in the Council of State, theoretically at any rate, three out of thirteen. But this calculation does not really reflect Holland's influence in either body. It will soon be seen that Holland's one vote dominated the States-General. In the Council of State a province had practically no opportunity to exert any influence. The members of the Council took an oath to the States-General to relinquish any particular relationship with the towns or provinces of their birth. Most of them took this oath seriously. It could not be combined with the predominance of Holland, nor was this all: in view of the particularistic mentality of the still-so-recently-united provinces, it was incompatible with a vigorous central government, however paradoxical this may sound. The five small provinces might be content to be directed by the most powerful sixth one, if in every case that arose they had the opportunity to put forward their interests and views and

[1] See Burghley's complaint to the Loozen–Valcke embassy, Calendar of State Papers, XXIII, 284.

to negotiate over them in a conference of ministers like the States-General. They could never agree to being ruled by a set of people nominated by themselves, but owing them no responsibility, and who would wish to use authority rather than consultation or persuasion in governing. Such authority was just what the Council did not possess.

There was also the fact that it had English members. Their presence was a lively reminder of the Leicester period, when the Council had debased itself to an instrument of the hated tyrant. Oldenbarnevelt made skilful use of this circumstance to realize his ideal all the sooner. Leicester and Willoughby having successively been removed, Oldenbarnevelt steered full course towards an independent Netherlands commonwealth, and that was inconsistent with a supreme governing body on which two foreign members had seats.

The course of this process of demotion can be followed from the behaviour of the new English envoy Bodley, who arrived at the beginning of 1589. Willoughby, as commander of the auxiliary troops, had continually protested against the new instructions of the Council of State and the powerlessness to which it was condemned both by its brief and in practice. Willoughby resented the affair but showed little political flair and moreover seldom appeared in The Hague.

However, in the new envoy, Oldenbarnevelt was to meet an opponent of a calibre he had not yet experienced. Bodley, given detailed instructions by Walsingham,[1] took the view that the Treaty of Nonsuch, in clauses 16 to 20, 23 and 24, gave certain powers to the Governor-General together with the Council of State. He claimed that these clauses had been violated by usurpation of power on the part of the States-General, but the clauses did not state what powers the Council of State would possess apart from the Governor-General. Bodley's assertion was largely based on the assumed spirit of the treaty, but nothing was to be proved by the spirit. By the nature of the matter Oldenbarnevelt must get the best of it. Relations between the Netherlands and England had been entirely changed by the failure of Leicester and the victory over the Armada from the disguised protectorate envisaged in 1585. The Netherlands were feeling independent and grudged anyone else a say in the way they wished to mould the government. When the Delft pensionary Leonard de Voocht returned from an embassy to England he presented the States-General with a report just as the Queen had requested him. Bodley protested because De Voocht had passed over the Council of State. But he had not a leg to stand on: the treaty said nothing about the handling of foreign affairs and the instructions were couched in such vague terms that they could mean everything or nothing. Oldenbarnevelt had decided to make nothing of them. He

---

[1] Calendar of State Papers, XXII, 324.

was not entirely successful, but before Bodley's mission was over he had come to the conclusion that no one but Oldenbarnevelt controlled the United Provinces' foreign policy. Succeeding ambassadors never doubted this. Oldenbarnevelt had made himself master of these affairs in the course of a few years without any formal competency, or with a formal competency varying from case to case. The procedure was as follows: if, for instance, an important despatch came in from a Netherlands ambassador abroad it went first to the clerk of the States-General, Cornelis van Aerssen, who was in daily contact with the Advocate of Holland. The despatch was then given to Oldenbarnevelt to read and the two of them discussed what action to take: an answer to the ambassador or a letter to the monarch to whom he was accredited. If this happened during a session of the States-General – and they were sitting most of the time – Oldenbarnevelt drafted the letter to be written and presented the draft to the States of Holland. It had become the custom for proposals not mentioned in the letter convening the States-General, and not of a purely financial nature, to originate with the province of Holland. As Advocate of Holland Oldenbarnevelt was able to put his draft letter on the agenda at once. There was hardly ever any opposition in the States of Holland, as most of the deputies knew little about foreign affairs. Once the matter had gone through the States of Holland, Oldenbarnevelt, usually leader of their deputation in the States-General, could sometimes bring it up for discussion the same or the next day. If it was thought to be of fundamental importance, or if extra expense was attached to it, the deputies 'took report', as indeed sometimes happened in the States of Holland: they wrote to their principals for instructions or sometimes made the trip to Leeuwarden or Middelburg, especially if there were several matters at issue. If the matter seemed less important, but they were still afraid to make a snap decision, a commission was appointed to draw up the definitive text of such a letter. This almost always happened when instructions were issued to departing envoys. Oldenbarnevelt generally had himself appointed to the commission; if, as an exception, he was not on it, because he was away or fully occupied with other work, one of the others, not always the Holland member, was someone so subservient to him that the result was eventually what Oldenbarnevelt had intended.

The Council of State, as can be seen, did not fit into this procedure. At most it was asked for advice in the last stage but one, but, as De Bye complained, they were not given data on which to base their advice. De Bye is certainly right in attributing this to a trick of Oldenbarnevelt's. By concentrating information,[1] by building up a sort of rudimentary intelligence

---

[1] Gilpin complained in February 1589: '(The Minister of Navarre, Du Fay) writes his particular news to Barnevelt, who keeps it to himself.' Calendar of State Papers, XXIII, 114.

service, Oldenbarnevelt managed to establish the monopoly in foreign relations so characteristic of the ensuing period.

Of course it was not an ideal system for waging war vigorously. To anyone like Bodley, accustomed to monarchical rule, this government by persuasion must have seemed a monstrosity. Therefore when Bodley time and again advocates the extension of the Council's powers he does not use only juridical arguments, nor promote solely English interests. He had indeed got the Netherlands' interests in view. Certainly he looked on Oldenbarnevelt as anti-English, but also primarily as a man who was destroying his own country, either from blindness or spite. His oral instructions said that he should try to win over Oldenbarnevelt to England's side,[1] but indignation at his behaviour prevented him from carrying out this part of his assignment. He regarded the military and political situation on his arrival as desperate,[2] mainly owing to the irresponsible behaviour of a small group of people, of whom Oldenbarnevelt was no doubt number one, described as

aulcuns ambitieux et factionaires, lesquels sans due considération tachent satisfaire a leur naturel et propres desseings, les poursuivant (ce quest grandement a craindre) jusques a leur ruine, et hazard de cest estat.

That was in February 1589. The loss of Geertruidenberg in April intensified his feelings. He could not regard such a loss as anything but the result of Oldenbarnevelt's personal ambition and blind anti-Englishness.[3] Bodley's tone became 'intemperate and impassioned' to such an extent as to madden Walsingham, who shortly before his death in 1590 expressed to the Dutch agent Ortel his regret at having sent such a hot-headed diplomat to upset Anglo-Netherlands relations. Bodley again and again urged the States-General to change the form of government, particularly the pernicious *ruggespraak* that had annoyed the Prince so much too. Each time he was put off with an evasion. Then Burghley sent Thomas Wilkes as special envoy to discuss a change in the treaty; he was probably chosen because he got on well with Oldenbarnevelt. For the last time we see the two envoys appear before the States-General to ask for respect for the Council of State. They cannot have had much hope of achieving anything. Bodley had expressed himself rather pessimistically and more or less resignedly on the matter. After 1 August 1590 he definitely reconciled himself to the position of the Council, as

---

[1] He mentions this later in a letter to Walsingham: Conyers Read, *Mr Secretary Walsingham*, Oxford, 1923-5.

[2] 'Unless by her Majesty's extraordinary assistance and counsel they be presently holpen, there is little appearance that they can hold it out long.' Calendar of State Papers, XXIII, 195.

[3] Calendar of State Papers, XXIII, 155, 167, 195 (where Oldenbarnevelt as well as Maurice and Villiers are made responsible for the siege), 288 ('passion and wilfilness of some few, who sought afterwards to cover up their folly by this placard').

intended by Oldenbarnevelt. It may have been partly Wilkes's influence, but it was largely because the war was beginning to go well. In 1589 the Netherlands were still on the defensive, but in 1590 a series of successes, starting with the surprise of Breda, made Bodley think again. Evidently it was possible to wage war efficiently even with this theoretically inadequate system of polyarchy and *ruggespraak*. One could talk to Oldenbarnevelt as long as one confined oneself to the protection of English interests and did not try to act the guardian and counsellor. Previously he had complained to Burghley about Oldenbarnevelt's 'rude and untractable nature, delighting continuously to oppose himself against the English government (i.e. English intervention in internal affairs) for so it pleaseth him and some others to term her Majesty's directions'.[1] As soon as Elizabeth stopped giving 'directions' Oldenbarnevelt suddenly turned out not to be so rude and intractable. The new state was found to be viable and Oldenbarnevelt had brought it into the world. He could not be disturbed in his work by importunate advisers. Bodley understood this, as did the Netherlands members of the Council, who confined themselves, not without heartache but with a certain amount of relief, to the still useful task allotted them in Oldenbarnevelt's scheme of government: military administration and financial control. They also had a certain juridical and undefined administrative capacity. It was enough.

As the repartition system was carried out more and more consistently, an increasing number of troops was withdrawn from the authority of the Council of State. Originally a kind of banking system had been intended, by which the provinces paid money they owed the States-General to the latter's creditors. This background was forgotten when it was in Holland's interest to do so. The companies paid by Holland were regarded as being in Holland's service. Obedience to the paying province was taken for granted. It was postulated by Grotius, who as a good jurist should have known better. More than any other single factor this tragic assumption led Oldenbarnevelt to the scaffold.

The Council allowed itself, disgruntled but not too deeply embittered, to be eliminated from the taking of military decisions in the course of these ten years. They only carried on military administration in a more narrow sense, though entirely under the orders of the States-General. It was a thorn in the flesh of Anthonie Duyck, the diarist, at this time *fiscaal* (a judicial officer) to the Council of State, later first *fiscaal* to the judges delegated to try Oldenbarnevelt. On the occasion of the dispute that broke out with Maurice at Arnhem after the capture of Groningen[2] he accused the States-General of

[1] Read, *Mr Secretary Walsingham*, III, 355.
[2] See p. 18.

handling this matter in too sovereign a manner, without the knowledge of his Excellency and the Council of State, as if the Council served a monarchy... whereas in fact they were bound by an oath, just like the deputies to the States-General ...

Both Oldenbarnevelt's contention and the objection that could be raised against it are summarized here. On principle as well as by temperament Oldenbarnevelt liked to handle affairs in a 'sovereign' manner and this was bound to cause trouble with the Council of State. When on 8 January 1590 the question of the Mint at Gorcum was being dealt with by the Council, Oldenbarnevelt came in unannounced to give his opinion. He often did so, usually with an assignment from the States-General, who met only a few yards away. This time apparently he came without an assignment on a matter on which Holland was not entirely at one with the States-General. Oldenbarnevelt's tone must have been on the peremptory side, as it so often was when he was not quite sure where he stood. That is undoubtedly why the Council next day passed a resolution denying Oldenbarnevelt, 'the Advocate of Holland' and other deputies from the States of Holland admittance to the Council. The reason given, that 'some of the deputies of the provinces raised objections', takes away some of the import of this gesture. The Council was not so much affronted by Oldenbarnevelt's masterful conduct as that the other provinces disliked the States of Holland affecting the Council's deliberations in a way that the States of the five other provinces were in the nature of things unable to do. Decisive importance should not be ascribed to this resolution in Oldenbarnevelt's efforts to reduce the Council's power. It was no more than one of the many symptoms of tension.

It was tension and not enmity. In many matters then and for years to come the Advocate and the Council of State cooperated admirably, particularly on finance. In Leicester's period something like annual budgets were made for the first time. They were called variously 'war statement', 'general petition' or 'war petition'. Some years later two documents appear in which the general petition is comparable with a modern budget, a war statement with a memorandum for information. Both were drawn up by the Council of State, especially by the treasurer-general, De Bye, and presented to the States-General around November of each year. Part of the petition was an assessment, a system of dividing the amounts requested among the provinces. The States of each province met separately to discuss it and gave their assent sooner or later; the consent was never unconditional and sometimes so full of saving clauses that it was of little use. It was of course important to take care beforehand that this was not the case with Holland, in other words that the war petition was previously gone over with Holland. At first this was done

quite officially. On 16 January 1588 the States-General commissioned Oldenbarnevelt and five others, one from each province, to draw up the war statement jointly with the Council of State. Later on consultation became
unofficial; only on one occasion is there any trace of this, where some
unimportant changes have been made to a general petition in Oldenbarnevelt's handwriting. In any case it is clear, and was a natural consequence, that
Oldenbarnevelt was controlling the republic, not only in foreign and military
affairs but in finance as well.

Change in the English membership and a change of mood in some others
was not the least of the reasons for his attaining this position smoothly. When
Willoughby left in March 1589, full of resentment towards the States and
Oldenbarnevelt personally, his last act was of decisive importance to better
relations between the leader of Netherlands policy and the English ally.
Willoughby's wife had a young cousin, Francis Vere, who had followed him
to the Netherlands in the hope of making himself a career quickly. Willoughby
had given him a company at Bergen-op-Zoom at the same time that he himself was commandant there. When his brother-in-law Wingfield was given
command of the Geertruidenberg garrison Willoughby wanted to give him
Vere, again as company commander. The appointment did not go through:
the mutineers had enough with one English officer. It led, however, to a sad
misunderstanding and a remarkable coincidence, for Willoughby recommended his cousin as his successor in command of the English auxiliaries in the
Netherlands. When Elizabeth, after her usual hesitation, had decided to
oblige her favourite in this matter – promotion over the heads of twenty
senior officers was not without its dangers – Oldenbarnevelt's edict against
the betrayers of Geertruidenberg had just appeared, and Vere's name was
prominent in the list of those to be hanged without form of trial, if they were
caught. The misunderstanding was soon settled. It is typical of Vere's genial
character that his relations with the man who would have had him hanged
were not adversely affected. On the contrary: it may be assumed, though it is
not known, that Oldenbarnevelt offered his excuses so politely as to form the
basis for their future friendship. It had other causes: Vere became his
cousin's successor only in a relative sense. He was not made general or
colonel, but 'sergeant-major', a much higher rank than it denotes at present,
but still not one of the high-ranking officers. From the start, owing to his low
rank, combined with a complete lack of interest in politics, he never laid
claim to the powers allotted to the governor-general by the treaty. Military
matters were his concern and here he had a common interest with Maurice,
with whom he collaborated excellently for many years. Where Willoughby
had been pessimistic, Vere made light of his difficulties. Walsingham, who

had him appointed, thus symbolized, as it were, his difficult decision to be reconciled with Oldenbarnevelt. He wrote to Bodley in August 1589: 'I wish that our fortune and theirs were not so straightly tied as it is, so as we cannot well untie without great hazard, and then there would easily be found some way to free us from them without peril.'[1] But young Robert Cecil, son of Walsingham's opponent Burghley, was Vere's intimate friend. References to Vere in the letters written home by the English in the Netherlands form a chorus of eulogy. Bodley praised him repeatedly, among other things for making himself liked by the Hollanders. Elizabeth herself, who hardly knew him, once called him 'the worthiest captain of her time'.

Oldenbarnevelt was fond of Vere both because of his bad and his undeniable good qualities. His limited interests made him an easy partner to deal with; his impressionable nature made him accept uncritically a lot of things against which a more forceful character would have rebelled. He was so pro-Dutch that he was more than once rebuked by Burghley and even by the Queen herself, and that he irritated Willoughby. In short, Vere seemed to have been sent by heaven to help Oldenbarnevelt on his course and the latter would have been very shortsighted if he had not appreciated it. In 1593 the States-General, no doubt at Oldenbarnevelt's instigation, resolved to appoint Vere colonel in the States' service

providing that His Honour shall be obliged to serve the country in the quality of colonel, beside the person of His Excellency or elsewhere, at sea, on land, in fortresses or towns, where the service of the country shall demand and His Honour be commanded . . .

He took the oath on 15 July of that year, after which he was bound both to the Queen and the States-General; to our ideas an undesirable combination, though it does not seem to have caused any difficulties.

A change in Oldenbarnevelt's favour came about in these years in the Council of State too. In Leicester's time the English members had often complained about the discussions being held in Dutch, a language which, of course, they had not mastered. Their complaints led nowhere, perhaps not so much from unwillingness as from the fact that it was unnatural to hold discussions in French in a four-fifths Netherlands body, where usually only one or two of the English members were present. When Bodley accepted the appointment as ambassador–councillor he therefore demanded that he should always be accompanied by an interpreter. The choice of interpreter was easy: it could only be George Gilpin, an Englishman who had lived for a long time

[1] Read, *Mr Secretary Walsingham*, III, 358.
[2] Clements R. Markham, *The Fighting Veres*, London, 1888.

in Antwerp and was used by other English merchants as a sort of consul before he was attached to the Council of State as secretary. He soon became friendly with Oldenbarnevelt, for much the same reasons as Vere. He was primarily interested in military affairs, without much knowledge of statesmanship. He is therefore not a good reporter of the political scene, though much devoted to the alliance between England and Holland, of which he saw Oldenbarnevelt as the embodiment. He had become quite Dutch in his ways, sent his sons to the university at Franeker and lived at Delft where in 1600 he was exempted from tax. Like Vere, his relations with his English masters benefited from the goodwill he had acquired from the States-General. When Bodley left for England in 1593 Gilpin succeeded him as member of the Council of State and thus for years held the position, though without the title, of English ambassador in the Netherlands.

Everything ran smoothly too with the other English officers in service with or under Vere. The new commander of Flushing, Robert Sidney, seems to have inherited some of his brother Philip's tact; at any rate we hear of no serious difficulties during the fifteen years of his office, such as those for which his predecessor Russell was notorious. The new replacement in command of Ostend, Edward Norris, a troublesome and hot-tempered man, regarded Oldenbarnevelt, his brother's friend, as the protector who would constantly save him from the dangerous situations in which his temperament placed him.

The predominance Oldenbarnevelt was able to bring to bear in all such matters of finance, conduct of the war, relations with England and the English higher ranks, was primarily due to the semi-voluntary abdication of the Council of State. An extension of the States-General's field of operation complemented this, and by 1593 the sessions had become permanent. Oldenbarnevelt's control of the States-General was clearly strengthened by this change in its character. As long as the States-General were a congress of envoys from the provinces, the deputies went to The Hague with well-defined briefing as to all the points reported in the 'recesses'[1] and no other matters were usually put on the agenda. It was different when the States-General constantly had to pass resolutions that would not allow of delay and on which the deputies had no mandate. They had to give their views impromptu at the sessions, only the Hollanders being able to consult their principals. In these circumstances it was natural for the deputies almost always to vote in favour of Oldenbarnevelt's proposals, well prepared in the States of Holland. They were of course always entitled to abstain from voting, saying that they had not been instructed. In practice that was only the case with proposals, usually

[1] The Dutch word *reces* meant at that time the document the deputies took home when they went into recess, containing the points on which they had to obtain orders from their principals.

financial, directly affecting a particular province. They did not regard themselves as experts in matters touching the Union as such – the war effort, foreign
affairs – and their votes did not carry much weight. In this hydra-headed
government the power of one man, terminable only by death or revolution,
was created in this way, making the administration of the republic feasible.
It was Oldenbarnevelt who succeeded, where Prince William had failed, in
giving firm leadership to an emergent state. He was able to do so by setting
a different course: he set his compass by Holland's preponderance in a loose
federation instead of by an inherently powerless central body. It was not an
ideal solution but the best available.

To exercise his power Oldenbarnevelt had to see that he was present as
often as possible. In these years he had himself deputed without exception
to the States-General by the States of Holland, sometimes with the addition
'if he should be available'. All the other delegates, or the majority of them,
were his adherents or dependants. The clerk to the States-General, Cornelis
van Aerssen, an indispensable instrument for the control of that body, was
like putty in Oldenbarnevelt's hands, at any rate till 1613, when his son
François lost his honoured position as ambassador in Paris by Oldenbarnevelt's doing. Till then he let the Advocate rummage freely in his papers.
Many minutes of the States-General's resolutions are in Oldenbarnevelt's
handwriting. A scribble like the following typifies the relationship still
better. Oldenbarnevelt wrote the minute of a letter from the States-General
to the assay-master of the Mint, instructing him to examine two dollars as
to their quality. Underneath he wrote:

Mr. Clerk, send this note at once enclosing these two dollars. I shall be glad to
have a copy of the answer of Her Majesty of England to the ambassador of
Poland, if one is ready.

The man who could give such orders certainly had the whip hand. The
treasurer-general, De Bye, noted early on that he had 'most trust and authority'. He gave two secondary reasons, too amusing not to mention. In the first
place, he said, his life had been greatly endangered in Leicester's time, considered greatly to his credit. There was also a bit of jugglery arising from his dual
membership of the States-General and States of Holland: in the first body
he used the authority of Holland and in the States of that province he got his
way by saying that it was the desire of the States-General.

Foreign diplomats too began soon to realize that nothing happened in the
States-General without Oldenbarnevelt. As early as 1589 Bodley was writing
to his minister that the States-General 'proceed very slowly, unless those of
Holland and especially the Advocate are present'.[1]

[1] 11 March (O.S., 21 March N.S.) 1589: Calendar of State Papers, XXIII, 140.

This is just one of many observations of the same trend. Oldenbarnevelt was the dynamo of the assembly, which adjourned its session if he was away from the town for a day or if the States of Holland were very much occupied. Oldenbarnevelt could not be in two places at the same time, even when they were so close together as the two assembly halls to the left and right of the Hofkapel. His ascendancy was not confined to foreign affairs. In June 1595 there was again trouble with Zeeland, mainly about money matters. The Council of State was instructed to send two of its members to settle the affair, but they would not leave without Oldenbarnevelt.

seeing that no one will be able to confront the men of Zeeland with reasons better than the said Advocate . . . regarding the quota, the closing of the harbours of Dunkirk and Nieuwpoort, the tax on peat and other matters . . .

Oldenbarnevelt, not usually keen on missions to the provinces except on military matters, allowed himself to be persuaded and left a few days later. We can see at once how far his authority reached: in almost every sphere, in particular that of finance. Both before and during the Leicester period we have seen Oldenbarnevelt engaged in politics on the grand scale, on which our attention will of necessity have to be concentrated from now on. It is the aspect of his work that is visible from a distance and had the most lasting results. It must not be forgotten though that in all these years his time was largely taken up by questions of quotas and taxes on peat, petty but necessary worries, from which he constantly had to disengage himself in order to attend to larger matters in the troubled field of European politics.

Thus Oldenbarnevelt had his own way in nearly everything concerning the constitution of the growing state, the United Provinces. The position of the Council of State, the States-General's sphere of influence, the preponderance of Holland, the retention of the repartition and quota systems, were all settled, for two centuries, in accordance with his wishes. In a few years he rose to mastery over Holland and thus over the States-General. How did he exercise this mastery?

During most of the daytime he was at the Binnenhof, at the meetings either of the States-General or the States of Holland or their *Gecommitteerde Raden*, the States' executive committee that governed the province during recess. Each body had its assembly hall. It is not known whether the Advocate had a study of his own there, besides the clerk's office of the different bodies. He probably worked at home, where he was often to be found for conferences or meetings. He drafted his letters there himself and had fair copies made by one of the clerks of the States. These clerks must have acquired great skill in deciphering his handwriting, as it is sometimes illegible, full of abbreviations and with letters mixed up.

These clerks worked not only for him but for the secretary of the States. We do not know in detail how the work was divided between them. It seems that Oldenbarnevelt himself 'extended' the more important resolutions passed on the 'points of convocation', the previously circulated agenda, and left the less important ones to the clerk's office. The texts of the edicts in Maurice's name, in fact issued by the States, were of course always drawn up by Oldenbarnevelt. Very important edicts or decrees were made the subject of a committee; the different trends of opinion were represented in it but Oldenbarnevelt was the moving spirit and, as the chief expert, usually had what he wanted. Monetary questions caused him more difficulty as unanimity was required, at least to the extent that opponents were not bound by the decision of the majority. Amsterdam, especially strong because of its high quota (18% to 37% according to the purpose of the apportionment) was often recalcitrant. Leiden tried in vain to introduce a two-thirds majority vote in 1589.

An ancient privilege of the towns of Holland was involved here and Oldenbarnevelt was not in a position to alter one of the main things for which, according to his own contention, the war had been begun. He was to be given special responsibility with regard to these privileges: in 1604 he was appointed registrar of the land tenure department and as such entrusted with the 'keeping of charters and letters'. In 1590 the original privileges of the towns of Holland were transferred from Gouda to The Hague. Most of them were kept at Oldenbarnevelt's house, where they were catalogued after his death. As a matter of fact correspondence and other official papers which now fill the archives of the ministries were kept by Oldenbarnevelt at home. Evidently it did not occur to anyone to ask him to give an account of how he kept them.

It is a source of constant surprise, how the Advocate was able to accumulate so many functions. It is sometimes a mystery that he found time to attend all the meetings, to draw up all important state papers for Holland, as well as many for the States-General, and then to hold the numerous conferences needed in the intrigue for power. It is not surprising that with so much activity he often acted in an authoritarian way: if the Advocate was expecting opposition he confronted the States with a *fait accompli*. In some cases this must have been the reason for by-passing the States, as for instance in the case of help for Kamerijk (Cambrai) in 1593. In other cases criticized by his opponents, it was probably more a question of shortage of time. Nevertheless he took on more and more appointments, partly perhaps because of the emoluments attached, partly no doubt so as to be involved in yet more fields of activity. In 1593 he became Lord Privy Seal of Holland, a function not lucrative in itself, but influential, probably in terms of cash, since all individuals requiring a document under the seal – mostly tenants who wished to transfer their fiefs – were dependent on Oldenbarnevelt's cooperation. It was thus a useful supplement to two other functions filled by Oldenbarnevelt after this period: those of registrar and official dealing with tenancies held in fief from the States as feudal lord.[1]

The most important body to acquire a definite shape at this time under Oldenbarnevelt's impact was the *Gecommitteerde Raden*. Its shape was not entirely logical. Oldenbarnevelt wished to establish a body composed of the minimum number of towns in Holland under his own chairmanship: when the 'big' States were not in session such a body would handle current affairs with ample powers, especially money matters, and also act as an advisory body to Maurice. As such it should greatly have increased Oldenbarnevelt's preponderance. He was not able to effect this, however, and had to put up with a double subdivision.

The first was in West Friesland. As a result of the Spanish occupation of Haarlem and Amsterdam, by which West Friesland had been cut off from the rest of Holland, the towns of North Holland had set up a number of authorities of their own which could not be dissolved immediately after communication with the south was restored in 1577. The chief one was a separate body of *Gecommitteerde Raden* at Hoorn. After the Prince's death West Friesland showed its separatist inclinations clearly, and even appointed its own 'syndic', a position equivalent to that of Oldenbarnevelt in the southern part. It came to a crisis in 1589, when it seemed that West Friesland was to be subordinated to the admiralty of Amsterdam. Enkhuizen, Hoorn and Medemblik stopped attending the meetings of the States of Holland. It was only the fact that Alkmaar and the three towns in Waterland outvoted these three in meetings at Hoorn that prevented complete separation. One commission after another was sent north to bring the secession to an end. One of the commissions was given a memorandum by Oldenbarnevelt from which they had to produce arguments for bringing West Friesland back into the fold. The memorandum contains no mention of any concessions or any understanding of the harassed West Frisians' grievances. It is a sermon in favour of unity, supported by historical references, in particular to the revolt of 1491, and was therefore intended to prove that the West Frisians had always fared badly if separated from the rest of Holland. It was not a felicitous example, as the impoverishment of this district after 1491 was not caused by the extremely short period of separation but by a merciless oppression after

---

[1] *Stadhouder van de lenen*, not to be confused with the much higher office of stadtholder, or governor, of the province.

the revolt had been put down that had left bitter memories in West Friesland. In vain did Oldenbarnevelt introduce a for him unusually pious tone into his sermon. He declared unctuously that the war had been undertaken to propagate God's holy word and to champion the rights and liberties of provinces and towns; thus contrary to his custom making religion – *haec religionis ergo* – a more important reason for war than the privileges – *haec libertatis ergo* – as inscribed on a medal during the siege of Leiden. Once again it was Adriaen van der Mijle who was sent north as mediator.

The West Frisians were given guarantees regarding their admiralty and against being outvoted by Monnikendam and the towns that voted with it. The States of Holland met in session at Alkmaar in 1589 so as to meet them halfway physically and, as it were, symbolically. Peace was thus signed on 20 October, certainly not against Oldenbarnevelt's wishes, but setting aside his excessive presumptions. There was never again any question of a unification of the *Gecommitteerde Raden* till the end of the Republic.

The second subdivision of the *Gecommitteerde Raden*, this time a functional one, was introduced against Oldenbarnevelt's wishes. They acted not only as executive and interim representatives of the States, with Oldenbarnevelt as their natural head, but also as an advisory council to Prince Maurice. The States now suggested a separate commission for this function on which Oldenbarnevelt was not to have a seat. This was impractical for more than one reason, and as a general Maurice was under the jurisdiction of the States-General, not of those of Holland. After three years Oldenbarnevelt managed to have the experiment brought to an end.

Almost all the institutions of the republic were thus created or fashioned by Oldenbarnevelt's hand in the years after Leicester had left. The result was not perfect. Later statesmen were highly critical of Oldenbarnevelt's form of government, certainly quite out of date in the eighteenth century. In the seventeenth century, however, it was adequate. Neither the entourage of Maurice in 1619, nor Frederick Henry, Jan de Witt or William III at the highest peaks of their power tried to alter it in any essential respect. The people of the Netherlands might well revere Oldenbarnevelt as their Lycurgus[1].

The very fact that the Netherlands were a republic at all had been brought bout by Oldenbarnevelt. The word appears at the end of the period we are lealing with. In 1598, in a conversation at Nantes, Oldenbarnevelt expressed it thus: 'L'inclination (meaning of course his own inclination, though he was speaking in the name of the Netherlands people) est plus à une bonne république sous la conduite de quelque seigneur de qualité qu'a une principauté.'

---

[1] *Foppens Bibliotheca Belgica* 574: 'quem suum velut Lycurgum hactenus Batavi coluerant'.

It is no exaggeration then to regard Oldenbarnevelt as the founder of the Republic of the United Netherlands. All the institutions existing on his appointment as Advocate: States-General, States of Holland, Council of State, *Gecommitteerde Raden*, Stadtholdership, fitted well into a monarchical system of government: it was Oldenbarnevelt who changed their direction to one consonant only with a republic. This view was not always taken later, and institutions from after 1589 were backdated to a time when monarchy was taken for granted. That is partly because the present meaning of the word republic only grew up slowly, as a result of more accurate study of Roman historians. As early as 1580 the States of Zeeland spoke of a 'joint republic', meaning the Holland–Zeeland community under the Union of Delft. But there is no question here of a contrast with a monarchy. When De Bye, writing about 1620, calls the Netherlands of 1585 'a republic in which the States remained sovereign', in contrast to the monarchical government of England, he is committing an anachronism.

There was one more thing that Oldenbarnevelt perhaps did not establish but to a great extent promoted: the principle of the constitutional state. The rule of law was on the point of disappearing throughout the whole of Europe under the effect of rising absolutism. In the Netherlands alone its strength was growing. The Advocate of Holland, so conservative, indeed reactionary in many ways, thus pointed to the future, the foundation of the liberal era.[1]

All this was conditional on the preservation of the young state against the *reconquista* attempts of the Spanish crown. It will be seen how this was managed by a combination of incomprehensible miracles and very comprehensible opportunism.

[1] Clark, 'Birth of the Dutch Republic', p. 195.

CHAPTER 5

A turn in the fortunes of war

THE future looked gloomy for the Netherlands when Geertruidenberg changed hands. Not only this secession but also the departure of a number of their best troops for Portugal had weakened the military power of the States. Parma's troops, on the other hand, still had their reinforcements, brought in to support the Armada, and nothing seemed to stand in the way of a victorious advance across the rivers in the following summer.

It was the course of events in France that saved the Netherlands and made the establishment of an independent state possible in the ensuing years. Since 1585 one of a succession of religious wars had been raging in that country, this time with Henry of Navarre, heir to the throne since the death of Anjou, at the head of the Huguenots, and Henry III, constrained against his will to be head of the Catholic Ligue. At the end of November 1587 Navarre gained a shattering victory at the battle of Coutras. If he won the war too there was every likelihood that France, thus become much more powerful, would join England and the Netherlands in an anti-Spanish coalition, so that Philip II decided to use part of Parma's troops to help the Ligue. A year later, on 23 December 1588, Henry III succeeded in cutting loose from the Guises' domination by having two of the three brothers murdered at Blois. Parma was now ordered by the King, greatly against his inclination, to reduce his offensive operations in the Netherlands to a minimum. The attitude of the Netherlands towards the French Protestants also underwent a noticeable change, in which Oldenbarnevelt's guidance can be seen.

When in the spring of 1588 an ambassador came from the King of Navarre to ask for help and at the same time to propose a general Protestant alliance, he was received with due honours at a formal session of the States of Holland. But he obtained less than he wanted. Oldenbarnevelt's reaction was in this vein: we in the Netherlands are full of sympathy with the struggle in which your King is engaged with the King of France, the captive of the Guises. We will give you some surreptitious help, a small sum of money and a few cannons. But we cannot and must not side with you openly. The King of France must sooner or later counterbalance the King of Spain in Europe. We must not risk that possible alliance by openly fomenting a rebellious faction.

That was the policy towards France inaugurated by the Prince after the massacre of St Bartholomew's Day. The Anjou episode had been its logical outcome. It was to be Oldenbarnevelt's policy as long as he was in power, in spite of growing and, towards the end, embittered opposition from theological Calvinists and emotional anti-Spaniards. There was not much opposition in 1588 and a lot to be said for a policy of caution, with the Armada approaching and every penny needed for self-defence.

The resolution in which the States-General granted the relatively small sum of 90,000 livres is a little masterpiece of Oldenbarnevelt's statecraft. Ample expressions of goodwill gloss over the fact that the Netherlands were unwilling to accept the proposed alliance. It was put so nicely that the ambassador could only show gratitude and satisfaction. The objective had been attained: the friendship of the rebels' leader, who was also heir to the throne, had been preserved without affronting the King of France.

These considerations no longer applied when the Guises had been murdered and it soon became apparent that the King would have to form an alliance with his brother-in-law of Navarre. Arms and money were at once voted in support of the anti-Ligue governors of Boulogne and Dieppe, partly because of the Netherlands' vital interest in keeping these ports, so close to Belgium, out of the hands of the Ligue.

In the first few months of 1589 Henry III advanced with Navarre on Paris, which was in the hands of the Ligue. Before he could begin a serious siege he was murdered on 1 August. Now there was no more need for either Philip or the States to exercise caution. Henry IV was now the legal King of France, and it was just as obviously in the Netherlands' interest to support him in this position as it was in Philip's to oppose him, by means of the Ligue and its head, the surviving Guise brother, Mayenne. Parma was therefore given orders to concentrate his whole war effort on France instead of on the Netherlands. The first result was the relief of the little town of Heusden, suddenly deserted by the Spanish troops which, after some months of siege, were diverted to France.

The Netherlands' assistance to the lawful King had of its nature to be more limited and slower. There was still no question of military support. This came from Elizabeth. She sent her favourite, Willoughby, who could do with some rehabilitation after his failure in the Netherlands, with a fair number of troops to Normandy, where he arrived just too late to help Henry IV, on 21 September 1589, in his somewhat unprofitable victory at Arques. The battle is briefly described in the Resolutions of the States of Holland, in which from now on can regularly be heard the echo of Holland's rejoicing at the successes of their French ally.

Help from Holland also came too late for the battle. On 18 August, when the news of Henry III's murder reached The Hague, a new ambassador from the King of Navarre, La Thuillerie, had just arrived. He had come to ask for a subsidy of 50,000 *écus*. The States-General were still unaware of Parma's plans and the extent of the relief it would afford them. The finances of the inland provinces were still in a bad way too: Gelderland and Overijsel were contributing nothing and Utrecht with reluctance to the cost of the war. So when the States-General decided to grant only 30,000 *écus* of the amount requested, Utrecht, which had voted against it, refused to bear its share. This naturally caused delay, particularly because Friesland had been put down for double the quota of Utrecht, and on the basis of this not very objective calculation claimed the right not to pay as long as Utrecht did not do so.

After his accession Henry IV sent a second envoy, Saldaigne, to act as receiver of any amount voted and at once return via England with as much money as he could acquire from the States, as the King needed it badly for paying his troops. As Utrecht had refused and those provinces willing to pay had not the cash in hand, it was three weeks till Saldaigne could leave The Hague. Then he had only had payment of the quota from Holland, £57,826 5s 2¼d., or about 65%; it is not clear how this far from round sum was calculated. He hoped to pick up the Zeeland quota while passing through Middelburg, the Frisian contribution would be forwarded later, and the Council of State had, after some hesitation, stood surety for the Utrecht quota. What this meant exactly from the point of view of accountancy is not evident. The Council had no reserves available it could freely dispose of. It is likely that the members personally guaranteed an eventual grant by the province of Utrecht, amounting to only 5% of the total. It often happened in Oldenbarnevelt's time that personal credit was used to further affairs of state.

A matter like this involving a few thousand pounds could therefore take up quite a lot of Oldenbarnevelt's time and diplomatic powers, for we need not doubt that it was he who induced the Council of State, Friesland and finally Utrecht too, to agree to this ingenious solution.

Oldenbarnevelt and La Thuillerie discussed the great anti-Spanish alliance – anti-Spanish, no longer Protestant. Both La Thuillerie and Oldenbarnevelt surely realized that if Henry wanted to be King of all France and all Frenchmen he could not follow a Protestant policy, even though the former had not been in touch with the King since his succession. We can imagine the discussions between Oldenbarnevelt and La Thuillerie to some extent in the light of his subsequent policy regarding the alliance. He must have felt more drawn towards an anti-Spanish alliance than one based on religion, though even for this he cannot have felt much enthusiasm. Alliances have the troublesome characteristic of binding their signatories in a future they cannot foresee. If one party reluctantly keeps to his contract he does so at the expense of his own defence measures. If he does not, the other party is angry. He professes great loyalty to the alliance, but if he presently finds himself in the same position he is not to be counted on. In 1598 we shall see Oldenbarnevelt bewailing French disloyalty in concluding the Peace of Vervins contrary to the 1596 treaty. In 1648 – a long time afterwards on this occasion, but retribution is not always swift – the Netherlands concluded the Peace of Munster contrary to the terms of the treaty of 1635. Oldenbarnevelt was therefore more in favour of fostering a spirit of joint resistance to the threatened domination of Europe by the Habsburgs. It could be fostered by way of drumming up recruits for the great alliance and no harm in this. Oldenbarnevelt had done so as far as he was able in Germany, Scotland and elsewhere. But when it took a long time for the alliance to be formed he cannot have been sorry, and the somewhat shaky *Union* of German Protestant Princes was entirely the work of Henry IV, not of Oldenbarnevelt, who was at most a benevolent spectator. Herein lies the difference of temperament between the two leaders, with Elizabeth, of the opposition to the Habsburgs. Both Henry IV and Oldenbarnevelt were realists, but all his life the Gascon mixed his realism with chimeras – or rather fine phrases. What was missing in Oldenbarnevelt – and this was an advantage as well as a disadvantage – was the *panache* to fire the enthusiasm of his followers.

That *panache blanc* was soon to glitter in Henry's finest feat of arms, the battle of Ivry on 14 March 1590. The victory was gained without any actual help from the allies: Willoughby's expedition, arriving too late for Arques, had taken ship again before Ivry. The financial help from the States, not completely paid up, did however enable the King to recruit German auxiliaries, who had a substantial share in his success. Mayenne, on the other hand, had been given a considerable contingent of auxiliaries by Parma; it is certainly the absence of these forces that brought about, not the surprise of Breda but the retention of the surprised town. Oldenbarnevelt could be satisfied: rather niggardly help had scored 'surprising' results.

Saldaigne returned in the summer of 1590 to collect the rest of the subsidy of 30,000 *écus* granted. He was successful in this after a two months' tour of the provincial capitals; in Middelburg he pleaded for permission to export food and war *matériel* to Dieppe, a town to which a list of *licenten* tariffs, drawn up by the States-General, had forbidden exports of any kind.[1]

The *Gecommitteerde Raden* of Zeeland, identical with the admiralty in

---

[1] The list of convoy taxes was graded according to the port of destination: Dieppe was not on the list, which means that exportation to it was prohibited.

charge of the collection of these taxes, were not able to resist Saldaigne's eloquence, and informed the States-General of this on 29 September 1590.

Oldenbarnevelt was faced with a dilemma. From the point of view of foreign policy it was quite justifiable to accede to Saldaigne's request. Dieppe was Henry IV's chief base in the north-west. It was threatened on all sides by the Ligue and the provisions, the import of which was requested at a reduced *licent*, were of prime necessity for the preservation of the town. On the other hand the States-General, to whom Saldaigne had first submitted the question, had rightly or wrongly passed a contrary resolution on 3 August, and for reasons of domestic policy it was most desirable to support their authority. The States-General therefore resolved, after deliberation and by a majority vote, to quash the Zeeland decision and point out to the Middelburg admiralty that they were to be given instructions by no one but the States-General and the superintendent body, and in particular not by the *Gecommitteerde Raden* of Zeeland. At this theoretical distinction the members of the Middelburg admiralty, at the same time *Gecommitteerde Raden*, probably laughed up their sleeves.

Oldenbarnevelt therefore set principle above an incidental foreign interest.

Saldaigne obtained satisfaction on almost all the other points, thanks no doubt to Oldenbarnevelt; payment of another subsidy for war *matériel* of which the King was in urgent need; naval help for the Seine and Loire areas and strict maintenance of the embargo on exports to Ligue towns.

During these negotiations the joyful tidings were received that Parma had left for France on 27 July at the head of an army of 14,000 foot and 2,800 horse. They must have made the States-General feel more generous to the envoy, though at the same time realizing that they would have to take advantage of Parma's withdrawal by an offensive that would also cost money. It would take time to prepare as well, since the news of Parma's departure seems to have taken the States unawares. It shows that their intelligence service was far from efficient and is also perhaps an indication that Oldenbarnevelt's understanding of French affairs was still limited, for after Ivry the conquering King had begun a second siege of Paris. The town was hard pressed and cut off from all access. Its loss would be an irremediable blow to the Spanish cause. Only Parma could save it and had no choice but to advance upon it. But Maurice was not yet ready. He had just failed in an assault on Nijmegen, his first offensive of this period, except for the surprise of Breda.

How could he make further use of Parma's departure? Maurice wanted to aim for the towns on the IJsel, but he was not the war planner: the direction of the crushing offensive intended by the States was partly determined by large-scale policy. Elizabeth, uneasy about Parma's threat, in which her own auxiliaries were involved, was repeatedly insisting on a southward offensive. Oldenbarnevelt set out to army headquarters at the head of practically the entire States-General to discuss plans with Maurice. That was on 13 August, but it is not till 27 September that Maurice in Brabant satisfied English requirements. The war season was nearly over and there was not more time for spectacular successes, though reports from France gave hope that Parma would not return so soon. His campaign in France was a success, but dearly bought. He relieved and provisioned Paris, made his entry on 19 September and reinforced Spanish prestige in the town, an important move in view of the impending election of a Catholic King. On the other hand Maurice was able to terrorize Brabant with impunity, though without doing much damage, and the majority of Parma's veterans did not come back from the French expedition. Only 4,000 men followed him on his entry into Brussels on 4 December: the hospitals in Artois and Hainault were full of wounded. If an expedition to France should be needed again in 1591 – and there was every indication that it would be – the Netherlands would certainly be able to take much greater advantage of Parma's absence. Oldenbarnevelt determined not to miss this chance.

The close interaction of French and Netherlands interests during Parma's first French campaign induced Henry IV to set up permanent diplomatic representation in the Netherlands. In October 1590 he sent Turenne (later Duke of Bouillon) to England to coordinate the war effort. He was accompanied by Paul de Choart, Seigneur de Buzanval, who had often acted as agent in England. Turenne was to go on from England to Germany, while Buzanval was to act as permanent agent in the Netherlands. Buzanval was regarded as a henchman of Du Plessis Mornay, with whom he had been a student at Heidelberg at the same time as Oldenbarnevelt; they must have known each other there. He was a Protestant from the neighbourhood of Paris and like Mornay belonged to the National–Protestant group, always trying to avoid bringing political differences with Catholics to a head and setting loyalty to King and country above the immediate party interests of the Huguenots. Turenne was as a rule the head of the other faction, the militant Huguenots who, some from religious fanaticism, others from political ambition, usually felt more Protestant than French. At the moment the two factions were working in harmony, but it was plain that both Henry IV and Oldenbarnevelt would have to rely more on the national than the religious faction.

Owing to their views on the prime importance of politics, the two alumni of Heidelberg, Oldenbarnevelt and Buzanval, were predestined to get on well together. There was also a third reason. Oldenbarnevelt was not eloquent.

Speeches by him which have been preserved are long-winded, full of historical digressions and constantly betraying suppressed irritation at the stupidity of his audience. He therefore often had trouble in putting across his French policy, in itself sensible and moderate. That French policy, as we have seen, consisted in providing the strongest possible help to the legitimate monarch, involved in civil war. Without neglecting its impact on the conduct of the war in the north, this help was primarily intended with an eye to the future. Gratitude and self-interest were to combine in making the King of a united France the paladin of the anti-Habsburg cause in Europe. It was of course the policy Buzanval was charged with impressing on the States. Buzanval however was eloquent. It must have been a pleasure to listen to him, even for those to whom the sound of the words said more than their meaning – for one must not overestimate the knowledge of French possessed by the States deputies at this time.

At his first audience, introducing another request for a subsidy, he gave a flowery exposition of the reasons for French and Netherlands solidarity in the war against Spain and why the Netherlands were better served by the ultimate victory of Henry IV than by local military success in the country itself. He referred to history, but not beyond the negotiations with Anjou – mentioned by name – which imperilled the liberty of the Netherlands in a desperate and unsuccessful attempt to make France take part in the war. Well now – according to Buzanval, and it is as if one can hear Oldenbarnevelt speaking: 'You now have what you desire: France is involved with Spain in a cruel war, and that without your having risked anything by it.' For this reason, he continued: 'the continual assaults which they made on these noble provinces (*ces nobles provinces*) have been weakened and postponed, so that they have quitted what they thought to be their own to attack that of another, to which they have no right.'

Noble provinces! The States were not used to being addressed like this by the English envoys or by their master Oldenbarnevelt. Some people thought he was laying it on too thick and Duyck writes scornfully about Buzanval's 'useless and unimportant words'. But he could be harsh when occasion demanded and even when it did not. He had made his position in England impossible by indiscreet observations on the more ludicrous aspects of the Virgin Queen. That must have appealed to Oldenbarnevelt too, and the two statesmen were soon on cordial terms. Buzanval never went to the States-General without first sounding the Advocate. He was soon entirely familiar with the labyrinth of the Netherlands constitution and the peculiarities of the national character. A remark such as the following is revealing both of the writer and his subject: 'Le fondement de leur Estat', he wrote on 20 August

1597 to Du Plessis Mornay, 'est la Religion, mais en effet y a plus d'autre chose que de celle-là.' Surprisingly, he adds, 'Ils sont du naturel des peuples qui, en laissant le milieu, suivent ordinairement les extrémités.'

The subsidy was granted and the English troops, sent in 1591 by Elizabeth first to Brittany and then to Normandy, were in a certain sense assistance from the Netherlands, being largely drawn from there and leaving smaller forces behind than provided for by the Treaty of Nonsuch. The Netherlands constitution and the poverty of the inland provinces did indeed cause a delay of four months before the 100,000 guilders asked for by Buzanval left the Netherlands – a delay with serious consequences for Henry IV. The German troops to be recruited with this money could not set out before the autumn of 1591, so that it was too late for Henry to capture Rouen. Masterly manoeuvring in Parma's second French expedition in December 1591 succeeded in provisioning the town, so that Henry nearly gave up hope. By providing guns and ammunition and by brilliant diversionary tactics along the IJsel Oldenbarnevelt had made a great effort to help the King take Rouen, so important for Rotterdam's trade.

Oldenbarnevelt then went further. For the first time he considered the possibility of supporting the King not only by money, arms, ammunition and warships, but by an auxiliary corps in the Netherlands service. The money was there. The fall of Antwerp, followed by famine in the south and another famine in the Mediterranean countries had caused an unprecedented trade boom in Holland and Zeeland, affecting not only the convoy tax and *licenten* collected but other taxes as well. Furthermore, after the change from defensive to offensive strategy, levies, plundering and destruction had greatly decreased in Friesland, Overijsel, Utrecht and Gelderland. Holland and Zeeland therefore urged that the customary annual contribution to the cost of the war in France should be doubled and Oldenbarnevelt took great personal care to secure a vote for an auxiliary corps under Maurice's twenty-five-year-old cousin, Philip of Nassau. It was intended not merely to help in the capture of Rouen but either to pin down Parma's army in France longer than he had planned, or even to defeat it, thus making it possible for the campaign in 1592 to be more successful than that of the previous year.

Oldenbarnevelt had his way, both with regard to the despatch of auxiliaries and the doubled subsidy, but not with the results expected. When Philip of Nassau, after much delay, at last approached Rouen in March 1592, exactly two months after taking ship at Brill, the town had offered such stout resistance as a result of Parma's aid that the King had to give up the siege. He asked the States-General if he could keep Philip in France for a time for another undertaking, but Oldenbarnevelt could not spare the troops for so long and they were home again in August, just in time to provide rearguard help in Maurice's attack on Koevorden.

Parma died on 3 December, just as he was preparing for another expedition into France. It set out under much less capable leadership, and when Buzanval, given the rank of ambassador in April, made a fresh request in August for a subsidy, earmarked for raising a regiment of infantry 3,000 strong, the States-General kept him waiting six months for their answer. Oldenbarnevelt then reduced the subsidy to two-thirds of the sum requested, considering a regiment of 2,000 men sufficient after Parma's death. He was right in taking this risk. The Spanish expedition achieved nothing this time and Parma's interim successor was recalled when Maurice started to besiege Geertruidenberg in the spring. The focal point of Oldenbarnevelt's concern with France shifted to the political plane. He was confronted with an action of Henry IV, his reaction to which would be a test of the Netherlands' friendship for France. The step was Henry's second conversion to Catholicism, and Oldenbarnevelt withstood the test brilliantly, though at the expense of his popularity.

Since the death of the shadow king, Charles of Bourbon, the Ligue no longer had a candidate for the crown usurped by Navarre. It could also be said that there were too many candidates, whose mutual rivalry precluded the success of any one. Philip II decided in the winter of 1592–3 to resolve the impasse in favour of his daughter, the Infanta Isabella. This placed the nationalist Ligue members in a quandary. Their leader Mayenne was too much of a lightweight to put in the scales even against Isabella. The Spaniards were detested everywhere. The 'usurper' was, as a Protestant, unacceptable. It looked as if they would have to accept the Spanish candidate and by so doing brand themselves as traitors. Henry IV saved them from this dilemma. He caused a report to be spread that he considered the time had come for his long-contemplated conversion. The Ligue reacted immediately by making the States-General of France, assembled for the election of a new King, rise with nothing accomplished; the Paris Parliament, till recently still terrorized by the extremists, plucked up courage and refused to recognize the States-General as competent to elect. The Ligue gave up the hope of winning the civil war and continued it with the sole object of selling their submission to the converted but still suspect King as dearly as possible. At the moment they were asking too much and Henry offering too little. On 26 June 1593 Buzanval was able to reassure the Netherlands States-General concerning rumours of peace: the war would go on as usual and would the States please continue their assistance.

Perhaps the States wanted to, but they were disturbed by these negotiations, though so far unsuccessful, and by Henry's promise, made in the course of them, to be instructed in the Catholic religion by the prelates of his kingdom. The States therefore decided to send a new agent to France with instructions to investigate, as far as possible, what was going on in the country.

The choice, one which Oldenbarnevelt never had seriously to regret, fell upon Lieven Calvart. In the four years that Calvart still had to live he inundated Oldenbarnevelt, in personal and official letters, with a large quantity of useful details which formed the basis of the latter's French policy. Unlike his rather stiff predecessor he was soon in high favour with Henry IV, which could only be an advantage. Less advantageous was his own bias in favour of the King, so that it was only shortly before his death that he saw through the apparent candour disguising Gascon cunning.

The envoy's ingenuousness was, however, not altogether unsuited to Oldenbarnevelt's book. He was able to temper the excessive enthusiasm of Calvart's despatches with his own natural scepticism and still maintain enough arguments to justify his consistently pro-French policy.

He had great need of such arguments at this time. The King's conversion was a bitter pill for the States-General, with their ever increasing number of inveterate Calvinists. Outside the States there were many who would not swallow it at all. What had become of solidarity between allies when one of them defected to the Antichrist? It could only have been the prompting of Satan. How else to explain that someone who had once seen the light of the Gospel should relapse into the superstitions of popery? People must have spoken thus, in church and at their work: their comments have not been preserved for us, as Oldenbarnevelt and his adherents took care to suppress them.

Oldenbarnevelt was in quite a different mood. He must have regarded the conversion as a new obstacle to the realization of his French policy and as such deplored it. But from the point of view not of domestic but of foreign, European, policy, he may have welcomed it, though with reservations. Welcomed it, because what he needed was a counterpoise, not only to Philip but even more to Elizabeth. It had much better be the powerful and generally acknowledged King of the first state in Europe than a partisan leader, however likeable and heroic. A partisan leader was largely dependent in war on the help of the States and what Elizabeth had to offer: the former dependence was financially ruinous for the States, the latter undesirable politically. The King of Europe's foremost state could make Elizabeth change her tune and make some return to the Republic for the help so loyally given for four years. Would he do so? Could his gratitude be relied on? It could not be relied but speculated on. Gratitude was in France's interest, which was not served by pressure on three sides from the Spanish empire. Far-sighted French policy would always in the long run have to be anti-Spanish as long as this pressure continued. Indeed, for more than a hundred years the world could witness France's efforts to break the Spanish grip in a series of wars, with short breathing spaces, only to end when Spain, powerless, was on the eve of disintegration.

It was indeed the long run to which this prognosis applied. But there were short-term considerations to be dealt with, which Oldenbarnevelt may have underestimated. In both the long and the short run, however, it was of the first importance, whether one welcomed or deplored Henry's reversion, not to jeopardize relations with Philip's mortal enemy by tactless reproaches. The States of Holland, in a long session on the subject on 16 and 17 July 1593, did not at first appreciate this; they contemplated, following Elizabeth's example, sending an agent to France, actually accompanied by a professor of theology to dissuade the King from his impious intent. Fortunately Oldenbarnevelt managed to prevent anything so preposterous. The States' resolution passed at his instigation, on the other hand, is of exemplary moderation and as such won much admiration from Elizabeth. The States expressed their regret and concern at the conversion, but resolved to pray and leave the outcome to God, and not to propose a mission to France. The town governors were to see to it that 'the said affair should not be spoken of but with all modesty and discretion', while the ministers were ordered to keep quiet about it in the pulpit and to continue to remember the King of France in their prayers.

The preachers can hardly have been pleased at this admonition. They were told to be quiet while Satan's friend in France was given their compulsory prayers and the flattery of those in office. Once more Oldenbarnevelt was too clever for the people. He was proud of it and boasted of it at a most unsuitable time, namely during his interrogation in 1618. He spoke of his conversation with Henry IV at Nantes in 1598, and of how the latter had stated

that it was agreeable to him that his Dr Morlans, sent to this country after his conversion, and being welcomed in Zeeland with a most vehement sermon against this conversion, in Holland on the other hand by means of him who spoke it was ordered that the same course was not followed, which was very agreeable to him, as touching his honour.

The judges whom Oldenbarnevelt was addressing at that moment were the spiritual descendants of the scolding Zeeland and muzzled Holland preachers. Oldenbarnevelt's behaviour in obtaining the friendship of the apostate King, plus a not inconsiderable *douceur*, did not appeal to them at all. He was right, if not in the acceptance of the present, at any rate in gaining his friendship. But there is often mortal danger in being right.

Morlans, speaking on 26 August in the States-General, conveyed the message that in spite of the armistice concluded on 31 July the war would be carried on; however, Oldenbarnevelt learnt at the same time from Calvart that Henry had sent a secret envoy to Spain to negotiate peace. The truth was that France, exhausted by more than thirty years of religious strife, needed peace badly, but it was only to be had through strong pressure on the Spanish Netherlands. Such pressure presupposed active help from England and the Republic, help that in its turn would only be given on the understanding that France was not going to make peace. So for the next five years we shall see the French King playing a double game, further complicated by the fact that though he was not always sincere he was seldom entirely insincere, being by nature pugnacious, hating the Spaniards for entirely comprehensible reasons, and afraid of trouble with the Huguenots if he showed Spain too much favour; moreover his repeatedly proclaimed gratitude to the Republic still had a solid basis in the lively expectation of benefits to come.[1]

Oldenbarnevelt always seems a little optimistic in playing this equivocal game, but not to the extent of losing his head. There were critics enough in the Netherlands who grudged every penny spent on the untrustworthy King; in view of the, in this respect, democratic nature of the 'government by persuasion' Oldenbarnevelt was constantly having to justify, to himself and others, continued confidence in the man most unpopular with the Netherlands public. In his own rather lax and indifferent way Maurice was one of the critics, especially of Oldenbarnevelt's attitude towards the Huguenots, which was too cautious in his view. The two Huguenot leaders, Bouillon and La Trémouille, married two of Maurice's half-sisters in 1595 and 1597. With other Huguenots such as Du Plessis Mornay, Rosny (later Duke of Sully) and Buzanval, they were the principal instigators and instruments of Franco-Netherlands cooperation. Oldenbarnevelt, however, did not give way to the natural inclination of some in the country to identify themselves with the Huguenots. They no longer had the King's ear as they used to. What was worse, he had every reason to distrust them. The ministers in the south-west of France did not all practise the discretion enjoined upon their colleagues in Holland by Oldenbarnevelt. The French Huguenots felt they had been betrayed and were the victims of political horse-trading, their leader having declared that Paris was well worth a Mass. They became divided among themselves: the moderates, or those whose employment depended on the King's favour, were more inclined to trust him. The majority, including the

---

[1] Chamfort's definition.

high Protestant nobility, formed a pressure group and openly sought support from England and Holland. Elizabeth consoled them with kind words and an occasional protest to the French King. Oldenbarnevelt would not commit himself, especially as the activities of the Huguenot leaders began to assume treasonable shape. In this he was continuing the policy of William of Orange, who had sooner cooperated with Anjou and Henry III than with Navarre and Condé. The result was in both cases the same: loss of popularity with the man in the street.

Opposition showed itself first when Buzanval asked for help on 8 December 1593. It took Oldenbarnevelt a long time and all his personal influence to get the subsidy voted, in the teeth of an unfavourable report from the Council of State.

In 1594 one high noble after another and one town before another submitted to the recatholicized King.

The most important and expensive conversion was that of Paris, which the King entered on 22 March. The same evening he wrote a triumphant letter to the States-General, which Buzanval was not able to deliver to them till 9 April. They had known of this success for some days, which led Oldenbarnevelt to propose two measures with unsuspected consequences. One was that 'tokens of joy' were prescribed throughout the Netherlands on Sunday 24 April. It was an innovation that was not welcomed everywhere. Religiously minded people regarded the turncoat's triumph as anything but one of God's blessings; it was not psalms of praise but the reverse that they would have liked to sing. The politically minded were afraid of too swift a victory by Henry IV, enabling him to make a peace by which the entire dreaded power of the new regent, Ernest of Austria, would be turned on to the unfortunate Netherlands. These Machiavellians were glad, now and later, of every Spanish conquest in France, as keeping France engaged in war. So the compulsory rejoicing certainly did not add to the popularity of those who ordained it, and Oldenbarnevelt, though in the right, began to become the prophet not without honour save in his own country.

The other measure was to cause still more trouble and grief. Another auxiliary expedition, this time of 500 horse and 3,000 foot, was voted on Oldenbarnevelt's insistence. They were to be sent on demand, but only after the successful conclusion of the siege of Groningen that had just begun. But when the town was captured at the end of July the troops stayed where they were. Henry asked for them several times, but without saying where he wanted to use them, on what date he expected them or how he would receive them. Oldenbarnevelt rightly refused to send his soldiers on these terms. It was not a matter of indifference to him where they were employed. If they could harass the Archduke on his frontiers, as near as possible to States territory, this was of course preferable to their being used to besiege some town deep in the interior of France. War, therefore, ought to be waged in Artois and Hainault, and this involved an open declaration of war by Henry IV on Spain. Although the earliest possible peace would have been welcome to France in its exhausted state, Henry had promised to declare war on Spain before the beginning of the next campaign. It was in the first place the result of intrigue by those around him, especially the Huguenots among them under their acknowledged leader, the Duke of Bouillon. But apart from this, constant pressure from Elizabeth and Oldenbarnevelt, holding out hopes of grand military victories, was an important factor in Henry's decision. He later reproached Calvart, saying that he had only declared war on account of his attractive offers. It was of course an exaggeration but it is a fact that when Oldenbarnevelt grasped that the King badly wanted auxiliaries, Calvart was ordered to make the condition that their despatch should be contingent on a promise by Henry to declare war on the Netherlands frontiers. Henry was somewhat alarmed and this may be one reason why there were no concrete plans till September. Meanwhile, after the capture of Groningen, the States had disbanded ten newly recruited German companies. They received a letter that Calvart had written on 3 July to Oldenbarnevelt personally, saying that after the capture of Groningen the troops requested would no longer be necessary, as the season was advancing and Henry's plans were constantly changing. Though he wrote quite differently to the States-General the next day, Oldenbarnevelt gathered that the more or less confidential letter of 3rd more truly represented the state of affairs. The troops earmarked for auxiliaries could therefore be used for another 'exploit'. There was a delay of another six weeks, to the annoyance of Maurice, who had returned to The Hague on 28 August, in the middle of the good war season, to accept with his usual surliness the honours due for the capture of Groningen. At last, when Calvart wrote that they were not getting down to business, it was decided on 24 September to use the money and troops intended for France for an expedition nearer home: to invade the south-east corner of Gelderland and besiege Groenlo.

In spite of the lateness of the season Maurice hastened to make every preparation for the siege. On 4 October he came to take leave of the States-General. But since the day before the situation had completely changed there: Buzanval had at last received letters from his King with detailed plans for the use of the auxiliaries allocated: they were to join a newly recruited French army in Luxemburg under the Duke of Bouillon as soon as possible; it was apparent from Calvart's letters that after the arrival of the auxiliaries a declaration of war on Spain could be confidently expected.

Maurice left for Arnhem, where he was to meet his troops, knowing that he would have to send twenty-two companies to France, again under Philip of Nassau, but assuming that it could be done after the capture of Groenlo, which he thought he could accomplish in a short time. Buzanval travelled after him, however, to tell him that this was not the idea. Henry had been awaiting the auxiliaries for a long time and they should set out immediately, if the promise was not to be broken. Oldenbarnevelt made no objection: the siege of Groenlo could be continued with the remaining forces. Maurice did not agree. The outcome was that the troops left and the capture of Groenlo was deferred for three years. Maurice was angry with Oldenbarnevelt for first letting him make unnecessary preparations and then demanding the militarily impossible of him.

Both the military and, with one exception, the political results of the expedition were as Maurice and Oldenbarnevelt had foreseen. Militarily it was a complete fiasco. Soldiers, not used to fighting so far from home, deserted. The troops narrowly escaped destruction by a strong Spanish army that tried to block their way. On arrival they were neither fed nor otherwise provided for; they took to plundering and were reduced by their hardships. Bouillon's army was small and unpaid. Comradeship left everything to be desired. Finally Philip of Nassau was forced to return his troops by sea, as otherwise they would have deserted *en bloc*. The bitterness against Oldenbarnevelt felt by the officers and men can be better imagined than described. Once again Oldenbarnevelt's French policy had earned him the hatred of influential people.

The King was satisfied. He kept his promise and declared war on Spain. When in the spring he received absolution from Clement VIII and allowed the head of the League to be restored to favour, there was no need for his allies to fear an imminent peace. The expectation of a joint French and Netherlands attack on the Southern Netherlands seemed likely of fulfilment. The extravagantly wasted soldiers had paid a political dividend.

Only with regard to Elizabeth does Oldenbarnevelt seem to have made a mistake, and then only a short-term one. She had welcomed Philip of Nassau's first expedition, and even suggested doubling the contingent sent. Her reaction to the second expedition was different: it had taken place without her agreement, far away from the maritime provinces of France where her interests lay. The States-General, she wrote, evidently had too many troops, so she would withdraw her own auxiliaries from the Netherlands and expected the States at once to start repayment of the advances, which since 1586 had reached staggering proportions. The reason for this change of attitude lay in the way relations between England and Holland had developed.

In this period (1589–95) policy towards England bears Oldenbarnevelt's stamp much less than that towards France. Not that he did not lead it. It was he who conferred with the English diplomatic representatives, alone or at the head of a States-General commission. Conversely, if envoys were sent from the Netherlands to England it was he who drew up, or helped to draw up, their brief. All foreign affairs were his department, with England as much as any other. But there was a noticeable relaxation since the great days of Leicester and Willoughby; not in the sense of a weak or timorous attitude, but a relaxation of tension. The great problem had been whether the Netherlands could maintain their independence of their powerful English ally. Oldenbarnevelt had found a solution to it which he had made to prevail with passion and ability. His success caused a slackening of the reins. The English were continually making certain claims to suzerainty. On one occasion Elizabeth's admirals called the Netherlanders 'allies and almost, as it were, subjects of Her Majesty'. The English government persisted in intervening in the trial of Leicester's followers, though ceasing to try to bring them into power. Oldenbarnevelt rejected any claim to supremacy on principle. He was prepared to spare the lives of the losers in exchange for a formal disavowal from Elizabeth. The Queen was reluctant to agree to this and when in 1590 Wilkes eventually produced it, it was rather late in the day and Oldenbarnevelt was no longer greatly interested. His position was indeed much strengthened since the removal of the Geertruidenberg problem; the States-General were undisputed masters of the Republic and with the fall of Breda the offensive stage of the Eighty Years' War had started. He could therefore bargain from strength and made full use of this fact in the principal problem affecting relations with England at this time: English interference with Dutch shipping.

Netherlands shipping in the Channel suffered heavy losses at the hands of the English, along whose coast they sailed. They were brought about by three different categories of agencies, sometimes overlapping. First, there were genuine pirates, uninhibited by either law or justice and sometimes protected even by English government circles and nobility. Secondly, there were reprisals, a word that had another meaning than the present one. Freebooters were equipped by English merchants and sought to indemnify themselves for losses incurred in the Netherlands; for capturing Dutch ships they obtained letters of marque from the English government, saving them from execution if they were captured by the Netherlanders. The final category was the most dangerous. This was the capture of ships and seizure of their cargoes, regarded as contraband if the ships were sailing to or from Spanish domains. It was an insoluble problem: England could neither be defied nor pacified. The English government did not want the Spaniards provided with military supplies by their subjects or by their allies, especially since it had been discovered that the Armada had been equipped with wood, pitch and rope almost entirely conveyed on Netherlands ships from the Baltic. When about 1590 a shortage of grain occurred in the Mediterranean area, it was placed as a matter of course on the extensive English contraband list, which comprised the most important goods for trade with Spain. Oldenbarnevelt produced exhaustive arguments in the spirit of his well-known memorandum of 1586.[1] Pamphlets said to have been printed on the instructions of the States-General and full of virulent attacks on English 'piracy' appeared in Zeeland.[2] One delegation after another was sent to England to explain why the Netherlands could not relinquish their profitable trade with Spain, which would anyhow fall into the hands of the Danes and the Hanseatic League if Holland stopped supplying its customers. It was an endless battle of wits, tiring for both parties, neither conceding anything substantial nor allowing matters to come to a head. Every so often Elizabeth allowed the return of captured ships with compensation and showed her appreciation of Holland's *navigare necesse est*. Nor were demonstrations lacking from the Netherlands of willingness to stop delivery of materials for war, provided ... and then followed some unfulfillable condition, such as an English guarantee that neither English subjects nor Scandinavian or Hanseatic merchants should deliver military supplies to Spain if the Hollanders gave up exporting them. Elizabeth for her part was willing to give official permission for sailing to Spain, provided ... and then she too made stipulations the Hollanders could not accept. So there was always something to negotiate; the diplomats had their hands full; the English took a lot and occasionally gave something back, but most ships escaped the English navy. The Spaniards were supplied by the Hollanders with enough material for a number of unsuccessful Armadas; but as time went by and no serious danger threatened, England and the Netherlands grew used to each other's faults, like a moderately happy married couple, and the comradeship in arms between Vere's and Maurice's forces was not seriously affected.

Oldenbarnevelt had little taste for all these dealings. They stood in the way of his chief objective: close military alliance with the English; they were enacted, moreover, against a background of domestic string-pulling between two contenders, both antipathetic to Oldenbarnevelt, the Amsterdammers and the Zeelanders. The former took the stance that typifies them for the next two centuries: their trade came first. They demanded that everything should be done, that the Republic's resources should be strained to the utmost to promote it, without any consideration for the carefully balanced

[1] See page 58.   [2] Calendar of State Papers, XXIII, 299.

foreign policy of the government in The Hague. So while temperament and self-interest – since they did little trade with England themselves – made Amsterdam follow an intransigent policy, detested by Oldenbarnevelt unless it concerned the authority of the state, Zeeland was following exactly the opposite course, one that might be called appeasement. They were not much interested in the grain trade, but very much in trade with England, which they did not want endangered by hostile treatment at the hands of that country's authorities. Zeeland therefore placed little trust in the long memoranda Oldenbarnevelt was so good at, but much more in far-reaching concessions and then in obtaining the goodwill of the English prize-court judges by bribery. The future was thus to be sacrificed to the present, not at all Olden-barnevelt's policy. A clash resulted with Zeeland, though not with Amsterdam, as they repeatedly sent their own delegates to England for underhand bargaining without Ortel's knowledge. When the official Netherlands envoys early in 1591 again complained about the private delegation from Middelburg and Flushing, these towns were reprimanded by the States-General – no doubt under Oldenbarnevelt's directions. In this way he made enemies in Zeeland, in particular of the powerful Moucheron family, without getting Amsterdam on his side. Might not this foreshadow the Amsterdam–Zeeland alliance against Oldenbarnevelt in 1617?

Apart from incessant wrangling about the seizure of ships, Oldenbarnevelt gradually came to be on better terms with the English themselves. A Netherlands delegation sent to England in the summer of 1589 ran up against the strong prejudice shown by both Walsingham and Burghley against the Advocate, whom they both considered omnipotent in foreign politics. But this was not quite true. When the States-General had conferred on the delegates' instructions, Oldenbarnevelt proposed to write to the Queen 'threatening to publish to the world the whole course of the English here, unless she will take order for the governing of her people'.[1] The deputies realized that Oldenbarnevelt was in one of his fits of bad temper and sent a letter in much milder terms. When the delegation was back Walsingham wrote to the English ambassador in the Netherlands at that time, Bodley, that its members must have conveyed a detailed and exaggerated account of his criticism of Oldenbarnevelt 'with the malicious intent of stirring up his wrath to such a pitch as to make him intolerable'.[2]

If this was indeed the aim of the envoys' report they did not achieve it. The States-General had gradually gained confidence in Oldenbarnevelt and this

[1] Bodley to Burghley, 10 June (O.S., 20 June N.S.) 1589, Calendar of State Papers, XXIII, 311.
[2] Résumé by Conyers Read, *Mr Secretary Walsingham*, of Walsingham's letter to Bodley of 28 July (O.S., 7 August N.S.), Calendar of State Papers, XXIII, 404.

was not shaken, on the contrary, it was strengthened by the passage of time, as first his French and then his English policy were seen to be paying off.

Evidence of this was given while the delegation was still in England. Elizabeth was dissatisfied with its restricted powers: it could voice complaints and listen to English objections but not negotiate, still less conclude anything. Elizabeth had various wishes of her own, *inter alia* alterations in her favour of the Treaty of Nonsuch. She haughtily demanded that the delegates' powers should be amplified. Oldenbarnevelt felt strong enough to refuse the demand in lofty terms. Negotiations would have to be conducted in the Netherlands. The Queen was asked some awkward questions. Alterations to the treaty were not mentioned again for some time.

The States were of course emboldened by the changed political circumstances. Now the enemy proved unable to take advantage of the secession of Geertruidenberg there was no more need to approach the English Queen as petitioners. The allies' affairs were to be dealt with on a basis of equality and not otherwise. Walsingham grasped the fact, even if not without regret. On 30 June 1589 Ortel wrote that he had had a stormy interview with Walsingham and that Oldenbarnevelt should do everything to avoid a 'regrettable breach', but a letter of 12 August from Walsingham to Bodley shows that the storm was only a stage effect: he strongly urges Bodley not to do anything to unsettle friendship with the Hollanders, however damaging the necessity might be to English pride. Alteration of the treaty in England's favour was not discussed again in Walsingham's lifetime. Bodley, at first desirous of enforcing such a modification by the withdrawal of troops, was now advising against any such insistence; so was Gilpin, who with his first-hand knowledge of Netherlands affairs, was at this time coming more and more to agree with Oldenbarnevelt. After Walsingham's death, when the parsimonious Burghley was dominating the Royal Council unopposed, the matter was brought up again: the Hollanders, made overbold by incipient military success, were beginning to interpret the treaty in a way so increasingly onerous for England that Bodley wrote in 1592: 'There was never no Contract, so wrested from the purpose, that was first intended by the parties, as that had bin by them.'[1] It was not till 1598, however, in the totally changed circumstances that year produced, that Elizabeth managed to effect the economies she had been working for by means of a fresh treaty.

She did make a last effort in this direction after Walsingham's death, when deciding once more to send Lord Buckhurst as ambassador extraordinary to the Netherlands, where he was well-known and respected by the States party. Again the Queen was concerned with economies, the gradual withdrawal of

---

[1] State Papers 84/45/237.

her troops from the Netherlands. After the capture of Breda and the battle of Ivry, and the effects on the course of the war promised by these events, it was thought in England the Netherlands could manage with less assistance. This was the drawback to the strong position so useful to Oldenbarnevelt in the defence of Netherlands independence. The more help England offered, the greater the English government's tendency to meddle in Netherlands affairs: as this tendency diminished so did the help provided.

When Oldenbarnevelt's old friend Wilkes arrived in June 1590 as ambassador in the Netherlands, his behaviour reflected the change of mood in England. He came with orders to win Oldenbarnevelt and other politicians over to England – and against France; for this purpose he was authorized to spend a maximum of 300 pounds. It is not known whether Oldenbarnevelt enjoyed his share of this. Probably he had nothing. At any rate it never leaked out and it must soon have become clear to Wilkes that though the Advocate was pro-French he was not for that reason half so anti-English as Bodley had supposed in his despatches. Sternly opposed to Elizabeth's claims to protectorship, once she abandoned them he proved most amenable in other difficulties. The anarchy that had threatened for a short time after the fall of Geertruidenberg had vanished; the authority of the young Prince, now also stadtholder of Utrecht, Gelderland and Overijsel, was reinforced; opposition to Oldenbarnevelt was confined to matters of detail; in short, the emergent Republic had been changed from a set of quarrelsome and ungrateful tradesmen into a worthy ally, controlled by a shrewd man of affairs knowing how to give and take and neither to be intimidated nor flattered. A business man who, as is said of the Dutch, would sometimes give too little and ask too much, but one who, when negotiating from a position of weakness, was prepared to give more and ask less. That was the tone of the English despatches of the ensuing years. It is the measure of Oldenbarnevelt's greatness to have been able to give this impression not only to a somewhat ingenuous soldier like Sir Francis Vere, but also to capable diplomats like Bodley, Wilkes and, later, Robert Cecil.

The first effects of restored confidence had already become apparent a few days after Wilkes's arrival. The subject of his first proposal had been the mustering of the English troops. It included several demands unacceptable to the States-General, as involving a considerable increase in the charges put upon them. They therefore decided to reject the demands one by one, and this was done in the turbulent manner customary since Leicester's days in dealings with England. Was it wise now to arouse Elizabeth's anger again by unnecessary asperity? It was decided to defer discussion. Then the matter came up once more and Oldenbarnevelt seems to have proposed bringing the tone into harmony with the spirit of 4 July (the date of the meeting between Wilkes and Oldenbarnevelt at which a new course became apparent). The States thereupon resolved to confirm the answer in substance, but to commission Oldenbarnevelt to 'sweeten' it, after which operation, and when it appeared that the intrinsic content was the same, it was given definitive form.

We see Oldenbarnevelt here in an unfamiliar role. Sweetening was not usually in his line, and the product is not particularly palatable according to our ideas. It merely lacked the embittered tone of some previous state documents addressed to England. Naturally the envoys came to the States-General protesting loudly at the Queen's not being accommodated in such a trifle. It might almost be thought that they meant it. In reality it was a tactic aimed at obtaining as much as possible in the negotiations. Oldenbarnevelt knew his position was strong, he conceded nothing and relations with Elizabeth were none the worse for it. From his own point of view he could therefore be satisfied with the results of Wilkes's ambassadorship. He persuaded the States-General to express it by offering Wilkes an unusually splendid present: four first-class matching horses, worth 600 guilders.

A fresh delegation was sent by the States-General to England in December of the same year at the request of Zeeland, which had been suffering severely during these months from the prize-making of ships to and from Spain. Elizabeth was again displeased at the delegation's limited powers, one of the weak sides of the Republic's government system, and of Oldenbarnevelt's personal system too. Every obligation entered into by the States-General needed the confirmation of all the principals and of the principals' principals. Because of mutual mistrust carte blanche could not be given. Any treaty concluded abroad, indeed any compact not in the form of a treaty, could therefore only be concluded after ratification by these principals, so that the delegates did not have a free hand. Now it happened that most of the principals had little interest in foreign affairs and still less knowledge of them. If an oligarchy like that of Venice had existed in the Netherlands some of the most influential members of the establishment could have been sent abroad, well enough acquainted with their fellow-oligarchs to know what concessions they would sanction. But the Netherlands were only formally an oligarchy. In practice foreign policy was already, and to be increasingly, managed by one man who, like most great men, knew that he was surrounded by enemies or second-rate supporters, and so could not trust anyone enough to delegate authority. That could be called lust for power, but it is better regarded as the consequence of rulership. When a delegation was really intended to get down to business Oldenbarnevelt himself went with it, once to France and three times to England.

The delegation got nothing out of Elizabeth except some kind words and promises of redress. Elizabeth got nothing out of the delegates, who had been given no powers. Then Elizabeth's displeasure at trade with the enemy was superseded in her mind by her desire to recover 3,000 of her auxiliaries as soon as possible, so as to be able to use them in France. John Norris, England's best general, was appointed commander of the intended expedition. The majority of his troops would have to consist of veterans of the wars in the Netherlands. Elizabeth sent him at the end of January 1591 to the Netherlands with orders to locate the companies he wanted and take them with him. He was to ask the States-General politely for permission, but if it were not granted the troops were to be put on board ship without it.

The intended mission aroused great alarm in the States-General, who were still trying to have it cancelled. It was too late: on 6 February Norris appeared before them in person and made his demand, at first politely, and then, in answer to the 'refusal' with which the States had wanted to 'content' him, announcing in very rude terms that he would take no notice of the Netherlanders but order the troops to leave on his own authority.

Oldenbarnevelt was in a quandary. He was convinced, more than anyone else, of the need for strong and efficient help for Henry IV, especially in Brittany, for which the troops demanded were destined and where the Spaniards were threatening to dig themselves in, to the inestimable detriment of Netherlands shipping to the west. The moment for withdrawal was however psychologically most unfortunately chosen. After years of defensive warfare the first town of importance, Breda, had been captured from the Spaniards in 1590. Parma's departure on his first French expedition had given the Netherlanders some advantage, but not much. In the expectation of a second move southwards by Parma they wanted to undertake a definitely aggressive campaign. The plans had been made, the money voted: the towns on the IJsel were to be the first objective. The English troops were indispensable here. They formed the nucleus, indeed the majority of the army in the field: their quality was highly praised, especially since being paid regularly and systematically trained by Vere in cooperation with Maurice and William Louis. If the greater and better part of the English now left it was goodbye to any hopes of taking Zutfen and Deventer; much dissatisfaction would be caused among the military leaders and the civilian population; and the French policy, of which Oldenbarnevelt was the embodiment, would become highly unpopular. He therefore decided to take the risk of using every means to prevent the transfer of the English troops.

Bodley and Gilpin, the two English members of the Council of State, were no less convinced than their Netherlands colleagues of the perniciousness of

Norris's mission. With their help Oldenbarnevelt persuaded Norris to return to England to propose a compromise. The latter had been confronted not only with an order from the Council of State prohibiting the commanders of the English garrison towns from letting their troops leave, but also with a collective refusal to obey by the English officers led by their commander Francis Vere, who told Oldenbarnevelt that he considered himself cashiered by Her Majesty for refusing to be sent to France. Norris came back on 18 March with altered instructions: only part of the troops were diverted to Brittany, twenty companies remaining available for the operations against the IJsel towns. It was enough. Oldenbarnevelt had once more gained his point by that attractive mixture of boldness and guile which was his speciality. Zutfen and Deventer were the prizes it won for the Netherlands.

The situation was quite different when in November of the same year, 1591, Elizabeth again summoned a thousand of her auxiliaries for temporary service in Normandy. The victorious campaign was finished, the season, still tolerable in France, was unsuitable for war in the Netherlands. The States-General left the decision to the Council of State; Bodley, Vere and Maurice too advised in favour of it. The troops left, allegedly for two months.

Before the beginning of the siege of Steenwijk in the late spring of 1592 the auxiliaries do indeed seem to have been at their full strength again. The siege had scarcely begun when the Queen again summoned troops to be sent to Brittany. Bodley, who does not appear to have grasped that neither Maurice nor the Council of State were competent to decide this, had gone to Overijsel to consult with Maurice as to how the auxiliaries should be used. He was a day's journey from Maurice's headquarters when the order for the recall of the troops reached him. He went on at once, but both Maurice and the Council of State, present at headquarters, took refuge behind the States-General. Bodley then went back to The Hague and delivered the letter to the States, from which Oldenbarnevelt was absent during these weeks. They naturally began by refusing. If Elizabeth persisted they could always see what could be done. Elizabeth did persist and ordered Bodley to hasten the return of almost the entire English auxiliary force. Bodley left for the second time for Zwolle and had various unpleasant interviews with the military leaders, who again referred him to the States-General. The letter to the States was in a sealed envelope and Bodley had not been given a copy. When the States opened the letter it was found to contain a clause to which Oldenbarnevelt could cling so as once more to stop the immediate withdrawal of the troops. In view of the news, received meanwhile, of the capture of Steenwijk, the Queen wrote: '. . . pourveu que vostre armée se puisse bonnement dissouldre et que nos gens qui vous y ont servi sen puissent librement retourner, nous avons absolument promis au Roy, et résolument arresté de lui envoier 2,500 hommes, ou environ de nos forces par delà'.

The English troops had in the meantime left for Koevorden, which Maurice had laid under siege. They could certainly not leave 'bonnement'. In spite of repeated insistence from England, where the restrictive clause was already regretted, Oldenbarnevelt, loyally helped by Vere, managed to postpone the departure of the troops till Koevorden too had been taken from the enemy. Winter was then approaching and it did not matter if the English soldiers left.

Vere, alarmed at the repeated encroachments on the strength of his forces, again seriously warned Burghley in June 1593 against neglecting 'the very root' (the Netherlands) in favour of 'the top branches' (France). The Netherlands could count themselves lucky to have a commander of auxiliaries who championed their interests so forcefully.

In the following winter the auxiliaries were gradually augmented. Vere went to England to raise a regiment. He did not return till the middle of May with 'a fine troop from this nation', as he wrote to Oldenbarnevelt, whose ears must have tingled with the praise Vere heaped upon him and Maurice during his stay in England. These troops did splendid service at the siege of Groningen.

After the siege and before the capitulation became known in England, Elizabeth summoned the envoy Caron, to whom she made a new request for help. This time it was not a recall of troops but an amphibious expedition, for which the Netherlanders were requested to equip ten ships with food for 2,000 landing troops, to be provided by Elizabeth. The reason that this request is mentioned here is its motivation, which must have given Oldenbarnevelt food for thought. The States had constantly been sending help to France and that very summer a large expedition of this kind was being prepared, for which the States had given Henry their consent. Elizabeth did not grudge him the help, but she did grudge the States the honour and status to which it entitled them. She therefore asked if the States would send her ships, sailors and provisions for a new expedition to France 'not by force of any previous agreements or promises made to the King of France, but really for her sake, and to show the world that there was such a good and firm alliance between them, that they would always help each other faithfully in their enterprises of importance'.

There is something pathetic in this begging for sympathy. The sympathy did not exist at all and the prestige reasons, which Elizabeth naively used, and which Caron evidently appreciated, were valid for Oldenbarnevelt in exactly the opposite sense. He did not refuse the help asked for, thankful that this time Elizabeth was not recalling troops. But the land expedition was of most importance for him, and Henry IV's gratitude important directly rather than indirectly via the English Queen.

In 1595 Elizabeth began vigorously to claim repayment of the sums advanced on the strength of the Treaty of Nonsuch. Thanks to Oldenbarnevelt's excellent delaying tactics she had no success till three years later. The claim was not based on the treaty, in which it was stipulated that repayment should begin when peace was established. No one had then foreseen, apparently, that the war would last so long. Everything shows that Elizabeth and Burghley, but not Walsingham, had in 1585 counted on a sort of *Blitzkrieg*, soon to be ended by the triumph of Leicester's brave men. The reason for the delayed repayment was no doubt that the war had brought the provinces into sore financial straits, only to be put right by peace. However, a government that was equipping expeditions to France year in, year out, or voting large subsidies for their French allies, could not plausibly plead poverty when it came to the repayment of the subsidies that had made this prosperity possible. As early as the beginning of 1594, when Bodley was on long leave in England, Gilpin had been given instructions to find out how the States-General would react to such a request for repayment. He had not found that moment opportune, as the allowance for the coming season had not yet come in and the siege of Groningen was involving great expenditure. If Groningen were captured time would be needed to recover from the financial bloodletting. After that though, Gilpin thought, it would be a good thing to bring the matter up. Elizabeth was easily persuaded: just then she was having to ask the States for twofold help – against Brittany and against an expected second Armada. So when Bodley returned to the Netherlands in May 1594 he did not mention the subject of repayment. His mission revolved entirely round help in Brittany, about which he shared Oldenbarnevelt's views. He was displeased with Burghley for not giving him adequate information and so was not really suited for another ambassadorship in the Netherlands. However, after some months' stay in England, Elizabeth sent him again. The idea was most likely that being on good terms with the Netherlands statesmen he would be better than anyone else in extracting ready money out of the rich Hollanders.

He appeared in the States-General on 14 February 1595 and in a long and courteously phrased speech asked for a start to be made in repaying the advances, notwithstanding the letter of the Nonsuch Treaty. The States turned the request down, and continued to do so when Bodley, who would be in real trouble if he went back to England empty-handed, again implored them to produce some money. Oldenbarnevelt expressed the opinion that it would even be bad tactics to inform the provinces of the English claims, as it might make them less inclined to give their normal contribution for war purposes, or even induce them to enter into the peace proposals that had just come from Belgium in the spring. In a secret interview, however, just before Bodley was leaving for England with his disappointing results, Oldenbarnevelt was much more forthcoming. The debt to England had risen in the course of nine and a half years to 7 or 8 million guilders. It would be ostrich policy to let it mount up, with the obvious attendant danger that one awful day Elizabeth would recall all her troops, and make a separate peace with Spain, probably surrendering the cautionary towns. It might take time and trouble to convince the States of the need for financial sacrifice despite the letter of the treaty. Oldenbarnevelt was confident, however, that it could be done, provided Elizabeth bound herself to leave 4,000 English soldiers in the Netherlands for the duration of the war and to continue the alliance entered into at Nonsuch unimpaired in the eyes of the world, even if on different terms. He made a proposal of this tenor with express instructions that his name was not to be mentioned, for if that were known it would hamper his efforts to work upon the tight-fisted Netherlands politicians.

However, before Bodley, back in England, could apply this balm to the wound, Elizabeth threw one of her familiar tantrums and implacably banned Bodley from Court. The good man became ill with fright and it was July before he managed to get a report of this interview to Elizabeth. She had calmed down a good deal in the meantime and was alive to the fact that 'none can better deal inwardly and privately with Mons. Barneville than yourself', as Burghley wrote to Bodley. She therefore sent him again and for the last time over the North Sea in August 1595 to press for a start in paying off the millions owing, on the basis of Oldenbarnevelt's suggestions and in close consultation with him regarding the time schedule.

It will be seen that during this ambassadorship the subtle development of the France–England–Netherlands triangular relationship altered the situation in such a way that repayment was once more put off for several years. This delay enabled the Netherlanders to 'mend their fence', as it was called in the catchphrase of the time, that is to drive the Spaniards back over the main rivers.

The year 1595 thus saw the Netherlands in a far better position with regard to both France and England than they had been in 1589. It was largely due to the military situation, considerably improved in these six years.

In the spring of 1589, after Geertruidenberg had gone over, four of the eleven provinces of the present-day Kingdom of the Netherlands (Groningen, Drente, North Brabant and Limburg) had been entirely recaptured by Parma; Gelderland, Overijsel and Zeeland (Zeeland–Flanders) to a great extent. This conquest had given Parma a firm foothold in Holland too.[1] Contemporaries, always tending to picture the future in terms of the recent past, reasonably enough supposed the downfall of the emergent republic to be imminent. Indeed the only result of a continued defensive war could be the further erosion of its territory. In that same year, 1589, William Louis went to The Hague to develop plans for offensive warfare in the States-General. His plans were not accepted. Van Reyd, his secretary, who accompanied him and later wrote a history of the beginning of the Eighty Years War, attributes it to opposition by timid 'pensionaries, burgomasters and others in the States', who thought it more advisable

to use the cessation of hostilities and rest, that the enemy was allowing them, to their advantage, with the building of necessary fortifications and putting everything in good order: contenting themselves with retaining what they still had and preventing the enemy's further invasion. They said also that by doing otherwise and seeking out the enemy they would arouse a sleeping dog and bring the war, now averted, upon themselves again. This opinion, that offensive war could not be waged, was immediately after the pacification of Ghent, when all the provinces still stood together, discussed in such a way, and now so deeply rooted . . . that it was impossible to make people change their minds.

At first sight it might seem as if a speech by Oldenbarnevelt, undoubtedly the most influential among the pensionaries and burgomasters quoted, were being retailed here, but a cautious interpretation is necessary. Oldenbarnevelt may have been conservative in his social aims, but he certainly was not in his methods of attaining them. The narrow-minded timidity reflected by the advocates of defensive tactics is hardly compatible with what we have seen of Oldenbarnevelt's penchant for taking a chance.

The reason for rejecting William Louis's plans – and we can safely assume that Oldenbarnevelt was behind the rejection – is more likely to have been that the time was not ripe in 1589 for a revolutionary change of tactics. The failure of the siege of Geertruidenberg had lowered the prestige of the States and exhausted their war funds. Far from allowing them 'cessation of hostilities and rest' the enemy had been besieging Heusden with might and main, a siege which was not broken till the middle of October. In the meantime a number of Spanish armed units had broken into the Bommelerwaard, and at the moment when William Louis was making his speech in the States-General, Maurice was exerting all his forces to get them out again. In these circumstances the expenditure of men and material on offensive action was not to be recommended, and certainly not to start in the north, as William Louis proposed.

[1] Geertruidenberg, today in North Brabant, was in Holland at the time of the Republic.

General war planning for the coming years was indeed considered desirable. It took place during a council of war at Maurice's headquarters, Alem, where besides Count William civilians, in accordance with Netherlands custom, had most to say: Oldenbarnevelt for Holland, Vosbergen for Zeeland, Roorda for Friesland.

The first part of the war plan could not be discussed at this meeting, as it was so secret that only Maurice and Oldenbarnevelt and those immediately involved in the plan were allowed to hear of it: the famous surprise capture of Breda by means of a sort of modern Trojan horse: a peat boat full of soldiers was to make its way into the castle, the soldiers were to gain control of the fort and open the gates to the approaching army. Everything went according to plan. The preparations were mainly in Oldenbarnevelt's hands, down to appointing the commander of the raiding party, a post Maurice had intended for his cousin Philip: but Oldenbarnevelt insisted on Charles de Héraugière, although he had been compromised in the Pescarengis affair: his name is still after four centuries familiar to all Dutch schoolchildren.

The surprise of Breda on 4 March 1590 was the dawn of a new epoch.[1]

The fundamental importance of this feat of arms was already realized at the time. It was the first Netherlands town to be captured from Spain since 1580 (Doesburg and Axel, the paltry fruits of Leicester's rule, can scarcely be counted) and the first Catholic town to fall into the hands of the reformed Netherlands. The solution of the problems this caused was more liberal than was to be the case later: though the principal church was allotted to the Protestants, the old religion was allowed to be practised in one other: a compromise in the spirit of Oldenbarnevelt's practical tolerance, which Maurice had no trouble in agreeing to.

Oldenbarnevelt was justly regarded as the principal architect of this victory. After the occupation of the town he again displayed 'very great trouble, industry and diligence' in supplying the town within twelve days not only with 'corn and powder, but also all kinds of provisions of victuals, ammunition and all necessities'.

Oldenbarnevelt received a presentation, from States-General funds. It was 'a large, fine gilt bowl and lid most ornamentally made and therein artistically portrayed the whole story of this matter, divided inside and out in various ovals and circles . . .' The inscription, a long Latin poem, did not mention his name, only that of 'Heraugerius'. Oldenbarnevelt was an opponent of personality cults. Breda had provided him with power and riches. That was better than fame.

[1] For Breda as a 'landmark' in the foundation of the Republic, see Clark, 'Birth of the Dutch Republic', p. 193.

It was not the only reward given. Furthermore the defence of the newly captured town and the construction of fortifications at the river crossings caused so much expense that the money was not forthcoming to take advantage of Parma's first expedition to France. Oldenbarnevelt left at the head of a large deputation of the States-General for headquarters in the Betuwe to spur Maurice on to greater activity, if only to relieve the French ally. Maurice promised, evidently after some objections, to undertake a campaign in Brabant, but only after a successful conclusion to his intended expedition in the neighbourhood of Cleves. He did not go into action in the direction Oldenbarnevelt desired till towards the end of September. He had some success, but nothing to boast about. The offensive planned was not to start in earnest till the following year.

The great question now was in what direction this offensive should be made. Everyone with a hand in determining the Netherlands' strategy had his own opinion, based on his own interests. The front – if the small effectives of those days can be called a front – stretched with several loops from Ostend to Groningen and could be divided into five sectors: the area south of the Scheldt, that between the Scheldt and the Maas; between the Maas and the Rhine; the area beyond the IJsel (south-east Gelderland and Twente); and the northern sector, with Groningen as chief objective.

Elizabeth was of course mainly interested in the first sector, in which Ostend, so vital to England, formed a sort of military exclave, separated from the rest of the Netherlands by Zeeland–Flanders and Sluis, still in Spanish hands. When she urged an offensive in Flanders on the States-General they answered with a letter in which Oldenbarnevelt's ideas can be seen at work: they were quite prepared for an expedition in Flanders provided Elizabeth took the initiative and sent an extra three or four thousand men to Ostend to take their part in the attack. This would be in Henry IV's interest too and the States would support her. There was of course no question of Elizabeth, who had long been groaning loudly about her understrength treaty troops, throwing in another three to four thousand. Nor did Oldenbarnevelt intend her to. A large-scale attack in Flanders did not suit the Hollanders' plans. The army would have to operate far away from its base, against objectives with which Holland and even Zeeland were not greatly concerned. Yes, if the pirates' lair Dunkirk, a thorn in the flesh for Holland and Zeeland shipping in the Channel, could be captured! It was unthinkable, however, without strong help both from England and from France. It was not till 1600 that Oldenbarnevelt let that plan loom up again, with the well-known glorious and harmful consequences.

The Zeelanders, for their part, could see only one objective in this sector to excite their interest: Hulst, an ideal centre for raising *brandschatten* in East Flanders, like Ostend in West Flanders. With Sluis, on the other hand, they were less concerned, as it formed an important transit centre for their profitable trade with the enemy. Hulst was then the only town captured by States forces in the period we are dealing with; actually this sector was not to play a significant part in the war till after 1600.

The second sector did not get its turn till later on either. The exception was the Holland town Geertruidenberg: though it did not prove to be such a danger as had been feared during the great mutiny, the authorities in Dordrecht, the oldest town in the province and a powerful one, became nervous at the proximity of Spanish troops. Dordrecht still had to wait a few years, for reasons partly of policy and partly of strategy, for its turn, but it came in 1593 and Maurice was despatched to Geertruidenberg, which he began to besiege *more romano*, that is to say according to the lessons learnt by him and William Louis from Vitruvius, Caesar and other Roman writers: a lot of trenches, fortifications and patience; great expense, little bloodshed. A great deal of time was used up in this way, and Oldenbarnevelt and the oligarchs objected to both the slowness and the cost of the siege: they had trouble in finding the money and needed the army quickly for other purposes. Oldenbarnevelt was repeatedly heading delegations of the States-General to the army to impress on Maurice the need for economy and speed. But the stadtholder's prestige had been so boosted by the surprise of Breda and the military successes of the intervening years that he was able to have his way in matters of war. So there were disputes, but there is nothing to show that they were acrimonious: a general with only 5,000 men at his disposal is bound to use conservative methods to contend not only with the occupying forces of a town but also with a 15,000-strong army returned from France. After three months of these cautious tactics the relieving forces had melted away and the town was forced to surrender. Maurice could return to The Hague for the third time as the victor in a successful campaign. For the time activity between Scheldt and Maas came to a halt, in spite of constant pressure by Buzanval, who stressed the importance of an offensive in the direction of France to the Netherlands' great ally.

In the third sector Nijmegen was at first the principal target, mainly for strategic reasons. It was the transit point and provisioning base for the Spanish troops in east Gelderland, Overijsel and Groningen and was therefore given high priority, partly on the insistence, again, of Dordrecht, which used to do a lot of trade with Germany along the River Waal, closed by Nijmegen. Nijmegen was already captured in the first campaign after the seizure of Breda, Maurice having driven the Spanish army command frantic by moving his troops along the inner lines first from Deventer to Hulst and then from Hulst to Nijmegen.

Nijmegen had originally fallen to Parma by means of a *coup de main*, helped by a considerable Catholic part of the population. That may be why Olden-barnevelt deprived Nijmegen, unlike other captured towns, of a substantial privilege: the right, as a free imperial town, to elect its own authorities. This election was in future to devolve on the stadtholder – a provision that was to play a great part in the conclusion of the religious disputes in 1618.

Henceforth the lines of communication between the main Spanish forces and their garrison in the north ran through Rheinberg, a Cologne enclave lying within neutral Jülich territory, which accordingly became a bone of contention between the parties. For the time, however, the States were not capable of such a distant expedition, and the third sector remained quiet throughout the rest of this period.

The fourth sector was another matter. In Zutfen and Deventer the Spaniards were closest to the heart of the Netherlands, and so these two towns were the first target of the war plans drawn up by Oldenbarnevelt. As the garrisons were small, the fortifications neglected and the distance from the centre of the Spanish forces great, both towns were taken in 1591 without long sieges: Zutfen in five days, Deventer in ten. Oldenbarnevelt was present at the capture of Zutfen and settled the terms of capitulation. The entire preparations had also been in his hands and he had earned the nation's gratitude in scarcely less measure than after Breda. The States-General expressed it by issuing a medal; Maurice and William Louis were presented with gold plate and a present of bonds.

In the fifth and last sector, the north, it was chiefly the Frisian stadtholder William Louis who kept on urging the overall command to subdue the towns in his area. Friesland was threatened by Steenwijk in the south, cutting off overland communications with the rest of the Netherlands, by Koevorden in the east and, most of all, by Groningen. Once the province of Groningen was taken the stadtholdership would most likely fall to him. It was not yet his turn in 1591, but in the next three years a sizeable part of the campaign was directed towards this region, Steenwijk and Koevorden being taken in 1592 and Groningen, of most importance, in 1594. Oldenbarnevelt had given powerful support to the action against Steenwijk and Groningen, but obsti-nately opposed that against Koevorden. That came about as follows: after the capture of Steenwijk on 5 July 1592, Maurice, united in comradeship in arms with William Louis, wanted to push on at once to Koevorden and asked for strong support from the States-General, from whom he was expecting war supplies, particularly transport. Two members of the Council of State and three deputies of the States-General in the field were sent with this message to The Hague, to the great perplexity of the States-General. Parma had returned from France in the meantime and they were not aware of the poor shape his forces were in. It seemed reasonable to expect him to start an offensive somewhere in the south immediately. The Dordrecht and Zeeland deputies present must have expressed special anxiety, while the two Councillors of State defended the views of the Nassaus. The debates took three days. The result was a victory for Zeeland and Dordrecht, who had evidently gained Oldenbarnevelt's support. The lengthy resolution contained detailed war plans for the coming weeks. The army must be divided, William Louis going one way, Maurice the other. Waggons must be provided, but not more than two hundred, not nearly enough for the assault on Koevorden envisaged by Maurice. Maurice was not to take any risks, taking note that the impending dog-days were the season 'when all wounds were the most perilous'. In short, the States-General, led by Oldenbarnevelt, well over a hundred miles behind the front, were usurping the commander-in-chief's place. But Maurice saw a fine military opening: he could profit from the fact that Vere and his troops were still at his disposal.[1] Verdugo, the Spanish commander at Groningen, was still west of the Rhine; so Maurice went his own way without waiting for the States-General's resolution, though with the authorization of the Council of State. The States of Holland, the main suppliers of waggons, thereupon refused to deliver the quota required, which must have angered Maurice most. He was now twenty-four and felt that he was not only an adult but a great man, after 1591 and the glorious siege of Steenwijk. He had experience of Parma. He was familiar with the possibilities of transporting troops and guns along the rivers. Could he not be allowed to take the responsibility for combining an actual attack and a potential defence?

The result proved Maurice right. Parma was not in a position to undertake any dangerous action on the southern front. He confined himself to sending a small auxiliary expedition, under Verdugo, across the Rhine, to relieve Koevorden. Thanks to stout support by Vere and his men Maurice was able to defeat this small relief army in the open field to the south of Koevorden: the first time that the Spanish *tercios*[2] had shown that they were not invincible in open battle either. Holland's sabotage in the matter of transport had not stopped Maurice winning. Koevorden was taken and the canker began to gnaw at the good relationship in the duumvirate of the Republic.

The taking of Groningen was the last great success in the period under review. The siege took two whole months, during which time Oldenbarnevelt went twice to Maurice's camp to supervise negotiations with delegates from a

---

[1] See p. 190. [2] Infantry regiments.

pro-States party in the town, who made more promises than they could keep and did not contribute to the eventual capitulation of the town on 24 July 1594.

During this siege Oldenbarnevelt had to deal with peace feelers put out by the new Spanish governor, Ernest of Austria, next eldest brother of the Emperor Rudolf II. He sent two envoys who at first secured passports for the Northern Netherlands by pretending to be representatives of the Belgian Prince of Chimay, whose Protestant wife had settled in Holland. On arrival they asked to speak to Oldenbarnevelt and told him that they had a letter with them addressed to 'the States of Holland, Gelderland etc.' which they had quite unexpectedly (!) found among the letters given to them at the last moment in Brussels. They asked him to bring this fact to the notice of the States-General. Oldenbarnevelt proposed in the States-General, at that moment with six persons in session, to open the letter and act as they thought fit. It was rumoured that the letter had not been opened, as the envoys had gone outside the scope of their passports and could not be regarded as emissaries; it was not till these men, Hartius and Coomans, had withdrawn the lies they had told Oldenbarnevelt at first, and said that they had been instructed to explain the contents of the letter further by word of mouth, that 'the States-General not only allowed the opening of the letter, both to satisfy the common people and to stop the mouths of the evil-minded, who always slandered the actions of the States, but also told them that they would be granted audience' (Duyck).

The envoys' oral message proved to be as vague as the letter, making no mention of terms except to invite the States to propose conditions for reconciliation.

Oldenbarnevelt's answer was in his habitual style, expatiating on the history of the war and the wrongs committed by the Spaniards, summing up all their peace efforts, contradicted by simultaneous or subsequent atrocities. In composing this document, intended of course solely for domestic use, a copy being sent to all the provinces, Oldenbarnevelt was glad to be able to make use of the arrest of a certain Michel Renichon, hired, probably with the Archduke's knowledge, to murder Maurice, Frederick Henry, then ten years old, and Oldenbarnevelt. The envoys went to see the would-be murderer in prison to convince themselves of his accusations against his principals; their own denials that Ernest had any knowledge of the matter, however, did not count for much.

Groningen fell two months later and decreased the desire for peace in the north as much as it increased it in the south. Ernest now approached Elizabeth, keen on taking advantage of the Spanish peacemaking mood since she need no longer fear France or the Netherlands being overwhelmed by Spain. She was considering a mission for Wilkes, her most experienced diplomat in continental affairs. But Oldenbarnevelt found out about this, probably owing to the diligence of Caron, who had a flair for that sort of thing. Strong protests from Oldenbarnevelt and Henry IV made her drop the scheme.

The Archduke was again obliged to summon the fractious States-General of the south. They asked anew for peace negotiations to be started, this time ostensibly originating with the South Netherlanders themselves, and with serious proposals to allay distrust in the north. A bailiff was sent to ask the Council of State in The Hague to grant a passport to the envoys to be appointed. This was done, and Oldenbarnevelt sent four points in writing by the returning bailiff, stating the basis of the negotiations into which the States-General of the north were willing to enter. The document was a clear proof of how the States-General's pretensions had risen after five years of uninterrupted successes. They required the southern provinces to treat in their own name without mentioning that of the King. Furthermore the Spanish troops had to leave at once. On the other hand, the States-General would graciously allow the southern provinces to arrange their religious affairs as they liked. It was another ruse typical of the working of Oldenbarnevelt's mind. Of course he did not for a moment suppose that the south would accept these terms, which in effect amounted to an annexation of the south by the north and could only have been the result of total victory by the latter, from which they were still far removed. If the southern provinces did accept the terms it would only be a matter of form. Ostensibly acting on their own account, in actual fact they would have to submit everything to the approval of Fuentes who, as interim governor since Ernest's death on 21 February 1595, exercised almost unlimited power. If they did that and the States-General found out, it meant that they were practising 'deception' and the north could break off the negotiations with loud vituperation, without incurring the odium of not having been willing to enter into them. That was exactly what happened. Oldenbarnevelt managed to get hold of the secret report made by Liesvelt, one of the Belgian negotiators, to Fuentes. Later a long letter from the former Spanish ambassador in France, Tassis, was intercepted, in which the King was advised to overlook his exclusion from the negotiations and to allow them to start, but in which it was clear that there was no question of all the Spanish troops ever being removed. The secret had leaked out and the negotiations were broken off. The envoys had not been allowed further than Zeeland, as in The Hague they might have talked to too many unreliable Holland oligarchs. Maurice had received Liesvelt and Jan Baptist Maes at

Middelburg surrounded by Zeelanders dependably opposed to peace. The States found the matter too delicate to handle and Oldenbarnevelt stayed at home.

This put an end to peace talks for the time: the capture of Cambrai by Spanish troops in October 1595 made peace seem less attractive in Belgium, while in the Netherlands such inclinations were also checked by the prospects of a Triple Alliance with France and England.

Meanwhile the Netherlands' five-year period of military success had come to an end. The first reverse was due to a plan forged by Maurice and Oldenbarnevelt together without apprising the States-General or the Council of State: the surprise capture of Huy. Both Henry IV and the States had long been feeling the need of safe lines of communication between France and the Netherlands. The Liége corridor straight through the Spanish Netherlands seemed to offer the best opportunity. It was actually neutral territory, but that did not worry Oldenbarnevelt greatly. The Bishop of Liége, Ernest of Bavaria, was at the same time Elector of Cologne, and in this capacity was tolerating a Spanish garrison in Rheinberg, stationed there for the same purpose for which the States wanted Huy: to provide a 'pass' for troops from one theatre of war to another. Oldenbarnevelt therefore had few scruples about violating this far from benevolent neutrality, even at the risk of the indignant Elector, with all his domains, officially siding with the Spaniards. Such action, without the consent of the States-General being asked for, could be interpreted as an infringement of the Union of Utrecht: clause 9 forbade 'accepting' war without joint consultation. Oldenbarnevelt's opponents did not deny themselves this pleasure and regarded this action as a proof of his tyranny.

There was little trouble in taking the stronghold, but could it be kept? The leader of the expedition, Héraugière, obsessed by its strong position, thought so at first, even when it appeared that the promised reinforcements from Maurice in the north and Bouillon in the south would not be forthcoming. He sent a sanguine letter to Maurice, who was attending the Gelderland Diet at Nijmegen, and who took it with him to The Hague. Two envoys from Ernest of Bavaria had arrived there to protest against the violation of neutrality and demand the immediate evacuation of the town, promising he would himself occupy it in force without admitting a Spanish garrison. On reading Héraugière's despatch Oldenbarnevelt bluntly refused to evacuate the town on the terms stated by the envoys, which involved a guarantee of free passage through Liége by Dutch troops. At that moment the town was already in Spanish hands. Even before the Spanish siege troops summoned by Ernest of Bavaria had opened a serviceable breach Héraugière surrendered the citadel, though he had allegedly promised to be able to hold it for two years without relief. It was generally expected that he would be called to account. The Council of State urged it strongly. The Council's legal officer, Anthonis Duyck, had, so to speak, already drawn up the points for interrogation, when the States-General, at Oldenbarnevelt's instigation, wiped the whole slate clean. Just then he and Maurice were not well placed for throwing brickbats.

The remainder of the year saw only the unsuccessful siege of Groenlo, intended to reinforce the Netherlands' defences. The town was relieved in time by a strong Spanish army. A sortie in the direction of Rheinberg was equally unsuccessful and cost the life of Philip of Nassau, who rode into an ambush near Bisselich on 5 September. Oldenbarnevelt had lost another potential supporter in Maurice's entourage.

The 1595 campaign was just coming to an end. The attempt to push the Spaniards back across the big rivers had not succeeded. Another year of military reverses was to pass before it was accomplished. The victory in 1597, like those in 1591 and 1594, also resulted from the development of affairs in France and from the way in which Oldenbarnevelt helped to determine and profit by it. The conquest of Twente and south-east Gelderland can be called an indirect result of the Triple Alliance, concluded by France and England with the Netherlands in 1596. How did it come about?

By the summer of 1595 Henry IV, Elizabeth and the United Provinces had been waging war together against Spanish world power for six years. Together, and yet each one separately. No official alliance had been concluded between the three countries. There was indeed the Treaty of Nonsuch between England and the Netherlands, but it was a sort of crypto-protectorate, no longer in line with changed conditions. It was regarded by both the Queen and the States-General only now and then, and when it suited them, as the basis of their relationship, otherwise it had become a dead letter. Neither of them had ever made an alliance with France, and the help often given to Henry had been of an adventitious nature. The absence of formal ties had advantages and disadvantages for all three parties. For France the main advantage was that the King could make peace at any time without letting his allies know. This advantage lapsed to a certain extent when in January 1595 Henry had been persuaded to declare war on Spain, formally and in insulting terms. On the other hand the disadvantages were clearly shown in September of that year, when the loss of the important town of Cambrai could be regarded as a direct consequence of the lack of formal alliance. All the summer Henry, while himself waging war in Burgundy, had in vain appealed for military support from England and the Netherlands.

He met with refusal from Elizabeth, who realized that decisive French victories over Spain would be more likely to lead to a separate peace between the two countries than a moderate defeat. We shall see that there were many in the Netherlands who shared this view. To keep France at war the King must only be supported if otherwise he would be reduced to despair.

Oldenbarnevelt did not take this view. He did not believe in the permanence of good relations between the two Catholic Kings. He knew Henry to be aggressive and, influenced by Calvart's optimistic despatches, held high hopes of a French invasion of the South Netherlands. Even apart from an invasion he thought that the more troops were engaged on the French northern frontier, the fewer the Spaniards could use against the Netherlands and the more chance there was for some more profitable operations by Maurice. That was why he did his best to accede to French requests for help in the summer of 1595.

Who was right in this difference of opinion, Elizabeth or Oldenbarnevelt? The surprising answer is: both – one after the other. For some years the heightened pressure Henry was able to exert on his northern frontier had exactly the military results Oldenbarnevelt hoped for. After that, Henry's successes and Spanish despondency led to the Peace of Vervins, which Elizabeth had wanted avoided at any price payable by France, but not at the price of substantial English engagement on the Continent. The peace, however – and here Oldenbarnevelt came into his own again – led to a sort of cold war between France and Spain which enabled the Hollanders ten years later to extort acknowledgment of their independence from the Spaniards. So the Advocate was right in the short run and the long run, the Queen in the intermediate run.

The States-General, for the time being, had to make more sacrifices so that Oldenbarnevelt's policy could bear fruit. In August 1595 a new French envoy appeared before the States-General with the request for another expedition. The military situation in Picardy was serious. Fuentes had taken a number of strongholds and was now threatening Cambrai to the left, Amiens in front and Calais on the right, three towns which the King did not think he could hold without Netherlands help.

Feeling in the Netherlands was not much in favour of a third expedition to France, since the first two had paid such small dividends. This was especially the case when it appeared that Cambrai and not Calais, as had been thought, was Fuentes's first objective. In Oldenbarnevelt's absence the States-General countermanded the five companies standing ready to leave for Calais. On his return Oldenbarnevelt, by pointing out the ill-effects of displeasing Henry, managed to have an auxiliary expedition equipped for Cambrai as well, and not of five but of twenty-two companies. His opponents accused him later of dictatorial behaviour in taking advantage of the fortuitous absence of some of the provinces. It is true that the States-General assembly was very small at this time, sometimes no more than six or seven people, but the arguments in favour of help for Cambrai were so strong that trickery need not be assumed. None the less, the resolution caused a lot of anger in the country. It was not without good results, however: the States-General received a letter from Henry IV in which he addressed and treated them as a sovereign power. The reward they gave him for this courtesy a little later was permission to use the regiments under Justin of Nassau, arrived too late for Cambrai, for the siege of La Fère.

When, however, towards the end of 1595 the siege of La Fère was making no progress, and the new Spanish regent Albert of Austria came to Belgium, like Ernest before him, with peace plans in one pocket and money for the war in the other, Henry's spirits sank. It was generally expected that he would listen to the proposals for mediation beginning to reach him from the Pope.

It was this discouragement that produced the result Oldenbarnevelt had long been hoping for: the conclusion of a formal alliance between France, England and the Netherlands, recognized as an independent power. Elizabeth was beginning to fear that Henry would not only make peace with Spain but join it by a *renversement des alliances*. Oldenbarnevelt did not share her fears. He had obtained a promise from the French King, who had just refused a similar one to Elizabeth, not to make peace with the Spaniards without the Netherlands. Henry, whose territory was hemmed in on three sides by the Spaniards, had no interest at all in an alliance with them. Such an alliance could only be a protectorate.

It suited Oldenbarnevelt, though, that Elizabeth should think differently. It might induce her to abandon her opposition to France's repeated attempts to form a grand alliance. The three fighting allies would of course form its core, in the expectation of gaining some German and Scandinavian rulers as participants.

First, however, the repayment of the debt to England had to be discussed. On 15 August Bodley appeared again before the States-General to hand over Elizabeth's ungracious message. The prospect of perhaps having to pay the capital sum of a million guilders at short notice had certainly curbed the generosity of the deputies towards the other ally – just as Elizabeth intended.

Oldenbarnevelt would not change his mind; in taking such a risk he showed his greatness. After ten weeks' mature deliberation he composed a purely delaying answer, overflowing with the gross flattery that never failed to mollify Elizabeth.

This attitude appears to contradict the far-reaching undertakings given to

Bodley in the spring. It was because the financial position of the United Provinces had since then greatly deteriorated. The summer campaign had been a failure – and unsuccessful enterprises always cost more than successful ones. It was a bad year for trade: many merchants had been ruined by a fresh embargo in Spain and help to France had cost more than Oldenbarnevelt could have foreseen in the spring. It was simply impossible to induce the provinces to vote an amount of the order of a million for liquidation of debts to England.

Fortunately Bodley realized this, which was a great support for Oldenbarnevelt at this time. He had taken the financial situation into account and believed unreservedly that it was not unwillingness but powerlessness that prevented the States-General from accepting his proposal.

Once again it was her need for support at sea that made Elizabeth climb down. At the end of October she waived the first instalment, on condition that the States supported her with thirty warships for an expedition to Spain that she wished to equip for the coming spring.

The immediate cause of this change of course was a victory of the Essex clique over the Cecil faction. The former were more in favour of the venture, the latter more for economy. The reason for the intended expedition was undoubtedly in the first place the fear of another Armada. But the temporary ascendancy of Essex's war party was also due to events in France and the threat of a separate peace. Feeling in England was evidently beginning to favour the formal alliance so long opposed. To further this mood, to thank Elizabeth for her munificence and at the same time to discuss how English wishes in the matter of trade with the enemy could best be met, Oldenbarnevelt decided to send another ceremonious delegation to England. At the same time Caron had a favourable audience of Elizabeth, sponsored by Essex, in which the Queen denied all rumours of her considering a separate peace, and in particular of her ever contemplating handing the cautionary towns over to Spain.

All this seemed very nice, but Oldenbarnevelt had to remember that the Cecil party at Court had by no means been overthrown. Burghley was still Elizabeth's chief minister and his son Robert was high up the ladder which the following summer was to lead him to the office of Secretary of State. Burghley continued to urge economy upon Elizabeth. He wrote to Bodley telling him to use his friendship with Oldenbarnevelt to persuade him to make at least as large an offer as the previous year, perhaps even a larger one. When no offer was forthcoming Elizabeth's mood changed. She would be glad to receive the envoys, she said, but only if they brought concrete proposals for the debt discharge, with powers to negotiate on it. If they only came with thanks for the postponement granted she would regard them as derisory. Shortly afterwards she recalled Vere, who was to be given command of the landing troops for the Spanish expedition, thus depriving the Gelderlanders of their commander at Zutfen. They now charged their deputy in the States-General to confer earnestly with Oldenbarnevelt and Bodley as to what sort of repayment terms could be made to satisfy Elizabeth.

The remarkable proposal that resulted was never carried out, but gives a good idea of how Oldenbarnevelt and Bodley had weighed up Elizabeth's character. The debt to England was to be converted into an annuity of 20,000 pounds sterling on Elizabeth's life: she was sixty-two and, according to statistics of expectation of royal lives in those days, had not much longer to live. Bodley and Oldenbarnevelt seem to have been speculating on Elizabeth's well-known disinclination to make any provisions for her own death; a similar psychological calculation is reflected in the decision that the annual tribute should be conveyed by an ad hoc delegation, which was to express the States' gratitude to the Queen for her magnanimity: she was regarded as 'desirous of worldly fanfare', that is pomp and circumstance, according to the extent of which she might be disposed to drop a million or so of her claim.

We do not know whether Bodley would have succeeded by personal influence in obtaining acceptance of this proposal by his royal mistress. Before this stage he had resigned after a quarrel, as he could no longer stand the constant reproaches by Burghley and Elizabeth herself. According to Markham,[1] 'This man was not endowed with that patience and unselfish zeal which enable public servants to bear unreasonable censure as part of the day's work.'

Buzanval, in a speech to the States-General on 18 December 1595, alluded again to a definite alliance of the three countries at war with Spain. If England would not take part, it should be confined for the time to France and the States-General. Oldenbarnevelt did not care much for this: a dual alliance with France would be rather one-sided. Three or four thousand men would have to be kept permanently in France without any certainty that it would enable Henry to launch a real offensive in the southern Netherlands. The worst part, however, was that such an alliance would alienate Elizabeth. An alliance without England could really only amount to an alliance against England as well. That was incompatible with the Treaty of Nonsuch. Moreover, far-reaching military obligations did not sound well in conjunction with protestations of inability to repay the money advanced by Elizabeth. Oldenbarnevelt therefore lay low for a time, till the English Queen should also have been persuaded by Henry to join the alliance.

[1] *The Fighting Veres*, p. 208.

Henry's efforts in this direction occupied all the winter and a great part of the spring. Elizabeth was not averse from an alliance with France, which would assure her against a separate peace urged by most of Henry's counsellors. But she wished to make the minimum of sacrifice herself, since both the action planned against Spain and the rebellion of Tyrone in Ireland taxed her military and monetary resources too much for her to consider a continental expedition of any size as well. Nor did she yet intend to allow the States-General, whom she still looked on as her protégés, to join the alliance on an equal footing. That was unacceptable to Henry. He found the States a much more dependable ally than Elizabeth, and if there was an alliance he wanted to be able to play one party off against the other. He did not fail to point out to Calvart that through his attitude in this matter at the intended Franco-English conference 'the establishment of the State of your Excellencies (the States-General) . . . will have stronger and deeper foundations than hitherto'.

Francis Vere too, who was in England in February, in a conversation with Essex advocated a realistic policy and the formal recognition of the de facto independence of the Netherlands state. He was right. Netherlands participation was, after all, of the highest importance for both parties, and was only to be had on this condition. Nobody who knew Oldenbarnevelt could disguise that from himself for a moment.

Yet it took three months for Elizabeth to agree. In March Robert Sidney, sent by Elizabeth as envoy to France, was still telling Calvart that the Queen would regard the States-General as subordinate to England in the alliance. Her attitude was changed, not by the persuasiveness of Essex, with his lack of diplomacy, nor by the modest soldier Vere, but by the military events in France.

At the end of March 1596 the newly appointed governor, Albert of Austria, made a surprise attack on Calais at the head of a considerable army. Henry was engaged in the siege of La Fère, that he did not wish to raise. From Boulogne, where he went in person, he appealed to his allies for help. He was lucky in that Essex was at that moment at Dover with 8,000 men, ready to set sail for the Spanish expedition. Nothing would have pleased him more than to use the soldiers for the relief of Calais. Elizabeth forbade it unless Henry would cede the town to her. She sent Sidney to Boulogne to practise this discreditable blackmail. Calvart went with the King to the shore to welcome Sidney and heard from the former, not from the shamefaced English nobleman, how their conversation had ended. The King had refused. He hoped that he would some time be able to recapture the town from the Spaniards, but not that it would be given back to him by the English.

The Netherlands were informed of the siege of Calais by a message from the governor of the town. Maurice left in haste for Zeeland to place himself at the head of an auxiliary operation by sea. He wrote Oldenbarnevelt a private letter from Delfshaven with a list of his military requirements. Oldenbarnevelt was the moving spirit of this enterprise as well. Again he tried to prevent Maurice from putting to sea himself and endangering his life. Again Maurice took no notice and sailed for Calais, but entry to the harbour was blocked by a fort taken by the Spaniards on the first day of the siege. Maurice could not see any chance of effecting a landing and went back to Flushing with nothing achieved. Calais fell to the Spaniards on 24 April. The Netherlands effort had failed and, like the previous ones, produced only immaterial benefit: the increased goodwill of the King.

The fall of Calais made Elizabeth much more amenable with regard to joining a firm alliance with France. While the siege was still going on Henry had sent his minister Sancy to England again; he was a converted Protestant who had the King's ear more than anyone at that time and could be called the spiritual father of the idea of a triple alliance. Henry's other influential minister, Villeroy, had a realistic mind that attached more importance to coincidence of interests than promises in treaties. He and Oldenbarnevelt were made to get on well together. The latter entered fully into the negotiations, but his main concern was not the military results – he was rather sceptical on that score – but the enhanced status of the Republic.

In the weeks following the fall of Calais negotiations were started in England about an alliance, at first only between England and France, but in which the participation of the Netherlands was aimed at from the beginning. Burghley, chief negotiator on the English side, was not originally enthusiastic about it. The object – for Elizabeth the only object – of such an alliance must be to keep the French King at war. But would not the effect be just the opposite? Might not Henry be wanting to use the alliance to put pressure on the Spaniards to agree to an acceptable peace? Would it not be better to forestall the French and make peace with Spain oneself? Burghley suggested this openly in his introductory speech at the conference; an allusion to the cautionary towns and Calais suggested to Bouillon a well-defined plan to exchange them for Calais. More was said about the Netherlanders, not yet present. The French envoys urged Burghley to persuade the Hollanders to impose a stringent prohibition on trade with the enemy. This request for intervention ran somewhat counter to the repeated insistence on recognition of Netherlands sovereignty by the English. Elizabeth was stubborn about this for a long time; the French began to speak of the Netherlands as being under an 'esclavage anglais'. Finally the negotiations, which for a long time had threatened to break down, led to the offensive and defensive Treaty of Greenwich. Elizabeth had succeeded in restricting her concrete undertakings to a minimum. Though the treaty mentioned grandiose plans for a joint offensive war in 1597 they were explicitly made subject to Elizabeth's approval. Her immediate obligations did not extend beyond the furnishing of 4,000 men for six months. This number was small enough even by the standards of the times – Albert had entered Picardy with 21,000. But the King was satisfied, especially as the Hollanders could thus be actuated by it to supply an equal number of auxiliaries. With this joint support of 8,000 men, mostly hardened veterans, there was hope of being able to take the offensive.

In reality the support granted by Elizabeth was only half the 4,000 provided for by the treaty. The other 2,000 were just to throw dust in the eyes of the States and of German and other rulers, who were to be invited to participate in the treaty.

Henry IV had thought of a Machiavellian trick to hoodwink the States still more. He had asked Calvart to accompany the French delegation to England, allegedly so as to be able to give the States an eye-witness account of the negotiations, in reality, by seeming to trust him, to pull the wool over his eyes more easily. Poor Calvart wrote touchingly about the complete confidence the King had in him, 'saying often expressly, and as I believe without dissembling (of which there is little in him) that he did not desire to withhold knowledge of his actions affecting this war from your Excellencies'.

During the conference he flitted busily among the English and the French. He ascribed to himself 'without boasting' a great deal of the merit for the negotiations not being broken off. Oldenbarnevelt, with a lower estimate of his fellow-men, must have smiled at Calvart's innocent bragging. But he too was taken in; the truth only came to light a year later through an indiscretion of Buzanval's.

The trickery by which Oldenbarnevelt too was duped was an advantage to him rather than the opposite. He was determined to do his utmost to support Henry militarily and financially, whatever England did or did not do. He could pursue this policy better in the States-General if England set a good example by promising a fair-sized contingent. He therefore had no reason to take it amiss that Calvart had let himself be used by the French King as an instrument of his policy. At first there was some indignation in the States-General at his unauthorized journey to England and the Netherlands. He was put on the carpet and reprimanded. Oldenbarnevelt's intercession and the general rejoicing at the Treaty of Greenwich saved him from further unpleasant consequences.

It was some time before the States-General were invited to join the alliance. Buzanval explained this by the necessity for ratification and the oath that Henry and Elizabeth had to swear before it came into force. Till then it was better for the States not to join. What he did not add was that Bouillon and Sancy were highly dissatisfied with the results obtained, that ratification by the French was far from certain and that the whole treaty might be cancelled if the peace proposals expected from Spain turned out favourably. Buzanval's concrete proposals were therefore confined to an urgent request for military aid against Albert, outside the scope of any treaty obligations.

Oldenbarnevelt proposed not answering this request at present. A refusal might offend the King just as he was needed for their official inclusion in the treaty. Consent was still less to the mind of the States. They were very short of soldiers that summer, especially after helping Elizabeth's Spanish expedition.

The expedition to Cadiz was undertaken with Oldenbarnevelt's full approval. He regarded it as the price of Elizabeth's agreement to the post-ponement – so badly needed by the States – of discharge of debt. Here again, as so often, he emphasized diplomatic expediency as compared with military disadvantage. He had the number of ships asked for by Elizabeth reduced from thirty to twenty-four. He also attempted to make Elizabeth reduce the number of auxiliaries required, but failing in this, with a heavy heart he had the States-General consent to the withdrawal of the 2,200 men requested. With his own hand he drew up the instructions for Admiral Warmond, who was to lead the Netherlands squadron under Howard.

The troops left for England at the end of April and were held up there for the whole of May. It was again apparent that long-distance troop movements were an uneconomic method of warfare and that landing operations without a nearby naval base held little chance of success. Cadiz was captured quickly, as well as enormous booty, but Howard, of the opinion that he could not hold the town, left after a few days in spite of furious opposition from Essex, Vere and Warmond, on the insistence of the officers and men who wanted to secure their loot as fast as possible. Militarily the venture was another fiasco, like that in 1589. Even the damage done to the preparations for the new Armada was not enough to stop it setting sail in the autumn, scarcely less formidable than that of 1588; only storms and inadequate Spanish seaman-ship prevented the fleet reaching the North Sea. Meanwhile Oldenbarnevelt had attained his political objective. Warmond's behaviour on the expedition had enhanced comradeship in arms with Vere and Essex. He was the only naval commander who gave help to Essex when he got separated from the main forces on the return voyage; he was rewarded with a most flattering letter from Elizabeth, whose suspicious attitude towards the Netherlands gave way in the next few months to positive benevolence. From now on her strong prejudice against Oldenbarnevelt seems to have vanished; indeed the only letter from her to Oldenbarnevelt that has been preserved expresses trust, as did his reception on his two embassies to England in 1598.

The Netherlands had been pretty well emptied of troops both by Justin of Nassau's expedition to France and the naval operation against Cadiz. When Albert, after the capture of Ardres, broke off his offensive in France to turn his attention to Zeeland–Flanders, Hulst, recaptured five years previously, was soon in the greatest danger. The town was invested by the Spaniards on 10 July 1596, three days after Justin's troops had returned to Flushing, exhausted and unfit for battle. The garrison of Hulst under the Count of Solms was of poor quality and he was himself incompetent and irresolute, without authority over his officers. Maurice set up his headquarters at Kruiningen, where he was visited by Oldenbarnevelt at the head of a States-General deputation. The fall of Hulst could be regarded as imminent.

Oldenbarnevelt had indeed made efforts to obtain help from his allies at the eleventh hour. Henry's inactivity after the capture of La Fère had aroused much anger in the Netherlands and was attributed to lack of fighting spirit among the French, though gratefully seized on as the chief cause of the loss of Hulst. Both accusations were unfounded. Shortage of money and poor discipline in the army had caused Henry's inactivity while neglect by the States-General and the stinginess of the States of Zeeland were more to blame for Hulst than France's lack of striking power, of which the Netherlands had long been aware.

Matters were different with England insofar as Elizabeth, when summoning the greater part of the auxiliaries for the voyage to Cadiz, had promised to support the States with an extra consignment of troops in case of need. She fulfilled her obligation by sending 500 men to Flushing; but, if they ever actually arrived, they were too late to save Hulst, which capitulated on 18 August.

Oldenbarnevelt had hurriedly forced through a fresh levy of 2,000 men, but that was not till 27 July, and was, in any case, intended more for withstanding further attack by the enemy once Hulst had been taken. All these measures came much too late and worked much too slowly. A good illustration of the drawbacks of Netherlands federalism.

The loss of Hulst was a sharp blow for Oldenbarnevelt's and Maurice's prestige. The simplest thing would have been to divert popular indignation to Solms, whose behaviour had certainly not been above criticism. The Zeelanders took this course, without consulting the Council of State or the States-General.

Oldenbarnevelt took Solms's side in this dispute and eventually found an acceptable solution, while still relieving Zeeland of an unwelcome regimental commander. Solms was promoted from lieutenant-colonel to colonel, with increase of pay but without a regiment. Oldenbarnevelt's motives in the matter, which made him many enemies in Zeeland, can only be guessed at: partly perhaps respect for Solms's noble rank, but mainly the maintenance of Maurice's authority as commander-in-chief. He and the Council of State had accepted Solms's explanations for reasons of their own, probably much the same as in the case of Héraugière. The fall of Hulst was the result of a complex of circumstances, for which the responsibility was greatly divided. Oldenbarnevelt himself, but also Maurice, the States-General, the Council of State and the States of Zeeland were all open to criticism. On a purely personal level the Advocate's brother, a captain in the defending garrison of Hulst, had compromised himself badly, which could reflect on his own position. In such cases it is always expedient to hush thingsup, as we have seen Oldenbarnevelt do before.

There was also another side to it. The consequences of the loss of Hulst were not nearly so serious as they had seemed at first. Spanish losses had been heavy, both of men and money. The surviving troops were in poor shape, so that Albert was unable to carry out any significant offensives for the rest of the year. Oldenbarnevelt's power was therefore not shaken for long. On the contrary, the fact that the Zeelanders were open to criticism made it easier for him next year to bring his long-drawn-out dispute with that province to a conclusion favourable to Holland. The wind was not so ill as to blow no one any good.

In September, Bouillon, having taken Elizabeth's oath on the Treaty of Greenwich, obtained her permission to go to the Netherlands, and invite them, both in her name and that of his King, to take part in the treaty. He arrived at The Hague with a brilliant retinue of more than sixty nobles. Oldenbarnevelt, responsible for housing them, had his worries. There was no question of putting these dignitaries up in the simple inns with which The Hague abounded. They had to be quartered on private people, as had been done before on similar occasions, but never on such a large scale. Either a costly agreement had to be made or the nobles would have to make do with smaller and less comfortable lodgings.

In spite of these pressing affairs Oldenbarnevelt found time to set out at the head of the almost complete States of Holland to visit Bouillon at his lodgings in the Noordeinde. He made an uncharacteristically short speech of welcome. The next day he delivered another welcoming speech, this time in the name of the States-General, who had also proceeded in a body from the

Binnenhof to Noordeinde. Bouillon invited the Advocate to a *tête à tête* in the afternoon, when they got down to business, with the special object of speeding matters up, Bouillon having heard in England how difficult it was to negotiate in the Netherlands because of time-wasting *ruggespraak*. Oldenbarnevelt promised to meet his wishes and impress on the provinces the need for haste. He was successful. Scarcely a month later the deputies, who had taken Bouillon's proposal back to their provincial capitals, returned with complete authorization, and after a few days of intense negotiations the text of the Triple Alliance was drafted.

The text was not as advantageous in every respect as Oldenbarnevelt had hoped. The impression that he had insufficiently disguised his joy at the honour shown to the Netherlands cannot be avoided. Bouillon could see with half an eye that his own negotiating position was a strong one. The result was that the States entered into more obligations to France than Elizabeth had done, even without taking the secret treaty into account. They promised to assist the French King with troops and the substantial annual sum of 450,000 guilders without, like Elizabeth, bringing up the subject of repayment. They did get it back later, but only because Henry wanted to make the subsidies that it was in his interest to grant the States look like obligatory discharges of debt.

Another point which the Netherlands negotiators pressed in vain was that Henry and Elizabeth should give them the undertaking they had given each other, not to make a separate peace with Spain. Oldenbarnevelt may not have insisted on this too strongly. He was realistic enough to know how little value such a clause usually has when circumstances change.

The main thing was, and continued to be, the definitive inclusion of the Netherlands republic among the independent powers, on a level with Venice. It was what Oldenbarnevelt had been aiming at for years. Only as to the nomenclature of the new state was there still any uncertainty. In the pre-amble to the treaty the separate provinces were named as contracting parties: the child had as yet no name. Oldenbarnevelt, never a great one for formalities, probably did not worry much about it.

The public was to take part exuberantly in the rejoicings: there was a banquet for 'the quality', the bells were rung, barrels of tar were burnt to feast the ears and eyes of the people. But the joy was not unanimous. In the short run the grumblers were right: nothing came of the plans of which the Triple Alliance was the expression and hardly a year after its merry launching the little ship was wrecked on cliffs already in sight. Yet Bouillon need not have been grudged his six carriage horses, his chest of linen, his boxful of gold and silver and his pension of 1,000 pounds: a framework had been created within which national history was to be enacted till the end of the Republic in 1795.

An end had now been put to Elizabeth's uncertain and disputed protectorate. She did not deem it necessary to have it confirmed by a Duke; plain Mr Gilpin signed on her behalf. She also expressed her dissatisfaction to the envoys Oldenbarnevelt sent to thank her for her obliging attitude, and at the same time to try and reach agreement on repayment terms on the basis of the annuity project suggested by Bodley. Elizabeth had rejected this when it had been submitted by Bodley, so the embassy did not succeed and the question remained in the air for two years. Oldenbarnevelt knew that it was a moral impossibility for Elizabeth to let this matter lead to a breach in the same month that she had assented to the Triple Alliance. He also knew that at some time he would have to make a more liberal offer, but the later the better.

The Triple Alliance was intended to be enlarged into an anti-Spanish coalition including German Protestant princes, and perhaps Denmark and Sweden as well. Henry in particular was very keen on persuading the Germans to join his team and sent envoys round with high hopes, but without any results. Oldenbarnevelt sent a Netherlands envoy round too, with the same purpose and the same result. He, however, had been sceptical from the start about any such chances and was chiefly concerned to oblige Henry and keep him in the Alliance, there being almost at once indications that he was considering breaking away from it.

Negligible as the diplomatic effects of the Triple Alliance still were, from a military point of view it was equally disappointing.

Maurice gained his first important victory in the open field in January 1597. Vere states in his memoirs that the plan for a hit-and-run offensive against the main Spanish forces encamped near Turnhout was first suggested by him in a conversation with Oldenbarnevelt, whom he often met that winter. It is remarkable that Vere mentions Oldenbarnevelt and not Maurice, a proof that it was the former and not the latter who was considered the decisive factor in planning operations of importance.

The Spaniards suffered a shattering defeat on 24 January 1597. But it is typical of the cautious strategic methods of those days that Maurice did not think he was able to take advantage of his victory. He was back at Geertruidenberg almost as soon as he had left. He seems to have expected Henry to make use of Turnhout. Calvart was ordered to complain to Henry about his inactivity. That was unreasonable. The King did not dispose of a mobile field army that he could use at short notice for a powerful offensive. He had one in mind, but it needed preparation and depended on the military help that Elizabeth and the States had led him to expect. Elizabeth had only sent him the 2,000 men that she had promised him for immediate use in the secret clause of the Treaty of Greenwich. The States did not as yet send any soldiers; they were waiting till a proper plan of campaign should be drawn up in joint consultation with an invasion of Artois and Hainault. Furthermore Oldenbarnevelt greatly mistrusted Henry's intentions, which might be to use any reinforcements in Picardy as a basis for negotiations for obtaining favourable peace conditions from Spain more quickly.

The situation changed radically, both for the better and for the worse, when the Spaniards succeeded on 11 March 1597 in surprising Amiens, the supply base for the French army in the coming campaign. For the worse because now nothing would come of any French or allied offensive in Artois. But in Oldenbarnevelt's opinion, though he could not say so openly, its advantages far outweighed its disadvantages. The Great Offensive had now definitely been relegated to the fiction department, without the need to antagonize Henry by throwing doubts on the realism of his plans. On the other hand he would now be obliged to make a great effort of his own accord: Albert's troops would have to be used to relieve Amiens if the King laid siege to it, and the absence of these troops could be put to good use in the Netherlands. The greatest advantage of all was that Henry would be certain not to make peace as long as the Spaniards were in the middle of his country, while the latter, intoxicated by victory, would raise their demands to a level not warranted by their financial position.

It was thus of vital interest to the Hollanders that their trusty ally should not succeed in recapturing his beloved Amiens too soon. They did not mind his regaining it, for it would humble their common enemy – provided it was long deferred.

These considerations explain the at first slight surprising fact that the States-General pretended to be deaf to Henry's repeated and increasingly urgent appeals for help. He twice wrote to Oldenbarnevelt personally, but gained nothing, getting a dusty answer each time.

Things went just as Oldenbarnevelt had predicted: Henry encamped before Amiens, Albert led a relief force to the south. There was a strong feeling in the country for Bouillon as head of the militant faction among the French Calvinists and Prince Maurice's brother-in-law. His efforts aimed at vigorous war against Spain, his opposition to the pacific tendencies of the majority of the Crown Council – all fitted in with Oldenbarnevelt's desires. But the line of his French policy was to give the dissatisfied Huguenots no official support should they cease to confine themselves to respectful protests and take direct action. The situation was similar to that under Henry III, with Bouillon in the role then filled by Henry of Navarre. Now too an extremely cautious policy was imperative; without entirely abandoning the Huguenots to their fate it took great care not to damage the King or virtually to force him into a pro-Spanish policy.

On 5 March 1597 the Huguenots met at Saumur, the town where Du Plessis Mornay was governor. The latter, head of the moderate Huguenot party, managed to prevent a decision in favour of renewed civil war. Buzanval in the Netherlands sent a warning that in such a case no support at all could be expected from the Netherlanders. The assembly therefore confined itself for the time being to a letter drafted by Bouillon, explaining the Huguenots' critical situation. Henry for his part instructed Buzanval on his return to the Netherlands to ask the States to exert a moderating influence on the assembly at Saumur. Oldenbarnevelt proposed that the States should write exactly as the King suggested. Once more the States were persuaded; the letter went off as Oldenbarnevelt wished. A fresh Huguenot meeting decided to answer this letter, obviously inspired by Buzanval, the lukewarm royal servant, by sending a delegate, La Forest. He was given credentials to Oldenbarnevelt personally. The time had not yet come when the French Huguenots would try to achieve their own ends by stirring up Oldenbarnevelt's opponents.

It was the middle of September before La Forest arrived at The Hague. He had a list with him of nobles and towns who had united to exert armed pressure on the King if need be. It could have been dangerous for Oldenbarnevelt's statecraft to let this likeable Calvinist loose on the States-General unprepared. He therefore pursued an unusual course. Before La Forest obtained an official audience, Oldenbarnevelt wormed the entire content of his mission out of him and communicated it, without his being present, to the States, strongly spiced with his own comments.

The dangerous man could not be refused admittance. After waiting a fortnight he obtained his hearing. The States-General had by then been sufficiently worked upon. Oldenbarnevelt was charged with answering La Forest's request in complete cooperation with Buzanval. The short summary of the letter to be written was quite non-committal, a sort of explanation in general terms of the letter of 7 May, with the declaration that they pinned their faith to peace and friendship in France. However, Oldenbarnevelt and Buzanval went far beyond the States' resolution in drafting the letter. They wrote that they had learnt with satisfaction from the churches' letter that they would accommodate themselves to the service of His Majesty – a *protestatio actui contraria*, occurring indeed in the letter but not intended to be taken seriously. The States further expressed their opinion that there was no remedy but to reunite the whole body of the kingdom under prompt and voluntary obedience to His Majesty – thus hardly expressing the opinion of the majority of the States. The wording of the letter was not so divergent from the resolution as to prevent the president for that week from signing it without suspicion.

The summer of 1597 saw the beginning of the end of the still fresh Triple Alliance. Three events on the military plane contributed to it.

In the first place there was the Island Voyage, the unfortunate Anglo-Netherlands expedition to the Azores, on which the troops, so badly needed by Henry at Amiens, were wasted far away.

The Netherlands attitude to France, though in accordance with the letter of the treaty, was not quite that of an ally. No Netherlands soldiers appeared before Amiens. No diversionary manoeuvre had prevented Albert taking the field for its relief. This lack of enterprise was certainly largely due to lack of money. Albert had then directed his troops towards the south and there seemed to be a chance of gaining ground in the east. Shortage of money was not entirely over. This shortage became apparent when, after Rheinberg on the left bank of the Rhine had been taken, 170 carts and the necessary food had to be provided to transfer the army to Gelderland, Oldenbarnevelt did not succeed in getting the money required sent to the army. Maurice was forced to make a collection from the nobles in the army: only then, on 8 September, was he able to transport it across the Rhine towards the north.

It made little difference to Henry whether his ally's uselessness was caused by impotence or unwillingness. On 8 August he wrote to Oldenbarnevelt personally – the third letter in four months – asking for 10,000 guilders to be sent him. Oldenbarnevelt wanted nothing better than to oblige the King, but the amount, though so small, was too high now money was so scarce; the States resolved on his suggestion to divide the money into four monthly instalments.

Henry put a good face on it. He dutifully congratulated the States on every conquest, but after Rheinberg he added the request that the next town to be attacked should be a little nearer Amiens. Exactly the opposite happened. In September and October Maurice mopped up parts of Gelderland and Overijsel still held by the enemy – Groenlo fell on 27 September – and Lingen. The fence was mended, but the French ally was lost.

Naturally the connection was not so straightforward as it is pictured here. The main factor that forced Henry on to the path of negotiation was not the Island Voyage or Maurice's unfriendly procedure. It was the recapture of Amiens, after the failure of a seemingly dangerous relief attempt by Albert. The States demonstrated their joy at their ally's success just as dutifully as Henry had that of Rheinberg. But the ringing of the great bells of triumph in the tower at The Hague, ordained at Oldenbarnevelt's instigation on

5 October, found no general echo in the hearts of the people. It was too clearly realized that these bells were ringing out the Triple Alliance that they had so joyfully rung in a year before with such hopeful expectations.

Before going on to the consequences of these affairs abroad, we will first outline some developments in home politics, and the relationship between Oldenbarnevelt, his supporters, and his opponents.

CHAPTER 6

Supporters and opponents

W E are all familiar with the teachings of Marx. We know that a
revolution like that which occurred in 1618 cannot be explained
by personal antitheses. The historian must take account of the
great waves of culture determining the rise and fall of Arminianism, the keen
and, for the present-day sceptic, surprising reaction of Calvinism. Beneath
these waves he will surmise class struggles, not visible on the surface. He
will point out the progressiveness of intolerance reminiscent of the Middle
Ages. The conservatism of the seventeenth-century liberals will be an open
book to him. The inevitable victory of the former over the latter he will
regard as determined by history and see in Oldenbarnevelt's downfall
nothing but a link in an inescapable chain of development.

All these points of view have their *raison d'être*, but they exclude the tragic
element that grows only in the atmosphere of personal relations. According to
pure philosophy they may not be weighty, but they are decisive. Oldenbarnevelt fell because of his vain resistance to the course of events. He was
destroyed by his antagonists: Amsterdam, Zeeland, the clerics and a few other
elements; factors whose weight will have to be estimated. And then there was
hatred by individual enemies, in whose gaze tragedy culminates. Foremost
among them was Prince Maurice, whose choice of party in 1617 was
ultimately decisive.

The breach between the two founders of Netherlands independence,
ending in the bloody scene on the Binnenhof – no wonder that this eminently
dramatic circumstance enthralled our forefathers. We too will be enthralled,
following the growing hatred and aversion between Maurice and Oldenbarnevelt, but then we will turn our attention to the part played by other prominent
figures. At present we are confining ourselves to the first fourteen years of
Oldenbarnevelt's period of office, from his appointment in 1586 till the
preparation of the campaign in Flanders in 1600.

At the beginning of this period there was a close relationship between
Maurice and Oldenbarnevelt, almost that of ward and guardian. It was
Oldenbarnevelt who, after Prince William's death, advocated on behalf of
Rotterdam young Maurice's promotion to the rank of Count of Holland. It

was he again, still pensionary of Rotterdam, who took the initiative in making him stadtholder or governor of that province and of Zeeland shortly before Leicester's arrival. Later, at the time of Leicester's claims to supreme power, it was again Maurice who was a target of these 'usurpations', and Oldenbarnevelt who gave his protégé every possible support against the dangerous Governor-General. Soon Oldenbarnevelt was the overt head of an opposition, whose activities were carried on largely in the name of Maurice's threatened rights. The young man went along with this entirely, particularly when his power was considerably extended after the fall of Deventer and he had the feeling that he himself was the saviour of his country. During these years Maurice was full of gratitude and respect for his patron and first counsellor, and Oldenbarnevelt for his part took a liking to the son of his hero and *Bezugsperson*,[1] William of Orange, with his docile character and apparent lack of any troublesome interest in politics.

But from the start there were other facets. To begin with there was Maurice's mother, Anna of Saxony. She was not mentioned in Prince William's household after the break-up of the marriage and her imprisonment. The effects of such family catastrophes on different characters are not uniform, but assumptions can be made: it undermined Maurice's trust in humanity and made him an introverted, inhibited celibate, one of the still waters that run deep, much more dangerous than he would appear to anyone who only saw him in his lighter moments at parties with Hohenlohe, Solms or Philip of Nassau.

His entourage gave no less cause for concern. Marnix and Villiers, friends of his father, William, were independent theologians, not on bad terms with Oldenbarnevelt, but not at all to be regarded as subservient. Still less was that the case with his master of horse, Malderé, later to turn out an inveterate enemy of Oldenbarnevelt, when he was appointed by Maurice as his representative in the States of Zeeland as *Eerste Edele*.[2] The head of Maurice's secretarial office, Nicolaas Bruynincx, also inherited from the late Prince, was an exile for his faith from 's Hertogenbosch, still in Spanish hands. All his life Oldenbarnevelt was averse to refugees from the south, and though we know nothing of Bruynincx to indicate hostility to the Advocate, his loyalty was entirely to his old master's son, and at the least hint of trouble Oldenbarnevelt would not be able to rely on him. Maurice's ex-tutor, still with great influence over him, was a German, like his second secretary, and his legal adviser was another refugee from Brabant. He was the only one whom there was reason to

---

[1] Role-model; exemplar.
[2] As premier noble of the province Maurice had the right of voting first in the States, a right he exercised by proxy.

count as a supporter of Oldenbarnevelt, as he had lost his previous position to Leicester's notorious favourite, Ringault, and had probably not obtained his present one without the Advocate's efforts. But there is nothing to show that Oldenbarnevelt gained anything from this relationship, hypothetical in any case.

So there were four Belgians, two Germans and a Frenchman (Villiers). Not one Hollander or Zeelander, though it was obvious that the stadtholder of these two provinces, the servant of the States, should have composed his somewhat meagre 'court' largely of such people. Oldenbarnevelt would surely have wished it, but these men, mostly taken on from Prince William, were already in office when he came to power and he did not feel himself firmly enough in the saddle in the 1590s to make any changes in this entourage. It was much later that he managed to get his son-in-law, Cornelis van der Mijle, appointed to Maurice's 'Council', after Villiers had been superseded some years before as court chaplain by Uyttenbogaert; the latter hailed from Utrecht like Oldenbarnevelt himself and was on the way to becoming Oldenbarnevelt's best friend. But in the first few years of his stadt-holdership we can confidently say that Maurice's milieu, and the influences exerted on him in his youth, were not such as to win him over to Oldenbarnevelt personally or to the oligarchic interests he represented.

It would have been different if Maurice's stepmother, Louise de Coligny, had been much about him or influenced him greatly. She was on good terms, eventually almost friendly, with Oldenbarnevelt. Later on, right up to the night before Oldenbarnevelt's execution, she repeatedly used her influence with Maurice in his favour. But her influence was not great. During the fifteen months of Louise's marriage to the Prince, Maurice was a student at Leiden; after the assassination Louise, with her baby son and five young stepdaughters, did not join Maurice in the Binnenhof but set up a separate household at the Oude Hof of Brantwijck, later Noordeinde Palace. So Louise and Maurice never lived under the same roof. Psychologically it is reasonable to suppose that the lad of fifteen did not welcome his new step-mother. When she had had a son, she fervently championed his interests, not always parallel with those of his half-brother. Furthermore she remained heart and soul a Frenchwoman, as can be imagined. She could sometimes almost be regarded as an agent of Henry IV in the Netherlands; Maurice was rather sceptical of Oldenbarnevelt's French policy and undoubtedly did not like this. Their relations cannot be called bad, strained is too strong a word, cool they certainly were. If Oldenbarnevelt fell out with Maurice, he could not expect much help from Louise.

More was to be expected of Maurice's comrades in arms, he supposed. The

young Prince had soon shown that, unlike his father, war in the field interested him more than war in the council chamber. That was of course just
what Oldenbarnevelt wanted, and it is not hard to imagine that he did everything to stimulate this interest, to satisfy this need for action. He had long
known how to get on with soldiers; he had many good contacts among the
higher officers of the Leicester period, those most suited to giving Maurice
guidance in this field and to divert him from any opposition to the powerful
Advocate.

It was a grave miscalculation. Fate on the one hand, Maurice's very great
though highly specialized capability on the other, frustrated Oldenbarnevelt's
intentions. Three of the four high-ranking officers in the Netherlands army at
the time of Leicester's departure were killed in 1589. The fourth and highest
in rank, Hohenlohe, with whom Oldenbarnevelt was on particularly good
terms, fell out with the stadtholder, who was his opposite in almost every
respect, as cautious as Hohenlohe was reckless, as thoughtful as the other was
unthinking. He had nothing to learn from this firebrand seventeen years his
elder. It enraged him that Hohenlohe never went so far that he could decently
dismiss him; he insulted him when he had the chance and used him when he
had no other choice. Oldenbarnevelt took great pains all this time to patch up
the quarrels between these two chief army leaders. One wonders why he did
not let Hohenlohe go, even when he himself occasionally urged it and Maurice
keenly desired it. It is possible to set up an acceptable hypothesis for his
motives in the matter. First there was his permanent prejudice in favour of
coronets, attributable not only to snobbishness but also to the fact that ruling
counts in Germany were still well looked upon and enjoyed some prestige
with the German troops. A disgruntled count in Germany could do the States
a lot of harm, especially when it came to recruiting troops. In Hohenlohe's
case it also happened that years of acquaintanceship and alliance against
Leicester had brought about a sort of friendship between these dissimilar
characters. Hohenlohe let himself be advised and led by Oldenbarnevelt in all
his actions. He went about a lot with the top people in the States of Holland,
which could not be said of Maurice. He was much more affable and stood
drinks freely to everyone he met, so that he was popular among the oligarchs
and loved by his soldiers, in the first few years certainly more than the cool
and strict captain-general. It is therefore natural that Oldenbarnevelt should
have done his best to maintain this weak figure as number two in the army;
nor is there need for suspecting Oldenbarnevelt of desiring a counterpoise to
the increasingly powerful commander and so controlling the Netherlands
army on the principle of *divide et impera*. The idea must sometimes have
occurred to Oldenbarnevelt but it is most unlikely that he let himself be

influenced by it. In the first place poor Hohenlohe was no match, either personally or by his position, for Prince William's son, as Oldenbarnevelt knew very well. Moreover the temptation to create a counterpoise to Maurice was not great for someone who did not know what was going to happen in 1617–19. Maurice was and remained a docile executant of the orders of the States, whose purse-strings, incidentally, kept him efficiently under control. Differences of opinion occasionally caused ruffled feelings. Maurice got out of control sometimes, but not for long. The basis of mutual trust, an accurate estimate of each side's power, was at this time not yet shaken, as Oldenbarnevelt knew.

Primarily that was due to Maurice's character but also to that of his staff, the senior officers who, in the summer campaigning season, were his only companions, and in the winter his chief ones. They might be called his council of war, as they were by the English in 1589.[1]

It is typical, and from Oldenbarnevelt's point of view slightly disturbing, that the four officers mentioned in this context were all Belgians. They could not, however, be regarded as confidants of the commander-in-chief, especially after the oldest, bearing the then not very exalted rank of 'field marshal', died in 1589. The advantage of their South-Netherlands origin was that they had no political ambitions, nor did they steer Maurice on that course, which would have been dangerous for Oldenbarnevelt.

Two other foreigners were indeed Maurice's confidants, an Englishman and a German, whose position involved a somewhat equivocal subordination to him. Maurice consulted them as equals, and not as their superior, as in the case of the others. They were independent of their commander-in-chief and accordingly had their own access to Oldenbarnevelt, not gained through Maurice.

One was the commander of the English auxiliaries, Sir Francis Vere. He was on friendly terms with both Maurice and Oldenbarnevelt. When he returned to England for good in 1606 it was a loss for Oldenbarnevelt in his relations with Maurice, who was becoming less compliant.

Maurice's chief confidant, from the earliest years till after Oldenbarnevelt's death, was naturally the Frisian stadtholder, William Louis. It was he who in 1589 took the initiative in the army reforms *more romano*, from which Maurice gained immortal fame; his share in Maurice's campaign plans was a large one, preponderant in some cases. Though he voluntarily kept in the background as far as Maurice's genius and prestige was concerned, we need not doubt that his influence over his cousin, seven years his junior, was great and only exceeded by that of Oldenbarnevelt himself. What was the effect of this influence with regard to Oldenbarnevelt?

[1] Calendar of State Papers, XXIII, 237.

Politically speaking William Louis was certainly further to the 'right' than Oldenbarnevelt – if nineteenth-century ecclesiastical–political oppositions may be projected into the sixteenth century. He was further to the right not only than Oldenbarnevelt but also than Maurice, in this respect moderate and indifferent. In so far then as we can speak of people being to the right and left of Maurice at that time, William Louis and Oldenbarnevelt were pulling in opposite directions. The former, a devout Calvinist, had been highly praised by Leicester, had respected him as long as at all possible, and, under Maurice's influence, was late in joining his antagonists. He was a personal friend of Sonoy; he tried to mediate in his dispute with the States of Holland in 1587 in a way Oldenbarnevelt cannot have liked.

If then the state of affairs in the 1590s is regarded in terms of sharply outlined right and left antitheses, foreshadowing, as it were, the disputes during the truce, William Louis was definitely among Oldenbarnevelt's opponents. But matters were not nearly so simple as that. Disagreements in those years, both in politics and between the military and political leaders, were largely outside the right–left domain. That applied particularly to the great dispute that angered William Louis from 1593 to 1597: the fierce opposition of Carel Roorda and his supporters to the stadtholder's policy and to the Nassaus in general. Oldenbarnevelt sided entirely with the Nassaus in this quarrel. That was only natural, as Frisian opposition was particularistic and anti-Holland, whereas Oldenbarnevelt was always a centralist, provided the central authority was not anti-Holland. Such a political alliance of course benefited their personal relations. Moreover, William Louis was easier to get on with than Maurice, less reserved, suspicious and frigid: in short, the product of a happy family, and not, like Maurice, of a broken marriage. He found it easier to express himself in his letters, of which some have come down to us. Those to Oldenbarnevelt reflect trust and appreciation, but their religious views and their characters differed too much for close friendship. If a difference of opinion should arise between Maurice and Oldenbarnevelt the Frisian stadtholder would take Maurice's side as a matter of course. He could even be expected to egg Maurice on to resistance, if through insouciance or indifference he tended to acquiesce too far in the States' views. There are indications that this was the case at Arnhem.[1] It was certainly so in the religious troubles during the truce. On the other hand his warmer humanity would always try to avoid bringing issues to a head.

Now in the years we are speaking of, and long afterwards, there was really no question of any substantial conflict between Maurice and Oldenbarnevelt. There were differences of opinion such as occur among the managers of any

---

[1] See p. 181 above.

large concern. Such differences are not carried to extremes. One does not seek supporters to help push one's views through. One does not concentrate one's energies for months on the points of difference. One of the parties manages to get his way and the other resigns himself to it with a more or less good grace. In this case it was usually Oldenbarnevelt who was in a position to get his way, and the good grace part was left to Maurice. It was nothing to worry about. But there was an incidental circumstance, explaining why these differences of opinion left some iron in Maurice's soul. It was Maurice's ambivalent position – not perhaps in his own eyes and certainly not in Oldenbarnevelt's – but as seen in the world at large, by the people of the Netherlands and by their allies. Maurice was undeniably the first person in the Republic, by descent, stadtholdership and command of the forces. It was accentuated when in 1590 he was elected stadtholder of the three provinces Utrecht, Gelderland and Overijsel, as well as of Holland and Zeeland. Oldenbarnevelt had taken a lot of trouble about this, not out of personal liking for Maurice, but to strengthen Holland's grip on the eastern provinces and reinforce the authority of the States. Perhaps he did not realize that he was thus aggravating the abnormality of Maurice's position. Maurice, who with his five provinces was outstripping his cousin still further – he only had Friesland, and from 1594 the newly won provinces of Groningen and Drente, the latter not being represented in the States-General – bore, in contrast to his cousin, the title of Excellency, which sounded quite different in the sixteenth century from now, and was the only Netherlander to do so. He was also Prince, though the States avoided the title in their official documents. To the outside world he nevertheless looked like Prince of the country, comparable with the Doge of Venice, but hereditary, the commander-in-chief and therefore in a higher position. Yet the imperfections of this apparent monarch's power were alarming; we have already seen many examples and will soon see some more. It was the contrast between external splendour and actual servitude that more than anything else, certainly more than the servitude itself, turned Maurice into a discontented sour person. He was discredited by reverses for which he was not responsible and fulsomely congratulated on successes in which his part was purposely exaggerated. The latter was not less irritating than the former.

Of course it must not be supposed that in this period Maurice was forced by Oldenbarnevelt to do things that he was definitely against. It was more subtle: he was obliged to do things that he did not agree to, from which he felt an inner revulsion, without regarding them as utterly wrong. Sometimes his aversion can only be presumed, sometimes there is documentary evidence.

An instance of the first is the attempted subjection of Sonoy in the spring of 1587. It must have been repugnant to Maurice to suppress his father's old comrade in arms by extremes of force, as Oldenbarnevelt wished. He will have been glad that a milder attitude was urged upon him by Van der Mijle, also an old supporter of Prince William, after Oldenbarnevelt had left Hoorn.[1] When next year the attempt was repeated and brought to a successful conclusion, however, Maurice gives the impression of working for it heart and soul.[2] By then he had been accustomed for a year to the captain-generalship. He felt less unsure of himself after Leicester's final departure. His high office must be maintained against what he regarded as mutiny. Oldenbarnevelt and he took the same line here. Again in the following year, at the unsuccessful siege of Geertruidenberg,[3] we see that Maurice was almost as keen if not keener than Oldenbarnevelt. For the latter the supremacy of the authorities over the army was at stake in both cases, for Maurice his own supremacy. As long as both interests ran parallel there was cordial alliance in this sphere between Prince and Advocate.

We can though, after Leicester's return to the Netherlands, find a second example of how Maurice was forced by Oldenbarnevelt into a path he would rather not have trodden. At the Pescarengis trial the powerful statesman made use of him as president of the special court which, on purely political grounds, passed the death sentence not only on the Italian captain, but also on his far less guilty and most likeable partisan Maulde.[4] One can safely presume that Maurice signed this sentence with great reluctance.

One cannot find any clues to differences of opinion in the next few years. On the contrary: both Maurice's elevation to stadtholder of the three inland provinces and their close cooperation in the surprise capture of Breda cannot have affected their relationship other than favourably. At most one may suspect that Maurice, as he grew older, sometimes felt impatience at the constant tutelary attitude of the States, even in military matters. It was also due to the rough form in which the States' orders were sometimes phrased. When in 1590 they wanted a raid, which turned out not to be feasible, to be made on Namur and Hainault, they stated that if Maurice ventured to carry out the Council of State's plans for besieging some castles in Brabant, no gunpowder or other requirements would be provided.

If Maurice was affected by such pieces of tactlessness he did not show it. Oldenbarnevelt was thus encouraged to continue the dangerous course he had started. After the siege of Steenwijk he could not induce the States-General to give imperative instructions as to whether the campaign should be continued or not. He made the States of Holland refuse to deliver waggons and other requisites if Maurice carried out his plans for an offensive.[5]

[1] See p. 105.   [2] See p. 128.   [3] See pp. 148 ff.   [4] See p. 120.   [5] See pp. 197 ff.

From then onwards differences of opinion were the order of the day. They were often caused by Oldenbarnevelt's advocating more economical methods of warfare than Maurice considered necessary. The most serious clash before 1600, however, did not concern money but the extent to which Henry IV should be met half-way – in the literal sense as well. It was the dispute at Arnhem in October 1594.[1]

This shows for the first time the acute irritation Oldenbarnevelt's behaviour could arouse in Maurice. May one assume that the former made honourable amends, when it appeared that the haste had been entirely unnecessary, as far as France was concerned? It would be in character: like most short-tempered people, he did not mind admitting himself to have been wrong, at any rate in matters of minor importance. During the next few years relations seem to have been good again. The States-General resolutions, however, always struck a masterful note that must have originated with Oldenbarnevelt. When Maurice left in April 1596 to get the auxiliary expedition to Calais to sea[2], Oldenbarnevelt had reason to suppose that Maurice would go with the fleet himself. The Advocate was against this on various grounds and had an order issued by the States-General forbidding him to do so. It was quite nicely worded, in the form of a request, but with a sting in the tail: 'it had also been approved that the States of Zeeland shall be advised of this resolution and their Lordships requested to take good care that his Excellency follow the good opinion and intention of the States in this matter'.

Maurice had been at sea for some days when the letter reached Middelburg. When he heard of the resolution on his return he must have felt that he had been treated like a small boy, and that when he was nearly thirty. Oldenbarnevelt repeatedly committed such blunders – they cannot be called anything else.

There was another question two years afterwards in which the requirements of foreign policy conflicted with those of military strategy. Bouillon was then in the country to conclude the Triple Alliance,[3] and was pressing for a raid deep into Brabant to keep the enemy on his toes and stop him doing anything serious on the French frontiers. Maurice offered objections on military grounds. The Council of State agreed with him and there was a lengthy discussion with the States-General. Oldenbarnevelt had political reasons for wanting the raid and tried to weaken the military arguments. Eventually he made the States-General settle the question. They retired for consultation apart from Maurice and the Council of State and returned with the statement that they considered the expedition necessary and applied to His Excellency and the Council to advise, under whose leadership and in what strong and good form the

---

[1] See above p. 181. [2] See above p. 208. [3] See above pp. 212ff.

expedition shall be able to be made; and further stated, since they had declared and approved it, that it should not be further questioned or deliberated by the Council.

This sounds very peremptory and one might think that the campaign would progress rapidly. Nothing of the kind. The two cavalry leaders chosen to command the raid made it known – perhaps at Maurice's secret instigation – that the operation was impracticable owing to high water levels in Belgium. The military opposition was too strong for Oldenbarnevelt and on 12 November, eleven days after the imperious resolution just quoted, the Brabant expedition was cancelled. Maurice had once more succeeded, with the help of his faithful cavalrymen, in prevailing over the powerful statesman.

Obviously the question was being raised in Maurice's entourage whether it would not be better and more logical to provide him in actual fact with the sovereignty which in foreign eyes he appeared to possess. As early as 1590 Valcke had spoken to the English envoy Wilkes about the drawbacks of a polyarchy. The plan had then been put forward to appoint Maurice English Governor-General, a post stipulated in the Treaty of Nonsuch and vacant since Willoughby had left. It seemed attractive at first sight, but was unacceptable to Elizabeth, to Oldenbarnevelt and to Maurice himself, who would rather serve a few Netherlands masters, even if they were know-alls, than a capricious old woman across the sea. Those who conceived the plan showed little sense of realism.

In 1594 Maurice's secretary Nicolaes Bruynincx and his treasurer, Jasper van Kinschot, brought the matter up once more, perhaps at first with Oldenbarnevelt himself. He could see something in it, but it depended on what was understood by sovereignty. Maurice could be allowed to acquire it in the way the title Count of Holland had once been offered to William, heavily restricted by *capitulaties*. It could even be beneficial to Holland. Maurice's power *vis à vis* the States of Holland would not be increased, or only slightly, but his prestige would, in the other provinces and abroad. That, however, was not the sort of sovereignty desired by Maurice's friends or acceptable to politicians from the smaller provinces. The latter, men like Valcke and Roelsius, grand pensionary of Zeeland, or Everhart van Reyd, William Louis' counsellor, regarded Maurice's elevation as a means of strengthening the Union without adding to Holland's preponderance. This, however, necessitated that the sovereignty to be conferred should be more than a mere formality. It does not seem to have occurred to the planners to wonder whether this was compatible with the old privileges and the new rights acquired by the States since 1572, which could almost count as new privileges. Maurice himself understood this difficulty much better and was therefore all his life averse from accepting higher authority. He was not cut out for it and knew it. When sent in April 1598 to Utrecht to calm down the unrest that had broken out there, he behaved very unwisely, and the French ambassador Buzanval did not expect anything else of him. 'Vous sçavez', he wrote to Du Plessis, 'ce que je vous ai dict *de eo nostro heroe quo nihil* ἀπολιτικώτερόν ἐστιν.[1] Il est bien tard d'apprendre cette science, en laquelle son père a tant excellé.'

Prince William had exercised a high degree of authority as a result of his persuasiveness and generally acknowledged wisdom. His second son possessed neither. His tactics in the 1618 crisis show him as not altogether devoid of aptitude for affairs of state, but they did not attract him. He might have made a good absolute monarch, but not a constitutional one.

Rather than dispute an order, given him by those ultimately responsible, he complied with it. Sovereignty with restrictive stipulations would have enlarged his responsibility, but without increasing his power in proportion. Oldenbarnevelt appreciated these considerations. The question of sovereignty did not cause any of the friction between the two men during this period. A slow change only came about after the battle of Nieuwpoort.

To recapitulate, it can be said that till 1600 relations between Maurice and Oldenbarnevelt were good, but that the seeds of future hostility had been sown. They were not produced by religious questions, nor by that of sovereignty, nor by the possibility of peace with Spain. On Maurice's side they were the result of increasing irritation at Oldenbarnevelt's interference and a certain lack of enthusiasm for his French policy. Oldenbarnevelt found Maurice irritating too. His almost lethargic slowness in taking decisions and his exaggerated caution often made Oldenbarnevelt impatient; his expensive conduct of the war made Oldenbarnevelt's work in the States more difficult. De Bye, the Treasurer of the generality, describes most graphically in his memoirs how the rift came about. After explaining how Oldenbarnevelt treated and hampered the Prince and his war council, if they did not do what he wanted, by resolutions procured from the States-General or the States of Holland, he goes on to say:

Such procedures ran their course for a time, but could not last long, which the Advocate did not seem to pay heed to as he should, nor to remember that one can play with lions while they are still cubs, but not when they are fully grown. The Prince, after a time taking offence at this, began to show more and more aversion instead of the previous agreement, even against the Advocate personally, who seemed unable to moderate his daily actions according to the Prince's position, which he thought to maintain in the old fashion, not heeding the old proverb: omnisque potestas impatiens consortis erit.[2]

---

[1] About our hero, who has no political sense at all.
[2] Lucan I, 93 et seq. ('and all power will be impatient of an associate').

De Bye, as the only permanent member of the Council of State, was well placed for watching the Nassau lion cub grow up. In 1598 his claws had not been sharpened.

Maurice was the person, more than any other, whose cooperation or opposition Oldenbarnevelt had to take into account. But there were other political figures in this period whose dispositions towards Oldenbarnevelt affected him too. We can say that in the twenty years before the truce he was a ruler, and so he was, because he nearly always got his own way; but he was not a ruler without opposition. There was no opposition party but there were some people who at times thought that their interests or their views were being disregarded, and so opposed the great man's wishes. They had to be won over, and Oldenbarnevelt had no force at his disposal, except persuasion. Persuasiveness in personal contacts, though his public speeches were often insufferable, was his forte; however, he had more success with some people than with others.

We can distinguish various categories of people whose collaboration and active or passive agreement Oldenbarnevelt needed at this time. In the first place, there were the paid functionaries and bodies of the States-General: their clerk, the members of the Council of State and in particular the treasurer-general of the Union. Their agents or ambassadors as the case might be in France, England, Germany and, till 1603, in Scotland too, came under the same heading. Secondly, there were Oldenbarnevelt's fellow-deputies in the States-General from the six other provinces, who had to be induced to accept the proposals proceeding from Holland. Thirdly, there were the nobles of Holland, representing the rural districts in the States of Holland, without however having been elected by anyone there. They appeared individually at the meetings and had one joint vote, the first one, given by the Advocate of Holland as their pensionary. This vote was only one of nineteen but it was of paramount importance, firstly because the nobility, by casting the first vote, used to set the tone of the discussions, secondly owing to the prestige possessed by them of old. It was therefore vital for Oldenbarnevelt to keep on good terms with these aristocrats, a political necessity which his innate snobbishness can only have reinforced. The last category of friends and foes was that of the changing deputies of the eighteen franchised towns of Holland. They were the most troublesome to manipulate and their ranks produced the first opponents, then adversaries and antagonists and finally the determined enemies who brought about Oldenbarnevelt's fall.

Oldenbarnevelt was in almost daily contact with the clerk of the States-General, Cornelis van Aerssen. He came from Antwerp, was four years older than Oldenbarnevelt, and like him had studied at Cologne. In the year that

Oldenbarnevelt became pensionary of Rotterdam, Aerssen was appointed to the same post in Brussels, and that at a time when one had to be a good Roman Catholic. He was appointed clerk in August 1584, eighteen months before Oldenbarnevelt became Advocate of Holland. He was older and more experienced and, as former pensionary of Brussels, the superior rather than the inferior of the former servant of the small town of Rotterdam. Yet almost from the start we find Aerssen in a subordinate relationship to the powerful Advocate. We see the latter constantly making alterations to minutes written by the former in accordance with resolutions by the States. Sometimes Oldenbarnevelt wrote the whole of a minute himself, especially in the case of letters to ambassadors or foreign potentates. French texts, however, were usually written by Aerssen, who at Brussels had been the head of a department working entirely in French. Oldenbarnevelt's interference with the affairs of the clerk's office went still further: he tampered with the minutes files entrusted to Aerssen, sometimes giving the impression that Oldenbarnevelt was actually in charge of the department. Oldenbarnevelt must have had a great ascendancy and Aerssen a most servile character. The tone of the few terse scrawls from the former to the latter that have been preserved is of a staggering hauteur.

One wonders if there was not something here besides the obsequiousness one fancies can be discerned in Mierevelt's portrait. On 19 May 1586 Aerssen was suspended from office under suspicion of collusion with the enemy. Oldenbarnevelt, just appointed Advocate, was the moving spirit of the commission of enquiry, which after a week recommended rehabilitation. So Aerssen was under an obligation to Oldenbarnevelt, constantly renewed whenever unpleasant rumours circulated about him and were scotched by the Advocate. In 1589 Aerssen bought a house in Spuistraat opposite Oldenbarnevelt's. He had it demolished and a new one built in 1592 in the same place, for which the States-General, undoubtedly on Oldenbarnevelt's suggestion, voted him a present of three hundred guilders, intended for furnishings. So there was great cause for gratitude, perhaps mixed with a measure of fear; his gratitude reached its peak when in 1598 Aerssen's son François was appointed agent of the States-General in France at the age of twenty-six. As long as Oldenbarnevelt could use such bait, the clerk remained his loyal henchman.

We need not concern ourselves with Oldenbarnevelt's relations with the constantly changing ordinary members of the Council of State. As has been seen, he had tamed this body in the first few years after Leicester's departure. They were now entirely subordinated to the States-General, except for the rare occasions when, incited by the two stadtholders who were members as of right, they opposed Oldenbarnevelt's wishes, inspired by considerations of foreign policy or finance, on military grounds. It was not, however, resistance by individual members of the Council; rather, it reflected the protests of the stadtholders, whose officials the Council were coming more and more to consider themselves.

Apart from the stadtholders and the receiver-general, a typical civil servant who need not be discussed here, the only *ex officio* member of the Council was the treasurer-general, De Bye. He was responsible for grants coming in on time, especially of the amounts voted by the provinces. As this was a subject of special interest to Oldenbarnevelt, the two men were in continuous and on the whole friendly cooperation. De Bye wrote his memoirs after Oldenbarnevelt's death, criticizing him a good deal; but the tone is more that of a friend who records with regret that Oldenbarnevelt had antagonized his fellow-men by his ambition and tactlessness, sometimes amounting to contempt. He certainly did not consider Oldenbarnevelt innocent of causing the disorders, but he also strongly emphasized the guilt of the other party.

We can therefore regard the treasurer-general, at any rate in the period under review, as a younger friend of Oldenbarnevelt's, full of admiration for him and his capability in financial matters, but not blind to the flaws in his character. In his view they were due first and last to ambition, an opinion that seems rather exaggerated to later generations, though too lenient with regard to Oldenbarnevelt's love of money, sometimes leading to a form of corruption, a subject De Bye does not mention at all. He makes four specific accusations: firstly that he induced the ambassadors to address their important secret news to him personally, filling their official letters to the States-General with routine matters, which gave a monopoly of news, with the consequence that some deputies attributed great wisdom to him.

Obviously most of them were more likely to resent this, being obliged to cast their votes without the complete knowledge of the circumstances possessed by Oldenbarnevelt. The feelings of the Council of State were hurt in the same way. It is remarkable that De Bye, who says nothing about religion or the *waardgelders*, lays far the most stress on this point, while it is also the only point to which Oldenbarnevelt pleaded guilty in his interrogation and appealed to the judges for clemency.

A second accusation was that Oldenbarnevelt arrogated to himself the administration of foreign subsidies. He simply told the receiver-general to transfer the money by draft without any order for payment signed by those empowered to do so by resolution of the States-General. The receiver-general naturally got into trouble with the Audit Office and complained about the informal and authoritarian Advocate behind his back 'although he had not dared refuse out of respect for his person'.

De Bye does not suggest that Oldenbarnevelt made any personal profit out of these transactions. His sources of income were sometimes questionable according to modern ideas, but he never descended to embezzlement. His mistake was that he never cared what other people would think of him. This singular disregard for his own reputation had already been evident in the matter of his marriage. It was to be one of the main causes of his downfall.

The third accusation made by De Bye sounds rather strange. Oldenbarnevelt corresponded not only with Netherlands ambassadors abroad but also with various ministers of foreign princes,

whom he knew to be in favour with their masters. If anyone else had done this, he would certainly have managed to bring him to trial, as this obviously should not be allowed in a properly ordered government; but he thought that the brilliance of his prestige would counterbalance it.

Such an accusation is only comprehensible in the context of the disputes during the truce. In the present connection it is only of significance in that De Bye does not accuse Oldenbarnevelt of treason or any serious moral shortcomings, but of imprudence or, worse, recklessness. De Bye wonders, as did Professor Wenckebach when considering his design for Oldenbarnevelt's statue on Lange Vijverberg in The Hague, how this great statesman, also a good man, managed to arouse such hatred among his fellows that they cut his head off. The sculptor expressed these feelings in a conversation with the author at the unveiling of the statue on 14 October 1954. De Bye does not share this hatred. He explicitly disapproves but tries to explain it. He does so eventually by Oldenbarnevelt's *goût du risque* that we have noticed here and there already. Statesmen cannot do without it, but those who have it to excess fall into the traps laid for them by their enemies.

The fourth accusation concerns the assumption of a title which in his view Oldenbarnevelt had no right to: 'First Councillor and Advocate of Holland'. It is interesting because it is only here that we can find an allusion to vanity, a vice to which Oldenbarnevelt does not seem otherwise to have been prone.

The *fiscaal* of the Council of State, the official who acted as prosecutor in actions brought on behalf of the Council, mostly of a military nature, was Anthonie Duyck; he was also to act as first *fiscaal* at Oldenbarnevelt's trial and became his successor two years later with the title of *raadpensionaris*, rendered in English by 'Grand Pensionary'. He is one of the best-known Netherlanders of his time, not because of his ability or the importance of his position – he was one of the most obscure Grand Pensionaries – but owing to the trouble he took in keeping a diary for eleven years, in which, besides notes on the weather and troop movements, many political and moral judgments occur, often drawn on as a source in the preceding chapters. Some of them are extremely critical of Oldenbarnevelt, often with inadequate reason. He has been called an enemy of Oldenbarnevelt, but that seems exaggerated. He is also very critical of Maurice; in these writings, not intended for publication, he lets himself go and does not give considered opinions, but rather an echo of chats over drinks in the officers' tents. He often wrote to Oldenbarnevelt, without being obliged to, about army movements, and in most of the difficulties experienced by the Advocate in the 1590s was on his side. Only about Oldenbarnevelt's French policy he was not happy – but who was in the Netherlands, after 1593 ? – and when Oldenbarnevelt clashed with the army leadership, Duyck, usually with the troops, took Maurice's part. To this extent the beginning can be observed in Duyck of the crystallization of what was later on to become the counter-remonstrant party; this group was to consolidate itself also, though not primarily, around the dispute between Maurice and Oldenbarnevelt and the latter's pro-government policy towards France. But it was no more than a beginning and this conscientious official was certainly not an adversary in the 1590s.

Nor can adversaries be traced among another group of paid servants of the state, the career diplomats.

It was Oldenbarnevelt who created the diplomatic service, at first as an organ of the jointly working provinces of Holland and Zeeland, not of the States-General. Prince William had of course always had many contacts abroad, but always incidentally: for a well-defined purpose an envoy, usually a whole embassy, was sent abroad for a short time. Permanent embassies had existed in Europe for about a century, but they were costly, not merely because of the salaries of those employed but owing to the ceremony that had to be kept up for prestige purposes and the communications that had to be provided. The rebels were too poor for that. The Prince relied for the information from abroad that he so badly needed on humbly situated spies, occasional travellers and solemn delegations. The latter were frequently composed of delegates from each province wishing to take part, and were judges, pensionaries or nobles, chosen not for their diplomatic ability but owing to their position in the province.

During the Leicester period Oldenbarnevelt could not manage with only such incidental intelligence from England. The curious triangular relationship between Elizabeth, Leicester and the States-General made it indispensable for the Hollanders to have a permanent agent in London to keep them informed of court intrigues and on occasion to be the channel through which something could be imparted to the Queen or her ministers without Leicester knowing. There was someone to hand for this task. He was not a diplomat, but when Oldenbarnevelt got to know him he discovered in him full aptitude for learning the job and had complete trust in him. It was Joachim Ortel, a South Netherlander, like almost all the career diplomats of the 1590s. He had been sent to England in the Prince's lifetime as 'agent-general' of Holland and Zeeland, a post which was not of a diplomatic nature and did not confer diplomatic status, but was comparable with what was later to be called a consulate. The circumstances during Leicester's rule and Oldenbarnevelt's personal confidence in him made Ortel the first permanent ambassador in the service of the Netherlands. In this respect, however, he was handicapped in two ways. In the first place Elizabeth as yet refused to recognize the Netherlands as an independent state, entitled to issue ambassadors with credentials. Nothing could be done about that for the time. The other cause of Ortel's difficulties was his lack of rank and private means, so that he could not take part in court life on an equal footing. Oldenbarnevelt decided to bring about an improvement in the latter point at any rate when Ortel died in 1590. The appointment was given to a Flemish nobleman, Noël de Caron, Lord of Schoonewalle. Zeeland, which had more trade with England than Holland had, pushed the appointment through. It was considered reasonable that this province should have a voice in the appointment of a London ambassador, principally concerned with commercial matters; on the other hand it was the custom for Holland to designate the ambassador to France.

The custom probably arose in the 1590s. Whether and why Caron was particularly favoured by Zeeland does not appear in the records; at first cooperation with Oldenbarnevelt did not run smoothly. Caron addressed his letters quite formally to the States-General. The first detailed letter preserved, written to Oldenbarnevelt personally, dates from the end of 1595, when Caron had been in London for six years. In the following year he informed the States-General that he had written about a certain point 'in more detail to Mr van Oldenbarnevelt, because their Lordships of Holland and Zeeland were most concerned'.

Caron evidently thought it necessary to inform the States-General apologetically about his correspondence with Oldenbarnevelt. The latter may not have welcomed the ambassador's scruples. Caron was also greatly influenced by the English ministers. Now and then he behaved more like Elizabeth's representative to the States-General than vice-versa. Thus he energetically supported Elizabeth's request for the return of troops in 1592 and when on leave in The Hague had discussions about it with Bodley, which he concealed from the States. It was no wonder Bodley wrote home that Oldenbarnevelt mistrusted Caron and would like to dismiss him if he could find a suitable successor.

The absence of a successor saved him. Caron was a nobleman and had experience, an unusual combination. Moreover he was a man who had found out, though rather slowly, on which side his bread was buttered. He submitted entirely to Oldenbarnevelt, whom he thenceforth supplied with information just as faithfully as Ortel and Calvart had long done, behind the backs of the States. Oldenbarnevelt had his salary raised to 6,000 guilders – in those days a considerable sum. He remained diplomatic representative of the Netherlands, first as agent, later as ambassador, till his death in 1624. Oldenbarnevelt, during his interrogation in 1618, spoke about him as of an old friend, but on the last night of his life appears to have accused him of treachery in sending his confidential letters to Maurice to be used against him at his trial: this accusation is mentioned only by Carleton.[1]

In France too Oldenbarnevelt at first appointed a somewhat undistinguished person with the status of agent: Lieven Calvaert, or Calvart (the French form of his name that was generally used), from Antwerp, a member of the bourgeoisie who had fitted himself out with a title by the purchase of an estate. His humble origin, when he was sent as permanent agent to Henry IV in 1593, was not such a handicap as it would have been in England, as the French King, accustomed to simpler conditions in the south-west, cared much less for etiquette than Elizabeth. He liked doing business most informally and as man to man. He had neither wife nor palace, no regular household and held few or no ceremonies, in which order of precedence would play a part. Calvart's humble origin therefore did the Netherlands no harm: on the contrary, it sometimes enabled him to disregard decorum for the sake of more efficient reporting, for instance when he hid himself to eavesdrop on a conversation between two French ministers. Oldenbarnevelt was in all likelihood not sorry to have appointed him. In spite of a certain innate ingenuousness and an excessive predisposition in favour of the French King, he was a capable diplomat.

Apart from Ortel, Caron and Calvart the other diplomats of the 1590s remain in the background. Oldenbarnevelt only listed them at his trial to demonstrate that he 'corresponded with them by order and charge . . . of the States-General and those of Holland, and had taken much trouble to inform them in writing of the state and course of this country's affairs'.

The 'order and charge' of the States-General is somewhat doubtful, but it is a fact that he corresponded with these men and in practice gave them briefings no less coercive than the documents from the States-General. They were willing tools in Oldenbarnevelt's hands, because and as long as they thought it suited their book.

So much for the exercise of power abroad, in which in the 1590s and long

---

[1] Carleton's Letters, p. 364.

after Oldenbarnevelt met with plenty of cooperation and certainly no systematic opposition from those, most of whom had been called upon, by him or by his predominant influence, to carry out his policies on the spot. With domestic policy it was different, but not greatly. There was more opposition, because the executants of policy, mainly States-General deputies, were not appointed and paid but elected and unpaid. They felt that they were lords and masters, and so they would have been, if they had known how to organize themselves. That was just what they would not and could not do. Until the beginning of the truce negotiations they agreed with Oldenbarnevelt on the main issues in Netherlands politics: vigorous and efficient conduct of the war; no concession to deceptive peace negotiations; maintenance of the alliances with France and England; provincial autonomy in all matters in which centralization was not urgently required by the war; support of the repartition and quota system; promotion of the Reformation in the Netherlands and in the world, but in moderation and without fanaticism or anything approaching it, and in particular without domination of the state by the church and without harsh religious persecution: all these were programme points which every budding political party had to subscribe to. These points were scrupulously and conscientiously carried out by the Oldenbarnevelt government – to use nineteenth-century terminology. Most people were satisfied and showed it by cooperating with Oldenbarnevelt.

Of course there was indeed one point which caused some discord in the provinces outside Holland and was not part of the 'government programme': breaking the oppressive hegemony of Holland in the Republic. It is one of the points on which five of the seven provinces came to terms in 1617 and scored a precarious victory. Then, however, religion acted as a catalyst. Without it the affinity among the provinces was too slight to overcome the great obstacles to agreement, since almost every province took up a different position towards this problem.

Zeeland, though Oldenbarnevelt tried as far as possible to form a 'maritime provinces front' with it, caused him grave trouble in this period, which will be discussed at the end of this chapter. On the other hand relations with Utrecht were such that the province, under the leadership of its secretary, Ledenberg, could almost be regarded as a satellite. This man, with a position corresponding to Oldenbarnevelt's in Holland, was a *homo novus*, the son of an illiterate mason, a strange and almost unheard-of phenomenon on the aristocratic Utrecht horizon. To ward off the rather dangerous 'democratic' opposition he had to be permanently active and on the spot; in contrast to Oldenbarnevelt, who until the beginning of the truce negotiations was constantly on the move, Ledenberg hardly ever left Utrecht or its immediate environs. Oldenbarnevelt only saw him when he went himself to Utrecht. Then he was received like a prince. On one occasion he was entertained to a sumptuous dinner *chez* Ledenberg's titled father-in-law, Willem van Rijsenburg, leader of the nobility. Otherwise they only had indirect contact, in the States-General through the Utrecht deputies, who in the circumstances could not of course carry much weight. The impression is given that the main point of their briefing, even though it had to be read between the lines, was always to support Oldenbarnevelt's plans, except in finance matters, where this impoverished province had to practise the greatest economy. This is typified in a description by the Advocate of the States of Utrecht of his arrival in The Hague at the beginning of a session of the States-General, to which he was deputed. He first conferred with his co-deputies and they decided first of all to pay their respects to Oldenbarnevelt

and recommend to him in general the affairs of the province of Utrecht, which was accordingly done; and being there, submitted to His Lordship the commission of the States of Utrecht; and so it was approved that we should be present at ten o'clock in the chamber of the States-General, so that the commission should be shown there . . .

It can be seen that Oldenbarnevelt had little trouble with these gentlemen. Their support, though, was not worth much, as Utrecht was a small province, meeting only 5% of the cost of war, a third of Zeeland's contribution, with only a few companies in its repartition. It weighed little in the balance, either figuratively or literally in the coin contributed.

The inland provinces of Gelderland and Overijsel were in much the same case. Actually nothing is ever heard about Overijsel. In the first few years it paid no contribution at all, three-quarters of its area being occupied by the enemy; afterwards it was assessed at $3\frac{1}{2}$%. It was often too poor to maintain a deputy in The Hague; when there was one he voted regularly with the majority and had not the slightest influence, either for or against Oldenbarnevelt's rule.

Gelderland's influence was a little greater, although the province made no contribution for a long time, afterwards being allotted the same quota as Utrecht. But being a duchy, Gelderland was the first province in rank; it contained the most 'frontier towns', controlled Holland's trade with Germany and formed the base for most of the military operations. On the one hand these circumstances gave Gelderland greater influence in the Republic than accorded with its financial contribution, on the other hand they kept it largely under Holland's thumb for the duration of the war. Only a light hand on the reins was needed for the Gelderland deputies in the States-General and the Council of State.

Relations with Friesland were less good than with the other provinces, but did not cause Oldenbarnevelt much trouble. Friesland was isolationist, from natural causes, it might almost be said. Till the capture of Steenwijk in 1592 it had no common frontier with other provinces within the Union of Utrecht. It had a different theatre of war, its own stadtholder, its own language, its own university and finally its own admiralty. It was therefore largely un-interested in the political goings-on in The Hague, except when they began to assume a centralistic character or interfere too much with the north of the country outside Friesland, which the Frisians regarded as their private hunting-ground. When we recall their ancestral hatred of the Hollanders since the battle of Stavoren in 1345,[1] we can understand that the Frisians in the States-General and the Council of State would always be ready to join in a rebellion against Oldenbarnevelt, but that they were incapable of leadership and organization. Indeed they were too divided among themselves for such a purpose. Their stadtholder, William Louis, was at first distrusted as a foreigner and suspected of a pro-Holland policy. An influential agitator, Carel Roorda, fomented unrest for years about the status of the adjacent province of Drente and the frontier with Overijsel, during which everything to do with Nassau was shouted down. Oldenbarnevelt sided entirely with William Louis in this dispute, in spite of the fact that Roorda had been a stout fellow-campaigner against Leicester. Much later Oldenbarnevelt was himself to become anti-Nassau and his supporters were to use arguments very similar to those of the fiercely republican Frisian. Such arguments were often reproduced in the rivalry between States and Orange party that was to dominate Netherlands politics till the end of the Republic in 1795. Olden-barnevelt did not sympathize, particularly in the 1590s, when he was still on good terms with Maurice. He was not a republican on principle. He worked hand in glove with the Nassaus as long as it seemed useful for the efficient conduct of war, and afterwards too, as long as Nassau could be used as a symbol of national unity. Oldenbarnevelt had as little political philosophy as any other great statesman in world history.

If then opposition from Friesland, arising occasionally, was not a matter of principle, still less was it the case in Groningen, when this region joined the Union of Utrecht as seventh province in 1594. In 1600, however, a bitter quarrel blew up over money matters which made Oldenbarnevelt a number of enemies, not only in Groningen, and which he was to rue until and during his trial. For reasons connected with its internal constitution the province had paid no contribution for years, so that arrears of 600,000 guilders had

---

[1] In this year William IV, Count of Holland, attempted to conquer Friesland, but immediately on landing he was defeated and killed by the massed peasantry.

mounted up. There was no procedure provided in the Union of Utrecht, which for better or worse served as the constitution of the young state, for enforcing payment on defaulting provinces. Contemporaries could see four possibilities within the framework of the Union. The most stringent was to build a castle, a measure savouring of slavery which would arouse resistance not only in Groningen. At first Oldenbarnevelt only had recourse to the least severe means of coercion: disarming the citizenry and the occupation of the town by a small garrison. When Groningen remained intransigent, Olden-barnevelt had the States-General despatch a small army, accompanied by a commissioner, the judge in the Hoge Raad, Adriaen Junius, with instructions in the form of an ultimatum. As could be expected from Oldenbarnevelt, these instructions were very harshly worded. Impossibly large amounts had to be paid within a month, otherwise the troops would be billeted on the inhabitants till the money was raised. Furthermore the local government was to be dismissed and ten named ringleaders were to be 'seized' in consultation with the stadtholder, with the implicit intention of subjecting them to criminal proceedings, very likely leading to capital punishment. Oldenbarne-velt was in a rage and really hitting out, though he might have secretly hoped that William Louis and the moderate Junius would do their best to sweeten the pill. It had long been known that the stadtholder was not in favour of all this sabre-rattling and wanted to take a milder course. The billeting caused a lot of bad blood, but the arrests did not take place, even when the town took up a defiant stance and stopped the government of the province for eight weeks. The effect on Oldenbarnevelt was predictable by anyone moderately versed in psychology: he resorted to the strong-arm policy of building a castle, had three of the Groningen resistance leaders brought to The Hague to answer for their conduct and kept them there nearly a year as hostages with limited freedom of movement.

The building of a citadel in Groningen was a huge sensation in the country. A citadel was equated with a symbol of tyrannical power; Junius was compared with the member of the Council of Blood, Juan de Vargas. Moreover the building of a citadel was expressly prohibited by the conditions of Groningen's surrender in 1594. Oldenbarnevelt countered that Groningen had forfeited the right to appeal to these conditions by not submitting to the States-General's arbitration in its quarrel with the Ommelanden.[1] It did not avail him. Public opinion, which had been with him at first, now turned against him. Furthermore, once the citadel was being built, a certain catharsis seems to have occurred, first in public opinion and then in Olden-barnevelt himself. It was enough to have shown one's claws and then leave

---

[1] Rural distict around the town of Groningen.

well alone. It left a bit of a hangover too. Junius had lightheartedly estimated the bill for the castle at 70,000 guilders, but when it was presented it came to over 400,000, more than the town's arrears. When Junius returned to The Hague next winter he came under heavy fire in the States-General for this and for his drastic measures. The Groningen deputies said roundly that he had made profit and commissions on the building. Oldenbarnevelt defended him vigorously and perhaps saved him from prosecution, which helps to explain Junius' comparatively mild attitude at the trial in 1618, where he acted as one of the judges.

The result of the whole story was that the States-General had gained little financial benefit from their action and Oldenbarnevelt's unpopularity had slightly increased, not only in the town of Groningen but in the Ommelanden, whose delegates left The Hague in May 'with great bitterness . . . imputing it mostly to Mr Oldenbarnevelt, whom they considered to have been too exacting and hard in this matter, and therefore rejected everything in order to ruin the land with distraint and entirely to impoverish it'.[1]

There was displeasure at the matter outside the provinces concerned as well, and the disapproval of men such as William Louis and Duyck must have enhanced the difficulties Oldenbarnevelt had to endure in the summer of 1600.

This shows that Oldenbarnevelt met with little or no resistance and enjoyed considerable support in the States-General from those on a lower plane, the only ones he could tolerate beside him. This was due to the enormous financial and moral predominance of Holland. What was the situation in Holland itself?

Constitutionally things were different in the States of Holland and the States-General, but in fact analogous. In the States of Holland too it was his overwhelming personality that made his power irresistible, but there was also his complete control of one of the deputations, that of the nobility, in this case combined with no less complete control of the equivalent in Holland of the Council of State: the *Gecommitteerde Raden*. In addition there was the psychological advantage that in Holland he exercised his power quite officially by virtue of his twofold office of Advocate of the province and pensionary of the nobles, whereas he had no office at all in the States-General and had usurped all his power. In the States of Holland he was in effect president and permanent president at that; as pensionary of the nobility he cast the first vote and benefited by the historical prestige still possessed by the nobles, although their economic position was not what it had been. Oldenbarnevelt, who himself had aspirations towards noble rank, always defended their views,

[1] Duyck.

when they had any, loyally and energetically, and the position was now that the nobles were more dependent on Oldenbarnevelt for the exercise of political influence than he was on them. So a bond of mutual gratitude was forged, never broken till the end. The nobles were by nature inclined to be conservative. Most of them lived in the country, seldom went to The Hague and were often either Catholics themselves or married to Catholics. The result of all this was that they displayed little interest in politics. There is scarcely a single nobleman who played a significant part in the politics of the sixteenth century. Most prominent were Noordwijk, better known for his Latin verse written under the pseudonym Janus Dousa, and the older Mathenesse, for many years a member of the Council of State despite the double handicap of being a practising Catholic and a former 'collaborator' during the Four Years War (1572–6). They were both faithful adherents of Oldenbarnevelt. Only with the senior noble of Holland, Walrave van Brederode, was the position rather different. He had been appointed to the Council of State through Leicester and as such had had a most disagreeable scene with Oldenbarnevelt. Probably that is one reason why he spent more and more time in this period at his home at Vianen. In 1594 he served as an ambassador to Scotland and in 1597 for a short time as deputy to the States-General. He was the only nobleman who can be presumed to have had something against Oldenbarnevelt. The family was staunchly Calvinist: his nephew and successor Walrave IV was commissioned by the States-General to the Dordrecht synod and a younger nephew, Joan Wolfert, commanded a company at the Binnenhof during Oldenbarnevelt's execution, presumably because he liked the job.

There was thus one possible dissident among the nobles; rather more, yet not many, among the towns. Neither Amsterdam nor Dordrecht, later the leaders of the opposition, sent antagonists to the States assembly in the 1590s. Amsterdam's position is thus to a certain extent comparable with that of Friesland. The impression is gained that the town was only faintly interested in what was happening at the States meetings in The Hague. It was the richest and most powerful town in Holland and had other means, in particular economic ones, of getting what it wanted. As far as we know not a single political initiative was taken by Amsterdam during Oldenbarnevelt's period of power. Their disputes with him – and there were many – were confined to money matters directly concerning Amsterdam. The fact that they did not become more acute and at first did not spoil the atmosphere was largely due to the personal characters of those employed by Amsterdam for 'public relations'. In the first place there was the pensionary Sille, from Mechelen, often at Oldenbarnevelt's side on committees and missions. That they were good friends is shown by the words addressed by Oldenbarnevelt to Sille's son, Laurens, when as third *fiscaal* of the special court he announced the death sentence to him: 'Thy father would stare to seet hee let thyself be used in this affair!' He was an exception to the rule that Oldenbarnevelt could not get on with Belgians. But he did not really represent Amsterdam.

The oligarchs who did do so had not the time to attend meetings regularly. It is typical that in all these years Amsterdam was not represented on the Council of State, to which pensionaries were not eligible. Among the older generation of oligarchs Cant and Hooft were Oldenbarnevelt's kindred spirits, exiles during Amsterdam's Catholic period, without having become members of the Reformed Church. Cornelis Pieterszoon Hooft, father of the famous poet and historian P. C. Hooft, was to remain one of Oldenbarnevelt's most loyal adherents, even after being unseated as burgomaster by the rising Calvinist party. After Cant's death he was usually Amsterdam's deputy in the States-General. It would not be correct to state that Oldenbarnevelt had queered his own pitch for good with Amsterdam by his obstinate litigation in 1581. Things were more subtle: in that year originated the hatred for him of Reynier Pauw and his fellow-Calvinists on the *Vroedschap*, which was to be augmented by later clashes and was finally to be fatal for Oldenbarnevelt.

The set-up was much the same in Dordrecht, the other main centre of opposition during the truce years. Here again there was a Belgian pensionary who had escaped dismissal in 1586, here too a number of burgomasters, of whom at least one (Cornelis Fransz Wittensz (= de Witt), grandfather of the Grand Pensionary) was later to become Oldenbarnevelt's enemy, though now working with him in the States-General and the *Gecommitteerde Raden* without any sign of discord. The difference lay in the character of the pensionary Joost Menijn, who in some respects had been the leader of the Leicester faction in Holland. He was a scholar rather than a politician: he had not enough self-control, tact and judgment of character for the latter role, qualities that rarely deserted Oldenbarnevelt, for all his vehemence. When the Leicester period was over so was his part in politics in general. He was only heard of as an over-violent champion of Dordrecht's rights, so much so that the oligarchs of the town, at this time on a good personal footing with Oldenbarnevelt, became impatient. They were glad thus to make use of a piece of imprudence on Menijn's part. His old friend Arend van Dorp, a noble not summoned to the States assembly, asked Menijn for a look at certain documents, entrusted to him in his official capacity, saying that he wanted to have them copied out of curiosity, for his own pleasure. In fact the copies went direct to the South Netherlands negotiator, Otto Hartius, who was staying with Van Dorp at The Hague at the time. There followed a rumpus: Van

Dorp was arrested and Menijn subjected to repeated and unpleasant interrogation. As far as Van Dorp, the more guilty party, was concerned, the matter fizzled out; he could thank his wealth for that, insinuates Duyck, who would have liked to see the Catholic, pro-peace nobleman beheaded. Menijn sought protection from Oldenbarnevelt, whom he still regarded as his friend in spite of quarrels about Leicester – another sign of his naiveté, already shown by the favour he did Van Dorp. Hadn't they met as students in France? Hadn't they fought together, under Prince William's rule, for honour and decency, against the intrigues of Paulus Buys? And could the Dordrecht authorities dismiss him without more ado, while though *in reatu* (under accusation) he must still be considered innocent till he was found guilty?

Oldenbarnevelt knew all this. He had no intention of entirely destroying his old friend and new enemy. It is not known how he answered this letter. He said only one thing to Menijn: the Dordrecht authorities wanted to be rid of him, and for good. He did not add that he himself wanted Menijn out of politics, and for good. So as not to drive him to desperation he offered him a post more suited to his temperament: historian of the States. He did not produce anything to show that he deserved the appointment. Nor did Oldenbarnevelt expect it; his idea was to provide the fallen politician with a sinecure without influence, so that he should not do anything desperate. At about the same time he had provided another statesman, of great service in the past, but now become impossible, with the job of Bible translator: Marnix, the Prince's right-hand man. He certainly had the qualifications, but he was decrepit and Oldenbarnevelt must have realized that he would not produce anything useful.

With Menijn one of the last of the leading figures in the Leicester epoch disappeared. It is surprising how quickly Oldenbarnevelt managed to dispose of nearly all the chief personalities of those troublous times. True, fate lent him a hand, with friends and foes alike. He had no use for either, he had to dominate the Netherlands alone. He could not tolerate partly subjected opponents or independent supporters. The extremists of the Leicester party, Sonoy, Meetkerken, Borchgrave and Prouninck, had long been rendered harmless and driven into exile; among the moderates, Brederode had faded into the background, Loozen was stowed away in the Hoge Raad, Menijn had been brought down; only Valcke was still living to stir up trouble for him in Zeeland.

The leaders of the anti-Leicester party could not compete long either, once their bogeyman had crossed the North Sea. The two neighbours in Oude Delft, Brasser and Van der Meer, were growing old and fat; they played second fiddle for a short time in the States and then lost interest in politics that had become rather tame. Paulus Buys had blotted his copybook in both

Utrecht and Holland: when Leicester left he was only curator of the university at Leiden, but he became quarrelsome there too and was dismissed. Roorda was toppled with a great crash and Francken had had enough of active politics and had himself appointed to the Hoge Raad; Adriaen van der Mijle, Thin and Nieuwenaar were dead. Oldenbarnevelt was thus left standing on a lonely pedestal.

Only the Zeelanders now and again dared to speak against him. This led to the most dangerous and lengthy conflict in which Oldenbarnevelt was involved before the truce negotiations, and one from which, for once, he did not emerge as victor.

Generally Holland and Zeeland followed the same course in the States-General. Their interests mostly ran parallel and Zeeland's best chance of promoting them was to keep in the shadow of its big neighbour in the north. But there was one discordant note: control of maritime affairs. It had already been a sore point under the Emperor Charles. Leicester had taken it into account in setting up the admiralties: whereas Holland possessed two admiralties, each having other provinces under them, Zeeland only had one, whose area coincided with that of the province, and its board of control was identical with the *Gecommitteerde Raden*, the executive body of the Zeeland States. As the Zeelanders had their own vice-admiral under Maurice, who as overall admiral had little opportunity to carry out his coordinating function, the position was in effect that the growing Republic did not possess a unified navy but two fleets working together.

Oldenbarnevelt wanted to put an end to this by the well-tried recipe: a central body sitting at The Hague, under Maurice's presidency and daily supervision by the States-General. Here, as in the States, urgent decisions would continually have to be made, for which the States of Holland could be consulted but not those of the other provinces. Thus Holland's wishes were practically bound to prevail. This was of particular importance for the adjustment of convoy taxes and *licenten*, and deciding which harbours might be exported to, questions closely connected with Oldenbarnevelt's foreign policy. He wanted to dominate the body making these decisions, and it had to control the various admiralties: the collectors of the taxes had to account for them to the new body. Early in 1589 the States-General set up this superintendent body.

It proved ineffective: the admiralties of Holland cooperated reluctantly and under coercion, that of Rotterdam was soon pressing for its abolition. Friesland and the inland provinces were indifferent, till Friesland, having set up its own admiralty, resented intervention by Holland or The Hague in its private concerns.

The greatest opposition was, predictably, from Zeeland. Oldenbarnevelt was never in so strong a position with this province as with the others. Zeeland had been Holland's ally in the difficult years from 1572 to 1576. Voting together against the other provinces had almost become a tradition, and Holland needed this vote to maintain its preponderance. So when Zeeland, having pointedly dissociated itself from the setting up of the superintendent body, refused and continued to refuse to recognize it, Oldenbarnevelt had no choice but to agree to its abolition: it never established itself and the experiment was ended on 31 December 1593.

Now not only control of the fleet but the collection of convoy taxes and *licenten* was again legally in Zeeland's hands, as it had never in practice ceased to be. Disagreement on these matters between Holland and Zeeland, temporarily laid aside, was however bound to exacerbate relations between the two provinces now that the opportunity for a master body had disappeared. The difficulties mainly concerned the collection of *licenten* from exporters from Amsterdam and Rotterdam to the South Netherlands. Their exports were almost all carried along the Scheldt, destined for Antwerp, Sluis or the Belgian North Sea ports. The question was now where the export tax should be paid. In theory it was of no consequence, the *licenten* were part of the national revenue, spent on the fleet, wherever they had been paid. A surplus at one admiralty was credited to another. As there were uniform rates fixed by the States-General it was all the same to the merchants and the admiralties where the *licenten* were paid: at the harbour of shipment, at their last Netherlands harbour, or at their destination.

In practice, though, things were different from this slick theory. Merchants in every port tried to have the lowest possible *licent* charged on their exports to Belgium. It could be done by having their exports taxed at a lower rate than that laid down by the States-General, or by false description of the goods, or in the last resort by pure fraud, tax evasion made possible by insufficient inspection. All these methods promoted competition among the merchants, the 'trade was diverted', as it was said, and it benefited not only the individual merchant and the corrupt tax official but also the town or province to which the trade was diverted. In addition, fraud in one province led to fraud in another: if a merchant suffered loss from these malpractices elsewhere he tried to recoup himself by committing them in his own town. It could only be prevented by a strictly centralized control, with inspectors from another province in each place: it had perhaps been Oldenbarnevelt's chief reason for insistence on a superintendent body.

Zeeland, however, looked upon this whole effort as a 'racket' designed by Holland to make smuggling easier for the Amsterdam merchants and only to clamp down on the Zeelanders. There may have been some truth in this, though it was not what Oldenbarnevelt intended. The Zeelanders therefore kept on the safe side by charging *licent* for all goods destined for Belgium trans-shipped in their harbours, or even sailing to it through their waters without trans-shipment. The Hollanders, and particularly the Rotterdammers, were highly indignant. Their reaction was drastic: they began to charge *licenten* on all goods transported in the direction of Zeeland, alleging that they might well be eventually destined for Belgium, the bill of lading being only marked for Zeeland in order to profit from the lower *licenten* charged: it was aimed at preventing merchants enabling Zeeland to charge *licenten*, illegal according to Rotterdam, by means of the double charter-parties which would have made such a levy legal. Afterwards the levy of *licenten* on internal shipments was mitigated by demanding only the deposit of a surety that the goods were in fact for consumption in Zeeland: inspectors were sent from Holland to Zeeland to check this.

But the result of the Rotterdam regulations was that exporters from Holland were forced to pay the already high taxation twice, first in Rotterdam and then at Tholen or Middelburg, an intolerable state of affairs. While the impression of the capture of Breda was still fresh Maurice managed to bring about a 'provisional agreement' between Holland and Zeeland in 1590. Following the example of some of the temporary measures in previous years, Holland and Zeeland agreed to share the proceeds: in future half the *licent* was to be levied at the port of first shipment, the other half at the place of final export.

The agreement, signed by Oldenbarnevelt with undoubted reluctance, was an unsatisfactory compromise, pleasing neither party and hampering trade. Furthermore there was not enough check on its being carried out. Though it was stipulated that inspectors from Holland should be admitted to offices in Zeeland – for the sake of formal equality Zeeland inspectors were to go to Holland too – it was obvious that nothing would come of this cooperation, especially as it extended to higher levels: the Zeeland admiralty was ultimately responsible for accurate levying and there were no Hollanders on this board, identical with the *Gecommitteerde Raden* of Zeeland. The agreement was only to be valid for a year but was tacitly prolonged, so that the Zeelanders began to regard the situation as an acquired right, notwithstanding ominous rumblings on the horizon, when the Hollanders started complaining of various abuses in the performance of the agreement.

The Zeelanders had complaints as well, principally regarding the growing habit of Holland merchants of going direct by sea to the Flemish North Sea ports instead of to Antwerp and Ghent through Zeeland waters: this had always been the trade route taken to avoid the dangers of the open sea. The

Hollanders were doing so with the obvious intention of by-passing the agreement. Dissatisfaction on both sides was allowed to simmer for years without any attempt being made to put an end to it at top level.

There was constant trouble about interpreting the provisional agreement and putting it into practice, with Oldenbarnevelt vigorously supporting the Holland merchants, especially when their cause was championed by the Amsterdam admiralty, with whom he was on amicable terms, evidenced by the presents he was given by them from time to time.

Embitterment was intensified on both sides by disputes resulting from the coinage edict of 2 September 1594. Among other things it ordered a reduction in the value of some of the gold and silver pieces used in particular in trade with France and therefore circulating in large numbers in Middelburg. The town, feebly supported by the States of Zeeland, refused to publish this reduction. Apparently the gold coins especially were undervalued by the latest reduction. The result was of course that they were sent out of the country to other countries where the rate was considerably higher, and a great shortage of gold coin occurred.

Oldenbarnevelt, as was so often the case, was not interested in economic equity but in the constitutional question. It was intolerable that a town should actively resist the execution of an edict properly enacted by the States-General, 'thus causing', as Duyck wrote,

no little loss of prestige to all the resolutions of the States-General, and opening the door to all other towns to be allowed and dare to resist and contravene similar resolutions of the States-General, while the present times do not permit of remedying such matters by force of arms.

Oldenbarnevelt was not so sure about that. He began with a peaceful mission, but with a sanction available if needed. In February 1595 two members of the Hof van Holland, and the *fiscaal* of the Council of State, Duyck, were sent to Zeeland to address the Middelburg *vroedschap* in a fatherly way. On their persistent refusal Duyck had to serve a writ on them from the Hof van Holland, whose jurisdiction extended to Zeeland as well. This action was provided for in the delegation's draft instructions. Oldenbarnevelt had been given the draft to read and marked it: 'this to be entered separately in the *fiscaal*'s orders and deleted here'. The delegates were probably to show their instructions to the Middelburg *vroedschap*: it was more prudent not to let them see the threat. Duyck was told not to go to Middelburg but to await the course of events at Veere. The two councillors, however, talked too much: when Middelburg remained recalcitrant they made it quite plain what they had up their sleeves, whereupon the Middelburg *vroedschap* refused service of the writ or admittance to the servers. The delegates then backed down and went back to The Hague with nothing accomplished.

After long hesitation Oldenbarnevelt decided to take action. Maurice himself was to come forward to make the refractory town see reason. Two members of the Council of State travelled ahead of him to announce his coming and report that the States-General had planned all the measures necessary for the use of military force. Now it was the Middelburgers who took in their sails, allegedly so as not to offer the stadtholder the affront of a vain journey. On 25 April a deputation from Middelburg to the States-General complained of the harsh threats by which the town had been coerced – a sort of boycott had been intended – and also asked permission to continue the higher valuation of two of the coins in most extensive use. Oldenbarnevelt answered with a long sermon on the need for States-General supremacy. He ended it, however, by declaring himself ready to discuss not only the two coins in question but all the errors that the Middelburgers might allege pertained to the edict. This took place in the course of 1595 and 1596. The result was that everyone seemed to have a different opinion, that the arduously achieved edict of 2 September 1594 was weakened, and that the much-needed currency reform was wrecked by the particularism of the provinces.

In the last stage of the dispute with Middelburg the States of Zeeland had sided with the States-General, but immediately after the capitulation there, the Middelburgers naturally resumed their predominance in the States of Zeeland and it now appeared how much ill-feeling Oldenbarnevelt had caused by his intransigence. When the grants from Zeeland came in they were couched in such terms as to make the intended campaign in the east of Gelderland impossible for the time being.

The Council of State was instructed to send a mission to Zeeland to obtain better grants. But they were only willing to go if Oldenbarnevelt went with them. He alone was able, they considered, to confront the Zeelanders with reasons on such diverse subjects as the quota, the closure of the harbours of Dunkirk and Nieuwpoort and the tax on peat. It was a tribute to Oldenbarnevelt's wide knowledge and versatility, doubly valuable as coming from a body that in many respects thought it had reason to complain of his autocratic behaviour.

Oldenbarnevelt let himself be persuaded and left on 23 June with two members of the Council of State. The journey became superfluous in so far as the States of Zeeland were induced by their special deputation, on their return, to make their grants absolute, without any restrictions. The news of this came on the same day that Oldenbarnevelt was leaving, but he decided to go all the same, as the three points mentioned were of enough consequence to justify a conference with Zeeland.

The deputies decided to inspect the new fortifications at Bergen-op-Zoom and Hulst on the way, another typically military assignment which Oldenbarnevelt may have carried out with greater expertness than his fellow-travellers, who had more right to do so. They arrived at the session of the States at Middelburg on 1 July; after long discussions Zeeland gained a victory in one respect: Oldenbarnevelt agreed to prohibit trade from Holland by the sea route to the Flemish coastal ports. It was a concession that must have been difficult to obtain, especially from Rotterdam, which was now entirely dependent on Zeeland's wishes in its trade with Belgium. To counterbalance the closing of the two harbours mentioned they now obtained a committee of enquiry, appointed by the States-General, in which two members of the Rotterdam admiralty played a leading part. The committee had to join the fleet in the West Scheldt and, cooperating with the Zeeland admiralty and their *fiscaal*, conduct a close investigation into possible fraud.

The report of the committee showed that corruption in the Zeeland customs was simply boundless, with obvious discrimination in favour of Zeeland exporters. Extirpation of fraud was not feasible, as the defrauders came under the jurisdiction of the Zeeland admiralty, who took good care not to deal too hardly with their friends, the Zeeland merchants. In letters to the States-General they expressed their indignation at these frauds and their determination to restrain them, but they named no names, so that the States-General, in a letter probably drafted by Oldenbarnevelt, asked with some asperity to be informed

when the punishments were carried out, on what persons, for what reasons, what persons were still under arrest there, what their names were, where the seizure of the ships took place and for how much those ships and goods were sold . . .

The letter was not answered. The Zeelanders only protested that they would not tolerate any inspection in Zeeland waters by the Rotterdam admiralty, even if it was acting on orders from the States-General. It was obvious that a crisis was rapidly approaching. Furthermore there was no question of accounting to the Council of State for *licenten* received in Zeeland.

Oldenbarnevelt then proposed heading a large deputation of the States of Holland to Zeeland, if their States were willing to convene a 'solemn' meeting. Zeeland agreed to this summit conference and by 12 January had summoned a States meeting at Zierikzee, so as not to make the journey too long for the Hollanders. They arrived on the 16th and were entertained to a dinner for twenty-eight in the Huis d'Apteeke,[1] owned by Ocker Jacobse Boeye. Next day Oldenbarnevelt wrote to the States-General that the States of Zeeland had promised to make their grants, unlike those of the previous year, short and effective. They were also accommodating on a number of points of secondary importance to the admiralty question, for the very purpose of gaining acceptance of their intransigent views on this last matter. They stoutly refused to pay the convoy tax and the *licenten* into one fund. The reason given was that the admiralties in Holland were so overdrawn that the fitting out of the Zeeland fleet would be endangered by pouring the *licenten* raised in Zeeland into their empty coffers. With regard to fraud, the Zeelanders said that the Hollanders were the last people to make such accusations, as just as much fraud went on in Holland as in Zeeland. They thought the best plan would be to appoint representatives of other provinces in the admiralties.

Though a step forward in the direction Oldenbarnevelt wanted, it was not nearly enough. The example of the Holland convoy tax collectors in Zeeland showed that a stranger would not make much headway among the clique on the Scheldt. A Hollander and, say, a Gelderlander, sitting on a board consisting otherwise entirely of the *Gecommitteerde Raden* of Zeeland, would be almost entirely dependent on the cooperation of the latter; if it were not forthcoming the result could only be a clash. Though the proposal regarding the appointment of councillors from other provinces had originated in Holland, it was only one in a package deal, and Oldenbarnevelt and his circle did not feel obliged to accept the one proposal when the others had been rejected. The negotiations had to be broken off and on the 29th Oldenbarnevelt and Boom, the Amsterdam deputy, were back in The Hague and gave a gloomy report to the States-General.

Though united against Zeeland, Amsterdam and Oldenbarnevelt were at loggerheads among themselves about another question concerning *licenten*: the prolongation of the export embargo on grain, issued the previous year owing to the disastrous shrinkage of stocks in the Amsterdam warehouses. The embargo was stifling for Amsterdam, largely living on the grain trade; the town was vainly using pressure to have the embargo raised, and when it was nevertheless renewed, began shipping clandestine cargoes of grain to Italy. The admiralty needed the convoy tax just as much as the merchants needed the trade. They took advantage of the absence of a joint fund or overall accounting; it was the only reason for the infringement remaining secret for some time. But eventually it came to light in Zeeland and then the merchants there began exporting grain, so that prices rose to an unprece-

[1] 'The Pharmacy'.

dented level. Once more, as so frequently, Oldenbarnevelt had to fight on two fronts, as each admiralty in turn was taking advantage of the anarchy to which he was so strenuously trying to put an end.

One result of these disputes between Amsterdam and Zeeland was the reopening of the prohibited harbour of Sluis by the Zeelanders, just after the delegation from Holland had left Zierikzee. The agreement with Bruges, by which Zeeland merchants could sail there unmolested through the Sluis estuary, had been constantly violated by the Spanish authorities and had gradually fallen into disuse. It was renewed on 24 February 1596, causing much ill-feeling in Holland. Not only were agreements with the enemy a matter for the States-General, owing to their political consequences; the Zeelanders also required the sea route to Sluis to be used, that is to say without trans-shipment, as had formerly been the custom. They brought every ship from Holland that tried to profit by the agreement into a Zeeland harbour, to pay again half the *licent* that had already been levied in full in Amsterdam or Rotterdam.

Fuel was being added to the flames of the dispute. On 2 March the States-General passed a resolution on the revaluation of gold coins, meeting the valid objections made by Zeeland in the previous year. The resolution caused a 'tumult', according to Duyck, everyone speaking at the same time. The Zeeland president, Van de Warcke, was against the proposal formulated by Oldenbarnevelt, in which the value of the silver coins, according to Zeeland also undervalued, was not raised. Before anyone knew what was really happening the Hollanders shouted that the proposal had been accepted and that the change in the edict must be printed immediately, to the considerable annoyance of the Zeeland deputies present, who felt that they had been taken off their guard. The next day the States decided to send a committee to Zeeland to effect publication of the resolution; the president Van de Warcke refused to countersign the order for the committee; Oldenbarnevelt signed it himself, without any authority to do so. The committee failed, Zeeland adhered to its own views on the matter and another attempt to unify the coinage in the United Provinces was frustrated.

Zeeland was visited by Maurice again in April 1596 in connection with the endeavour to relieve Calais.[1] As stadtholder of each province and author of the provisional agreement of 1590 he enjoyed the trust of both parties, particularly of Zeeland, since their becoming aware that he was no longer so exclusively on Oldenbarnevelt's leading-strings. The foremost Zeelanders learnt in conversations with him that they had put themselves in the wrong by continuing to refuse the unification of the convoy taxes and settlement with

---

[1] See p. 208.

the Council of State. They therefore decided to employ delaying tactics. In May and June they sent delegations to Holland who were to see that Zeeland was not 'precipitated', as their instructions put it, and to 'proceed *pede plumbeo*' (to drag their feet) but in such a way that 'no subterfuge or cause of delay in these tasks can be noticed by the other provinces'.

It was an unwise stratagem and merely infuriated the Hollanders. Their countermove was just as crafty as the Zeelanders' obstructionism.

Oldenbarnevelt decided to collect evidence of the frauds in the collection of convoy taxes and *licenten*. He told the general inspector of convoy taxes in Amsterdam to make a tour of inspection round all the local convoy tax collectors' offices and to report his findings to him, Oldenbarnevelt, personally. His report showed the existence of a great deal of corruption in almost all ports; it was difficult to put a stop to, as the one collector claimed the right to do what the other was allowed to do elsewhere and there was no overall authority to take standard measures against venality.

Oldenbarnevelt then drafted an edict appearing at first sight to comprise nothing but the closure of the Flemish ports, which Zeeland had so long been pressing for, and the stressing of certain regulations, only adhered to by Zeeland and the other admiralties as it suited them. The Zeeland deputies present voted with the other provinces in favour of Holland's draft on the basis of a general authorization by the States of Zeeland. It did not appear till later that some of the stipulations in the edict could be read as meaning that the whole *licent* was to be levied as of old in the port of first shipment, thus cancelling the provisional agreement of 1590. The two deputies had fallen into the trap.

Oldenbarnevelt alleged later that this cancelled the agreement of 1590. It is difficult to sustain. It is more likely that Oldenbarnevelt hinted at it when he left for Zeeland at the beginning of August for Zeeland to discuss the relief of Hulst with Maurice and make a tour of inspection in Zeeland–Flanders. He was accompanied by Van de Warcke and the clerk, Aerssen, who had made the fair copy of the edict of 24 July, and the leader of Zeeland's maritime policy, Caspar van Vosbergen. They sailed close by Lillo and Sas-van-Gent, the two main centres for levying the Zeeland *licenten*, and it is probable that the Hollanders' intention not to abide by the provisional agreement was sometimes mentioned on this occasion. In any case, official cancellation did not take place and for the time being the Holland admiralties went on claiming only half the *licent*.

The reason is obvious: Oldenbarnevelt wanted the rates for convoy taxes and *licenten* revised, mainly by codifying the changes of detail made from time to time. The instructions for inspectors-general, collectors and super-

visors ought also to be changed, especially so as to give them wider powers
and at the same time to tighten the check by the higher on the lower officials.
All this had to be accomplished in the States-General in cooperation with
Zeeland, and if the Hollanders showed their cards too soon this help would be
jeopardized. The vengeful Holland admiralties were thus forced to postpone
the use of the dubious right granted them in July. The final form of the
convoy tax collectors' instructions contained a clearly worded stipulation that
the *licenten* were to be levied at the place of first shipment. Strangely enough
the Zeeland deputies again let this clear stipulation pass, just as they had
approved the equivocal edict of 24 July. This can only be explained by
assuming that the cancellation of the provisional agreement in July or
August had been in such vague terms that the Zeelanders had not grasped it
and thought that an agreement between Holland and Zeeland could not be
nullified by a resolution of members of the States-General. It shows how
unstable the Netherlands constitution was and how little it was understood by
interested parties. The taxes were a matter for the States-General with
which the provinces had nothing to do in theory, though in practice matters
were very different.

That autumn the Zeelanders again acted with a compliance only explicable
if it is assumed that the province was indifferent to what the States-General
decided about convoy taxes and *licenten*, as it in any case did what it chose.
Oldenbarnevelt, on the strength of the Amsterdam inspector-general's report,
proposed sending a number of committees to all the convoy tax offices to keep
a closer check on all ships waiting for an east wind before putting out to sea.
The list of councillors on the committees showed obvious discrimination
against Zeeland. Whereas the inspection in Zeeland was to be carried out by
three members of Zeeland's great enemy, the Rotterdam admiralty, the
Zeelanders were allowed to have only one inspector to work with two
Amsterdammers in the check on Brill. Naturally nothing came of the
inspection in Zeeland; the officials met with passive resistance from all Zeelanders and could only surmise, but not prove, that fraud was going on.

Once the resolution had been passed in the States-General and the cooperation of Zeeland was therefore no longer indispensable, the Rotterdam
admiralty began to charge the full *licent* on goods destined for Antwerp.
Zeeland kept to the provisional agreement and refused passage to cargoes
without further payment of half the *licent*. After animated debate in the
session of 26 November Oldenbarnevelt pushed through a brusque resolution, giving the Rotterdam admiralty a free hand 'to maintain, have prosecuted and effected the prescribed instruction and list by such means as they
shall consider serve the purpose'.

The Zeeland deputies Van de Warcke and Hermansz protested 'that this should not be done without first hearing the States of Zeeland, nor should they be outvoted and contrary to all proper procedure and without their knowledge of the matter authority over them be given to the admiralty of Rotterdam'.

It now became a tug-of-war. Rotterdam took advantage of the freedom granted to charge *licent* on all goods exported to Zeeland, on the pretext that some exporters were using falsified bills of lading, pretending to convey to Zeeland cargoes in fact intended for Belgium.

Obviously something had to be done to settle the dispute. After Christmas, when the States of Holland had expressly approved their stringent counter-measures, the States of Zeeland appealed to the stadtholder as intermediary. On New Year's Eve 1596 he summoned Oldenbarnevelt together with the *Gecommitteerde Raden* and requested them to proceed in a more orderly manner, or at least to wait for ten days for the execution of the resolution, so as meanwhile to let deputies of both sides meet; but the Advocate and the *Gecommitteerde Raden* of South Holland expressly refused this, saying that they had already put up with enough from Zeeland.

Oldenbarnevelt now proceeded recklessly, without noticing that he was losing the sympathy both of the Prince and of the neutral provinces, who at first had certainly been on Holland's side. Measures against Zeeland became more stringent. When Holland placed men-of-war off Bommenee, a Holland outpost on the Zeeland island of Schouwen, a stage had been reached that could be called a breach of the Union. Zeeland would be deprived of basic necessities unless prepared to pay the prices the Belgians paid for them. They then proceeded to prohibit the export of grain, which they had no right to do at all, certainly not with regard to the transit traffic in grain from Holland. They sent delegates to Holland to settle the dispute, but with explicit instructions not to enter into negotiations before Holland had withdrawn the coercive measures against the provisional agreement. Holland was concerned with its prestige, as it would have meant that the deviation from the provisional agreement was illegal. The negotiations were broken off and the mercantile civil war continued. The other admiralties in Holland had been following Rotterdam's example regarding the imposing of *licenten* since 1 January. To help fill the exchequers of the Holland admiralties, which had been suffering since trade with Zeeland had virtually ceased, Oldenbarnevelt connived at the despatch of 400 grain ships to Italy, against the still valid prohibition by the States-General. Within Holland, however, it was as usual Rotterdam that gave the lead; in Zeeland Middelburg and Veere exacerbated the conflict. Oldenbarnevelt, as was his custom, regarded the matter less

255

from the angle of economic equity than from that of the States-General's authority, complaining bitterly at Zeeland's autonomous conduct, as reducing the prestige and reputation of the States. His remedy, to make Holland disregard States-General orders, was worse than the disease. The States of Holland decided to trade with Antwerp by land and on their own authority to open the closed Flemish ports, Gravelines and Nieuwpoort. Oldenbarnevelt delivered a fiery speech in the States-General and the Zeeland delegate answered a good week later with vehement countercharges. The other provinces did not understand much of all this disturbance: what was all this dispute about convoy taxes, which after all belonged to the States-General? They proposed a compromise giving Zeeland partial satisfaction, but Van de Warcke refused to negotiate on it till Holland's 'innovations' had been withdrawn. An impasse had been reached. The States-General, otherwise the natural arbitrators in disputes between provinces, were mistrusted by the Zeelanders: they had more or less taken sides in the contest under the influence of resolutions passed by Holland.

Oldenbarnevelt then tried to win the day by inciting the smaller Zeeland towns against the fanatics at Middelburg and Veere. When this failed he asked his old friends Jacob Valcke, who had been on an embassy with him to England, and Jan van Santen, from Delft, the pensionary of Middelburg, to meet him on the island of Putten, halfway between The Hague and Zeeland, where he had some private business to do for a few days. 'But the others', Duyck wrote,

either ignoring the letter, or fearing to become suspect themselves among their own people, did not answer, so that he returned on 24th *re infecta*. This private letter from the Advocate, without the knowledge of the States, was not well interpreted by some, as though too ambitious and smacking of sovereignty, or as if he wished to ingratiate himself with the Zeelanders; others considered it permissible, as all persons in service ought and may seek to act for the general good and peace.

A glimpse is given here of the demoralization always resulting from internal discord. Valcke and Van Santen were afraid of being suspected if they showed the least sign of moderation. Oldenbarnevelt's constancy was doubted by the extremists in Rotterdam and Amsterdam and he was forced to make a conciliatory gesture by stealth. The gesture became known though, and earned him the reputation of a power-maniac, as was to appear so clearly later on. Oldenbarnevelt was not brought down by going to Putten in 1597, but his trip caused the reactions foreboding the criticism that brought about his fall twenty years later.

Now that the States-General through ignorance, and the Council of State owing to its civil-service mentality, had shown themselves unsuited to the role of arbitrator, another had to be found. The obvious thing was to look abroad. Gilpin was the first to suggest Elizabeth. At the same time Caron, on leave in The Hague, was returning to his post via Zeeland. Both in The Hague and Middelburg he gained the impression that intervention was necessary, and in Middelburg perhaps the false one that the Zeelanders would like Elizabeth make the Hollanders see reason; she seemed to be the appropriate person on the strength of the Treaty of Nonsuch, still lingering on. In actual fact the Zeelanders were no keener on foreign intervention than Oldenbarnevelt was. Elizabeth would be quite unable to understand what it was all about. She had a deep-rooted hatred of all trade with the enemy and her pronouncement could only be calculated to suppress this activity, dear both to Holland and Zeeland.

On 7 May 1597 (O.S., 17 May N.S.) a letter from Elizabeth to the States of Holland was read in the States-General, lecturing them in her usual haughty tone on harmful disunity under the enemy's eyes and desiring: 'that the States of Holland should state the reasons for it; that she had written the same to the States of Zeeland and insisted on their accounting to her for reconciliation and decision'.

Oldenbarnevelt then accused the Zeelanders of having provoked this unwelcome intervention. There were again high words between Oldenbarnevelt and Van de Warcke, the latter loftily denying any provocative acts by Zeeland. He was probably right. In spite of their trade disputes Zeeland and Holland took the same line regarding independence.

The Advocate was perhaps particularly bitter because he was facing a defeat.

In April Holland had resolved on still more drastic measures. On the 11th they had instructed their vice-admiral Pieter van der Does to keep open the harbours of Nieuwpoort and Gravelines by force for Holland merchant shipping, even if the Zeeland fleet tried to stop them. There is no record of any naval incidents off the Flemish coast. Perhaps the instructions were withdrawn too soon, for in the meantime Maurice had abandoned his usual modest reserve and taken an active part in the affair. Zeeland was once more ordered to send its delegates, but when Malderee, Maurice's former equerry, who had great influence over him, told him that he would never get the proud Zeelanders to do so till Holland's 'innovations' were cancelled, the stadtholder considered the time ripe for throwing the whole weight of his prestige into the scales in Zeeland's favour. On 9 May he convened a meeting of the Council of State, assisted by five 'neutral' deputies from the States-General. Maurice summoned Oldenbarnevelt and exerted such pressure on him that the next day the States of Holland announced, through their deputies in the States-General, that they would cancel the 'innovations' pending the negotiations.

There was an atmosphere of triumph at Middelburg. The Grand Pensionary Christoffel Roels was at the time on his deathbed. He heard of the success from friends: in their excitement the States had no opportunity to pay him an official visit. He therefore decided to address them a letter as his political testament; it was handed to the States by his widow when he died on 18 May. Dated the 15th, it points out the lesson to be learnt from what had happened with regard to the part taken, after long hesitation, by Maurice. He recommends the States to let it lead to Maurice's election as 'head of the Union' with monarchical powers. It should be done openly by the States-General and certainly not by a *coup d'état* emanating from Maurice's 'creatures', by which Roels was thinking mainly of Malderee and perhaps of the foreign senior officers too. It was some years before the Zeeland statesmen followed the suggestion of their dead pensionary. The idea had been launched, however, and aroused in Oldenbarnevelt and his adherents the hideous suspicions that contributed so much to the truce disputes and their fatal consequences.

The Zeeland deputation to settle the main question arrived in The Hague at the beginning of June, accompanied by Uyttenbogaert, Oldenbarnevelt's friend, a liberal churchman, who boasted that he had contributed to the eventual reconciliation by his conversations with Valcke, Reygersberg and Van Santen. They had to negotiate with a seven-strong committee of the States of Holland, largely composed of experts on trade with the enemy, at the same time interested parties. This did not yet look like an impending capitulation. Zeeland too had naturally sent its chief fanatics: Vosbergen and Jan van Santen, who had been allowed to draw up the delegates' instructions himself, and three others. Maurice insisted on the negotiations being conducted under his presidency and in his rooms at the Binnenhof.

Zeeland began by asking too much. They even had the cheek to propose that the whole of the *licent* should be raised in Zeeland on goods passing through. The admiralty would have nothing to do with a superintendent body, whatever it was called, nor with the appointment of counsellors by the States-General, as in the case of other admiralties: the Middelburg admiralty should and would remain identical with the seven members of the *Gecommitteerde Raden*, to which three members from other provinces were only to be admitted as a favour, when admiralty affairs were being dealt with. Oldenbarnevelt tried unsuccessfully to put through the same regulation for all the five admiralties in the States-General. Even if it could be held with some justification that a majority vote was constitutionally possible, it could not be effected against Zeeland's will. When the appointments for the reformed bodies were made on 13 August they were tacitly made in the form desired by Zeeland.

It was only in the matter of charging *licenten* that Maurice obtained from Zeeland a modification, probably contained in their instructions: they agreed to return to the régime of the provisional agreement of 1590. Seeing that the Zeelanders remained obstinate and that in view of the feelings of the other provinces and of Maurice it really was wiser to be the wisest, Holland then, according to Duyck,

thus accepted it and so largely put an end to the dispute and misunderstanding dragging on so many months. It showed how injudicious the States of Holland were, that they had to work so much to obtain that which they previously, after long deliberation and estimation, had rejected, to wit the provisional agreement . . .

It can hardly be put better. Oldenbarnevelt, influenced by extremists in Rotterdam, his old friends and his brother's, had overestimated his strength. He had suffered his first serious defeat. It had been proved that the great man could be resisted. Neither Maurice nor Zeeland would forget that lesson.

CHAPTER 7

Vervins and Nieuwpoort

Not long after the end of the 1597 campaign it began to be clear that Henry IV was about to break away from the Triple Alliance, so recently concluded. Though, on 5 November, Buzanval proposed an alternative, a joint conquest of Belgium, the demands he made in men and *matériel* were so great that the States could not meet them.

In the following months Oldenbarnevelt began to bargain with France about these demands and to use all his powers of persuasion to keep Henry in the war: he appealed to his honour, to his own interest in not letting the young Netherlands state be swallowed up again by Spain, and to the advantages for France of a continuation of the war. At the same time he tried to persuade Elizabeth to increase her meagre help, so as perhaps to be able after all to fulfil Henry's minimum demands. It soon appeared, however, that kind words but no intensification of the war effort could be expected from England.

Perhaps then it would be a good thing to accept Henry's offer, of which Elizabeth and in particular her minister Burghley were in favour: to take part in their peace negotiations with Philip II and with powerful diplomatic support from the allies to hold out for the best possible terms. True, they would not contain independence; but autonomy guaranteed by France and England, even with preservation of religious freedom, would probably be obtainable, now that Philip II, old and near death, had given up the idea of total victory. A rumour had just been going about that he wanted to marry his still husbandless eldest daughter Isabella to the Governor of the Southern Netherlands, Albert of Austria, and give her the Netherlands as her dowry. Would not the sovereignty of this couple, largely nominal, be much more tolerable for the Northern Netherlands than that of the man who had sent Alva?

There were many people in the country who would have accepted something like this. But the great majority of the oligarchs saw nothing in it. Even if the liberal terms that could be expected were kept to faithfully – which they had reason to doubt – they were still unacceptable. They would include religious freedom for Catholics in the north and exclude it for Protestants in the south. The prestige gained by the Republic in the last few years would be thrown away, there would be an end to its diplomatic representation abroad, Maurice's position in such a new state would be inconceivable, and, above all: the ruling oligarchy would be swept away to make room for the rulers superseded in 1572 or their descendants.

It was of course not practicable to inform the allies of the differences among people and cliques which, over and above religious objections and commercial interests, made the Netherlands oppose a peace. But it might be as well to bring the fact of this aversion to the notice of the allies; to point out to them that in the long run the United Provinces could not cope alone with the Spanish world-monarchy and the Spanish vassal state; and that the eventual inclusion of the rich Northern Netherlands in that monarchy would mean mortal danger both for an independent France, hemmed in on three sides by the Habsburgs, and for a heretical England, that would almost be inviting conversion by force.

Embassies had therefore to be sent to France and England. In Holland it was soon agreed that only Oldenbarnevelt was qualified to defend the policy, advocated by himself, to Henry IV. He had no confidants in the whole of Holland and a matter of such consequence could not be left to Zeelanders or Frisians; they were at most adequate for the secondary embassy despatched at the same time to England: Van de Warcke from Zeeland and Hottinga from Friesland were therefore appointed to it.

Oldenbarnevelt showed reluctance to accept the appointment, on the grounds that his presence was needed in Holland. As has been seen before, it was his regular practice to let himself be cajoled into doing something that he meant to do anyway, and it can safely be assumed that he was using this system now. Gilpin, who had known him well for twelve years, did not think he was being sincere on this occasion. He wrote on 31 December (O.S., 9 January 1598 N.S.) to the Royal Council:

Divers marvel Barnefield to be chosen thereto considering how ill he can be spared hence and that without him nothing is done of importance; (I) hear he refused the charge and alleged sundry reasons, but being thought that they shall not be kept long there, no excuses would hitherto serve, yet doth he still make show (if he can) to avoid and put it off to another. I am of opinion that the hope he hath to prevail in the business, and that he may there in place hear and see the proceedings of the French so to be the abler to judge of their causes hereafter, will make him take the charge upon him the sooner . . .[1]

The nominal head of the embassy to France was Maurice's illegitimate brother Justin of Nassau, well known to Henry IV, to whom he had twice

---

[1] Public Record Office, State Papers 85/55/277; spelling modernized.

led a Netherlands auxiliary contingent; the secretary was François van Aerssen, the twenty-five-year-old son of the clerk to the States-General. It was intended to leave him behind in France as successor to the ambassador Calvart, who had died a short time before.

Everything shows that Oldenbarnevelt thought that an attempt to save the Triple Alliance would succeed. It is not a compliment to his perspicacity. Here again, as in the negotiations with Amsterdam in 1580, he was so convinced of Holland's rightness that he disguised the weakness of his position from himself. He thought he knew better than the King and Villeroy what France's interests involved. It is almost amusing to notice, here and in his later addresses to the King, how he takes it for granted that the interests of France and the Republic coincide. Knowing that Philip II would necessarily use a peace in the Netherlands to recapture the absolute power he had lost, he presumed that the French would know it too. The embassy's instructions ignored the possibility that the French King might not be susceptible to Oldenbarnevelt's arguments. No mention was made of the position to be taken up in that case. But such a position existed Oldenbarnevelt was to take it during the negotiations and in the long run it was no less favourable to the Netherlands than maintenance of the Triple Alliance would have been. So Oldenbarnevelt learnt something during his mission. Perhaps it is the quality that distinguishes great from mediocre statesmen: the ability to learn. Oldenbarnevelt could do so, provided his teachers were called William of Orange, Henry IV or Elizabeth.

After two attempts prevented by adverse winds, the embassy, impatiently awaited by Henry IV, put to sea from Brill on 18 March 1598. Among the company were Oldenbarnevelt's eldest son, Reynier, whose youth – he must have been about nine – did not prevent him having this outing, and the eldest son of Oldenbarnevelt's friend Jan de Groot, the linguistic prodigy Hugo (Grotius), gladly entrusted by his father to the strict Advocate. Buzanval, a great opponent of Henry's peace plans, travelled with them to support Oldenbarnevelt's arguments.

At Dieppe, where they arrived two days later, they had to wait three days till horses and coaches were ready for them to continue the journey. The Protestant congregation at Dieppe approached the envoys and asked them to foster the Huguenots' interests. They had no personal complaints, as the governor, though 'very Catholic' favoured and 'tolerated' them. They invited the Netherlanders to the church service and Lord's Supper on Easter Day, 22 March, which they attended. With regard to politics Oldenbarnevelt lay low; though showing goodwill he made no more promises than were consistent with his status as envoy of a foreign power.

He learnt from the governor that on 20 March at Angers Henry had accepted the submission of the Duke of Mercœur, the last remaining leader of the Catholic Ligue, on terms favourable to the latter: it was generally expected in France that this would hasten the conclusion of the negotiations at Vervins. Oldenbarnevelt wrote at once to the envoys in England, repeatedly urging them to see that the English envoys, who had already arrived in France, would be empowered to offer substantial military help, as otherwise 'the matter would undoubtedly be difficult'. In the same letter he told them of his decision to travel direct from Rouen to Angers 'so that we can compensate for the delay caused by the contrary wind'.

In Rouen they heard that the English embassy under Robert Cecil had passed through eleven days before. One of its members, Oldenbarnevelt's old friend Thomas Wilkes, had died there after a short illness on 12 March. Politically too this was a loss for him: Wilkes understood better than anyone else in England the impossibility of Netherlands participation in peace negotiations, and the two other envoys, Cecil and the rather colourless career diplomat, John Herbert, were suspected of being pro-Spanish. Cecil, two years before, at a relatively early age, had become Secretary of State, the leader of foreign policy in his country; he had expressed himself cautiously about the purpose of his embassy, having told the governor of Normandy, the Duke of Montpensier, that he had been sent to adapt himself with regard to peace negotiations to the intentions of His Majesty.

Public opinion, in favour of peace, had received these words with relief. Oldenbarnevelt, still familiar with the missal of his childhood, notes sadly: 'that people had almost begun to cry: *Hosanna fili* etc., but *crucifige* about our opinions'.

It was to appear at Angers that Cecil's briefing was not so pacific as he had made it seem.

After two days' delay the company went on to the Loire via Anet – where Justin was able to see the battlefield of Ivry – Dreux and Chartres. On reaching Blois on 30 March they were told that Cecil and his party, coming from Paris, had passed there eight days before. Young Aerssen was sent ahead to get into touch with Cecil. Oldenbarnevelt let Cecil know that he had hoped to meet him on the way, but as this had not happened, he begged him for advice, as his instructions were to behave accordingly.

Tired by the long journey of the day before, the envoys decided to rest at Blois, and to have the horses reshod and a damaged coach repaired. They made use of their stay to look at the castle and bridge, listed together: the only record of any sightseeing on this trip; the cathedrals of Chartres and Rouen are not mentioned.

On 1 April they went by boat along the Loire; it was quicker and easier than by road. They had no difficulty in making the sixty kilometres to Tours in one day: the horses were led on the rein, the coaches drawn empty.

As at Blois, the envoys were not very well received at Tours. They were only visited, Oldenbarnevelt writes, 'by players and drummers, and were badly lodged and not very well fed, but otherwise Tours is a good town, also for trade, but its enlargement and fortification is left half finished'.

The want of hospitality at Tours was made good by courtesies paid at Saumur, where Oldenbarnevelt's old fellow-student Du Plessis Mornay was governor. He had followed the King to Angers, so that Oldenbarnevelt had no opportunity to seek advice from this kindred spirit. His wife, who was unwell, nevertheless entertained the company to wine, sweets and confectionery of various kinds, and in the evening sent them some more bottles of wine, the guests having no doubt acquired a taste for the famous Anjou rosé.

François van Aerssen came back from Angers with a royal courier, bringing important messages both from Buzanval, who had gone ahead, and from Cecil. During the last stage by water Oldenbarnevelt was able to read the reports and decide upon his attitude. A mile outside Angers they were welcomed by the governor of the castle with a great train of nobles, among them the fourteen-year-old Prince Henry, Louise de Coligny's son.[1] The governor had arranged for the envoys to stay with two leading citizens of Angers and accompanied them there in person; lodgings had not been provided for the rest of their party, but they too were made guests in private houses the next day.

Oldenbarnevelt's first visit, paid late in the evening after his arrival, was to the dowager Princess of Orange, both out of courtesy and to get some idea of the mood of the French court, where she had been for some weeks. She at once told him not to hope that the King could be induced to give up his peace plans. She considered 'that the necessities, especially of money, political difficulties and other considerations, impelled the King towards it'.

The Duke of Bouillon, a member of the Royal Council and an opponent of the peace, told the Princess to advise Oldenbarnevelt to take up the attitude that the Republic would continue the war alone, if necessary, even if left in the lurch by the French and the English. Oldenbarnevelt did not follow this advice. He thought it better to leave the King in uncertainty as to the future attitude of the Netherlands and, according to his instructions, to keep harping on honour and the duty – and self-interest – that the King had not to desert his allies. Not that Oldenbarnevelt was cherishing any hope at this stage of keeping the King at war. By pointing to his breach of treaty and with the offer of powerful help, from Elizabeth too, the matter would be made

[1] Later the stadtholder Frederick Henry.

plausible and the King would have qualms of conscience, which might be of some benefit to the Netherlands. Bouillon's plan, on the other hand, would have made it easier for the King to become angry and say something like: you obviously don't need me, get on with it.

The next day the official reception by the King took place in the sombre castle of Angers. Contrary to custom, Oldenbarnevelt embarked at once at this reception on the purpose of his mission and appealed 'gravi et pressa (qui mos ipsi) eloquentia',[1] as Grotius wrote, for the continuation of the war. His arguments were all based on French interests, which would be served by taking advantage of 'fair opportunities' and forcing the Spaniards to give back not only recently captured areas but also Navarre, wrested from the King's great-grandfather eighty years before. Oldenbarnevelt also mentioned the eternal obligation under which he would place the Netherlands, if he helped to drive the Spaniards and their followers out of the country for good; and further the great benefit to Philip II of peace, which, 'in a manner of speaking' would be worth a hundred times any French gain of territory.

Henry did not take the somewhat arrogant tone of this address amiss and answered with a lengthy apology for his desire to make peace. He let it be known, however, that his final decision had not yet been taken and hoped to be able to exchange ideas on the subject with the Netherlanders on a quieter occasion; but at the moment he was more in the mood for festivities, as the engagement of his illegitimate son to Mercœur's daughter was to be celebrated that afternoon. There was just time for the rest of the party to be presented, including young Grotius, and it was on this occasion that Henry applied to him his well-known description 'le miracle de la Hollande'.

At the reception in honour of the betrothal the Netherlands envoys had a brief contact with their English counterparts; Bouillon was attached to the embassy during their stay at Angers; he played the part of host on the King's behalf at a dinner in a 'small chamber' next to the hall where the royal banquet was taking place. The close contact into which Oldenbarnevelt was brought with Bouillon was tiresome rather than welcome. He was pro-Netherlands through thick and thin, both because of his religion and his family relationship to Prince Maurice. According to some reports he is said to have gone so far as to suggest to Oldenbarnevelt that the King should be forced by a Protestant rebellion to continue the war with Spain. The reports came from an adversary, Sully, and may be fictitious, but Bouillon's efforts for the cause, not unmixed with self-interest and ambition, were of a different kind from Oldenbarnevelt's: the latter needed to dissociate himself from Bouillon without antagonizing him. It was not the Republic's friends that Oldenbarnevelt

---

[1] With grave and persuasive eloquence, as was his custom.

had to contact; just because they were that they had not much influence. The only exception was Rosny, later Duke of Sully, a personal friend of the King's from his Huguenot period, superintendent of finance and head of the arsenal; but at that time he was just being sent to Brittany to incorporate that region into the French state after the submission of Mercœur. Oldenbarnevelt only spoke to him once before he left for Rennes. Although he took part in foreign affairs he did not carry much weight owing to the Protestant prejudices Henry rightly supposed him to possess. The King's chief adviser was Nicolas de Neufville, Lord of Villeroy, whose position as secretary of state corresponded to that of a modern foreign secretary. Oldenbarnevelt met him on the second morning after his arrival at Angers; he found that Villeroy was the chief driving force towards peace in Henry's circle, though not for that reason to be considered pro-Spanish or desirous of the subjection of the Netherlands to Spain or to Albert.

The greater part of the same morning, Monday 6 April, was devoted to introductory talks with the English envoys. Cecil stated at once and with the greatest emphasis that no offer of help from him to the King for the purpose of keeping him at war was to be expected. The Queen had too many burdens, most recently on account of the fresh Irish rebellion, for her to increase her war effort. She would be glad to see the Netherlands join her in taking advantage of the opportunity offered to reach general peace. The second envoy, John Herbert, who had been on a similar peace mission in Holland in 1587, outlined the possible peace terms that Elizabeth would guarantee, which came down to submission to the Archduke with retention of the privileges and practice of the Protestant religion. It was of course an illusion to suppose that the ruling party in the Republic would ever be prepared to make an agreement on such terms. Elizabeth's guarantee, even if backed up by a French one, would be valueless if the Archduke began converting nominal into actual authority. Oldenbarnevelt explained this patiently and really seems to have got somewhere. At any rate, the French noticed that before Oldenbarnevelt's arrival and on passing through Rouen, Cecil was full of talk about peace, whereas he afterwards inclined much more towards war. It was a result of his instructions, drawn up by his father, Burghley, that were based on the idea that the Netherlanders were to be protected from the French, who would try to force them to make peace with inadequate guarantees, whereas of course with guarantees from both France and England they would join them in making peace. Cecil was therefore told not to consent to a peace which was unacceptable to the Netherlanders. Now that it turned out that no sort of peace at all was acceptable to the Netherlanders, Cecil was in an uncomfortable situation, the more so as the other hypothesis in his briefing, namely that the French would offer insufficient guarantees, was wrong. On the contrary: Villeroy's ideas of peace terms acceptable to the Republic were identical with Burghley's. The spirit of Cecil's instructions would now have involved him in joining the French either by abandoning the Netherlanders or by forcing them to submit to the Archduke on the terms mentioned. But their letter told him to have nothing to do with a peace unacceptable to the Netherlanders. His attitude during the rest of the negotiations was therefore entirely negative and sterile, a circumstance in itself of help to the Netherlanders and gratefully made use of by Oldenbarnevelt. Actually it is not impossible that a present of tapestry worth 1,800 guilders, made to him by the States-General through Caron, was an incentive; he had not yet found out that the Spaniards were to be much more generous to influential English statesmen once peace had been concluded.

Cecil himself had the impression that Oldenbarnevelt was 'wholly French'. Henry had indeed assured him that he had Oldenbarnevelt in his pocket. It shows that in this conversation the Advocate took up a somewhat different attitude from that which he reported to The Hague. His whole mission pre-supposed great indignation at Henry's disloyalty. He was to reproach him with this, hoping to appeal to his honour and induce him to proceed with the war. According to Oldenbarnevelt's report to the States-General, he had faithfully carried out this assignment, which in fact he had worded himself. Everything shows, however, that with his usual arrogance he did not regard Henry's peace plans as disloyal so much as stupid. If the King could be per-suaded of that, so much the better; if not, he should not be put in an ill-humour by accusations of bad faith. It would be better to consult with him about how he could help the Netherlanders after a peace.

Such consultation must have been the main subject of the conference on 7 April with Villeroy, Maisse[1] and Buzanval. Villeroy, however pro-peace, was well disposed towards this help, since Spain, encircling France on three sides, remained a dreaded potential enemy whom it was in France's vital interest to keep occupied on the northern frontier. Oldenbarnevelt glossed over these discussions in his report to the States-General, as his instructions made no mention of them, nor was it in his interest to give the impression that he had resigned himself too easily to Henry's desertion. He did not men-tion the Huguenots' cause in his report either. The Edict of Nantes, by which they obtained a legal position in the country intended to make them safe, was being prepared, and both Cecil and Bouillon probably tried to persuade Oldenbarnevelt to elicit favourable terms from Henry. Oldenbarnevelt, how-ever, knew that intervention in French internal affairs would have angered

---

[1] French ambassador in England.

the King and jeopardized his help in the future. But this was not a consideration that would have been taken in good part by all the deputies from the
other provinces and so Oldenbarnevelt said nothing about it.

That evening Henry definitely decided to conclude peace. Both he and
Cecil made a last attempt to get the Hollanders to go with them to the conference table, but, Oldenbarnevelt writes, 'we found this highly objectionable
and a point outside our instructions that we could not enter into'.

Oldenbarnevelt might well fear that before long he would have to do without Elizabeth's help as well. He went to his first audience of the King that
evening with a heavy heart; it took place in his *garderobe*, probably in order
to avoid difficulties of protocol. Oldenbarnevelt once more delivered an eloquent speech in favour of carrying on the war, mentioning the damage to the
King's 'laudable reputation both within and without the country' if he violated his promise not to treat without the consent of the States, a promise which,
he said, the King had made not once but many times.

Of course Oldenbarnevelt was not hoping to stop the peace by this address,
having learnt since that morning that the opposite decision had been made.
His object was more subtle: by working upon the King's conscience, by
raising the offers from the States, which he would reject, as far as possible,
he was trying to get all the more undercover help out of him. This was a great
success. The King answered by cutting short any further discussion of peace
or otherwise, this time stressing his monetary difficulties. In the same breath,
however, he declared that he would not desert the States, 'but by restitution
of the money advanced assist them to keep their cause going, repeating the
same more than once in high-sounding words'.

He invited the envoys to follow him to Nantes, where he intended to go
the next day. When Cecil arrived there he appeared, on instructions received
from the Queen, much more in favour of war. He tried to win Oldenbarnevelt over to agree to a two months' armistice, during which he promised to do
all he could at Vervins to shipwreck the negotiations. Oldenbarnevelt did not
trust this promise, however, and Cecil noticed it. This cast a cloud over the
good relationship which till then had existed between the two statesmen.

The positions had now been clearly defined and there was really not much
more to be said, yet the negotiations dragged on for a time, all parties being
afraid to publicize the discord between the allies by breaking them off.

A plenary session was fixed, at which of course nothing was accomplished,
as is usual at plenary sessions. Oldenbarnevelt made a long speech. His unshakeable optimism as to a rapid and successful outcome of the war certainly
did not match up to his private opinion and cannot have made the least
impression on his audience, at any rate for the moment. The speech could

only be called masterly in so far as Oldenbarnevelt was looking ahead and already thinking of the possibility that Henry would resume the war sooner or later. The Netherlands' readiness to continue the war vigorously, expressed in the speech, might then affect Henry's decision; to hold the option open he would have to keep the States supplied with generous subsidies. The Princess of Orange had warned Oldenbarnevelt that Henry's original keenness in this direction seemed to be cooling. The speech and the prospects offered might thus well encourage him again. The King had offered Oldenbarnevelt a second private audience, an opportunity to exert further influence, after Villeroy had given him detailed and friendly information about what had happened.

The speech was also aimed at Elizabeth, over the heads of Cecil and Herbert, especially the allusions to Spanish perfidy and some flattering references to the Spanish expeditions in the two previous years. Cecil admitted next day 'that he would much like that Her Majesty could have heard it'.

He also told Oldenbarnevelt that the King was not pleased at the course matters had taken at the conference, not so much because of what had been said by Oldenbarnevelt but by Cecil himself, who had indeed spoken abrasively. They both agreed that it was time to leave, but Oldenbarnevelt took care not to tell Cecil that he hoped to get far more out of Henry for the Republic, but not for the Queen, than the conferences suggested. This was shown too by the interview the next day, 21 April, between Oldenbarnevelt and Villeroy; the King had let Oldenbarnevelt know that 'I should trust no one at our leave-taking but him'.

Villeroy now stated plainly that peace would proceed but that the King would none the less do everything in his power to continue to support the States; he also hinted that the rest needed by France would only be for a few years and that the war would be resumed at the first suitable opportunity. Probably Villeroy was not sincere about this and Henry was; at any rate in the next ten or twelve years Henry was constantly setting a course for war, applauded by Oldenbarnevelt, while Villeroy was doing everything to prevent it, though without for a moment stopping the supply of money and volunteers to the States. The Princess of Orange confirmed the reports of Henry's mood and boasted that she had helped to make it favourable through mediation of Gabrielle d'Estrées, Henry's mistress.

The next day Oldenbarnevelt, accompanied only by his young son, had a private audience with Henry, who repeated what Villeroy had said, adding some advice which may have been unwelcome to Oldenbarnevelt on two counts: firstly as savouring of intervention in the internal affairs of the Netherlands and secondly as impracticable in the circumstances, though it could not be rejected too brusquely. Would not the States do better, the

King asked, to strengthen the authority of their government by choosing a sovereign? Henry was probably thinking of himself, eventually he named Prince Maurice. What did Oldenbarnevelt think of that?

Oldenbarnevelt was of course not inclined to give an impromptu answer to the suggestion. We know that he had sometimes thought of Maurice's elevation himself, and there was something to be said for it. He probably agreed with the King's opinion that 'under a Prince all difficulties could be resisted better than under the government of the States'.

But there were objections, and serious ones: they stemmed on the one hand from the Prince's own unusually surly character, and on the other from the fact that the idea of sovereignty in the Netherlands had been launched by Zeeland as a countermove against Oldenbarnevelt and his followers. Oldenbarnevelt attempted to explain to the King that 'le parler seul d'une matière tant délicate pourroit causer divisions et aultres difficultés en l'estat'. He wanted delay for a time: such a step could not be taken without Elizabeth's agreement. Very well, the King said, I will get Bouillon to inform Cecil.

Eventually Oldenbarnevelt did so himself. Cecil afterwards spoke personally to Henry on the matter, the King telling him that he wished to help the Hollanders notwithstanding the peace. Oldenbarnevelt cannot have been pleased to hear this for, as we shall see, it only made his negotiations with Elizabeth more difficult. That these must now take place soon was obvious: Cecil had often discreetly hinted at repayment of the loans and now suggested that Oldenbarnevelt should go back with him to London, where he could at once have preliminary discussions with the Queen. He announced this invitation in a letter to Elizabeth, using some flattery and telling her how Oldenbarnevelt compared the Queen's solidarity with Henry's disloyalty; he also praised the Advocate as a wise man, with whom he had since his arrival enjoyed almost daily fruitful discussions. Made desperate by Henry's desertion he would no doubt 'do as much to ease you as can be found reasonable, rather than your Majesty should leave them'.[1]

Cecil expressed his extreme indignation to Oldenbarnevelt at the French King's behaviour, which had made his blood boil. He even mentioned his intention of refusing the customary parting present, though Oldenbarnevelt managed with difficulty to dissuade him. Cecil's invitation suited him, but for various reasons he wanted to go via Paris and not before having a last long conversation with the King, to put the finishing touches to the arrangements for financial aid. Cecil was in a hurry to leave and had ordered transport at Caen, so he took leave of Oldenbarnevelt, hoping to see him again soon in England.

[1] Salisbury Papers, VIII, 124.

On the day he left the Advocate was visited by Villeroy and Buzanval, with whom he held a sort of closing discussion. They promised in the King's name a subsidy of 200,000 crowns as repayment of the moneys voted by the States; half would be taken at once by Buzanval, the rest was promised by October. But this was not all: the King would receive Oldenbarnevelt the next day, Sunday, at a leave-taking audience and then name the total amount. At the audience, which was again held in the *garderobe*, Henry fixed the total amount of subsidy to be granted at 1,000,000 *écus* of three francs each, to be spread over four years. He also discussed military matters at length, particularly Albert's possible plan of campaign, if he should assume the offensive. He found that the Advocate was not afraid of the superior numbers of Spain, but worried about them; he tried to set his mind at rest by reference to the engineers (whom he mentioned first), commanders and soldiers who would become available as a result of the peace about to be concluded, and whom he was willing to send to the help of the Netherlanders. The King also returned to the subject of danger from the populace, described by Oldenbarnevelt as tepid and inclined to submission. Once more Henry suggested as a remedy the elevation of Maurice, emphasizing that he would not let him down; this could be interpreted as an indirect promise of continued subsidies after the repayment period of four years. Oldenbarnevelt may have wondered what could make Henry so keen on the promotion of a man whom he had never seen and to whom he was under no particular obligation, but rather the opposite. One wonders too. Knowing Henry's character one must most likely not expect to find an ulterior motive, however strange this may sound; one must assume that it was just disinterested advice by a monarch with personal experience of the harm done by republicanism and aware of Oldenbarnevelt's similar liking for autocracy and distrust of the masses. It can however be understood that Oldenbarnevelt's cynicism did not accept such disinterestedness without reservations and that it stimulated his unfortunate suspiciousness of the Prince.

The envoys left for home on 28 April, up the Loire, the same way they had come. At Saumur they found the *châtelain* at home this time. Oldenbarnevelt, who had to take a purge just then, spent a day of rest on this and a lengthy conference with Du Plessis Mornay. They had already had a long conversation at Nantes. Du Plessis painted a rather too rosy portrait of Henry which certainly affected Oldenbarnevelt's French policy strongly. He concluded by saying 'that we may indeed rely on his promises that he certainly believes that he will keep trust with us, and that he will maintain our state against anyone'.

On Friday 1 May he asked Oldenbarnevelt and Buzanval, who was with him again, to dinner; the Old Heidelbergians no doubt had plenty to talk about. So Du Plessis, a great enemy of his fellow-Huguenot Bouillon, must have informed Oldenbarnevelt of his intrigues. There is reason to suppose that Bouillon is identical with 'spy 49' mentioned by Cecil in his letters from Angers and with the anonymous author of the 'French Advertisements'.[1]

Continuing their journey the envoys attended the promotion of the youthful Hugo Grotius to *doctor utriusque juris* in Orléans on 5 May and reached Paris on 8 May, where Oldenbarnevelt spent his time, apart from sightseeing, on various contacts which were to stand him in good stead in the course of his career. The most important was the Venetian ambassador, from whom he learnt that Venetian policy, traditionally pro-Spanish, was then swinging in the direction of France, a turn which Oldenbarnevelt naturally tried to encourage by reference to Spanish power politics throughout Europe, recently exemplified by the forcible union of the duchy of Ferrara with the Papal state.

Two months all but a day after their arrival the envoys took ship at Dieppe, making first for Dover, where they hoped to find the States' envoys to England. But they had left on the 16th, probably because the wind was favourable then. Oldenbarnevelt was also in a hurry to get back to The Hague. He decided to ask Caron's and Cecil's advice before at this last moment accepting the English minister's invitation given four weeks previously. Both strongly advised the envoys to come to London, as did Essex, who was taking Burghley's place during his illness.

Essex had a good reason. He had always been pro-French and pro-war and had been closely connected with the Netherlands statesmen since being cavalry commander in the Netherlands under Leicester. His position had been considerably shaken by the outcome of Cecil's embassy: his friend Henry IV had proved an unreliable ally and his Netherlands friends had been unwilling to accept Elizabeth's good advice. His relations with the head of the peace party, Burghley, had always been excellent, in spite of stormy discussions in the Royal Council. In the absence of the latter, less scrupulous opponents like Buckhurst and Howard were representing the peace trend. Essex considered this tendency fatal to England's greatness and the interests of Protestantism, to which he was devoted heart and soul. Elizabeth was veering strongly towards participation in the negotiations at Vervins, the ending of which was not yet known. It can therefore be seen why Essex needed advice and support from Oldenbarnevelt, who, informed by Caron of circumstances at the English Court, saw the importance of granting it.

He therefore left at once with Justin for London, where Elizabeth received him immediately. The audience was stormy, as Oldenbarnevelt had no doubt

---

[1] Salisbury Papers, VIII, 109, 235 and elsewhere.

expected. Elizabeth was angry with herself and, as often happened, those around her suffered for it. She seems to have been certain that Cecil's embassy would be successful and that she would be able either to conclude a general peace, in which the Netherlands would be included on terms acceptable to them, or to postpone the negotiations at first and afterwards break them off without any sacrifice on her part. Neither of these objectives having been obtained she was faced with the choice of two evils. If she were to make peace without the Netherlanders the Spaniards would stipulate the cession of the cautionary towns, and she could not hand them over without mortal danger to England. It was anyhow most questionable whether surrender against the will of the Netherlanders was a military possibility. ('Comment deux villes!' she exclaimed, 'où ils ont plus de gens que moy!') And if the Spaniards succeeded in gaining total victory over the isolated Netherlanders – it was not likely in view of the support from France, but they might – the whole war for the last thirteen years would have been pointless and her popularity in England as champion of Protestantism and heroic Queen – 'illaque virgo vir', a quotation from Virgil she had once impressed upon the States – would be shattered.

The view in the other direction was not much more attractive: heavy expense without any profit. The Spaniards would invade Ireland. Who could tell if another Armada might not be prepared? Subversion would continue among the English Catholics. All this without anything to show for it, especially now that Calais was to be returned to France. No wonder Elizabeth was sorry she had ever started the war, and so her speech was querulous. Why would not the States join in the peace? Albert had let her know 'that the States, Count Maurice and also the towns would be left in their authority, government and rule, without admitting anyone else into the country'.

Oldenbarnevelt reminded the Queen of Warmond's recent embassy, that must have conveyed to her the reasons why the States could not join in the negotiations. He went on to gross flattery ('admirable, yea almost divine wisdom' is only one of the many hyperboles), to which he knew that she, unlike Henry IV, was extremely susceptible. It was of no use: the Queen remained 'in a peevish humour' till the end of the long audience. She did indeed promise to help the States but only if they were 'up to the neck' in trouble.

Immediately after the audience the envoys paid a call on Essex, who was ill in bed. He was able to reassure them, saying that Elizabeth's bark was worse than her bite and that everything would depend on what repayment scheme the States were prepared to draw up. If Oldenbarnevelt had no authorization on this point, it did not matter: the Queen would not make peace in such a hurry, provided fully empowered envoys were soon sent.

Oldenbarnevelt followed this line at the two meetings of the Royal Council, both presided over by Essex, at which the envoys were allowed to plead their cause. Cecil quoted what Oldenbarnevelt had said to him at Angers, which could be understood to mean that the States were willing to satisfy the Queen: Oldenbarnevelt answered that this was a private conversation and 'that they were not instructed on this point; nevertheless they firmly believed that the States would not desire Her Majesty to bear any other charges than she should herself be pleased to and deem necessary'.

Buckhurst, as keen on peace as he had been in 1587, considered that the Treaty of Nonsuch could not be used against the Queen, as it was only valid till the peace: well then: 'if the States, while having an opportunity to make peace, did not wish to, Her Majesty must be understood to be freed from the contract and entitled to claim her money'.

Oldenbarnevelt answered that the treaty presupposed a peace 'by which the Christian religion, the liberties, rights and freedoms of the country might be defended, and that such was not possible in dealing with the King of Spain or the Cardinal'.[1]

This passage is important, as here is one of the few occasions on which Oldenbarnevelt defines the States' war aims. It is noticeable that religion takes the first place here, supporting 'haec religionis causa' against 'haec libertatis causa'; it is however possible that this order of precedence was used to make a favourable impression on the English, or on the States, to whom the report was given. Opinion in the Royal Council seemed to incline more towards peace than to a continuation of the war, but Oldenbarnevelt did not lose courage and the second session of the Royal Council did indeed show that the Queen was taking just the line that Essex had said she would: she expected an embassy with generous offers as soon as possible, adding that the proposals made to Bodley in 1596[2] would not be regarded as adequate.

Elizabeth then received the envoys in audience to take their leave. This time she made herself agreeable; her debtors had to be put in a good mood. She no longer expressed regret for the thirteen years of war, only surprise that the States, who were now well off, had not yet done anything to satisfy her claims. Naturally the financial aid promised by Henry IV was a strong argument for diverting some funds to her own exchequer. Though he does not mention it in his report, Oldenbarnevelt must have been sorry that Henry IV had made this known. He found it more significant to state that the Queen allowed him and his little son to kiss her hand.

The last call was on Lord Burghley, who was ill but putting a good face on

[1] Albert.
[2] See above, pp. 192, 205.

it. He took great pains to explain that *raison d'état* took priority over conformation to treaties, which must always be interpreted 'civilly'; the French King, in contrast to his son and Elizabeth herself, he considered, had done 'well and wisely' to conclude peace and 'other Princes' should follow him in this. Oldenbarnevelt, no less proudly but a little unpractically, answered 'that kings and princes were also bound to their contracts, promises and oaths before God and the world'.

Three days later the envoys sailed into the Maas. It was high time that Oldenbarnevelt was back. A wave of defeatism had been caused by the news of the Treaty of Vervins, especially when it became known that the Archduke would be satisfied with an almost nominal submission. Oldenbarnevelt, however, succeeded in an incredibly short time in swinging public opinion away from this danger to himself by publishing the favourable results achieved in France and England. The impressions he had gained in England were indeed such that he dissuaded the States-General from agreeing to the stringent terms laid down by Elizabeth for remaining at war. Colonel Vere, accredited as ambassador for this occasion, brought them with him: cessation of payment by England of the English troops in the Netherlands, including those in the cautionary towns; immediate payment of 100,000 pounds sterling on account of the total debt; military help on sea and land for England, if attacked, and in Ireland at once. Vere was not empowered to negotiate, only to invite the States to send envoys with detailed authorizations.

This was decided upon and again it was Oldenbarnevelt who was expected to be able best to modify Elizabeth's demands. He resisted again, as in December, but this time apparently in earnest. After three months' absence there were great arrears of work to be attended to. Spanish troops were just then marching away from the French frontier, destination unknown. A formidable offensive could be expected and Oldenbarnevelt felt that he ought to stay at home to give Maurice moral support. He may also have wished to escape the odium of signing an agreement which, however hard the bargaining, was going to be a heavy burden on the exchequer. His resistance was of no avail: Oldenbarnevelt was with good reason expected to get more done than his colleagues Van de Warcke or Hottinga; it had only taken him three days to change Elizabeth's mood from peevishness to graciousness. Holland submitted to the majority vote. Oldenbarnevelt set out with wide powers. The embassy's instructions, again drawn up by Oldenbarnevelt, dealt with Elizabeth's demands one by one. Military help in Ireland was rejected out of hand. It would indeed have been foolish to send soldiers on distant campaigns when Albert's full power might be turned upon the Netherlands. Another demand was only to be complied with in the last resort: the payment of the

1,150 English soldiers in the cautionary towns. Liberal assent was given to assistance in the event of the invasion of England or of an English campaign in Belgium; there was little risk attached, as the likelihood of such eventualities was remote. The same applied to the promised participation in a fresh naval expedition against Spain; after the expensive lessons of 1589, 1596 and 1597 Elizabeth was not likely to burn her fingers again.

The biggest headache was of course the financial clause. There was no question of agreeing to the demand for a cash payment of 100,000 pounds sterling. The envoys were restricted to an offer of 20,000, or, in the last resort, 30,000, payable within six months and subsequently in equal annual instalments for at most twenty years, which payment would be increased after a peace acceptable to the States to 100,000 during four years. The total thus reached of one million sterling or 10 million guilders was to constitute complete liquidation of the English debt, assessed by England at 1,200,000 pounds, a total not accepted by the States, though without their ever explaining why; military administration was in such disorder that almost every item in the English bill could be made the subject of controversy. The agreement offered therefore bore the character of a compromise.

Of course this limit had to be kept strictly secret, in case it was possible to get away with a lower payment. Oldenbarnevelt therefore kept the instructions with him day and night and was convinced that no one could get a look at them, let alone make a copy. Yet one or the other must have happened. When Oldenbarnevelt, in repeated conferences with English ministers, dug his toes in and refused to go above 8 million guilders, the Queen sent for him and 'attacked him vigorously, saying that she well knew that he was charged to rate the debt to her at ten millions and to agree thereto, and that she was most surprised, seeing that she had advanced more than twelve millions in cash over so many years, that they refused to act according to their charges'.[1]

It does Oldenbarnevelt's resoluteness credit that he did not yield to this angry attack. Without actually denying that his limit was what the Queen had heard, he merely stated evasively that 'they had their order and charge in writing, which they had to follow faithfully'.

He knew that the negotiations would not break down on this point, the advantages to England of the settlement proposed being too great. As the States would have to pay for the auxiliaries, under the command of Vere, who was to be general in their service, the result would be that the war would provide Elizabeth with revenue instead of causing her expense. The only drawback to continuing the war now lay in the danger of a Spanish invasion of Ireland, which was, in fact, launched a year later but successfully repulsed at Kinsale.

[1] This and the following quotations are from Oldenbarnevelt's repo.t to the States-General.

Now again after the first audience one minister after the other was coming to the envoys to impress on them that they must not offer too little if they wanted to keep Elizabeth in the war. But Oldenbarnevelt would not change his mind, and he was supported by Essex, who stated plainly that he regarded the continuation of the war to be in England's interest. However, he had fallen from Elizabeth's favour shortly before the envoys' arrival on 20 July. Banned from the court he received them as a private person, full of bitter feelings about Elizabeth, now wholly influenced by his opponents.

When introduced to him Oldenbarnevelt had tactfully assumed that it was his 'indisposition' that prevented him from taking upon himself 'the direction of our cause', but Essex scorned any subterfuge. It was not his illness, he said, 'but other matters which the Lord God could judge, inspiring the heart of Her Majesty and disposing it to another resolution'.

He declared that he would give his life for the Netherlands cause. This was to be appreciated all the more, as he did not know at the time that the envoys had been instructed to buy him six horses as a gift from the States-General. The present was one of many that the envoys were empowered to give 'at their own discretion' to some persons in England; the report does not mention any other gifts.

Another request to speak to Burghley was refused owing to his illness. Before the bargaining was ended he died on 14 August. François van Aerssen considered, probably wrongly, that his death facilitated the conclusion of the new treaty, twelve days later at Westminster. The Queen remained at war, but relieved of all obligations stemming from the Treaty of Nonsuch. The political stipulations, in disuse for the last ten years, were formally cancelled, with the exception of that as to English representation on the Council of State, which was continued, though reduced to only one English member and only for the duration of the war. The total indebtedness was fixed at 800,000 pounds sterling, half to be paid in thirteen annual instalments of 30,000 pounds plus one of 10,000; the payment of the other half was postponed till after peace had been concluded.

The envoys got back to Holland on 30 August. Oldenbarnevelt could be satisfied. He had been made to yield a lot, but on the other hand, in his own words: 'Her Majesty's favour and friendship to this country has been preserved, diverted from the intention of the enemy, the further augmentation and canker of her debts prevented, her arrears regulated to a certain sum and fixed as to years and instalments . . .'

He could have added, though it was not a thing to say in public, that the King of France had been made jealous, which could only stimulate his willingness to give help. Experience was to show to what extent it would prove possible to combat Spanish power successfully with the open, but un-paid, help of the English, and the secret payments from France.

When Oldenbarnevelt returned to The Hague at the end of August, where the States-General soon ratified the treaty with relief, he was distracted from his accumulated back-log of work by two religious questions. Though a lay-man, he had to decide whether certain religious opinions could be tolerated in Holland.

The first one concerned two mysterious foreigners, a Pole and a German, who had come to Leiden as the mentors of young students from their coun-tries and were distributing pamphlets there which smelled of heresy. They had been making propaganda for their views in Amsterdam as well, but there their books were confiscated. They had connections with a councillor of the Hof van Holland, who now asked Oldenbarnevelt to intervene. When he learnt that the moving spirit behind the charge of heresy was the strict Calvinist professor at Leiden, Gomarus, he told his friend the councillor that he would receive them. He could not make much sense out of them; evidently they were outside the main Protestant current, but they would not commit themselves definitely as to what their opinions were. Eventually Oldenbarne-velt asked them if they were papists, a category that he knew; if so he also knew what to propose to the States of Holland. But they denied that stren-uously, probably without showing themselves to the Advocate in their true colours. They were the first Socinians to be met with in the Netherlands. They denied the divinity of Christ, and this aroused such passions in the States of Holland when they got to know it from the theological faculty at Leiden that Oldenbarnevelt could not have prevented the resolution to ban them and burn their books, even if he had wanted to. It did, however, go too much against the grain for him to tell the foreigners of it himself. At the end of their conversation, on a Sunday, he made another appointment for Monday, which was first postponed till Tuesday, the States not having met on Monday, and subsequently put off again and again till the Greek kalends. Perhaps Oldenbarnevelt was embarrassed at having confused Socinians with Romans.

The conversation was not an important event in Oldenbarnevelt's life, except for some details helpful to our imagination and our knowledge of his character. We can surmise that his house in Spuistraat was teeming with people who wanted something from him, but it is not mentioned elsewhere. Audiences were evidently difficult to get and then only through a friend at court; this explains some of the hatred felt for him later by many who had not had access to him and were sent away at the door by an underling. It is also interesting to see that Oldenbarnevelt did not mind sometimes making an appointment with people and then calmly having them told that 'mijnheer' had forgotten them and they must come again another time.

He was so arrogant he did not even think it necessary to make excuses.

The other religious question was a difference of opinion between the town government and the church council at Medemblik. A preacher liked by the former had annoyed the latter by casting doubts in the pulpit on the Calvinist doctrine of predestination.[1] Oldenbarnevelt had himself delegated, with a clerical friend, Uyttenbogaert, to settle this dispute peaceably. Generally the Advocate did not consider such trips as part of his job. This suggests that there was something else behind it. In the Zijpe, a reclaimed area a few miles west of Medemblik, Oldenbarnevelt had taken part in dyking this tract of land, the dyke of which had just been destroyed by floods. Perhaps the assignment had been taken on so as to be able to inspect the damage done at no expense. The polder accounts show that Oldenbarnevelt lodged at an inn at Schagen, paid for by the polder funds. This does not mean that he did not go to Medemblik or that the journey was of no use, but it might not have taken place unless there had been flooding.

It was certainly imprudent to leave The Hague for a week at the moment when the Spaniards were benefiting from the peace just concluded to transfer troops from France to the Netherlands, or rather, first to Germany, where the powerless Duke of Cleves and Jülich was unable to save his territory being used as a theatre of war between his western neighbours. As the Spanish troops were badly paid and mutinous, their commander gained no advantage beyond recapturing Rheinberg, a remote outpost belonging to the Elector of Cologne in Jülich territory, occupied some time before by States forces to deny the Spaniards a passage across the Rhine to the east of Gelderland.

The drawback to this gain was that the neighbouring German princes were worried about the Spanish invasion of the Empire and began to assemble an army to push them back.

That was one reason why the dreaded Spanish offensive in 1598 and 1599 achieved nothing. Another was the death of Philip II on 13 September, and a day later the departure of the Governor, Albert of Austria, for Italy and Spain to fetch his bride; in his absence the interim government at Brussels could not make any important decisions. Before leaving Albert gave instructions to try another peace offensive. His negotiator's offer was the same as in 1595: formal submission to Brussels, with privileges and freedom of worship guaranteed. Very well, Oldenbarnevelt replied, we too want the Netherlands reunited into the powerful state that they were under the Burgundians, but not annexation of the Northern by the Southern Netherlands, but reunion

[1] See p. 440 ff concerning these 'pre-Arminians', as they were called.

on a basis of equality, without being Spaniardized; this amounted in practice to an annexation of Belgium by the north, which would be generous enough to permit the Belgians freedom to practise their religion. It was an entirely unrealistic basis for negotiation. It is obvious to us, knowing the outcome, that peace was not to be obtained by reunion but only by the splitting up of the Netherlands. The idea of the Burgundian state was, however, still so strong on both sides of the front – it could be called pan-Netherlands national feeling, from Cambrai to Groningen – that years of useless bloodshed were to pass before the illusory reunion was given up in favour of the strong basis of the status quo.

Oldenbarnevelt's chief anxiety in the winter of 1598–9 was finance, which was in a bad way. The cost of the war was bound to be increased by the Peace of Vervins. Servicing the English loan cost hundreds of thousands annually. Tax revenue, on the other hand, was decreasing; Friesland and Groningen were years behindhand with their quotas; Zeeland was complaining bitterly about the new absolute embargo on trade with the rebels issued by the new Spanish King, and the growing presumptuousness of Dunkirk. The general revenue earmarked for the maintenance of the navy, convoy taxes and *licenten*, was stagnating for the same reason. Once more it was Holland, still relatively rich, that had to step into the breach for the other provinces. Increased taxation was needed but always extremely difficult to carry out owing to the voting method, the minority not being bound to the majority resolution. It was a great feat to propose taxation in a form that could eventually be agreed to by all, each town finding its tax burden counterbalanced by loss suffered by a competitor.

Oldenbarnevelt again attempted, as in the emergency in 1584, to introduce majority voting in financial matters as well; the towns, anxious about their trade, rejected it, lest cunning taxation might divert it to another town or province. In his interrogations Oldenbarnevelt recalled all the hard work and trouble involved in this delicate task.

What eventually resulted was an immediate levy of $\frac{1}{2}\%$ on property, with an inbuilt slight progressive rise, as well as a decrease for the largest properties: the first 3,000 guilders were tax-free, and anyone who paid 1,000 guilders voluntarily was not required to pay more, even if he owned more than 200,000 guilders. Some of those who owned less may have made use of this regulation to avoid the nuisance of assessment. Oldenbarnevelt himself managed even better: together with the thirteen nobles summoned to the States, he offered 9,000 guilders, 'which was gratefully accepted by the towns'. It is not known how much each of these fourteen people paid. The towns' gratitude may not have been so much for the generous offer as for the fact that the commissioners were spared the delicate task of assessing these highly placed personages impartially. We can assume that Oldenbarnevelt paid more than a fourteenth part, not only because he was richer than some of the nobles but because it was worth something to him to be on the same footing as the old nobility, the Duvenvoordes, Brederodes and Egmonds.

Another cause for concern was the countermeasures which had to be taken against the trade embargo pronounced in Spain and shortly afterwards in Belgium. The first step was the renewal of an old edict prohibiting neutrals conveying contraband to Spain. The neutrals did not all obey it. A Hamburg ship with munitions was brought in off the estuary of the Elbe. Oldenbarnevelt negotiated with the envoys who came to protest, and satisfied them in so far as the ship and the part of the cargo that was not contraband, although forfeit, was returned to the friendly town as an act of grace. This afterwards became the usual procedure with neutrals.

Many merchants wished to go further and make all trade with Spain and Belgium illegal for Netherlanders and foreigners alike, irrespective of the nature of the cargoes. Such a reaction was understandable but open to objections. A blockade of this kind, advocated by Amsterdam in particular, would have to be either partial or total. If partial, ships could be arrested anywhere but most of them would escape; it would be a matter of chance which ships suffered and the whole operation would assume the character of near-piracy, a sort of resurrection of the fierce Sea Beggars. On the other hand a total blockade, for actually cutting off the long Spanish coasts, in those waters would necessitate an expensive permanent fleet, difficult to operate without a base. The incensed merchants chose a cheap version of the second solution, partly with a view to the unemployed sailors, among whom there was unrest and who were thus given employment. Oldenbarnevelt's reaction to this proposal is not known. The whole winter and part of the spring passed before it was embodied in an edict on 2 April 1599 and the equipment of a large fleet under Pieter van der Does, whose instructions are dated 24 April: the texts both of the edict and the instructions were drafted by Oldenbarnevelt.

That some restraint would have to be placed on this privateering and that the edict, even if not formally withdrawn, could not be enforced, was clear to Oldenbarnevelt. The general embargo on trade with the enemy was merely a watered-down edition of Leicester's detested edict of 14 April 1586. Only the capital punishment of *lorrendraaiers* was dropped. Little opposition was aroused in the Netherlands, in contrast to thirteen years before, it being supposed that trade with the enemy had in any case been made impossible by the measures taken by the other side. Loopholes were presently discovered though, such as sailing under false colours, and then feeling against strict execution of the edict gradually increased. The strongest opposition, however, came from abroad. Oldenbarnevelt had foreseen that it would, but probably not to such an extent. Buzanval had warned him of the resentment that would be felt in France and his prophecy came true. Henry IV was extremely nettled, especially when a letter from Oldenbarnevelt to Aerssen, asking him to inform the King of the edict, got lost; at a later stage he even threatened a rupture of relations, if the trade with Calais, also forbidden under the edict, was not allowed. Loud complaints were heard from Scotland, the Hanseatic League and Denmark, to which country an embassy even had to be sent to convince the King of the rectitude of the blockade, without success of course.

The edict was therefore a resounding failure, at home as well as abroad. In part this was due to the outcome of Van der Does' naval expedition, which had been amazingly expensive. Even so it was far too small for a total blockade of the Spanish coast and was frittered away in attacks on the Azores and the islands off the Guinea coast, during which the commander died of a tropical disease. On its return the booty captured, after deduction of the percentage due to the crews, was not nearly enough to cover the outlay; the debts incurred for this adventure were a burden on the States-General for years. The only positive result was damage and alarm caused to the Spaniards and heightened prestige for the young state, that had sent its naval forces so far from home for the first time without English help.

Another naval expedition was for the time out of the question. The policy of partial blockade, which meant privateering, had therefore to be adopted. Once again Oldenbarnevelt does not seem to have given full consideration to the disadvantages of this sort of warfare for an established state; at any rate it was he who drafted the first instructions for privateers, a few days after the edict of 2 April. It was of course an endeavour to keep the privateers within bounds, soon forgotten once they were on the open sea. Some years later, when privateering was beginning to show a good profit, there was a tremendous rush to fit out freebooters. Soon the sea was crowded with Dutch buccaneers, sparing neither friend nor foe. The restrictions Oldenbarnevelt was then forced to introduce caused much bad feeling among the shipowners concerned, and shipping to Spain was not noticeably curbed. The matter was finally decided by a dispute with Venice. A Venetian merchantman was first captured by Van der Does' fleet, and although released without too much loss, was then plundered completely by a grim pirate serving the Dutch East Indies Company. Friendship with Venice, politically valuable, could only be retained at great financial sacrifice. Oldenbarnevelt saw that this must stop; even though the edict were not rescinded it must not be put into practice.

He could always be flexible in practice, but on the subject of texts he was most obdurate. Again and again he would incorporate, as in this case, a principle to which he was attached into a harsh resolution. He knew, though, that owing to the imperfections of the administrative system its execution left much to be desired. But then he did not always desire precise execution.

The Netherlands were on the defensive in 1599. They had to be, owing to Spanish superiority and the shortage of money in the tax collectors' coffers. Spanish troops crossed the Maas and encamped before Bommel.[1] Maurice realized that he could do no more than restore Bommel's neglected defences as quickly as possible and await the enemy in hastily prepared fortifications round the town. It cost a great deal of money, raised with extreme difficulty. The States-General calculated that at that moment and place Maurice was no less strong than the enemy. They sent him a message to go over to the offensive and if necessary force battle on the Spaniards. Maurice refused and asked the States to send a large deputation to Bommel to see the situation with their own eyes. When those deputed were not convinced the entire States transferred themselves to Bommel, still accessible by river. They allowed themselves, though only after a long discussion, to be persuaded that Maurice was right. When the siege had been raised the younger deputies in particular began to show aggressive tendencies, but this time Oldenbarnevelt was obviously not on their side. In the end they left everything to Maurice, with merely an admonition to practise the greatest economy.

Maurice was irritated at Oldenbarnevelt's inconsistency: on other occasions he had wished to avoid a battle at any price, and now he pressed for one, even bringing in the soldiers' health, which would suffer from staying in the damp fortifications – a concern he had never shown before. Even if the latter argument was just *pour le besoin de la cause*, the former makes sense psychologically. The numerous victorious campaigns and success in foreign policy had greatly enhanced Oldenbarnevelt's confidence in the strength of the young state, to such an extent that in the next few years one must sometimes shake one's head at so much optimism. Though he sometimes feigned depression to Buzanval when it was a matter of extracting subsidies from the King, as a rule he scarcely took into account the possibility of a serious defeat. The wild excesses of the Spanish army in the Rhineland and their constant mutinies had filled him with contempt for their military strength; the absence of Archduke Albert, followed by his evident unpopularity with the Belgian nobility after his return, raised his hopes of an imminent rebellion in the south. He also had great expectations of the army assembled by the German princes to drive the Spaniards out of Empire territory. These expectations

---

[1] Today Zalt-Bommel, on the river Waal, between Utrecht and 's Hertogenbosch.

proved baseless. The little army assembled with much delay by the German princes in the Westphalian district achieved nothing, partly owing to the incompetence and lack of authority of their commander, Simon von Lippe, partly because of rivalry among the princes who had equipped it. The campaign ended in September in an inglorious retreat by the Germans, not caused by any show of force by the Spaniards but simply because of lack of organization, munitions and provisions.

This incident was a lesson for Oldenbarnevelt, inasmuch as he never again tried to obtain military aid from German princes. Support was gratefully received, but it had to be in cash. It was what the States needed most in this winter of 1599–1600. Three provinces had stopped paying their contributions: Zeeland, Friesland and Groningen. The first two might, in Oldenbarnevelt's view, be more or less excused, but in the case of Groningen the time seemed ripe for intervention.[1]

Another source of anxiety for Oldenbarnevelt that winter was Elizabeth's renewed leanings towards peace. She had been disappointed by the reverses in Ireland, by the Netherlands' failure to make the repayments promised by Oldenbarnevelt and was no longer being prompted by Essex, the leader of the war party, disgraced after his mismanagement of the Irish campaign. The financial situation did not permit Oldenbarnevelt to keep her happy with money, and when the Spanish and Belgian envoys were appointed to a peace conference at Boulogne in April, it looked for a time as if the Netherlands would have to do without the English as well as the French alliance since, as two years before, Oldenbarnevelt steadfastly refused to take part in the negotiations. But then Caron reported that at an audience the Queen had mildly reproached him with doubting her loyalty, adding a quotation from the Bible: 'Modicae fidei, quid dubitasti?'[2]

In the spring Oldenbarnevelt's chief concern, apart from internal and foreign affairs, was the preparation of the campaign of 1600. As usual the provinces were pulling different strings as to where the army should be sent. That an offensive would have to be undertaken was agreed. No undertaking of any significance by the Spaniards was to be feared, on account of considerable mutinies and shortage of money, as well as the evident dissatisfaction of the southern States.

There was a great deal to be said for aiming the offensive at Flanders; relations between France and Spain were almost continuously tense: if a Netherlands army operated successfully in Flanders, the nearer the French frontier the better, another rupture between Henry IV and the Habsburgs

---

[1] See pp. 239 ff.
[2] Matthew xiv, 31: O thou of little faith, wherefore didst thou doubt?

was not unlikely. In spite of discouraging experiences in 1595–8 it still seemed as though such a rupture would guarantee speedy victory, liberating at any rate some of the 'disunited provinces'. Another argument was that it was from Flanders that much of the dissatisfaction with the new régime was being reported: it did not seem to be an illusion – though it was – that the appearance of a strong Netherlands army in that province would cause rebellion to flare up. But perhaps Zeeland's plight was the most weighty consideration.

This province had suffered more than any other from the export embargo imposed by Spain and Belgium. At Sluis, opposite Walcheren, Spanish galleys were lying in wait for Zeeland ships sailing in or out of the Scheldt. At any moment the Spanish armies might venture an attack on the heart of the province. Six of the companies in Zeeland's scanty repartition were garrisoned at Ostend and could only be brought back by sea. But the greatest harm was done by Dunkirk, where practically every male inhabitant was a privateer. Now that the Spanish army was disrupted by mutiny, a campaign in Flanders seemed a good opportunity to capture Sluis and Dunkirk, and free Ostend from continual fear of a siege.

If Oldenbarnevelt and the Zeelanders were in agreement on the plan there was always a good chance of it being carried out. Only Maurice had to be won over. He had begun the campaign with the siege of St Andries, a fort recently built by the Spaniards on the Maas as a convenient starting point for invading the Betuwe.

The Zeelanders came to see Maurice in the camp before St Andries near Alem on 3 April 1600. He had not yet discussed the Flemish campaign with Oldenbarnevelt and gave them an evasive answer: the time had not yet come for such an expensive expedition. St Andries had to be taken first, then the troops would have to be rested, and afterwards one could see what was to be done.

Some days later Oldenbarnevelt himself went to Alem with 60,000 guilders in his waggon. He walked with Maurice along the lines to inspect the fortifications and speed up the start of digging communication trenches. This time Maurice had a good reason for his slowness. The forces occupying St Andries had not been paid for many months and were in full mutiny. If they were not harrassed by too many bloody offensives there was a great chance that, in the absence of relief, they would sell the fort to the States-General. Oldenbarnevelt, usually more economical with money than with soldiers' lives, must now have agreed with Maurice, especially in view of the intended attack on Flanders, for which every available soldier would be needed. Negotiations as to the capitulation started while he was still there; he personally promised delegates from the mutineers 125,000 guilders, which he could well do, as an instalment of the French subsidy had just arrived. When the garrison did not accept this proposal immediately, Oldenbarnevelt left for The Hague, where he arrived on 6 May. The days that followed were devoted, after the St Andries force had gone over, to raising money for the great Flemish campaign, decided on in principle in the camp at Alem. The severe treatment of Groningen must be regarded in the light of these circumstances: the resolution to build a citadel is dated 13 April 1600; the Groningen ringleaders were taken hostage on 15 May and finally released in March 1601. Troop transport by sea to Ostend alone, for which 900 vessels were needed, cost a fortune. In addition there was the provisioning of the army and *matériel* for the siege, though with regard to the former Oldenbarnevelt expected large voluntary or requisitioned contributions from Flanders. This time money was raised by a tax on absentee landlords, who had benefited by non-inclusion in the poll tax of the previous year. They were now assessed at over 50% of their incomes in Holland.

Oldenbarnevelt had still not let it be disclosed what these preparations were for. This was not done till after another Zeeland delegation had come to complain in the States of Holland about their financial straits and Spanish plans for an attack. Oldenbarnevelt had already heard from Maurice that Zeeland was keen on a raid on Dunkirk and would make great sacrifices for it in spite of their desperate situation. Only when this had been confirmed by the Zeeland delegates did he reveal the plan to the States of Holland. It aroused great enthusiasm there: after the successful taking of St Andries people in Holland were in a victorious mood.

The prospects looked eminently propitious for this, the greatest military undertaking in the Eighty Years War. The enemy had active mutinies on his hands everywhere. Demoralized by reverses in the Betuwe he was practically defenceless. His available troops were in North Brabant, far from the scene of the projected invasion. Ostend was an ideal base, accessible by sea, like Nieuwpoort, the first objective of the attack. Within a week of embarkation at Dordrecht it could be surprised. It was hoped to leave on 5 June with a colossal army of 127 companies of foot and 25 squadrons of horse. Maurice could capture Nieuwpoort, with its poor defences, before the middle of June and then Dunkirk, just as weakly fortified and occupied, could not but fall to him. The gains would be of various kinds. The main one was relief of the severe pressure on the admiralties, accompanied by the expected increase in convoy tax and *licenten*. This was explicitly mentioned in the States' resolution, as was the raising of the blockade of Ostend, which would decrease army expenditure. As the war was to be waged on enemy territory, its effect would be felt by the inhabitants while the provisioning of the enemy army would be hampered by a systematic scorched earth policy. Strange as it may sound, it was principally a campaign for financial purposes; one might almost say, in order to save money. This aspect of it largely explained the trouble arising both before and after Nieuwpoort between civilians and soldiers, and especially between Oldenbarnevelt and Maurice. There was a foreign policy angle as well as an economic one; it was hoped that greater activity in the neighbourhood of Calais and Boulogne would bring Henry into the war again and keep Elizabeth in it.

These were considerations which had little appeal to Maurice, who was more concerned with strategy. The capture of a place over sixty miles from Flushing, leaving nearby fortresses like Sluis, Bruges and Ghent untouched, might seem inadvisable from a military point of view. Moreover much depended on wind and weather, which could nullify the surprise effect of a landing near Nieuwpoort. Mutinies could suddenly stop at the prospect of profitable action, as had been seen before. If the time schedule did not work out exactly, Maurice could expect the Archduke's main forces on his flank or in his rear before he was properly entrenched before Dunkirk, in which case the entire future of the state would be made dependent on the gamble of a battle.

These were sensible arguments, the only drawback to which was that they were brought up for discussion too late, actually not till the beginning of June, when it appeared that the ships would not be on the spot on the date arranged and that the voyage would have to be delayed at least a week. The Hollanders were all keyed up and said they would not agree to a change in the war plan: their great financial outlay was for an immediate sailing to that pirate's nest Dunkirk, and not for a slow advance by land according to the well-tried recipe, with one town after another in Flanders being subjugated after costly and lengthy trench work.

Maurice then withdrew his opposition, especially when fresh reports seemed to show that the Spanish mutineers were increasing in numbers and audacity. What he did ask, not too peremptorily, was that the States-General should themselves come with him not merely as advisers but active participants in the enterprise and be at hand in all difficulties; where possible, they should organize the contributions from Flanders and assess a high *brandschat* on all the villages; they relied on this so much that they took a special receiver with them.

When the States-General, accompanied by two members of the Council of State, arrived at Flushing, they found that the wind prevented the troops from sailing out of the Scheldt to reach Ostend by sea. After a day of deliberation it was decided to change the plan of campaign. The Scheldt was to be crossed above the estuary and Ostend to be approached by land from Philippine, passing by Bruges. This delay, costing nine days, was regrettable, but Oldenbarnevelt thought it was an advantage to be able to practise *brandschat* and incitement to rebellion at closer quarters.

The army landed at Philippine on Thursday 22 June, and moved on the next day to Assenede; the civilians remained behind for a time as no suitable waggons were to be found at Philippine and they wanted some sent across from Flushing. When this took too long they climbed on to munition carts, more suited to the conveyance of gunpowder than of elderly gentlemen. In this uncomfortable way they covered the fifty miles separating them from Ostend in four days and a half, escorted by the rearguard of the army. Such daily marches of not much more than ten miles do not seem much, but roads were poor and few, foraging had to be constantly undertaken, right up to the gates of Ghent; and without maps, since this march had not been prepared, proper plans could not be made, some units being lost for half a day. The States-General held a meeting at every stage and passed resolutions on *brandschat*. Oldenbarnevelt and Aerssen were busy writing letters to towns and villages. Even Ghent and Bruges, which they passed close by, were warned that they would have to pay large sums within a fortnight, not only for fear of the neighbourhood being burnt down, but in their own obvious interest in being at last liberated by the brave army of their northern brethren from the intolerable tyranny of the Spaniards. It was incredible optimism, but Oldenbarnevelt believed in every word of it. It was to be years till he – before Protestant public opinion – grasped the fact that the Flemings and Brabanders did not think the tyranny intolerable at all, although objecting to this or that measure taken by the Archduke. They wanted an end to the war, but by compromise and not by the victory of the far from brotherly heretics from the north, who had been doing them such untold harm for twenty years.

The threats therefore failed completely – partly too because the people of Ghent and Bruges realized that the large army could not hang around for a fortnight to carry them out.

The march was a nerve-racking affair, chaotic in fact. There was no reconnaissance. Nothing shows that Maurice worried at all about what Albert and Isabella were doing, though his strong objections to the expedition in The Hague had been principally based on the possibility of the main enemy forces attacking his communications at any moment. During the whole of the Eighty Years War there was scarcely any military intelligence service; the many reforms due to Maurice and William Louis did not extend to this necessary organization. Spying was done only at short range, during a siege for instance, or if inactive armies were confronting each other. There was indeed a long-range information service organized by the official agents of the States abroad, who sometimes sent out scouts for a particular purpose. The Netherlands agent at Calais, for example, Sailly, was told at this time by Oldenbarnevelt to send spies to Dunkirk; but this was primarily to gauge the financial capacity of the leading inhabitants with a view to *brandschat* and capitulation terms. The commander relied on farmers in the neighbourhood he was passing through for information as to the enemy's movements. The threats of arson and further unbrotherly behaviour by the States' army resulted in not a single farmer being found at home on the whole march from Assenede, the first halt, to Ostend. The army thus went on blindly, dependent on wild and mostly optimistic rumours brought back by the cavalry from their forays. It seems to us almost incredible that Maurice arrived on Friday 30 June at Ostend and the next day at Nieuwpoort without realizing that the news of his departure from Dordrecht had quelled the mutiny at Diest and that on the previous Thursday the Archduke had mustered over 10,000 men at Ghent, with whom he was advancing by rapid daily marches towards the coast.

Oldenbarnevelt was the first to hear of Albert's approach. According to the original plan he had stayed behind at Ostend with the civilians and the service corps while Maurice left for Nieuwpoort. On the Saturday afternoon a cavalry officer of the regiment left by Maurice to man the fortifications around Ostend reported that three of these sconces had fallen into enemy hands. The details indicated that the enemy's main force was about six miles from Ostend. Oldenbarnevelt sent the cavalryman to Nieuwpoort at once, while he himself took the necessary military measures to prevent a *coup de main* against Ostend. They did not include the defence or destruction of the bridge at Leffinge, for which Maurice immediately sent an order to Ostend on hearing the bad news: it was too late, and when Maurice sent a detachment under his cousin Ernst Casimir to hold Leffinge, the bridge had already been crossed and he suffered heavy losses.

Oldenbarnevelt, understandably and rightly, was more anxious about Ostend than about the beach. He sent the colonels from the captured fortifications to a redoubt called Albertus, the only one not taken. He had difficulty in persuading the utterly demoralized troops to defend this redoubt, the nearest to Ostend. Some of their comrades from the other fortifications had been killed after surrendering, contrary to the terms of their capitulation. This made them extremely nervous and greatly endangered Ostend.

Nobody can have slept much that night. Contact with Maurice seems to have been broken although he was only an hour's ride away along a beach where the enemy had not yet appeared. The danger was great, even if the enemy was not much stronger than Maurice's remaining forces. The approach of the Archduke had obviously sown panic among the army around Ostend. If it should extend to Nieuwpoort, defeat was inevitable – *mea culpa, mea maxima culpa*, Oldenbarnevelt must have thought for a moment. He later told Grotius that the more strongly a bold course had been advocated in the past, the more everybody was impressed by the danger. For consolation he had his friend Uyttenbogaert, who had joined the army as chaplain but had not gone on to Nieuwpoort. On Sunday morning he prepared to go there and hold a service for the troops, but the defeat at Leffinge had already taken place, the Spaniards had reached the coast and he had to return to Ostend with the remnants of Ernst Casimir's regiment. Uyttenbogaert preached that morning in the church at Ostend, while Oldenbarnevelt was trying in vain to bring the demoralized fugitives under some sort of military discipline and induce them to make an attack, even if it was only a show of force, on the rear of the Spanish army. Later he was accused of preventing some forces going out to see what was happening, to the great annoyance of some officers, as he thought that it was all over with the Netherlands troops. There may have been some truth in it, but in that form it is certainly incorrect. After the breakthrough at Leffinge the Spanish army turned westwards, away from Ostend, so there was no reason to give it strong cover, especially with regard to cavalry, which alone were suitable for such a show of force. There is an authentic ring though to the annoyance of the officers in the story. Most probably either Ernst Casimir wanted to send the demoralized infantry in useless pursuit of the enemy, or put the cavalry into action, after Oldenbarnevelt had realized that they could not be used till they had recuperated.

Cannon fire began after midday. Oldenbarnevelt cannot have been very hopeful of the result: one can only judge by what one sees, and for twenty-four hours he had seen nothing but panic-stricken fugitives, while Uyttenbogaert reported the hundreds of corpses with which the beach was strewn. Prayer was the only comfort. Uyttenbogaert went with the Ostend minister to the deputies' lodgings while they were in session. The ministers called on them to stop their useless deliberations and, according to Van Meteren

after the example of Moses while Joshua was fighting the Amalekites to help His Excellency and the army now engaged in battle with their prayers, requesting that the people of the town might be assembled by their Lordships' authority; then, as owing to the great dejection and other hindrances there was no convenient means of doing this, it was approved that prayers should be offered in their Excellencies' hall with open doors, calling in all those thereabouts, in the presence of their Lordships; this was done ... by Uyttenbogaert, with great attention and earnestness from all their Lordships.

While this praying was going on the first reports from the battlefield were coming in. On receiving news that the battle had started, Oldenbarnevelt directed some infantry with provisions and ammunition to fort Albertus, so that Maurice could fall back on it more safely. Soon afterwards one messenger after the other arrived, first with the news that the enemy was yielding, and later with the confirmation that Maurice, with the courage of despair, had won a brilliant victory – except for the cavalry engagement at Turnhout the only one in his thirty years career as commander.

Talks were held that evening in Westeinde, near Nieuwpoort, where Maurice was spending the night, the report of which cannot have pleased Oldenbarnevelt. When Maurice had had to decide in the morning whether to accept battle or not he had not taken into consideration whether the country's future hung on a thread, according to Duyck, 'since the States had so expressly desired this campaign, as though the state could not otherwise exist'.

After the battle, which for two hours had been a most precarious affair, it was typical of Maurice not to forget his grievances and say that all's well that ends well.

It was only human nature that Maurice, and in particular his circle, described (by Grotius) as cunning in sowing discord, preferred at that moment to forget how feeble Maurice's opposition had been and that his own mistakes had brought the army into such a dangerous situation. The loudest talkers among the officers were wondering what kind of motive Oldenbarnevelt and his pensionaries could have had in exposing them to so much danger. Soon the word 'treason' was heard on cynical lips. Maurice certainly did not encourage this sort of gossip, but seven years later, and again ten years after that, he remembered the expedition to Dunkirk as reflecting on Oldenbarnevelt's patriotism.

This sort of evil talk soon spread from the commander's tent to the camp fires of the other ranks and in a few days Oldenbarnevelt was the most hated man in the army. In 1618 he complained in his 'remonstrance' (self-defence) of the trials he had to undergo in 1600 after the battle in Flanders. Unfortunately this was not the only disagreement. Fresh difficulties cropped up after the battle about how the victory should be used to the best advantage. They were met with at once the next day after Uyttenbogaert's sermon on a text from Psalm 116: 'The sorrows of death compassed me, and the pains of hell gat hold upon me: I found trouble and sorrow. Then called I upon the Name of the Lord; O Lord, I beseech thee, deliver my soul.' Perhaps not a very tactful choice in view of Maurice's mood, but tact had never been the outspoken court chaplain's strong point, nor can he, any more than Oldenbarnevelt, have guessed the extent of Maurice's ill-humour.

Maurice had already made two decisions without consulting Oldenbarnevelt, who cannot have welcomed them. He had made no serious attempt to pursue the retreating enemy and instead of digging himself in before Nieuwpoort he had withdrawn his soldiers from the town and allowed them to rest at St Mariekerke. He excused both measures, on the one hand by a severe storm which made trench digging impossible, and on the other by the weariness of the soldiers and the lack of food supplies that had to be replenished. Oldenbarnevelt accepted both reasons and busied himself with provisioning, assembling prisoners, who had to be protected from the vengefulness of the troops, the burial of those killed – though the Spaniards were left unburied – care and transport for the wounded and finally the most important task: announcements at home and abroad.

Meanwhile there were fervid debates on the best means of exploiting the victory. To Oldenbarnevelt's straightforward way of thinking the only possible tactics were to go on with the plan conceived in Holland, to capture Nieuwpoort and then just push on to Dunkirk. It seemed logical: a plan was made which was obstructed by an advancing enemy; the enemy suffered a shattering defeat, the obstruction was removed and the plan was carried on. Neither at home nor abroad – always a great consideration with Oldenbarnevelt – would it be understood if things went differently. Both Henry IV and Francis Vere lost their respect for Maurice's gifts as a commander as a result of the barren victory at Nieuwpoort.

Maurice raised objections. The army was weakened, not only in numbers but in morale, which had not been strengthened, as is usually the case, after the victory. It was remarkable how little desire was shown by the troops to follow it up. They felt that they had been led into a trap, especially as the defeated enemy had not fled in the same direction as the advance, but back, quite near the lines of communication with the Netherlands. It was learnt that the Spanish army had gathered at Ghent and was drawing reinforcements from all sides. The Netherlanders could obtain only few reinforcements. Lack of numerical strength and bad weather made it impossible to encircle Nieuwpoort entirely, according to military precept. At any moment he liked the enemy could replenish the town's garrison. In such circumstances, and with an obviously reluctant commander, a siege of Nieuwpoort had little point. But Oldenbarnevelt persevered obstinately. On Thursday 6 July the army, grumbling in the rain, advanced along the beach to Nieuwpoort. Oldenbarnevelt, all for action as usual, promised to supplement the depleted companies, partly by a levy he intended to make in England. On the same day he twice sent reports to Maurice's headquarters not lacking in military advice about the occupation of this fort and that 'pass'. Maurice took his advice, though without much enthusiasm, and only so that he could not be blamed for the abandonment of the siege, which he regarded as certain.

Two days later he sent to Ostend to urge withdrawal. In answer to this the whole States-General descended upon him, conferring with him till late in the evening and spending the night in camp. They did not see much good in a siege of Nieuwpoort *more romano* either, but asked Maurice if it were not feasible to force the town with a few days heavy artillery bombardment, without surrounding it with entrenchments.

Maurice must certainly not have thought it feasible, but he was willing to try if the States insisted so strongly. A resolution, couched in most honeyed words, declared that they left everything to the commander, 'without otherwise standing by repute or disrepute', but it was impressed on him by word of mouth that he must do as much as possible to capture this place (they had already given up hope of Dunkirk) to bring the campaign and the contribution in Flanders into good repute again.

Maurice would now have been formally entitled to abandon the siege, of which he no longer expected anything, in the next few days. But he did not want to take the responsibility, knowing how peremptorily he had been ordered to take the army there. Moreover the weather was not favourable to a march, after which time would have to be spent on the building of hutments. Meanwhile the besiegers' camp was flooded. Maurice was in an evil temper and made unfair criticisms during his inspections of the fortifications.

On Wednesday 12 July the States decided to return to The Hague, where plenty of work was waiting for their attention. This did not suit Maurice, who would have to bear the responsibility for unpopular measures alone, with consequent loss of prestige, after his masters had left. He tried to obtain a positive order from the States for raising the siege. Oldenbarnevelt would not agree: the States had left everything in Maurice's hands.

Such evasion of responsibility on both sides was a sorry business. The chief blame for loss of blood, money and time, due to indecision, rests on Maurice, but Oldenbarnevelt was deeply involved as well: his arrogant behaviour, his constant insistence that *cedant arma togae*, stifled Maurice's initiative and it is not surprising that his overburdened spirits discharged an acrimoniousness of which only vague evidence can be found now, without any direct pointer to what actually happened.

At five o'clock in the evening of the same Wednesday the enemy launched a strong sortie. The States forces offered poor resistance; after all people do not much care for being killed in an enterprise considered futile by their own commander. Maurice decided to go to Ostend himself to persuade the States of the uselessness of continuing the siege and the need to use the troops for a more profitable undertaking: raising the blockade of Ostend by capturing the redoubts still occupied by the Spaniards after their defeat. The session lasted the whole morning and afternoon, resulting in a compromise, which in this case was the worst solution. Half the army was to continue the siege of Nieuwpoort, the other half to advance on Fort Isabella.

Next day, Friday the 14th, the ships for the deputies had still not arrived, but some envoys had come from Scotland, who had the opportunity of a long conference with Oldenbarnevelt and others concerning the purchase and transport of arms desired by James VI. The transport was allowed – perhaps the arms were to support James's claims to the English throne if Elizabeth died suddenly – but the States excused themselves from selling any: they needed all they had.

On the same day the resolution was taken to agree to the request by the southern States-General to enter upon peace negotiations. The Belgians were to come as representatives of their States, not of the Archduke. It was a good sign: in view of Albert's defeat it was possible that the southern provinces were softened up for the sort of peace envisaged by Oldenbarnevelt – reunion of the seventeen Netherlands provinces without the Archduke and without Spanish troops.

This resolution was not made without lengthy discussion. Not everyone had the same confidence in the Belgians' wish for reunion as Oldenbarnevelt, and in any case it was thought that an answer should not be sent to Brussels without letting Maurice know. Oldenbarnevelt was the obvious person to convince him. So he left on Saturday, in haste and unaccompanied, for Nieuwpoort, where he spoke to Maurice alone for an hour. Then he returned quickly, no doubt on horseback, to Ostend.

We know that the conversation dealt not only with the peace negotiations but with the entire abandonment of the siege. There are indications that it was not very friendly. There was a rumour in the army that His Excellency had struck the Advocate. It is not likely to be true, fisticuffs were not Maurice's line. It is clear, though, that his anger was roused and Oldenbarnevelt must have caused it in some way. By combining a statement by Grotius during his interrogation in 1618 with one made by Oldenbarnevelt to Dominie Walaeus, in the last night of his life, we can perhaps make a hypothetical reconstruction of the talk which probably had an adverse effect on their subsequent relations. Oldenbarnevelt began by again refusing to give, or have given by the States-General, the order for raising the siege. This made Maurice, who would now have to take the unpopular decision himself, somewhat disgruntled for a start. Then when Oldenbarnevelt asked for his approval of the peace negotiations at Bergen-op-Zoom, he objected, probably on the following lines: the proposed basis for peace was neither realistic nor desirable; what was the point of forming one state with those papists? It could only result in continual discord. Oldenbarnevelt, full of his own sanguine hopes for the future, thought that there was something else behind these arguments. He had heard indirectly that Maurice's entourage, enraged by the Nieuwpoort trap, had been indulging in wild talk of overthrowing the civilian régime and setting up Maurice as sovereign. It was of course true that reunion of the Netherlands would make a kingdom under Maurice impossible. If Oldenbarnevelt insinuated in the course of the conversation that Maurice's objections to the Bergen-op-Zoom conference sprang from monarchical aspirations, it can be imagined that Maurice, who had no such aspirations and was extremely touchy on the subject, took this imputation badly and expressed his anger in a way that gave rise to the legend that he came to blows with Oldenbarnevelt. He gave his consent to the negotiations; they could not do much harm after all. But the talk left Maurice with feelings of rancour and Oldenbarnevelt with ineradicable suspicions of Maurice's monarchical leanings.

It was of course not the case that from that moment the two became sworn enemies, their hatred only concluding with Oldenbarnevelt's execution. Human relationships do not develop as simply as that. But, just as we say of old people who have been ill, that it has taken it out of them, we can say that something was taken out of the still friendly relations between Prince and Advocate after the crisis of 1600.

In the States-General there was a debate over the instructions to be given to the delegates who were to meet the Belgians at Bergen-op-Zoom. They were to be required to take up arms against Spain, or at least allow the States troops to levy contributions in Flanders; they must also manage to wrest the castles from the Spaniards. If they were not prepared to do so, the negotiations were to go no further.

They began at Bergen-op-Zoom on 21 July. After an introductory address by Bassigny, head of the Belgian delegation, full of unctuous sentiments but devoid of concrete proposals, Oldenbarnevelt made a long speech, sounding a victorious note quite unjustified by the military situation. The Spaniards, he said, had not been so weak for thirty years; the conquering northern armies were in the middle of Flanders; now was the time to join forces to oust the foreigner; then they would all be Netherlanders together and easily agree to the terms of reunion, each side respecting developments of the last twenty years.

The southern delegates were painfully surprised. They had been authorized to accept almost any conditions to put an end to the disastrous war, but they could not play the part of turncoats; the southern States might be dissatisfied with some of the Archduke's measures, but they were loyal subjects and in no way disposed to hand themselves over bound hand and foot to the wild Beggars from the north. Bassigny explained this calmly to Oldenbarnevelt, but the latter replied with hauteur that he was not going to negotiate with the Archduke; if the Belgian delegates were his slaves they had better leave. The negotiations were broken off on the same day and only resulted in increased embitterment in the south against the proud Hollanders.

Oldenbarnevelt's attitude is a mystery. Did he really believe that he had brought the Belgians to their knees and that a mixture of intimidation and expressions of fraternal feeling would revive the good old days of the Pacification and put Albert and Isabella in the place of Don Juan? There are indications that his optimism was moving in that direction, at any rate at the beginning of the Dunkirk campaign, a month earlier. But it is difficult to conceive of Oldenbarnevelt so far removed from reality, especially after the passive and even hostile attitude shown by the Flemish populace during the army's passage, and when the battle of Nieuwpoort had not produced any military advantage. Conferences at Ostend must also have shown him that his fellow deputies had as little sympathy as Maurice with his vision of the reunited Netherlands. If Oldenbarnevelt was to retain his influence as leader he would have to follow public opinion, which considered that the time for peace had not yet come. An accommodating attitude – he had observed it during his conversation with Maurice – would expose him to serious suspicions. It is therefore possible that he went to Bergen-op-Zoom with the preconceived plan of making the negotiations fail in such an offensive way that no suspicion could attach itself to him.

It was of no avail. There was talk about him just the same. At some moment, during dinner on Thursday evening or during an adjournment on Friday he had a private interview with Bassigny, the son of one of his old clients. It was enough to suggest intrigue. A few months later the States of Holland resolved to sell the property of Count Aremberg, admiral of the southern forces, as a reprisal for the atrocities committed by the Dunkirkers under his vice-admiral, who was responsible to him. Aremberg threatened dire revenge on all concerned with the sale, either as commissioners or purchasers. Either as a result of these threats or owing to lack of money, no offers were made. Oldenbarnevelt was later blamed for this, as he might have been bribed by Aremberg, perhaps at Bergen-op-Zoom. The probably untrue accusation was made plausible by the fact that the property was later returned to Aremberg under the terms of the Truce; he then sold it himself at a good price, Oldenbarnevelt being the buyer of the principal lot, the Naaldwijk house in Kneuterdijk in The Hague.

Oldenbarnevelt therefore came back to The Hague on Sunday 23 July, exactly five weeks after he had left, with shaken prestige and serious worries. Bad news was coming in from north and south. Maurice had been unsuccessful in his attack on the Spanish fortifications near Ostend. He was beginning to insist on his recall. When the States withheld their consent longer than he liked he came back on his own account. Repeated letters from the States with serious requests – orders were no longer given – at any rate to attack the galleys at Sluis before the main body of the army crossed the Scheldt, reached him too late. The advance on Dunkirk had ended without anything being gained at all. Nonetheless the States of Zeeland and later the States-General were obliged to give Maurice festive banquets and create a 'See the conquering hero comes' atmosphere for the benefit of public opinion. It was an unpleasant state of affairs.

In the north a lively dispute had sprung up between William Louis and a section of the provincial States, only brought to a kind of reconciliation after a long time and a lot of excitement. It was also understood that William Louis was perhaps even more indignant at the 'Nieuwpoort trap' than his cousin Maurice, though contemporaries were not aware of the letter that William Louis' secretary wrote to a German friend: 'Barnefelt und die lanckrocke haben uns precipitiert; Gott gleichwol hat uns nit willen lassen verderben.'[1]

On 24 July two English courtiers, Lord Cobham and Sir Walter Raleigh, had been to Ostend on board two English warships to view the battlefield. They had spoken to Maurice there for a long time and also to the members of the Council of State who had remained behind there and were naturally dismayed at the discord between Maurice and Oldenbarnevelt. The English nobles gained the impression that it was a serious dispute and reported it to their Queen.

Elizabeth now decided to urge unity upon the States officially but discreetly. To avoid talk she used the Netherlands ambassador Caron for this purpose, and he appeared at her request before the States-General at the end of September. The next day Gilpin delivered a lecture on unity carefully confined to generalities. The occasion was far past: the quarrels had been composed and there was no intention of calling in foreign potentates as arbitrators. Oldenbarnevelt wrote a memorandum full of smooth talk for Caron to take back to England. Discord in the Netherlands? Well, there had been something of the kind in Friesland but it was settled. There was nothing to worry about and they thanked the Queen very much. Buzanval also denied, perhaps too eagerly, in all his letters that there was any trouble;

---

[1] 'Oldenbarnevelt and the longcoats led us to the edge of the precipice; God however would not let us be destroyed.'

only Sidney, the commander of Flushing, who was in The Hague in September, tells us that Oldenbarnevelt was 'much discontented with the bruit had bin spread of him of his being put in prison attributing it to some practice of the ennimy'.[1]

It was not the enemy abroad who was spreading such rumours but the increasing number of the Advocate's adversaries at home, encouraged by the catastrophic victory of Nieuwpoort. Oldenbarnevelt would need all his genius to regain his prestige and remain the master over his prematurely rejoicing opponents for the next eighteen years.

[1] Salisbury Papers 84/60/318, Sidney to Cecil, 25 September 1600 (O.S., 5 October N.S.).

CHAPTER 8

Towards a truce

TRADE with the enemy, Elizabeth's great concern, consisted, as far as export from Portugal was involved, largely of spices brought by the Portuguese from the East Indies, in particular the Moluccas. As such trade ran into more and more difficulties – risks of an embargo in Portugal, now become Spanish, and of English privateering on the outward or return voyage – enterprising Amsterdam merchants hit upon the idea of by-passing Lisbon and bringing the spices direct from the Indies. At first a northern route seemed most suitable. Without knowledge of the immensity of Eastern Siberia or of the obstacles, insuperable at the technical level of the time, to shipping in the Arctic, it had been calculated that the Northeast Passage, as it was called, was considerably shorter than the long way round the Cape of Good Hope.

Oldenbarnevelt, who regarded everything from the angle of its bearing on the Spanish war, could see three benefits which might accrue from the success of this endeavour. In the first place Spanish and Portuguese profits on the Indies trade would be cut down; in the second, Dutch traders' profits would be increased, bringing more revenue into the exchequer; and thirdly, the necessity of trade with Spain would be reduced, thus improving Netherlands relations with the English ally. So in 1593 and 1594 he was at great pains to support plans made by the pioneers in Holland and Zeeland. The first voyages to the north, which later came to a celebrated though unfortunate end in Willem Barentsz wintering on Nova Zembla in 1596–7, were largely financed by the admiralty of Amsterdam and the States-General on the recommendation of Oldenbarnevelt and Valcke, the Zeeland treasurer.

A little later Amsterdam merchants fitted out the first voyage to the Indies round the Cape: after many vicissitudes it reached its destination, whereupon companies for the promotion of this trade sprang up like mushrooms both in Zeeland and Holland. In August 1600, just as Oldenbarnevelt was back from Bergen-op-Zoom, a fleet came in for the third time with results apparently promising fine profits in the future, but also pointing to the dangers of cut-throat competition among the few shipowners with sufficient capital. To start with, this rivalry raised purchase prices as soon as the Moluccan and

Javanese sellers got to know of it. Then the different companies began to undersell one another, thus reducing the market value in Europe. The worst part, however, was that the Spaniards and Portuguese did not take kindly to being deprived of their monopoly. The arms that a small fleet could carry, though paid for by the States-General, were inadequate defence against such attacks. Trading posts had to be set up and remain occupied between voyages; they had to be fortified both against the natives and the Spanish and Portuguese enemies. A joint policy had to be established, both as regards the terms of business and the exclusion of interlopers. In short, circumstances here demanded what Oldenbarnevelt otherwise abominated: what would nowadays be called a trust, a United East Indies Company with a resolute management able to act on a majority vote. It would not be easy to arrange. Amsterdam had invested the largest amount of capital in the East Indies trade and felt entitled to be at the head of the new enterprise. But the Zeelanders, particularist as ever, in view of their own initiative and also considerable outlay of money, would not be easy to keep under control. Moreover Rotterdam, Delft (a port by virtue of its suburb, Delfshaven) and West Friesland would all want to have their say.

The rivals could only be brought together by a neutral outsider. Oldenbarnevelt, in charge – in practice at any rate – of the national exchequer, was in the fortunate position of not belonging to any of the competing towns, though a slight prejudice in favour of Rotterdam, where his brother was pensionary, and Delft, where he had a house and where his wife came from, might be surmised.

Oldenbarnevelt set to work in earnest in the winter of 1597-8. He was faced with applications for subsidies and guns from all the rival concerns: the powerful Amsterdam group under his later mortal enemy Reynier Pauw, and, one after another, a second group from Amsterdam and those from the various places mentioned.

How were the States-General to deal with these demands? There were three possible lines to take. A principle long followed by the States of Holland laid down that 'all exclusive charters in the matter of navigation, trade and commerce were prejudicial to the prosperity of the provinces, towns and inhabitants'. On this basis general regulations could be drawn up granting each group of shipowners the same rights. It would also have been possible to turn down all future applications and on the grounds of the expense incurred and losses suffered confer what would amount to a monopoly on the Pauw group, who would in the long run show their appreciation. Finally, pressure could be brought to bear on the various shipowners to combine under the threat of otherwise withdrawing support.

In his trial interrogation in 1618 Oldenbarnevelt gave fairly detailed reasons for not taking the first course, the traditional one of free competition. He said that he had given much time and trouble in 1595 and 1597 to examining the possibilities of East Indies trade,

the nations with which trade must be done there, and their character, the goods that must be traded in and purchased there, the kind of obstruction the Spaniards and Portuguese, either by violence or otherwise, were likely to offer in order to prevent the inhabitants of the Netherlands from navigating and trading there.

The conclusion he drew from thus studying the matter was that free competition was not suited to the East Indies trade, for the reasons mentioned. Oldenbarnevelt rejected, or perhaps did not even consider, the idea that the necessary military support in the Indies should be provided by the nation's naval forces. Such an expedition, or rather the permanent maintenance of a strong fleet in the East, would be far too expensive for the States-General, unless it could be paid for by spoils and profits.

Nor could the second possibility, granting this monopoly to the 'Old Company' of Hudde and Pauw, be considered by a statesman who was not from Amsterdam. The States of Holland, let alone the States-General, would not ever have granted subsidies and exemption from convoy tax to a group from one town. It would have meant that Rotterdam, West Friesland and Zeeland would have had to ruin their own people. The Amsterdam group pressed for this solution for a time, but were not supported by their own burgomasters, who were confronted with another group of aspiring East Indies merchants in the town.

In these circumstances the first discussions of a general concentration of interests were begun on Oldenbarnevelt's initiative.

The Advocate of Holland called a meeting for 15 January 1598, in the middle of the preparations for the embassy to France. All the shipowners concerned from Amsterdam, Rotterdam and Middelburg – West Friesland and Delft were evidently not yet interested – were to take part. To spare everyone's feelings – town authorities did not like being passed over by the States-General in their contacts with their citizens – the three towns mentioned were requested 'to have the companies appear before them and to have them send their authorized deputies by the date mentioned to The Hague'.

Only the Hollanders were on time. The Zeelanders were held up by drifting ice. There may also have been some suspicion of the Hollanders' intentions, for it was not long since they had found how hard and intractable Oldenbarnevelt, Amsterdam and Rotterdam could be, when defending their trade interests against their southern neighbours.[1] The Holland shipowners

---

[1] See pp. 254 ff.

put forward their points of view. Amsterdam and Rotterdam were in a hurry to get home. Perhaps they were no keener on a confrontation than the Zeelanders. When the latter arrived on 19 January their opposite numbers from the north had left, after giving Oldenbarnevelt their opinion of the uniform order and footing which he proposed. Zeeland had quite different plans. Their views differed too widely and negotiations were impossible. Oldenbarnevelt, who shortly afterwards left for France, did not exert any further pressure, and disastrous free competition was continued.

Eighteen months later the matter was more acute than ever. Two Amsterdam companies had formed a merger, but when results proved better than had been expected, more and more shipowners began to take part in the trade, and competition became keener, even ruinous. Oldenbarnevelt tried in vain to bring at least the shipowners in Holland into a merger, 'otherwise the result will be that the trade will come to nothing', as he wrote to them.

A year later, in 1600, the Amsterdammers had joined forces under pressure – not from Oldenbarnevelt but from their own burgomasters. The Amsterdam merchants all took the same line in the subsequent discussions of a merger on a national basis.

For the present Oldenbarnevelt had to let things run their course, in the expectation that the stubborn rivals would get such bloody heads that they would come to him for comfort. For one whole year we do not find his name mentioned in East Indies affairs. It was mentioned in those of the West Indies, which were developing parallel to those of the East Indies but on quite a different footing. The two urgent reasons for cooperation and formation of a trust in the East Indies trade were not applicable here. Prices were not affected by the appearance of Netherlands competitors, as there was enough Spanish competition. The watch kept by the Spaniards made one or two ships turning up briefly in a Central American harbour more effective than large, slow-moving convoys. Oldenbarnevelt's intervention was thus not aimed at mediation between rival merchants but at letting the national naval forces strike a blow at Brazilian harbours, reconnoitred by merchants sailing to the West Indies.

The enterprise came to nothing after all, for reasons which cannot be traced. It may be assumed that Oldenbarnevelt required the West Indies merchants to meet most of the expense, while they were envisaging an undertaking paid for by the States-General and of indirect benefit to trade. If this hypothesis is right, the later friction between Oldenbarnevelt and the West Indies merchants can be dated back to the beginning of the century.

Things were going from bad to worse in the East Indies trade, as far as amalgamation was concerned. On his return from Ostend and Bergen-op-Zoom Oldenbarnevelt thought that it was time to intervene with vigour and persistence. He had two reasons besides those already mentioned. Considerable capital was needed to equip merchant fleets to the Indies, which had to consist, as experience had shown, of at least three ships. That meant that the profits went only to the rich. People of slender means, mostly Calvinists, were dissatisfied. Oldenbarnevelt was neither a Calvinist nor poor, but he had two reasons for sharing this dissatisfaction, or at any rate feeling concern. Besides the poor, those among the rich who were not in trade were excluded from making money out of the East Indies and, further, an oligarch does not like to see too much wealth concentrated in the hands of a few merchants. This forms a nucleus of power around which, in certain circumstances, opposition can grow. History repeatedly shows us wise oligarchs fostering the interests of the less rich – not of paupers, of course – against those of the very rich.

Once this reason was involved it affected the character of the amalgamation proposed. Though till 1600 only the formation of a trust had been considered, in which existing shipping companies were to combine, or at the least of a cartel, in which they would retain their separate identities but demarcate their spheres of operation, after this year the plan was altered. The new East Indies Company was to be one in which everybody, whether a merchant or not, could participate to an amount decided by himself. This represents something resembling the modern joint stock company, though with considerable differences. Our sources do not tell us whether Oldenbarnevelt was the originator of this kind of undertaking. It is quite possible.

The second consideration referred to was concerned with foreign policy. The ships sailing to the Indies for the various owners were provided with ordnance and ammunition by the States-General, sometimes by the provincial States as well, purely for defence of course; it had to be possible to ward off both pirates and Spanish police vessels. But the guns could be used for attack too, for instance on a Portuguese competitor with a rich cargo; this not only enriched the admiral and his crew but scared competitors away from areas where the Netherlanders did not want them. This, it is true, was piracy, and went beyond the bounds of a norm of decency which Baptist shippers or investors in particular scrupulously maintained. Oldenbarnevelt and the majority of the States-General did not mind it in itself. Any harm done to the enemy was a good thing, and if it happened at the other end of the world the reputation of the Netherlands at sea, in any case not immaculate, was not too greatly damaged.

But things worsened when admirals and shipmasters, having acquired a taste for piracy, began to practice this occupation in European waters, and not by any means exclusively on enemy shipping. That could cause harm, not only indirectly to one's reputation but directly, in the form of demands for compensation. The complaint made by Venice[1] was against one of these maverick East Indiamen. Oldenbarnevelt realized that he had to keep a firm hold on these sailors carrying guns supplied by the government. There was no better remedy than to place trade with the East in the hands of a chartered company, but such a company could only be a public one. Here again was a good reason to prefer general amalgamation to self-interest.

Oldenbarnevelt did not yet venture in September to give the 'Order and Policy' of the East Indies trade the shape of a resolution on amalgamation. Only a cartel was described in the draft then submitted. A commission of six deputies in the States of Holland was appointed with the task of dividing trade geographically among the different companies, in the form of a separate lease for each trade territory.

When the commission began its consultations marked differences of opinion soon appeared. The different territories were not all equally profitable, and as most of the ships arrived through the Sunda Straits they would be dependent on the hospitality of the company to whom the ports of Bantam and Jakarta were allotted. After months of squabbling the members realized that they were not going to reach agreement on this footing and swung over from the cartel scheme to that of amalgamation, combined with a great deal of government supervision, in particular with regard to warding off foreign rivals by force of arms.

A resolution of this tenor was accepted by the States of Holland, though not unanimously. Oldenbarnevelt, with his sanguine temperament, seems to have thought that the matter was virtually settled. At any rate Gilpin, who generally obtained his information from the Advocate, wrote to Cecil on 12 May 1601:

It is sought by his Excellence and others of the chief to agree and drawe both [i.e. the Hollanders and the Zeelanders] into one company, so that they may goe the stronger, and consequently more assured of th' expected profitt, to which motion each part beginnes to enclyne and be conformable enough.[2]

Actually Oldenbarnevelt's biggest job only started after this resolution, which transferred responsibility for further measures to the States-General.

Gilpin was right up to a point. All those concerned were agreed that amalgamation must be brought about and a monopoly set up. Reports from a fleet reaching Texel in the late summer, with a large cargo of spices, show that the pepper prices had been sent up considerably by competition among

[1] See p. 282.
[2] Salisbury Papers 84/61/83.

the merchants and by the Portuguese. Resources had to be pooled to increase profits for everyone.

It was not possible, however, to reach an early agreement on the conditions for the amalgamation. Amsterdam stood by its ancient rights. It submitted a memorandum during the summer, recounting the history of the first voyages and the part that it had played in them with its mentor Plancius. It stressed the heavy initial losses while carefully not mentioning subsequent gains. It asked the States of Holland for a twenty-five-year monopoly as far as that province was concerned and said that it was prepared to open subscription to all other residents in Holland 'according to the demands of the fleet'. This phrase contained a material restriction: the company already existing in Amsterdam would determine the size of the fleet and only if more capital was needed than they could raise themselves would others be able to participate. In view of the fact that each fleet could easily be paid for by the profits of the preceding one the offer of public subscription was an empty formality. Even if it had not been, the proposal was unfair in Oldenbarnevelt's view, because it concentrated the fitting out of East Indies fleets in one port, to the detriment of the acquired rights of Rotterdam, West Friesland and Delft. It had the added disadvantage that Zeeland would be excluded from the amalgamation and the monopoly, which was undesirable for more than one reason.

Amsterdam's proposal was tabled at the session of the States of Holland beginning on 28 August 1601. The result of the vehement discussions it must have provoked was that the *Gecommitteerde Raden* were commissioned to see to it that 'the said Trade and Navigation may be quickly made and directed with good Order and Policy by one Company, seeing that otherwise what is done by different hands in this respect will involve general ruin of Navigation and Trade'.

They could go anywhere from there. Three points were to form the basis of negotiations: the charter was to be for twenty to twenty-five years, concession rights were to produce a handsome return and subscription was to be open to everyone.

No report of the discussions with the gentlemen from Amsterdam has been preserved. They must have been tempestuous when Pauw and his friends found out that Oldenbarnevelt meant to cut them down to size. The basis may well have been formed here for the subsequent personal hostility between Pauw and Oldenbarnevelt, which was only to reach a climax in West Indies affairs. The outcome was probably that the Amsterdam merchants resigned themselves to sharing their profitable East Indies trade equitably with shipowners from other towns.

The great thing was now to reach agreement with Zeeland. Oldenbarnevelt had to be in the province for other reasons and negotiated with them about his amalgamation plans. On his return in the middle of October, he pressed the States-General to convene a meeting of all interested parties for drawing up the new company's articles of association. This meeting, which Oldenbarnevelt was prevented from attending, was a failure, because although the extent of each party's participation was agreed, the method of voting and the number of members on the future board was not: Zeeland demanded equal votes on it with Amsterdam although its participation was smaller, and also wanted the body to meet at Middelburg from time to time as well. When Amsterdam and others from Holland would not accede to this, the Zeelanders refused to continue with the other points under discussion and came in high dudgeon to take leave of the States-General on 10 December. They said that they would report to the other shipowners at Middelburg and Veere, but not favourably: they were sorry, but the negotiations had foundered on Amsterdam's greed for power. The president of the meeting, no doubt instructed by Oldenbarnevelt, admonished the angry merchants 'to give heed to the harm that all companies in the East Indies trade would suffer, if they would not unite and agree to it, and for that purpose give every good report to their principals . . .'

A date for the next meeting was fixed: New Year's Eve 1601. Oldenbarnevelt was trying meanwhile to find a compromise on the question of the distribution of votes. The content of this compromise, to which Zeeland eventually agreed, shows Amsterdam's strong position: the number of governors was limited to seventeen, eight to be from Amsterdam, four from Zeeland, two from the Maas towns, including Delft, two from North Holland: the seventeenth member was to be appointed by rote by Zeeland, the Maas and North Holland. So Amsterdam had its own way at the expense of the other shipowners from Holland, whom the Zeelanders seem to have regarded as potential allies.

As always happened when members had to come from far and wide, this meeting began late, perhaps also owing to wintry conditions. Oldenbarnevelt was not able to open the meeting on behalf of the States-General till 15 January. After pointing out that Philip III had set his hopes on discord among the Netherlands East Indies merchants as the only means of keeping the trade profitable for his own subjects, Oldenbarnevelt continued: 'that all means should be used serving good mutual agreement and removing occasions of difference of opinion and disharmony'. It was therefore vital that the merchants present 'being agreed and united should put their means and equipment together, under one rule and joint dealing', for two reasons, 'for injury to the enemy and for the security of the country'.

It is strange that Oldenbarnevelt here only mentioned the political and military reasons for amalgamation and not the economic ones, which would have carried more weight with his audience. It shows again that Oldenbarnevelt was no merchant at heart, and also that occasionally he was given to sermonizing. Perhaps too the speech was intended to explain why the authorities were taking the initiative and the leading role in the discussions.

After ten days of meeting, at which Oldenbarnevelt was not always present but exerted predominant influence behind the scenes, the meeting reached an agreement. On 24 January 1602 the merchants submitted three proposals to the States-General for their approval. The first and third dealt with relations between the shipowners and, as it were, the articles of association of the company to be formed. Oldenbarnevelt was mainly concerned with the second, defining the company's position with regard to the government. Only the amount payable for the lease was not dealt with in the proposal: it seems to have been fixed orally at 30,000 guilders for the whole duration of the charter, which was to be fifty years.

The merchants promised to return on 11 February to hear the States-General's decision. It was thought that this would give time for *ruggespraak* with the provinces. The president of the week – Oldenbarnevelt himself – must have been showing his well-known optimism here. Except for the urgent handling of the Triple Alliance in 1596, the seven provinces had never yet been known to charge their deputies in a matter of such importance in a period of eighteen days, including the time needed for travelling. Five provinces did, as a matter of fact, come back to the reopened meeting with full powers, but Groningen seems not to have found the time – this was probably a sort of passive obstruction not unconnected with the building of the citadel[1] – and matters were even worse with Zeeland, running far less smoothly than Oldenbarnevelt had expected.

In the first place it was three weeks before the States of Zeeland met. When they began to discuss the documents there was strong opposition from the smaller towns, which thought that Middelburg had been shown too much favour. On the 21st the States decided to adjourn in a body to The Hague, where in fact they also had other matters to speak of. Fourteen members of the Zeeland States therefore arrived on 3 March at The Hague, headed by Malderee, as representative of the premier nobleman, and the Grand Pensionary Van de Warcke. Oldenbarnevelt went to welcome them at their lodgings at the head of a delegation from the States of Holland and to draw up an agenda for the discussions. The first item was the future position of Zeeland in the East Indies Company. The delegation had been given full powers for this

[1] See pp. 239 ff.

by the States of Holland after Oldenbarnevelt had submitted a long memorandum, which was later added to the text of the charter by way of preamble. In it he repeated the arguments in his speech of 15 January, but stressing the necessity of amalgamation, as well as the benefits of free share subscription, as enabling the less wealthy to have a share in the profits of the trade with the East. The document ends with an insinuation against the South Netherlanders, not only the refugees but also the Antwerp merchant houses, which had put a great deal of capital into the East Indies trade. Oldenbarnevelt suspected them of putting a 'new spoke in the wheel' and that 'by the intrigues of the common enemy'. The insinuation was baseless. The only opponents of amalgamation at that moment were Flushing and De Moucheron's company at Veere, which were certainly not in league with Spain. Such unjustifiable insinuations were, unfortunately, among the weapons Oldenbarnevelt was accustomed to use – as indeed did his opponents.

Some raised objections to the three points in the States of Holland. Subscription was open to the public but only for a limited time – originally till 1 May 1602. The opposition considered that everyone should be able to invest money in the company at any time. Obviously the dealing in shares begun as soon as the company had been founded was not expected. Secondly, in spite of capital distribution among so many there were still objections to excessive concentration of power among from twelve to sixteen principal shipowners. Thirdly, fifty years was thought too long for the duration of the charter: they did not want to do without convoy taxes for so long.

The first two objections could not be met. The company could not be forced to accept investment which it did not need, and to confer power upon a general shareholders' meeting would have been extremely impractical. On the last point Oldenbarnevelt gave way: he had found the merchants so keen on the advantages of amalgamation that he had every hope of making them pay practically the same sum for twenty-one years as for fifty. It was of course understood that it would not be paid in cash but in shares, reducing the risk to the merchants but showing a greater profit if things went well, as was to be expected. His arguments won the opposition over and during the session from 12 to 14 February Holland authorized its deputies to the States-General to help there to 'resolve what they should find to be of the greatest service to the country and the furtherance of the amalgamation'.

Oldenbarnevelt was therefore sure of complete backing by the States of Holland when he began negotiations. It was soon apparent, however, that Zeeland's opposition was due to internal dissensions in which he could not well intervene. Flushing and Veere were demanding certain privileges vis-à-vis Middelburg which that town considered excessive. Even if Middelburg made concessions, Zierikzee, Goes and Tholen claimed the same privileges, not that they wanted to take part in trade with the East, but purely as a matter of principle. Oldenbarnevelt could not cope with such hopeless squabbling and looked round for outside help. At his request Gilpin had an interview with Van de Warcke, and urged that all this pettiness should be dropped for the sake of the joint war effort with the English Queen, which would benefit from a strong and united East Indies Company. He was right here with regard to the war, but an English East India Company had recently been formed, a harbinger of the English merchantmen soon to appear in the Indies. This company was to become powerful at court, especially after Elizabeth's death, when the demands of war moved into the background, and the intended amalgamation of Netherlands interests was detrimental to it. Here we have another instance of how Gilpin, through long residence, had come to identify himself with Netherlands interests. Van de Warcke answered evasively, but Oldenbarnevelt was full of praise. Gilpin's action 'had done much good, and served fitly as a seconding to those that were well enclyned but overmatched by the others'.[1]

More effect was obtained by Maurice's mediation: he had been appealed to by Malderee who, as representative of the premier nobleman, was more or less obliged to take sides with Veere and Flushing, little as he may have sympathized with the recriminations by these towns' pensionaries. Maurice called these two, jointly with a delegation of Zeeland merchants, to the Binnenhof. In accordance with Oldenbarnevelt's ideas he persuaded Flushing and Veere to retract their demands: the States of Zeeland then declared their readiness to accept out of hand the charter, as altered by and after the merchants' meeting in January.

The Zeelanders were able to go home more or less satisfied. Before going they tackled Oldenbarnevelt on quite a different subject, disturbing him not a little. A lasting impression had been left in Zeeland by the political testament of their former Grand Pensionary, Roelsius.[2] The Zeeland treasurer, Jacob Valcke, had spoken to Oldenbarnevelt during his stay there in 1601 about the promotion of Maurice, recommended in that document. Oldenbarnevelt had evaded the issue and the Zeelanders now took advantage of their being in The Hague to do some lobbying among other Hollanders. The new Grand Pensionary, Van de Warcke, broached the subject in a talk with a Dordrecht burgomaster, who at once spoke to Oldenbarnevelt about it, and the next morning, 15 March, Van de Warcke and Malderee told him more precisely what they

---

[1] Salisbury Papers 84/62/33, dated 14 March 1602 (O.S., 24 March N.S.).
[2] See p. 228.

meant. Maurice was worthy, both 'with regard to his father's merits' – which still came first! – and on account of the great services he had himself rendered to the country, to be raised to the rank of Count. Holland would have to take the first step, as in 1583 in Prince William's case, and Zeeland would follow willingly.

Oldenbarnevelt immediately invited a number of prominent deputies from Holland to an informal meeting at his house to consider how to react to this challenge. It is instructive to note how he handled the matter. He was much less interested in whether it was intrinsically desirable to grant Maurice the title than in the question of whether the whole of Zeeland was behind what Van de Warcke and Malderee had said. He related all he knew about Valcke's intrigues, attributing them to ambition: his longing for a prominent position under Maurice. To this end Valcke had even made things up with Malderee, who had always been his opponent. Oldenbarnevelt went over the Zeeland towns one by one, to come to the conclusion that probably – he was not certain – the *démarche* by the two men stemmed from the States of Zeeland as such. If that were so, he said, Holland was not altogether free: 'If Zeeland takes the first step, we shall have to follow.'

Naturally the meeting wanted to know what Maurice's own attitude was in the matter. The Advocate did not know for certain. Maurice was very reserved. What he did know was that after the death of Paulus Buys his son-in-law had taken charge of the documents by which the towns had given their consent to the conferment of the title of Count on Prince William in 1584. And in August 1601, just as Valcke's intrigues were reaching their climax, Maurice had asked to see the documents. It showed how the wind was blowing. Oldenbarnevelt went on himself to praise Maurice's merits and those of Prince William. He must have pointed out the danger that Maurice, if he felt too little appreciated by Holland, but by Zeeland as much as he deserved, would be pressed by his clique to show Leicester-like aspirations and take by a *coup d'état* what Holland's ingratitude withheld from him. What did the meeting think about that?

The meeting brought forward four arguments against Maurice's elevation, distinguished neither by breadth nor depth of vision. The first was an economic one: the court would cost much more if Maurice were a Count. Some members thought that Maurice would be more exposed to the threat of assassination as a Count – a far-fetched argument, considering how many assassinations had been planned against him without his being Count. More to the point, but less effective, was the comment that in view of the treaties with England he should not be elevated without Elizabeth being previously informed. Lastly there was fear of Henry IV's jealousy: Oldenbarnevelt knew that this argument was not tenable as Henry had himself touched on the desirability of such a step in their conversations.

The objections were therefore either insignificant or non-existent. The real reasons why the assembled oligarchs were against Maurice's countship do not seem to have been expressed at the meeting, most probably in case one of those present should communicate them to Maurice. In the first place they were based on the difficulty of formulating the *capitulaties* in such a way as to form a guarantee against absolutism and at the same time to be acceptable to Maurice. In view of Maurice's character these two things were mutually exclusive. If Maurice were given a monarchical title, he or his entourage would do all they could to acquire the power presupposed by such a title. Secondly, Maurice had frequently shown a certain prejudice in favour of Zeeland's interests when they clashed with Holland's. If he were to be made Count on Zeeland's initiative this preference would be strengthened. Zeeland was manifestly reckoning on it. Holland could not tolerate it.

All this remained unsaid. The meeting pledged itself to strict secrecy and entrusted Oldenbarnevelt with the task of sounding Malderee and Van de Warcke as to what their intentions were based on.

Whether he did so or not we cannot tell. A curtain falls on the whole matter till a year later, when there was another meeting at Oldenbarnevelt's house. Also informal, and attended on 21 March 1603 by some of the same pensionaries, it had been convened for a different purpose – the discussion of new peace overtures from Belgium.

The Zeeland intrigues around Maurice were only spoken of incidentally, and Oldenbarnevelt said that he should be 'Prince of the country', indeed a more suitable title than the rather outworn countship, which would not have given him a higher title than William Louis and Hohenlohe. In the previous year people had been at work on the idea of Maurice's sovereignty in three provinces: in Holland, where it was asserted in his circle that he could claim a certain right from the letters under seal of 1584; in Gelderland, where quite a lot had been done to make him a duke; and in Zeeland, about which Oldenbarnevelt expressed himself in the most scornful terms. Zeeland, he said, was bowing and scraping and some, such as Valcke and Malderee, 'sought to be as the children of Zebedee'.

Oldenbarnevelt is evidently being quoted verbatim in the report of the meeting. If he remembered the Gospel context rightly, his remark is a proof that he did not suspect Maurice of personally striving to gain greater power. Indeed, Jesus rebuked his disciples with the words: 'Ye ask ye know not what.' At this time and for long after Oldenbarnevelt's suspicions were directed not against Maurice, but against his sycophantic adherents, whom he did not credit with any higher motive than that of ingratiating themselves with the Prince.

Perhaps he was right. There is no proof that the partisans of Maurice's elevation had any sounder motives. Of these there were in fact plenty. The United Provinces' prestige abroad would benefit by a monarchical form of government. As ambassadors of a republic the Netherlands representatives had low precedence, below those of Venice, whose republican rights were older. If the favour of Elizabeth and Henry were used to elevate Maurice to 'Prince of the country', it would certainly enhance the respect felt for the Netherlands at foreign courts, so sensitive in matters of rank. The revision of the Union of Utrecht, which Oldenbarnevelt was to aim at four years later, would be made easier; many excessively federalistic abuses could be tackled. But the matter was not regarded in this light. Maurice was looked upon as a sovereign prince only in dealings with Asian potentates. This may explain two obscure passages in the East Indies Company's charter, which was given its final form just at the time of this meeting on 15 March. They are the clauses defining the sovereign rights of the company in the East Indies. One provided for 'agreements and contracts in the name of the States-General of the United Netherlands or High Authority of the same'. Another stated that the governor, judicial officers and soldiery are to take the oath of loyalty to the same 'States-General and High Authority'. Probably Oldenbarnevelt, to whom we may well attribute this definitive form, purposely chose an obscure expression that could be applied to Maurice in the East and would not lead to false conclusions being drawn at home.

On 20 March, three days after the States of Zeeland had left, the charter was tabled in the States-General. It was not passed unanimously. Groningen still had no mandate and Friesland seems to have voted against it.

It was a matter for congratulation and many must have shaken Oldenbarnevelt's hand. The Almirante of Aragon, taken prisoner at the battle of Nieuwpoort,[1] is said to have admitted 'that the said amalgamation, together with the charter granted, would be found by the kingdoms of Spain and Portugal to be as harmful as the Union of Utrecht in the United Provinces had been'.

The comparison with the Union of Utrecht must have pleased Oldenbarnevelt, since he was not primarily concerned with the prosperity of Netherlands commerce, but with the damage which the amalgamation would inflict on Spain and Portugal.

Once the charter was passed subscription of capital began; the amount was fixed, but not made dependent on the success of the issue. The amount of

---

[1] See pp. 138, 315.

individual subscriptions was not limited: among the Amsterdam share-holders sums of 20,000 guilders were found and others of less than a hundred. Oldenbarnevelt decided to participate to the extent of just over 5,000 guilders in the Delft Chamber, in order to be taken not only for a *rader* (adviser) but for a *gelder* (partaker), as he was to express it sixteen years later. It was a fairly large sum compared with what others invested. The governors of the Amsterdam Chamber of the East Indies Company took only 12,000 guilders of stock, thus just a little more than double.

To the mention of his subscription Oldenbarnevelt added a few words that give food for thought: 'against all apparent difficulties which I well foresaw'. They can only mean that he did not expect a large or quick return on his investment. He looked upon it more as a contribution to a good cause, that of harming Spain, with the added bonus of a possible profit. For that time it was a good forecast. In the first few years dividends did not by any means come up to expectations. Oldenbarnevelt's creation, later to be the basis of fabulous commercial gains, was for the time what he intended it to be: an act of war, more important than the battle of Nieuwpoort or than the costly and long-drawn-out defence of Ostend.

This famous siege had begun in the previous year, 1601. The town, so far from the home front, was hard to defend, especially as neither Maurice nor William Louis wanted to chance his arm on a large-scale venture in Flanders – from the strategic point of view probably quite rightly. Diversion tactics were therefore the only means of holding Ostend; distant places were besieged in the hope that the Spaniards would go to their relief, thus weakening their strength outside Ostend. One of the first diversions was the siege of Rheinberg in 1601, shortly before the Spaniards encamped outside Ostend. This tactic led to the first dispute between Francis Vere and Maurice; Olden-barnevelt, who had vainly advised a fresh Flemish expedition, supported the former.

Vere, intended to act as commandant of Ostend, had gone to England to recruit troops, while Maurice had led the main part of the army in the field to Rheinberg. Some days after Maurice had encircled the town, Vere returned from England with a fair number of recruits, but said that they were not enough for the defence of Ostend. Oldenbarnevelt, pleased at this help, though maybe it was not unexpected, had instructions given to Maurice to send Horatio Vere's regiment, which he had available, to Ostend immediately. Francis Vere had explicitly refused to take over the command if this were not done. Maurice argued about it and obeyed only when a second order from The Hague said that he must let the troops go without 'further disputes'. The outcome vindicated Oldenbarnevelt's and Vere's view: the troops were badly needed at Ostend, when the Archduke appeared before the town with his main forces; and Maurice succeeded in forcing capitulation on Rheinberg without the twenty companies in question.

Ostend proved to be less strong than Oldenbarnevelt had optimistically supposed. Vere was desperate for reinforcement of the garrison, weakened by illness and hardship, and at the same time constantly demanding diversionary action to draw the enemy away from the town. The two things were incompatible. Maurice sent a memorandum, so confused as to be scarcely intelligible. The States-General were convinced of one thing: that the reputation of the United Provinces depended on holding the town 'as all neighbouring realms and countries have their eye upon it'. This expression was certainly included in the resolution by Oldenbarnevelt, always anxious about what neighbouring countries would think. Henry IV went to Calais to get a better view and to be able to intervene, if things went either badly or particularly well. Oldenbarnevelt also came nearer the theatre of war on another trip to Zeeland, where he crossed the Scheldt too and undertook the typically military work of inspecting the fortifications of Cadzand.

Another diversion now carried out was the siege of 's-Hertogenbosch. As a diversion the siege was a success in so far as the enemy had indeed withdrawn some regiments from Ostend. But the siege of Ostend was not raised and Vere got into such difficulties that at Christmas he could see no other way out than to open pseudo-negotiations for capitulation. The trick worked but caused great consternation in The Hague, especially among Vere's partisans in the dispute between him and Maurice – in the first place Oldenbarnevelt himself. Vere's behaviour did not accord with the code of chivalrous warfare. Furthermore it now came to light that he had made the situation worse than it need have been by negligence and quarrels with his second in command. Finally his opponents suspected him of having started negotiations that were only stopped by the timely arrival of reinforcements; otherwise they would have led to the actual surrender of Ostend at a moment when the position, according to the information available in The Hague, was still far from hopeless. The result of all this was that Vere could not be kept on as a commander. He realized it himself, and on 3 January 1602 offered his resignation, to the joy of some in the States-General, as Duyck wrote. Among them were of course the forerunners of the later Orangists, rubbing their hands at every setback suffered by their 'despot', as Oldenbarnevelt's followers had nicknamed him.

Oldenbarnevelt was not having this and refused to let the resignation be accepted. He knew that it would have to be granted, but for the sake of Elizabeth's friendship another pretext had to be found instead of the dishonourable suspicion of near-treachery. Vere supplied it later by demanding – in secret consultation with Oldenbarnevelt perhaps – reinforcements of 10,000 men for his garrison, failing which he again desired to be relieved of his post. It was an absurd demand, particularly as shortly before Vere had asked that the troops, who had been in the inhospitable and unhealthy town since the beginning of the siege, should be withdrawn and replaced by others. Maurice was highly irritated: there would be no troops for his own enterprises if Vere's request were met and the latter would take all the credit for the abandonment of the siege. Oldenbarnevelt and others who had stood up for Vere and tried to approve of all his actions now dropped him. He was called to The Hague for so-called consultations and did not return to Ostend. Relieved at his ultimatum not being taken literally, he undertook to go in person and inform Elizabeth of the situation at Ostend and the need for continued military support from across the North Sea. At the same time he promised to recruit troops and to make the English Treasury foot the bill as far as he could. He left for England at the beginning of April with this double assignment and a gold chain worth 1,500 guilders presented to him by the States-General to wipe out any idea of disgrace. Indeed he was not in disgrace and got on with Oldenbarnevelt as well as ever. But he had broken with Maurice, his popularity in the army was lost and Oldenbarnevelt had to realize that he could not keep this valued friend and ally in the States' service much longer.

Apart from Ostend, the matter which kept Oldenbarnevelt chiefly occupied during the whole of 1601 was the release of Francisco de Mendoza, Almirante of Aragon, commander-in-chief of the Spanish army in the Netherlands, taken prisoner at Nieuwpoort. Normally releases of this kind went quite smoothly. The captured officer was allocated to the commander of the unit which had taken him prisoner and short negotiations led to the captive's release at a rate that had gradually become a fixed scale, based on the prisoner's monthly pay. At first it seemed as if this procedure would be followed in the case of the Almirante, who had been allotted to Maurice's cousin Louis Gunther of Nassau. But Oldenbarnevelt brought forward objections. After all, not only Mendoza's family but King Philip himself stood to gain and Oldenbarnevelt wanted to release the captured commander for a comparatively low sum and for the return of all the Netherlands seamen who had fallen into Spanish hands in the autumn of 1598, at the time of the embargo issued by Philip III. With this in view the Almirante was taken over from young Nassau against a payment of 6,000 guilders per year, to be settled in a lump sum of 100,000 guilders. Oldenbarnevelt's opponents sneered that he could have had him for less, but it was a principle of his never to be stingy with the

Nassaus in money matters, so as to be in a stronger position in the event of any differences of opinion with Maurice or William Louis.

Negotiations in Spain were needed to effect the exchange desired, and the identification and counting of the Netherlands prisoners had to be done there too. This all involved time and constant consultations with the prisoner. It was noticed that Oldenbarnevelt kept in close touch with the Almirante, whom he treated with great respect, though care was taken that he should not escape. This led to slanderous rumours which did Oldenbarnevelt much harm in years to come. The pamphleteers in 1618 did not hesitate to accuse him of negotiating with the Spaniard and betraying secrets of state to him. It was said to appear from a report made by the Almirante on his return to Spain – pure supposition, for such a report was never published – as well as from the 'treacherous' truce concluded seven years afterwards. The accusation was ridiculous, even if only because Oldenbarnevelt took care to be accompanied by the States clerk or another deputy at every interview. But such slander was listened to eagerly. The old accusation of releasing prisoners for too low a ransom, made at the time of the Armada, was even brought up again with relation to a number of prisoners of lower rank released in April 1601. Oldenbarnevelt was said to have had a 'scout', who went to the prisoners to find out their financial position 'not so much for the ransom as for rewards for Meester Jan and his friends'.[1] The scout obtained permission to come to the meeting of the States-General, 'going in and out of the meeting-room at will'. When the money for Oldenbarnevelt had arrived, he explained in the States-General that they were 'skinny birds, threadbare nobles, from whom not much ransom or profit but rather loss to the country was to be expected. For Meester Jan and the scout had already bled them for all they were worth.'

All sheer slander, even if Oldenbarnevelt did sometimes make such remarks in the States-General. Settling the conditions on which prisoners could be released or exchanged was an important part of his task.

Another delaying factor was the attempt by Albert's chief minister, Richardot, to start peace negotiations through the intermediary of the Almirante. He was totally unfitted for such a task, not only because his position as a prisoner precluded him from receiving secret instructions, but because he lived by a military and not a diplomatic code. The basic points formulated by him after some pressure from Oldenbarnevelt, in which he attempted to reproduce what he had gathered from time to time from the Archduke, were unacceptable. Oldenbarnevelt objected in particular to the religious stipula-

---

[1] These quotations are from a pamphlet, *Gulden Legende van den Nieuwen St Jan*, which appeared after Oldenbarnevelt's imprisonment in 1618.

tions, the return of refugees and the restoration of their confiscated property. With regard to religion, though the enemy had relinquished the prohibition of Protestantism in the north, he was still demanding freedom of worship for the Roman Catholics there without reciprocal concessions to Protestants in the southern provinces. Oldenbarnevelt and his partisans might have permitted Roman rites if they were innocuous, not a nucleus of sedition. Public opinion, however, would not have tolerated Roman 'idolatry', although the majority of the population could still roughly be reckoned Catholic. But 'public opinion' meant the views of the urban citizenry, which affected the composition of the *vroedschappen*. Permission for Roman worship could not even be considered as long as no decisive defeat had been suffered. Without freedom of worship there was no question of the return of exiles, while the return of confiscated property, including the monastic estates, was equally unacceptable. Oldenbarnevelt expressed it thus: the proposed peace terms were neither honourable, Christian, nor safe. After Oldenbarnevelt had tried to make the Almirante moderate his terms in various discussions, the latter was ordered by the States-General not to concern himself any more with peace proposals, but rather to do more about the terms for his release.

Now it was not long before all the conditions had been accepted, and on 29 May 1602 the Almirante set foot on Belgian soil in Antwerp.

Oldenbarnevelt's popularity was increased when, a few months later, four hundred galley slaves came home again. It was remarked upon, not without surprise, that this proud and chilly man, with his aristocratic complexes, when occasion demanded still had compassion with the troubles of ordinary people.

His popularity with the merchants, gained by the formation of the East Indies Company, also rose at this time. He took decisions in the States-General for a permanent occupation of Emden, putting it on an equal footing with the Netherlands ports regarding trade with the enemy. It was thus possible to hamper the East Frisian port's foreign trade, so that an incipient rival to Amsterdam and Rotterdam was crippled.

Such had not been Oldenbarnevelt's primary intention, when in May 1602 he carried through the resolution to send Captain Hottinga with 600 men to Emden to defend the town against attacks by its ruler, Count Enno III of East Friesland. Still less had this result been foreseen by the town itself, when it asked first for intervention and then for occupation. Political and religious considerations had confused the economic ones. Count Enno, though a Protestant, was pro-Spanish. Two of his brothers were in the Archduke's service, and with their help and the Emperor's he was dreaming of setting up an admiralty at Emden of a strongly anti-Netherlands character, particularly in breaking the partial blockade by which the States made any trading with Spain impossible. In Emden there was naturally a party which entirely supported this programme, but the leading oligarchs were Calvinist and anti-Spanish and begged for help from the Netherlands, when the opposition party, assisted by the Count, attempted to seize power. Oldenbarnevelt had little relish for putting his hand into such a hornets' nest, but a coalition of keen churchmen and Amsterdam merchants forced him into an expansionist policy, and in May 1602 the town welcomed a Netherlands occupation force which was to smother their trade for a hundred and forty years.

The spring of 1602 had been productive for Oldenbarnevelt. The dispute with Vere at Christmas had been satisfactorily settled for the time; ties with Elizabeth had been strengthened by this same Vere, now on the point of returning with newly recruited English troops. The problem of the imprisoned Almirante had been solved with all kinds of political benefits, the East Indies Company had been founded, and East Friesland had been secured at a small outlay. Oldenbarnevelt could feel satisfied. But there were still two sore points: his relationship with Maurice had deteriorated and the relief of Ostend proved harder than had been thought. These two factors were connected.

There was still no question of a direct relief of Ostend, so a diversion had to be created. Maurice, as usual, was in favour of a siege, expensive but safe. Oldenbarnevelt, also as usual, preferred offensive action against the south. It was relatively economical, it might bring about a liaison with Henry IV, if he was in warlike mood, and, in particular, it might rouse the southern provinces to revolt, a prospect which Oldenbarnevelt always regarded optimistically. Moreover Elizabeth let it be known through Vere that she should prefer a diversion in the form of an expedition, if possible with a battle, to a siege which, as experience had shown, might very likely fail to divert the enemy from Ostend. Perhaps Elizabeth's strategic views had really been thought up by Vere, who had personal reasons for siding with Oldenbarnevelt in any dispute with Maurice.

However that might be, Oldenbarnevelt was in a very strong position in this difference of opinion. The diversion therefore took the form of an expedition in East Brabant, which turned into a fiasco, partly because of the false expectation that the Flemish-speakers in the south were yearning for liberation by their Protestant brethren. Maurice was thus shown to have been right, but it could be surmised that his own unwillingness had contributed to the failure of the campaign. It could not be proved. Oldenbarnevelt approved the decision taken at Tongeren, Maurice's return to base *re infecta*, without saying a word and personally helped in the successful conclusion of the siege of Grave, which now had to serve as a diversion for Ostend. But mutual distrust had risen a few more degrees, and for the rest of his life Maurice was never willing to undertake a campaign on enemy territory.

Though Oldenbarnevelt had raised no objections to Maurice's plan for besieging Grave, it worried him. By Maurice's well-known 'Roman' methods it was going to cost a fortune. Oldenbarnevelt hit on an idea that seems rather peculiar to us and must certainly have increased the suspicion with which he was regarded by advocates of a war *à outrance*. It would be possible to agree with the Spaniards to raise the siege of Grave, if on their side they were prepared to abandon the siege of Ostend. Such an agreement would amount to an armistice, and that was only to be thought of in terms of an introduction of peace negotiations. Perhaps this was the reason that Oldenbarnevelt met with unforeseen opposition in the States. It was evidently feared that he knew through secret dealings with the enemy that such a proposal might be accepted. Oldenbarnevelt had been given a warning that he was not omnipotent, even in his stronghold, the States of Holland.

The siege dragged on in the usual costly way. Oldenbarnevelt thought it necessary to see things from close quarters. He twice moved with the States-General to the camp before Grave, both to discuss the defence of Ostend with Maurice and to see that no unnecessary expense was incurred.

Meanwhile a remarkable change had taken place there. Maurice, who had pressed for the siege, was beginning to have doubts about it, perhaps because he saw how hard it would be to get the necessary money from the States. He felt inclined to turn his hand towards Flanders. Oldenbarnevelt found such vacillation intolerable. Now the siege had been started, Maurice must make a good job of it. As he went on dragging his feet Oldenbarnevelt had to warn him that if the approach trenches were not dug it would put heart into both the Almirante's relief army and the defenders of Grave. Maurice should attack the town in earnest 'without allowing himself to become uncertain or cast sidelong glances at any other design he might have in mind' (as the resolution put it). Maurice must work quickly, the resolution went on to say; in a few weeks there would be no more money, as he knew. He must also muster regularly and be more on his guard against traitors, as the enemy 'vaunts himself that he knows what is decided there and elsewhere, also what is planned, even better than the States themselves'.

That was not the way to speak to a general of thirty-five with a world reputation. Maurice felt that he was being treated like a child and became ill with resentment. The siege progressed if possible more slowly than before and in September, Oldenbarnevelt went to the scene himself for the second time, accompanied by the States-General and the Council of State and a cartload of money; the threatened shortage of money had already occurred in the middle of August; since the 13th there had not been a ducat in the paymaster's funds.

This time Oldenbarnevelt stayed longer than usual. A great mutiny had again broken out in the Almirante's army which, if the battle was fought properly, might be turned to the advantage of the States. Constructive decisions could not be made till Grave had fallen; Oldenbarnevelt waited for this and was wounded in the leg. The wound cannot have been serious, as Oldenbarnevelt was very active immediately after the capitulation. The presence of the States-General was useful, as terms had to be made not only with the defenders but also with the inhabitants, who made all kinds of demands, which Maurice could hardly have decided on by himself. Freedom of worship for Catholics was politely refused; they would 'be treated with all reasonableness without enquiry like other inhabitants of the country'. But safety of person and property, including that of the clergy, was assured.

During the siege of Grave the States-General appointed a third permanent ambassador, besides those in France and England. He was the keen Calvinist Pieter Brederode,[1] who was instructed to travel around and try to work up some enthusiasm among the German princes for a joint anti-Spanish union. He was to work in close liaison with his French colleague Bongars, who was traveling in Germany for a similar purpose. Their cooperation was not very smooth, because Brederode kept harping on religion, whereas Bongars, though himself a Protestant, had received just the opposite instructions from his King. Henry felt himself compromised by Brederode's activities in negotiating with the Pope and with Spain, and at the end of December 1602 he had Buzanval urge Brederode's recall. Oldenbarnevelt did not agree to the request. Henry IV had acted in a patronizing way before. The Republic was not dependent on him and a Netherlands ambassador could never compromise the King of France. We may surmise that Oldenbarnevelt wrote to Brederode, telling him to tighten his liaison with Bongars.

At the end of the year, though relations with Maurice were for various reasons not so good, there was still no question at all of hostility. When Maurice asked the deputies of the States of Holland to dine with him, one half at a time on 11 and 12 December, Oldenbarnevelt could sit down to one of the dinners without feeling unwelcome or putting on a grim expression at the toasts that were drunk.

That winter a new cloud appeared on the Netherlands horizon: Elizabeth's health was declining rapidly. There was no officially recognized heir to the throne, and a struggle for power might be damaging to the Netherlands.

[1] Not related to the titled family of that name.

Furthermore the favourite, James VI of Scotland, was an unknown about whom there were some suspicious rumours. For the Netherlands the worst of them were that he was pro-Spanish and favoured the Catholics – correspondence with Pope Clement VIII had been heard of. Others asserted that he was merely peace-loving and would endeavour to bring England over to the neutrality he had always maintained in his own kingdom of Scotland. It was the principal duty of Caron, the Netherlands ambassador in London, to investigate these rumours and maintain good relations with the influential statesmen who would have to give active help to the Scottish monarch, inexperienced in English affairs. Besides this he had to make constant excuses for the arrears of payment under the Treaty of Westminster, as Oldenbarnevelt was determined, if not to violate the treaty, at any rate to carry out its terms as little as possible. From the start it had been difficult to get the provinces to grant money for this purpose. One can see why: the English alliance gave the Netherlands nothing except the existence of a formal state of war between England and Spain, and even this was constantly threatened by open or secret negotiations between Elizabeth and envoys from Philip III or the Archduke. Poor Caron was therefore in the unfortunate position of a recalcitrant debtor; the only relief was an occasional spurt of warlike spirit in England, when Holland's help was needed against a fresh threat of an Armada.

In the first year after the treaty Caron was actively supported in his war propaganda by Essex and his faction. Essex, however, fell into disgrace after an unfortunate Irish campaign, and now the Secretary of State, Robert Cecil, was all-powerful; he was somewhat in the position of Villeroy, with whom Oldenbarnevelt was on good terms in spite of political differences. Cecil was in favour of peace on principle, now that England had nothing to gain by a war, as the Netherlands appeared to be safe. No more than Essex or any responsible French statesman could Cecil tolerate the effective subjugation of the seventeen Netherlands provinces under the Archduke. The difference was that Cecil was long convinced that a *modus vivendi* could be reached, in which the Archduke would only be recognized as sovereign in name, while the United Provinces' territory followed its own course in politics, religion and – the most important point for England – military matters. He preferred Spain to France as an ally, not so much because he received an annuity from Spain – he did not get this till his pro-Spanish tendencies had become known, and as an unsuccessful attempt to stimulate them – but because the balance of power in Europe seemed scarcely threatened by a weakened Spain, whereas France, nearby and in the ascendant, was in many respects a dangerous rival and an exacting partner. It was Oldenbarnevelt's task to underline the ever-present Spanish danger, to exaggerate the Netherlands' financial and military weakness and most of all, after the siege of Ostend had begun, to emphasize English interest in holding the town. As long as Elizabeth was alive he succeeded in this task. Cecil's peace moves were constantly frustrated by Spanish threats, which roused Elizabeth's Armada spirit. Even the ill-advised rising by Essex and his execution in 1601 did not change this pattern. Indeed, shortly after this drama, Elizabeth told Caron that she intended to continue the war throughout the whole of 1601 and if need be to take the offensive.

As Henry IV was beginning to show aggressive tendencies at the same time, the possibility of a new Triple Alliance arose, a renewal of the one concluded in 1596.

This French aggressiveness succeeded a period of acute displeasure with the States-General and Oldenbarnevelt personally at the blockade of Calais. Now the harbour of Dunkirk was being closely guarded by the States' fleet, Netherlanders and foreigners were doing most of their trade with Belgium via Calais. Henry IV had half-promised at Nantes to put a stop to this trade, Oldenbarnevelt having invoked the precedent of a similar measure by Henry III. Now that French ships too were being held by the States' fleet off Calais, and in one case chased right into the harbour, the King thought that this was going too far and made some sort of threat of war to the Netherlands ambassador. An ominous breach in the Netherlands front also came to light: Zeeland told Henry, though not through the ambassador, that it was Oldenbarnevelt alone who was behind the drastic action against Calais: Zeeland itself was against interference with trade. Oldenbarnevelt took no notice of this in public, but in private, when the Zeelanders were constantly coming in the spring of 1600 to Holland to beg for help, he no doubt told them what he thought of them. The upshot was that the States' fleet was ordered to give French and English shipping free passage to Calais, but to continue closing it to Dutch and 'Eastern' (Hanse) shipping.

In the ensuing years there frequently seemed to be a chance of a resumption of war between France and Spain, but each time it turned out to be a false alarm. Thus after the siege of Ostend had begun, Henry made a great fuss of going to Calais, the nearest French town, where he invited Oldenbarnevelt to discuss with him and Edmondes, the English ambassador who had followed him there, three-power action for Ostend's relief. It was much ado, but, as Aerssen, the Netherlands ambassador in Paris expected, about nothing. If Henry had been serious, he thought, he would have done better to stay at home himself and send two regiments of veterans to the frontier. The royal trip could only have one object: to push Elizabeth and the States into action without damaging his own position. When Aerssen, instead of agreeing to his plans for tripartite action on a grand scale, said he would prefer him to raise his subsidy, pointing out the Netherlands' financial weakness, Henry told him testily that he had learnt his lesson well. Three days after he had invited Oldenbarnevelt he received reports from Buzanval, who had caught the Advocate in a very cautious and parsimonious mood, knowing well that Elizabeth would not do much more than get her two allies to risk danger on her behalf. Henry felt that his bluff had been called, cancelled Oldenbarnevelt's journey and returned crossly to Paris on the pretext that Ostend was safe. He was no longer prepared to take open action against Spain; at most he secretly agreed to pay half the cost of an Anglo-Netherlands campaign.

Next summer there was a similar alarm, but the Calais episode had made Oldenbarnevelt sceptical and he hardly reacted at all when in the following spring the King made his customary complaint that the campaign was starting too late. Such complaints could be tolerated when Henry was himself engaged in mortal combat with Spain: now he was neutral and looked like remaining so they were out of place, as was his habit of warning England and the Netherlands against peace negotiations.

The fresh alarm, strangely enough, arose from French excuses for possible delay in the payment of subsidies promised for 1602 owing to the expense of armament, necessitated by the discovery of a conspiracy between Henry's principal general, Biron, and Spain and Savoy. Aerssen's letters once more brought up the subject of endeavours both in France and England to renew the Triple Alliance. Oldenbarnevelt spoke on the subject in the States-General in 1602. Of course such an alliance must be joined, he argued, as consolation for the absence of the subsidies, so badly needed for the intended campaign in Belgium, even if it might cause more hardship to the country.

It was decided to send Maurice's young half-brother, Frederick Henry, to France to give Henry detailed information about the position in the Netherlands, the siege of Ostend and the need of vigorous action by France, whether or not within the framework of a triple alliance. It was stated in a secret entry, however, that the resolution was not taken in order to be carried out but to deceive Maurice. He wanted to take his brother with him on the Brabant expedition, which was to start the next day. The eighteen-year-old Prince himself felt no desire to go and see his French friends, just as there was a chance of gaining honours on the battlefield. Oldenbarnevelt's motive was probably to have a successor in reserve in case anything should happen to Maurice during the campaign – there were plans for a new edition of the battle of Nieuwpoort. It was a transparent fraud, as everyone knew that Oldenbarnevelt no longer trusted in triple alliances. He was unable to keep

Frederick Henry back and the latter obtained his first important command after Vere had dropped out.

A journey to France was, however, made that June by an envoy from Elizabeth, Sir Thomas Parry. He arrived at a propitious moment, in that the King had just got hold of Biron, who was beheaded after a short trial. Henry put on very martial airs at first: he spoke about Ostend as if it belonged to him – anyone who did not want to save it was not a good Frenchman.

He soon calmed down. The second instalment of the subsidy was paid in July with only a slight delay, a certain sign that the war had been called off. Proof was mounting that, strangely enough, Bouillon, the Huguenot leader *par excellence*, had been deeply involved in Biron's plot. Now that the Huguenots had proved just as untrustworthy as the ultramontanes, Henry could no longer venture on a war and would do better to keep on good terms with the Netherlands, so that they should not harbour their Prince's brother-in-law and give him the opportunity to intrigue against his King.

He had come to the right person with this request. Oldenbarnevelt had never cared much for Bouillon, in spite of his constantly repeated professions of friendship for the Netherlands, ever since the time that he had concluded the Triple Alliance on behalf of Henry at The Hague in 1596. Maurice also willingly took the King's side. When Bouillon fled from Henry's clutches in the late autumn of 1602, it was not to the Netherlands but to another brother-in-law, the Elector Palatine Frederick, while Maurice, with his customary indifference, for months did not condescend to raise a finger for him or even send a message of sympathy.

When Philip III had smoothed over the Biron incident as much as possible, tension was, as so often before, succeeded by rapprochement. In August Villeroy asked Aerssen to tell him the Netherlands' war plans. One might just as well send them to the enemy, was his comment in a letter to Oldenbarnevelt. Jeannin, one of Henry's ministers, sounded him again a few days later about a triple alliance: at some time the King would have to resume the war, but circumstances were difficult. Could not the States be more obliging? But shortly afterwards Henry began to listen to a plan to marry the Dauphin to the Spanish Infanta – they were both one year old – and in December the King refused to make any promises as to subsidies for the following year, 1603.

So the five years following the Peace of Vervins formed a political lull. Many diplomatic comings and goings and discussions ended up where they had started, both in France and England. Elizabeth was annoyed at the way Henry had climbed down at Calais, though herself equally averse from any aggression in support of her Netherlands ally. For this she had an excuse soon after Calais: at the end of September a small Spanish force landed in the south of Ireland and threatened to wrest the whole country from English rule. Essex's successor forced it to capitulate at Kinsale after an arduous winter campaign of four months. The Spanish general had to evacuate his forces from Ireland, bringing the final 'pacification' of the country within view. This feat of arms became known in the Netherlands at the beginning of February 1602 and Oldenbarnevelt, as in duty bound, let the joy-bells ring in The Hague, though there were many in the country who felt a certain sympathy for the Irish fight for freedom against the somewhat unpopular English ally.

In September 1602 diplomatic business between England and the Netherlands was interrupted by the death of the ambassador, Gilpin, while Oldenbarnevelt was in the camp before Grave. For him it was both a personal and a political loss. A man in his sixties, George Gilpin had settled in the Netherlands long before, first in Antwerp, then for some years in Delft, and since the previous year, 1601, in part of the Naaldwijk House in Kneuterdijk at The Hague. He knew Dutch well, was regarded by the Council of State as one of themselves and took his turn in the chair. Not being of aristocratic lineage he did not share the class prejudice that distinguished most English nobles and courtiers in their dealings with the Netherlands merchant republic. 'A good man,' Duyck wrote, reporting his death, 'with whom the members of the government could get on well'. It was a long time before Elizabeth chose a successor from the many candidates. Bodley was approached, but refused on grounds of health. The Queen left the post vacant for a time and conducted all business through Caron. In the last few months of her life she became somewhat warlike again and pressed the States for help in another expedition to Spain, to be coordinated better this time. Oldenbarnevelt made his customary use of this to ask for a postponement of debt discharge, which was graciously granted.

Towards the end of the winter the States-General received an unexpected and unwelcome visitor. Count Enno of East Friesland came in person to Holland to appeal to the States to mediate in his dispute with the town of Emden, which was flaring up again. Oldenbarnevelt had been approached by both sides already in January. Each thought it was right in asserting that the other had broken the Treaty of Delfzijl.[1] As often happens in such cases, both were indeed right. The town felt that it was in favour with the States, since they had sent a garrison there. It was not willing to allow Enno any rights and was counting on help from its Calvinist brethren in The Hague and Groningen. As has been seen, Oldenbarnevelt could not give such aid unconditionally, even if only for the sake of the United Provinces' reputa-

---

[1] A treaty between the Count and Emden negotiated by the States-General in 1595.

tion abroad and the support enjoyed by the lawful Count from Elizabeth and, still more, from her probable successor James VI. He had to aim at guaranteeing Count Enno the maximum rights reconcilable with military impotence and inability to intrigue for seizure of power in the town, such as would bring the pro-Spanish party into power.

Neither party could agree to such objectives and they had to be enforced by the small States garrison in Emden. The parties could indeed be compelled to sign an agreement incorporating Oldenbarnevelt's wishes, and this was done during Enno's stay in The Hague on 8 April 1603. It put a stop to formal war between Count and town, but not to threats and incidents on both sides. James, by then King of England, doubted its legality, on the grounds that the Count had been in The Hague under the control of his enemies; the town felt itself deeply wronged by the Netherlands republicans for showing such favour to a tyrannous count. Emden thus remained a constant source of trouble till the end of the Truce.

That same spring the situation in Western Europe was changed by the death of Elizabeth on 3 April.[1] The first news of her serious illness reached the States only a few days before that of her death. Oldenbarnevelt made ready to intervene if the Protestant succession or the safety of the cautionary towns were to be threatened.

All concern and speculation abroad was superfluous. Robert Cecil, without his royal mistress's knowledge, had laid his plans so well that the succession of James of Scotland took place without the least friction or delay.

That was one worry out of the way, but great despondency was felt in Holland at the death of a rather capricious but yet sincere friend and her replacement by the son of Mary Stuart. It was hoped that he would show gratitude for the arms which, after initial refusal, he had been able to buy in Holland.[2] There were rumours, however, that the money for the arms had been supplied by Spain, with whom Scotland had always been entirely at peace. It was also well known that the new King usually let himself be influenced by the favourite of the moment, a fact that involved a good – or rather bad – chance of corruption.

Oldenbarnevelt was obliged to weigh up the advantages and disadvantages of the situation. Since his embassies in 1598 he had found how useful it was to know monarchs and their principal advisers and to adapt his instructions to Aerssen and Caron in the light of this knowledge. Moreover it would flatter James, if an embassy composed entirely of Netherlands notables were the first to congratulate him on his accession. A third reason for an embassy was to request help for Ostend, which without foreign support would soon be lost.

[1] N.S. (O.S. 24 March).   [2] See p. 294.

Only a fortnight after Elizabeth's death the States of Holland made their recommendations for the composition of the embassy. It was to be headed by the second in rank in the country: Frederick Henry, at nineteen already an accomplished courtier like his father. Holland sent its principal nobleman, Walrave van Brederode. He had represented the States-General at Edinburgh in 1594 at the baptism of James's eldest son, Henry, giving as a christening present an annuity of not less than 5,000 guilders: this offering was intended to lead to great rewards. Oldenbarnevelt was to be the third envoy; Valcke, Brederode's fellow-envoy in 1594, was deputed by Zeeland as the fourth. He knew England well, having been there among others with Oldenbarnevelt in 1585.

Oldenbarnevelt could be satisfied with the calibre of his embassy. To accompany them he recruited the largest possible number of nobles and pages, splendour which enhanced the prestige of the States and a mark of attention that would be appreciated in England.

Money had to be provided too, not only for the great expense of the embassy in itself, but also for discreet distribution among influential men and, not to be forgotten, women, in England, to counterbalance the bribes Spain could be expected to give. For those content with more modest gifts the envoys were given twelve gold victory medals, probably struck to commemorate the capture of Grave. They were economical with them, like good Dutchmen, and brought four back in July.

When the embassy landed on 14 May at Gravesend, Caron told Oldenbarnevelt, to his surprise, that the King had not yet reached London. The time had to be passed in showing the young people round London, which was tiresome, though it looked extremely well that the Netherlands delegation was the only one from abroad ready to join the King's subjects in welcoming him on his entry. Indeed, James showed himself at the first audience agreeably surprised at their promptitude. It was some consolation for their long and expensive wait, especially when it appeared that the embassy was a little premature. The King would need time to become sufficiently familiar with English problems to take a decision on war or peace, let alone how support could be given to Ostend at the same time as concluding peace, or else remaining at war without effort or expense, the two alternatives between which England was to vacillate for more than another year.

James himself, if it rested with him, would certainly choose the most pacific solution. Oldenbarnevelt had already gathered as much, and it was confirmed by the Netherlands ambassador to Scotland, Damman, who had accompanied the King to England. Though he had not been able to speak to James since his accession, talks with others on the journey and his knowledge of the King's character enabled him to enlighten Oldenbarnevelt considerably as to what he had to contend with. This appeared on 27 May, when the envoys at length succeeded in speaking to the King. The way in which the audience was granted does not seem to have been very dignified: the Netherlanders were placed under cover in a corridor, where the King was to pass, and thus an apparently chance meeting was organized.

The audience was not very satisfactory. The King regarded the Netherlanders as rebels against their lawful sovereign. He was of course too polite to stress this during the audience, but Oldenbarnevelt had heard that he had expressed himself in these terms to his courtiers. He was also known to be contemplating concessions to the English Catholics and was preparing an Order in Council prohibiting all hostile action against Spanish shipping. His refusal to comment on Oldenbarnevelt's proposals for a vigorous joint war effort, on the pretext of his inexperience, sounded like a rejection.

There were also favourable factors. James had written a warm tribute to Oldenbarnevelt in 1601. Though the letter could be regarded as the ordinary small change of diplomacy, the King had been to a certain extent impressed by Oldenbarnevelt's personality and political perspicacity, especially regarding the significance of Ostend for English interests. Oldenbarnevelt thought he detected a weak character, greatly swayed by Cecil and the Howards, but amenable to more favourable decisions under other influences. Whatever might be said of him, he was reasonable, one could talk to him. Oldenbarnevelt, firmly convinced of the reasonableness of his own views, need not give up hope.

A few days later the Zeeland envoy, Valcke, died of dropsy, according to contemporaries brought on by melancholy – was it because he felt himself eclipsed by Oldenbarnevelt? It was a reason for Oldenbarnevelt to make the States-General consider his recall. The embassy's powers were no longer valid without Zeeland's vote, and the appointment of a new Zeeland envoy, who would probably be sent too late, would take time. Frederick Henry was longing for the battlefield, Oldenbarnevelt for his desk. Yet in the same letter in which he recommended his recall he pointed out the desirability of waiting for the arrival of the French ambassador extraordinary, which must be soon. It had been announced that this was to be Henry's minister Rosny, as a Huguenot a well-tried friend to Netherlands interests, from whose influence over James only good was to be expected. The States-General attached the greatest weight to this last consideration. A new envoy from Zeeland was not appointed and the letters of credence were renewed to apply to the remaining three.

Oldenbarnevelt used the time till the long-awaited arrival of the French minister to take soundings in English court circles. He intercepted a rumour, probably put about by Cobham or Raleigh, two frustrated courtiers, in the hope of thwarting Cecil. The Archduke was said to have offered to help the English recapture the provinces of Guyenne, Poitou and Normandy, which had belonged to them a hundred and fifty years before, whereupon he and Isabella would take Burgundy and Brittany. Oldenbarnevelt reported this at once to Aerssen to pass on to Henry IV. The King thanked Oldenbarnevelt very much for the warning, but told Rosny that he could hardly take it seriously; he suspected Oldenbarnevelt of having invented this chimera to push him, Henry, into an offensive for the sole benefit of the States. Rosny was not to let Oldenbarnevelt know of this suspicion, but to ask him who his informants were. On doing so Rosny found that Oldenbarnevelt had merely been passing on untrue information; but he could and must have known it to be untrue and that Richardot, from whom such a plan would have had to originate, was not the man to make a new and unknown king nervous just at the moment that it was desired to make a simple peace with him. Henry had seen through Oldenbarnevelt's trick, but it did not impair their relations, as such deceptions were current diplomatic coin in those days.

On Tuesday, 17 June, Karel van Aremberg, the herald of the peace between England and Spain, arrived. He was a personal enemy of Oldenbarnevelt's, who had had his property in Holland confiscated, and he had uttered violent threats against the Advocate's life. There cannot therefore have been any question of personal contact. His behaviour was mysterious: for weeks he did not ask for an audience, to the astonishment of the King. The gout which he used as an excuse no doubt existed, but he was also suffering from lack of funds, so that he could not give or even promise any reward to his English and Scottish supporters. He informed Cecil that he was only a soldier, not empowered to negotiate; if he found England disposed towards peace and friendship with the Archduke he would return to Belgium and send a diplomat in his place.

Oldenbarnevelt had little to fear from this rival. A Spanish delegate had been announced in the person of Juan de Tassis, but he took months to come, which annoyed James as much as the early arrival of the Hollanders had flattered him.

Rosny arrived one day after Aremberg. He went to stay with the regular French ambassador and the next day received various fellow-envoys, including those of the States-General. At this first talk Oldenbarnevelt could count on a valuable ally in his efforts to get support for Ostend. Rosny's instructions, drawn up by Villeroy, were to consult the Netherlands envoys closely. More subtle distinctions were drawn than in Oldenbarnevelt's instructions, such being Villeroy's character: Rosny must in the first place try to establish good relations with James; for this he must watch closely how the King reacted to his introduction and accordingly advise either open war, covert war or sincere peace; though Henry had no intention at all of furthering the last-named course, Rosny must not let this show if he noticed that James had taken a firm decision in this direction. Oldenbarnevelt did not concern himself with such subtleties. He would never advise peace: support and still more support, for Ostend and in general, was what he had to wheedle out of the King. If support could not be given openly, then secretly, but openly was better and any friendship with Spain was objectionable.

These tactics had been used with success on Henry in 1598, but Villeroy's method, superbly executed by Rosny, was more applicable to James. Henry had a bad conscience and therefore put up with a lot from the Hollanders, who felt they had been let down. James was under no obligation to them at all and it irritated him when they told him what his own interests were. Unlike Elizabeth, he knew how to conceal his annoyance. As the Venetian agent Scaramelli astutely observed, he had learnt how to dissemble all through his youth and now he was putting it into practice. Oldenbarnevelt misread his character, as Grotius was to do in 1613:[1] as the King listened to him and endorsed some of his arguments regarding Ostend, he seems to have gained the impression that James was personally well-disposed towards him.

In his talks with Rosny he also soon reached his limit. Rosny was willing to support him in gaining English help but was not empowered to promise active help from France, apart from what the English would do. Olden-barnevelt tried to go beyond this limit in a clumsy way that earned him a reprimand from the French minister. He represented that if effective French or English help were not given soon, the States-General in their despair might well decide on submission to the King of Spain, in view of the intolerable expense to which they had been put since the Peace of Vervins. It was an argument that Rosny was to use successfully a few days later in a private inter-view with James, but he was not taken in by it himself. He had heard too often from Aerssen and Buzanval how determined the Hollanders were to defend their independence. So when Oldenbarnevelt began telling him tales about various oligarchs who had made up their minds to sell their estates if the embassy returned from England empty-handed, Rosny interrupted him by saying that such exaggeration did harm to the cause and did not increase Henry's goodwill.

At his trial in 1618 Oldenbarnevelt was charged with this defeatism. Fran-çois van Aerssen, from whom the accusation came indirectly, was not alto-

---

[1] See p. 547.

gether wrong. It was dangerous to represent the country's position to potential allies like James and Henry in such a bad light, even if for the 'good' purpose of obtaining subsidies and remission of debts. The Kings needed a determined and prosperous ally, not a desperate drowning man, grasping at them like a straw. It was better for the Republic's image to be respected than pitied. The Netherlands should approach the kings as a partner in a profitable business, not as a beggar. Usually Oldenbarnevelt realized this and could be very self-confident if necessary. But it was necessary more often than he thought, when his propensity for intrigue prompted him to unworthy mendacity.

Another accusation arising from these talks was that he had spoken to Rosny about the possibility of offering the sovereignty to Henry. This too originated with Aerssen, trying to defend himself against the imputation that the idea had been put forward by him.[1] Oldenbarnevelt denied the accusation, not on the grounds of national independence, which had to be defended against all comers, but owing to 'misunderstandings' between France and England which would result from the offer and involve the ruin of the Netherlands. A very apt answer, showing why Oldenbarnevelt did not yield in 1606 and 1607 to French pressure.

In the ensuing days of bilateral and trilateral conferences, Rosny managed to extract from James, against the wishes of his ministers, an agreement on joint support of the Netherlands: it fulfilled Oldenbarnevelt's short term requirements, but in the long run caused him recurrent trouble for ten years, only to be met by grave financial sacrifice. The Franco-English treaty, in which the States-General were interested but not contracting parties, was based on the fact that the French had received large advances from Elizabeth from 1589 to 1598 which, five years after the Peace of Vervins, they had not yet begun to pay back. Rosny and Cecil were now hatching out a complicated plan for providing the Netherlands with a subsidy. The French were to make a slight increase in the subsidy that they had been giving them since 1598, but a third of the total was to be regarded as repayment of the French debt to England. This sounded fine so far, but the catch in it for the Netherlands was that England reserved the right eventually to reclaim this subsidy-on-paper from the States. After some years the English claim was made and regarded as most unreasonable by the Netherlands. The French wrote off their subsidies – why should not the English do the same? They had, after all, the same interest as the French in seeing that the Archduke did not gain mastery over the Northern Netherlands. The affair, called that of the *tiers*, dragged on for years, till the States-General, after much altercation, felt compelled to satisfy the English demand.[2]

[1] See p. 354.   [2] See p. 483.

Oldenbarnevelt was not very communicative about his experiences during this embassy. All his letters to the States-General are not so long as one letter from Rosny to his King. This clearly indicates the difference in their positions: Oldenbarnevelt was in effect in charge and only told The Hague what he thought it was good for them to hear. In France it was the King who took decisions, only gave his minister limited powers, and had to be informed of every detail. Oldenbarnevelt's report to the States-General and the States of Holland is outstandingly laconic. Not a word is said of his dealings with Rosny. The only proof offered of James's goodwill is that he advanced the States-General 450,000 guilders, equal to a third of the subsidy of 1,350,000 guilders actually granted by the French. It shows that Oldenbarnevelt really did regard the *tiers*, about which there was so much fuss later, as an English advance. He took little account of the financial burden which the treaty laid on the States-General in the future. Everything had to give way to the idea that James had after all inaugurated his reign with a considerable subsidy, which was vital to the morale of the dispirited Netherlanders. They were in great need at the moment and it was relieved: repayment could be discussed after the peace, and they could take that hurdle when they came to it – it did not look as if there would be peace for some years to come. Oldenbarnevelt had indeed promised to repay the half million now granted, but he was not a party to the treaty ratified a month later at Hampton Court. This would be of use later. True, the treaty was silent as to a single levy of troops for the benefit of the Republic; on the other hand it was based on the supposition that the Spaniards would make an attack in force on the Netherlands, although the latter had behaved in accordance with the advice of the two contracting parties. In that case, it was stated, the two Kings would support the States immediately with a good sum of money and a sufficient number of soldiers.

In view of James's well-known irresolution it was doubtful if the treaty would ever be put into effect. In fact, owing to the Peace of London which soon followed, the stipulation concerning the *tiers* was the only one to have any effect in the future. But the mere possibility that the Triple Alliance might be revived as a result of the treaty was such a success that it was worth something to Oldenbarnevelt.

The question of repayment was the main but not the only difficulty attached to the *tiers*. In future the French subsidies would not be paid so promptly. Rosny, a good financier, would demand English recognizance for a third of every remittance and Cecil would not give it before his ambassador had actually seen the money on its way. This caused Aerssen great trouble in the next few years. As a result he was much annoyed at Oldenbarnevelt's short-sightedness, perhaps the basis of the ill-feeling to arise between them.

By and large Oldenbarnevelt had some reason to regard the embassy as more or less successful. At the farewell audience the King was much more affable than at the first one. Though he told Oldenbarnevelt he wished to live at peace with everyone, including the Spaniards, he promised that nothing detrimental to the Netherlands should be included in the treaty with Spain. When Oldenbarnevelt made a last effort to convince him of the righteousness of the Netherlands' cause and referred to the 'unity' of religion between England and the Netherlands, the King is said to have answered that if he were to make war for the sake of religious differences, he would have to declare it not only on the King of Spain, but also on the Kings of France and Denmark, the Elector of Saxony, the Duke of Brunswick, his brothers and brothers-in-law, as being of another religion than himself. It was not his intention, but the first argument that Oldenbarnevelt had used, the violation of all freedoms, rights and privileges was another matter.

The King may well have said something of the kind. But had he so emphasized the distinction *haec religionis – haec libertatis ergo*? Oldenbarnevelt needed to make this point when writing his self-defence in 1618, from which this discussion is taken, and represent James as his supporter in the battle being waged.

However this may be, the leave-taking audience deprived Oldenbarnevelt of any hope that England would decide to continue the war. He guarded, however, against any pessimistic tone in the report that he gave the States-General on 14 July, two days after his return. He handed over a friendly letter from James and further only mentioned the permission for recruitment and the subsidy granted. No doubt he boasted in private of the influential politicians he had bribed, but this is only based on a report by a Spanish spy.

A few days later the new English ambassador, Gilpin's successor, arrived at The Hague. He was Sir Ralph Winwood, till recently secretary to the English embassy in Paris. His appointment had been made by Elizabeth. He had often negotiated with Henry IV in his superiors' absence and belonged to the anti-Spanish war party, though of course as a good diplomat he subordinated his own views to his instructions from London. The first proposal he was charged with making was a formality: an invitation to the States-General to take part in the forthcoming peace negotiations. Since Oldenbarnevelt's stay, if not before, it was known in England that in the present circumstances the States could not enter into such negotiations, and why. Then the English would begin alone. But it was exactly a year after Winwood's proposal that the pact was signed in London. The Spaniards' progress was at a majestic pace. They were intriguing with English Catholics and other malcontents, causing James's keenness on their friendship to flag considerably.

333

Caron sometimes gained the impression that in the event nothing would come of the peace. Gifts of horses to suitable people might encourage the spirit of war. In October the newly recruited troops under Buccleuch arrived in the Netherlands and raised the people's hopes, especially when it was heard that James had promised Aremberg to hinder their despatch or to delay it so as to be useless. They were in fact useless for the current season, but Ostend had not yet fallen and they would come in handy in 1604. The English subsidy also became effective on their arrival, and all in all it was a proof of interest taken by the English, perhaps worth more than the couple of thousand Scots themselves.

There was trouble with Buccleuch in March, as he claimed the rank of general. Oldenbarnevelt would have been inclined to grant this to a Scottish nobleman of high rank, personally recommended to him by James, but in a long, intimate talk with Winwood he had to explain that this was impossible for military reasons: the other Scottish colonels, who had seen long service under the States, would be jealous, to the detriment of discipline. These military reasons may have been put forward by Maurice, but Oldenbarnevelt, with his knowledge of senior officers' mentality, must have understood them. Buccleuch, very popular with his fellow-officers in Holland since he was wounded as a volunteer at the siege of Grave, did not take the refusal too seriously. He remained in service as a colonel, without too much grumbling, till the beginning of the truce negotiations in 1607.

In September, two months after Oldenbarnevelt's return, Aerssen arrived in Holland on leave. His visit was partly connected with the *tiers* question, as he wanted specific authorization for signing any documents necessary for collecting the subsidy, if necessary including an acknowledgment of indebtedness to be handed to the English ambassador in Paris. At the same time Oldenbarnevelt asked Buzanval to urge Henry through Rosny's and Villeroy's intermediary not to make a great formality of the matter of the *tiers*, so that payment of the badly needed subsidies to the Netherlands should not fall in arrears.

In the same autumn of 1603 an altercation arose between Oldenbarnevelt and Maurice over a seemingly insignificant question, but the Advocate's autocratic behaviour must have made bad blood between him and the Stadtholder.

In the previous year mutiny had broken out among the troops of the Almirante. They chose an 'eletto' and established themselves in the town of Hoogstraten, in the Southern Netherlands, where, tolerated by both sides, they remained neutral till August 1603. However, when in June the Archduke made preparations for besieging Hoogstraten, it got too hot for the mutineers

– usually referred to as 'the squadron'. They asked the States-General for asylum.

Everyone agreed that this asylum should be granted. On the other hand, use had to be made by the States of the squadron's services. It had been done before; such ex-mutineers from the enemy ranks sometimes became good and reliable soldiers, but always if the enemy forgave them for changing sides and made them a substantial offer of back pay, the new States troops were liable to make friends again with their old employers. Great care had thus to be taken where they were placed.

Maurice wanted to use them first of all for the siege of 's-Hertogenbosch, intended to divert the Spaniards from Ostend. Oldenbarnevelt would not agree. Then Maurice wanted to allocate them to Rheinberg, a distant and unpopular garrison town. The inhabitants, who would not be at all keen on the presence of such lawless gangs, were in this case Germans and subjects of the Elector of Cologne. It would be better to lay the burden on them than on the inhabitants of Netherlands garrison towns, already anxiously wondering what the States-General would decide.

Oldenbarnevelt could not sanction this idea either: Rheinberg was in Empire territory and its occupation by the States-General was not acknowledged as legal by either the Elector or the Emperor, and if those fellows in the squadron followed the normal practice of pillaging within a wide radius, the diplomatic repercussions might be far-reaching: indeed, it was not improbable that the sorely tried Elector, Ernest of Bavaria, an uncle of the Queen of Spain, would openly side with his nephews. Oldenbarnevelt proposed that the squadron should be garrisoned at Grave: it was reasonable for a newly conquered town to be treated more harshly than another: furthermore it was papist and probably pro-Spanish. Unfortunately its inhabitants were Maurice's personal subjects and he vigorously resisted their maltreatment. He went so far as to obtain a majority against Holland in the States-General, in this one respect foreshadowing the pattern which was to become normal during the Truce.

Oldenbarnevelt thought the matter important enough to refuse to accept the majority vote. For a moment it looked like a head-on clash. If Holland had ordered the troops under its repartition not to evacuate Rheinberg, the situation in 1618 would have come about fifteen years sooner. But things were not pushed so far: Maurice, the Council of State and six provinces yielded to Oldenbarnevelt's persuasion and the squadron went to Grave.

In the ensuing siege of 's-Hertogenbosch, Francis Vere was no longer at the head of his English troops. His relations with Maurice had deteriorated steadily since his resignation as commandant of Ostend. At the siege of Grave things were so bad that Maurice showed pleasure at Vere being wounded and having to hand over his command to young Frederick Henry. To bait Vere still further Maurice started exercising a right he had never used before, that of appointing captains to the English companies. Oldenbarnevelt did all he could to keep Vere in service, for the Netherlands and in his own interest, but he could hardly side with the foreigner against the revered commander-in-chief, who in any case was in the right. Vere asked to go to England on leave, alleging that he had the King's permission to see to private affairs. The States-General authorized Oldenbarnevelt to tell him that his leave was granted; he was to add, however, that they would have preferred him in the circumstances to remain in the country.

Vere handed in his resignation from England in October. Oldenbarnevelt consulted Winwood about it: the enemy would regard Vere's throwing up his commission as a sign that King James was about to desert the Netherlands, or at any rate that Vere no longer had any confidence in their cause.

Winwood approached the States-General in January 1604 with a compromise, approved by Vere, but Maurice was adamant. The States rejected the compromise and in April Vere left the Netherlands' service for good. He was succeeded by his brother Horatio, a less overbearing man and in the course of time to become a willing instrument in Maurice's hands.

Oldenbarnevelt greatly took to heart the loss of influence in the States-General revealed by this affair. He had only been able to get his own way in the matter of the squadron by bringing heavy pressure to bear on the six provinces and Maurice: the power of the latter was on the up-grade, as everyone including Winwood knew. Now the Spanish assaults on Ostend were becoming fiercer. Maurice could be expected again to oppose a direct attempt at relief and the States-General to side with him. Ostend would fall, the Netherlands' reputation abroad would suffer and Oldenbarnevelt would be held responsible. On 24 February 1604, a few days after the States-General had rejected Vere's request, Oldenbarnevelt submitted his resignation for the fifth time to the States of Holland. He asked in any case to be excused from the obligation to attend meetings of the States-General. What the States did to mollify their Advocate is not known.

Things were going wrong at Ostend. Enormous sums were being spent: the monthly expenditure on the siege was estimated at 100,000 guilders. It was to no purpose: the sea and Spain's new commander-in-chief, the Genoese banker, Ambrogio Spinola, destroyed the outworks faster than the defenders could rebuild them. The counterscarp was lost early in the spring and the defence reduced to the town itself.

Oldenbarnevelt had already told Rosny in the previous June that without vigorous help from abroad the town could not be held another three months. This was, of course, exaggerated pessimism to further his argument, but now it was beginning to seem that the estimate was only a few months out.

The soldiers in Ostend were getting restive: they were being led to the slaughter without anything at all being done to relieve the town. Something had to be done and in earnest, but what was it to be?

Diversions were no use, as had become apparent in the past year. A second Flanders campaign was the only solution, and this was undertaken, in spite of serious objections by the two stadtholders, who pointed out that the circumstances were far less propitious than in 1600. Then the Spanish army had been far away, badly paid and mutinous. Now it was on the spot in strength, Spinola's money was keeping the soldiers contented and no further mutinies had broken out since that of the squadron. Oldenbarnevelt realized all this, but Maurice's tried skill as a commander, even with these handicaps, had a good chance against the inexperience of the Genoese banker. Things might take a surprise turn, as they had done before. For the sake of the Netherlands' reputation abroad Ostend simply could not be surrendered without the utmost prior effort. Maurice would have to obey, if possible less reluctantly than four years previously. The States-General were therefore again to go with the army and Oldenbarnevelt would drag the recalcitrant general to Ostend even against his will.

The attempt failed, because it seems that it really was impossible. On various occasions Oldenbarnevelt pressed for more daring action. He was very proud of this: in his short autobiography, written in 1618, he devotes more space to 1604 than to any other year in his career. The narrative is made much livelier, as he quotes both Maurice and himself verbatim.

The first altercation recorded was on 1 May, when the army had advanced between the redoubts of Cathelijne and Philippine, to force them to capitulate after a short bombardment, in the usual style of warfare. However, the artillery did not arrive till the evening because of a spring tide. Maurice considered it too late to attack and wanted to retreat. Oldenbarnevelt spoke, as he recalled, more or less as follows in the council of war:

I must admit that it is very late. Although we are in the middle of the summer, attack by night is liable to difficulty, confusion and disorder. I think it is best, as darkness can only last three or four hours, to remain on the spot, in good order, and start the operation at dawn, especially as the soldiers would need two hours to take up their previous positions again and our retreat would give courage to the Spaniards.

He cannot have spoken exactly like this. 1 May is a long way from midsummer and darkness lasts much longer than three hours. Further on he shows again that when writing his autobiography he was no longer quite clear about the chronology of the campaign. But he recollected the main point: that he wanted to stay and Maurice to retreat; also that Maurice had his way, but that owing to a series of strange misunderstandings the enemy fled during the night, so that both the strongholds were taken the next day without a blow.

The immediate result of this success was the siege and capture of IJzendijke, about which there was no disagreement. But then 'there was discussion as to whether it were not better to be satisfied with what had been taken and to secure it'. Many voted in the affirmative for these proposals, even that the commander of Ostend should be given written orders to save himself and his soldiers by capitulating or otherwise.[1] Fortunately a sufficient number of the States-General and Council of State was present, so that at their instance it was resolved 'to continue the campaign, either by advancing on Ostend or besieging Sluis.'

This looks very much like a direct attack on Maurice's laxity or reluctance; it contains some self-advertisement, partly accounting for the unfavourable impression made by the remonstrance, as this short autobiography was entitled, on many more or less neutral observers.

The general and the Advocate were not always quarrelling. The following reminiscence by Oldenbarnevelt has no point and is therefore pleasant to quote, as it shows that the wound in the leg he had collected at the siege of Grave had not put him off the front line of the battlefield.

At the first battle at Damme he met the Prince, who was joining the 'troops in battle'. Oldenbarnevelt asked him how things were going, to which the Prince gave the not very memorable answer: 'We must charge, or they will charge us.'

He added that the enemy was commanded by Don Luis de Velasco.

On the dikes many horse and foot could be seen from afar coming to reinforce them. His Excellency put on his arms and changed horses. Shortly afterwards our men charged the Spaniards and put them to flight . . .

As he recalls, Oldenbarnevelt afterwards remained with the army, which now started the siege of Sluis, till Marquette, after several of his predecessors had been killed, was sent as the last commander to Ostend. Afterwards Oldenbarnevelt travelled a few times from The Hague to Flanders and back 'to further everything necessary for the holding of Ostend and the capture of Sluis, with the Spanish galleys . . . as was done with great promptitude'.

Marquette was in Middelburg when on 22 June he received Maurice's

---

[1] i.e. by breaking out.

order to take over the command of Ostend. He wrote on that date to the States-General, in session at The Hague, about an ambiguous passage in Maurice's instructions, requiring him to be sparing of his soldiers but none the less to hold the town a long time. Oldenbarnevelt drafted an answer evading the question: he was to 'defend the town with all his power and rouse the soldiers to his support'. Were the States disavowing their commander-in-chief?

Oldenbarnevelt left for Flanders once more on 13 August, this time without the States-General. He was just in time to witness Spinola's last attempt at relief. On landing at Aardenburg he heard the thunder of artillery from the direction of Cadzand. He went there at great speed and arrived just as the attack had been repulsed with great difficulty. Colonel Van Dorp, the former commander of Ostend, was wounded but talkative; he told him how the battle had gone. Oldenbarnevelt seems only to have met Maurice later.

The repulse of this assault was the sign for the capitulation of Sluis on 19 August. Cooperation with Maurice seems to have gone smoothly during the whole siege. On 20 August Oldenbarnevelt wrote to the States-General: 'God the Lord must be praised and thanked, and His Excellency for his great trouble, care and diligence. It cost a great deal of money but it was well spent.' The capitulation, however, gave rise to a dispute, which had always been latent. Oldenbarnevelt, though he had not made this explicit in his letter to Marquette, had only regarded Sluis as a secondary objective, the relief of Ostend being the primary one. This can be seen from the resolution whereby the States took leave of the army on 23 May and again in a letter which Oldenbarnevelt caused the States to write to Maurice on 6 July. It stated that the enemy was set on the capture of Ostend, on which so much depended for him, especially the 'restoration of his honour, with regard to which', the letter continued, 'it must be concluded, in case His Excellency captures the town of Sluis before the town of Ostend, that we must both preserve the latter town and secure our gains'.

Maurice had always thought differently and still did not intend risking his troops in an enterprise likely to fail and which would make the chance of favourable capitulation terms more difficult.

As usual, when faced with a task he did not like, Maurice asked the States-General to come in person to view the situation and take personal responsibility for a strategically wrong decision. Oldenbarnevelt, who had returned to The Hague on 23 August, supported Maurice's request, and on 1 September the States informed Maurice and Marquette that they would soon arrive. The deputies at the front agreed with Maurice entirely, but the Council of State advised another relief attempt.

After long consultations Maurice and William Louis were given a definite order to move the army up to the relief of Ostend. Nevertheless, it was not done. There must have been some passive resistance. The States-General for their part did not oppose Marquette being allowed to negotiate a capitulation on favourable terms. Unlike previous occasions, the tone on either side was not harsh. When the States-General, against Maurice's advice, ordered the march to Ostend, they expressly stated that they 'found difficulties' put forward by Maurice 'of great importance and founded on security, wisdom and caution'; if, then, their resolution was different, it was mainly to save the States and Maurice's own reputation and also in order to meet the French King's wishes. Ostend had become a sort of status symbol abroad and Oldenbarnevelt was very sensitive on this point. Strategically Sluis was much better placed. From the military point of view the Netherlanders had made a good exchange. Nor did they lose much face; the defence of more than three years had lasted longer than that of any other town within living memory. At their departure on 20 September 1604 Spinola invited the officers to a splendid banquet. Maurice's opposition had been proved essentially right. Really the States should have been glad: they had disposed honourably of a sandy, rubble-strewn desert which had devoured blood and money. Oldenbarnevelt must have been glad too. Unlike previous differences of opinion, the discussions on Sluis and Ostend did not worsen relations between him and Maurice; it seems that in the next few years, despite renewed arguments, relations left little to be desired.

The Netherlands closed their ranks for grim resistance, as their last ally, England, left them during this year, and the hope of once more involving Henry IV in the war became fainter and fainter.

When Ostend fell the Peace of London had just been signed. In spite of James's overt inclination towards peace the negotiations had been long and arduous, largely owing to Spanish endeavours to obtain terms incompatible with the benevolent neutrality towards the Netherlands that Cecil intended to observe thenceforth. Thus the Spaniards had demanded the cession of the cautionary towns; it was refused, but the English agreed to a clause that made Oldenbarnevelt very uneasy, till Caron, after an interview with Cecil, put his mind at rest. The clause stated that James would not hand over the cautionary towns as yet, but that he would set a period within which the States-General were to reach agreement with the Archduke; if they refused James would regard himself as released from his obligation towards them and act as he considered just and reasonable, in accordance with the friendship he bore Albert and Isabella.

A captious king could have used this to put pressure on the Netherlands to conclude an unwelcome peace. But Cecil explained that the clause was only intended to throw dust in the Spaniards' eyes; neither he nor the King would ever lend themselves to using the cautionary towns to blackmail the Hollanders into submission to the Archduke. The clause could be, as was intended, interpreted as meaning that the Treaty of Westminster of 1598 had become void and should be superseded. Oldenbarnevelt had admitted this in an interview with Winwood on 5 July.[1] Cecil had wanted an embassy from the States-General sent during the negotiations with the Spaniards to conclude a new treaty. Oldenbarnevelt had refused: both at home and abroad it might lead to misunderstanding if Netherlands negotiators were in London at the same time as the Spanish and Belgian ones. The embassy had better be sent after the Spaniards had left.

The way in which another demand made by Spain was dealt with was to be an example for the Netherlands five years later. It concerned the East Indies trade, which England was required to renounce. In clause 9 of the treaty this trade was permitted in all territories where it had been allowed before the war and in accordance with the old treaties. The English could interpret this as meaning that trade with the East Indies was permitted, and the Spaniards that it was prohibited.

The Spanish negotiators also endeavoured to involve the Netherlands in the peace. To this end they made a declaration, never made explicitly and gratefully noted in the Netherlands, although not satisfactory: Albert was prepared to allow Maurice and William Louis to exercise their office of stadtholder on the customary footing, if the seven provinces were willing to recognize Albert and Isabella as nominal sovereigns.

Apprehension as to the consequences of the peace for the Netherlands was thus reduced by various factors, but not wholly allayed. England had not left the country entirely in the lurch. Buccleuch's Scottish troops were there to prove it and the English auxiliaries under Horatio Vere continued their normal service despite Spanish protests. Furthermore, James gave Caron leave to change his title of agent to that of ambassador: he sent him to Holland to assure Oldenbarnevelt of his continuing sympathy with the Netherlands' cause; in return Oldenbarnevelt himself was convinced by Cecil's explanations[2] that the peace did not really mean the end of the alliance, any more than that of Vervins had. His first comment to Winwood, when he heard of its signing, was: *Litera occidit, spiritus autem vivificat*.[3] Cecil had got him where he wanted him.

---

[1] Salisbury Papers, 84/64/170.
[2] In a letter to Winwood of 14/24 September, intended to be shown to Oldenbarnevelt. *Memorials of. . .the Right Honourable Sir Ralph Winwood, Kt.*, London, 1725, II, 27.
[3] 'The letter killeth, but the spirit giveth life', II Cor. iii, 6.

Yet it is not certain that Oldenbarnevelt was entirely serious about this. He must sometimes have wondered: who is being deceived, we or the Spaniards? The answer was of course that they both were, to a certain extent. The English would interpret the peace terms as it suited their book, but the Republic was not the only item in this volume: sometimes the Netherlands would gain, often they would not. In spite of all the aid still to be offered by Henry and James, the fact remained that in future the Netherlands would have to fight alone against Spain and Belgium together. It was becoming more and more doubtful how long they could continue to do so.

Meanwhile Oldenbarnevelt's family circle had been spreading owing to the marriage of his two daughters, Geertrui and Maria. The former married a Brederode in 1597; though of an illegitimate branch, his aunt was the widow of the Elector Palatine, a circumstance which was no doubt a great attraction for Oldenbarnevelt. Reinoud van Brederode, Lord of Veenhuizen through his mother, was a promising young lawyer who at the age of thirty, before his marriage, had become a member of the Hoge Raad. Though but little interested in politics he got on well with his father-in-law, and continued to do so after the early death of Geertrui in 1601. In the following year the president of the Hoge Raad died, and Oldenbarnevelt took the opportunity of having Veenhuizen appointed his successor, though he was the youngest councillor and not on the short list. Maurice chose him solely to do Oldenbarnevelt a favour, 'against the wishes of many', as he stated later. It was indeed a blow to many of the senior members. A man like François Francken must have taken this nepotism by Oldenbarnevelt amiss, though he himself had no chance or even ambition to be appointed to this office.

A year later Veenhuizen was the first of his name to be summoned among the nobles of Holland to the States assembly, where, though not outstanding, he loyally supported his father-in-law till his execution, after which he was expelled from the nobility.

The second daughter, Maria, married in 1603 the only son of Oldenbarnevelt's late friend Adriaen van der Mijle, formerly president of the Hof van Holland. It is remarkable that Oldenbarnevelt, unlike his fourth successor, Jan de Witt, did not make marriage ties for his family in the circle of the prominent Dutch oligarchs, but in that of the old or new nobility. Young Van der Mijle, who had been at Padua like his father, Veenhuizen and Oldenbarnevelt himself, was a much pleasanter son-in-law than the president of the Hoge Raad. At first he lived with Oldenbarnevelt for a long time, and later, when the Advocate moved to Kneuterdijk, he bought Van der Mijle the adjoining house, which often served as an antechamber for visitors who could not see Oldenbarnevelt at once.

He surpassed himself in his expenditure on the wedding celebrations on 4 February 1603. On three evenings guests were entertained practically the whole night long, at the house in Spuistraat. Louise de Coligny was there with her son, Frederick Henry and her stepson, Prince Maurice. In a letter to her stepdaughter in France she described the party:

Monsieur de Barnevelt has recently married his young daughter to the Sieur VanderMyle, whom you saw as a student at Leiden; he is a very fine young man. We were there for three evenings of celebration, that is to say, five hours at table, and then the ball, at which your elder brother[1] succeeded in executing all kinds of dances to show me that he has not forgotten anything; but my son[2] only does German dances. You have never seen such seriousness; I think he must have learnt it in Germany.

After the marriage Oldenbarnevelt started the advancement of this son-in-law too, having him appointed not only as governor of Leiden University but also as a member of Prince Maurice's council. This post did not involve much work and enabled him to gain the Prince's friendship in a short time. He long acted as a sort of buffer between the two headstrong leaders of the Republic. Oldenbarnevelt wanted more for him. When the first signs of strain began to show in his relations with François van Aerssen, he wanted to have his son-in-law appointed his successor, but Van der Mijle had no intention of leaving his beloved country again so soon after spending six years on study abroad; it was not till seven years after his marriage that he was willing to undertake an embassy, and then only a temporary mission, not a permanent post.

Compared with his sons-in-law, Oldenbarnevelt's own sons, Reinier, later Lord of Groeneveld, and Willem, Lord of Stoutenburg, did not turn out so well. In 1605, when the younger was still only fourteen, he sent them with a tutor on a long tour of study through France and Italy; but Reinier was too lazy and Willem too undisciplined to profit much by it; perhaps they were too young as well: the tour had more of a snob value than an educational one. In spite of the paternal bandwagon neither got very far: Reinier was given the sinecure of Forester of Holland, Willem became a cavalry captain. They were of no use to their father in politics.

In money matters, the Advocate was doing better and better. His salary was not exceptionally high, but his office involved a number of more or less secret emoluments to which no one took exception as long as they did not look like bribes. He took part in various dyking enterprises and bought

---

[1] Maurice.

[2] Frederick Henry, who had spent some time in November 1601 at the strict Calvinist court at Heidelberg.

manors and plots of land. All this demanded attention in addition to his already extensive work as the leading spirit of at least five bodies in The Hague: the States of Holland and their *Gecommitteerde Raden*, the States-General, the assembly of the nobles of Holland and the Delfland dykereeves, to which Oldenbarnevelt, as one of the principal owners of polder land, had been elected in 1595. His capacity for work must have been enormous, as indeed contemporaries testify, and it is not surprising that as he grew older he wanted to be relieved of some of it. Only the way in which he did so at first seems strange. In 1605 and again in 1606 he asked to be released from the obligation to represent Holland in the States-General, giving as a reason that his private affairs needed attention.

Since Oldenbarnevelt's interest had been mainly in foreign affairs, the States-General's domain, it might be wondered if he intended to leave them to others in future, in order to concentrate on provincial matters with the *Gecommitteerde Raden*. Nothing could be further from the truth. The fact was that the gradually consolidated preponderance of Holland had reduced the States-General's meetings, in most cases, to insignificant evening talks. Once Holland had let its views on foreign affairs be known nobody could care less what point the honourable deputy from Friesland or Gelderland wanted to raise. Things had usually been fixed with Zeeland beforehand, and Utrecht, under Ledenberg's leadership, had become a satellite of Holland. The deputies from the inland provinces wanted to have their say of course, long-winded and often inexpert, so that the long, almost daily sessions of the States-General had become an irritating waste of time. The views of Holland and Zeeland could quite well be stated by the Holland deputies to the States-General. Oldenbarnevelt considered his own time too valuable.

It is equally easy to see, though, why his request was turned down each time. Everyone realized that Oldenbarnevelt would remain the real leader of Netherlands foreign policy through his unofficial contacts with the Netherlands ambassadors abroad and the foreign ambassadors in the country. There seemed to be some disparagement of the 'allies' in the Union of Utrecht, if the great man did not deign to come and defend this policy in the body where it belonged. Nor did the Holland deputies care to be treated like errand boys, constantly obliged to go and ask for Oldenbarnevelt's instructions and never allowed to take responsible decisions.

Surprisingly, Oldenbarnevelt did not realize, even after it had first been rejected, that his request could not be granted, and did not sense that its inherent arrogance was bound to arouse widespread hatred. It was one of his blind spots and perhaps the chief cause of his fall.

After the Peace of London the situation of the Netherlands abroad was serious but not hopeless. There were encouraging reports that the Peace was unpopular in England, where it was thought humiliating to have conceded so much to the Spanish kingdom, whose incipient decrepitude was clearly perceived. Though he had spoken unfavourably of the Netherlands' war aims, King James had after all promised secret help and would certainly not allow the country to capitulate. Redemption of the war debt had been postponed till peace was made. This gave room for manoeuvring, but the principal, and indispensable, hope of foreign aid was still France.

The first principle of Oldenbarnevelt's foreign policy during these years was that Henry IV's friendship must be kept, except that the price must not be too high.

A Portuguese carack with a cargo of porcelain and other valuables had been captured off Malacca in 1603. The booty was brought into Flushing and, after a lengthy procedure, a large share was allotted to the States-General. Young Grotius, probably in part at Oldenbarnevelt's request, had written a dissertation on prize law to put uneasy consciences at rest. This bonus was a good opportunity for giving presents to important foreigners. Henry IV was the first choice and Buzanval and Louise de Coligny were consulted as to what he would like most.

But presents alone would not secure the strong and disinterested help needed. In a long interview with Buzanval, still deeply moved by the fall of Ostend, Oldenbarnevelt complained bitterly of the King's attitude in the last six years. He specially pointed out the flaccid way in which Rosny had conducted the negotiations in 1603. If Henry had then promised strenuous military aid for a joint offensive war, Oldenbarnevelt thought, peace between England and Spain would never have come about. Of course Oldenbarnevelt 'thought' nothing of the kind. In 1603 it had been clearer than daylight that James was not to be talked into any offensive action against Spain. Oldenbarnevelt was hoping, by voicing his complaint, to stimulate Henry to renewal of hostilities, constantly stressing the miserable state of the Republic and threatening to conclude a peace that would amount to a capitulation. Buzanval complained in his turn to Winwood that he thought this was a strange way to speak, especially just as he, Buzanval, had succeeded during a journey to Fontainebleau in inducing the King to raise the subsidy to two millions per year.

That was true enough, but there were strings attached to the increase, described by Henry in further detail in the course of the winter. Among others Aerssen was used for this purpose; he came home unexpectedly on 1 January 1605 for the first of a series of winter visits. Henry rebutted Oldenbarnevelt's accusations with countercharges that the Netherlands did not show enough aggressive spirit in their war effort. He could only conclude that the

Hollanders did not seriously wish to drive the Spaniards out of Belgium. Why should he trouble with such fainthearts, let alone involve himself in war? He peremptorily demanded an offensive in Flanders, for preference an attack on Grevelingen, threatening otherwise to stop all assistance. Henry was no more serious about this threat than Oldenbarnevelt about his, and as each saw through the other the effect was nil. An offensive in Flanders was an impossibility, strategically, financially and in particular psychologically: since the fall of Ostend the Spaniards' morale was improved and Spinola had returned from Spain with a commission as commander-in-chief and fresh troops.

When Henry learnt from Aerssen that there would be no question of a Netherlands offensive in Belgium and that he would not be allowed to dictate Netherlands strategy, he cancelled his decision to recruit two regiments he was going to send to the Netherlands' assistance under Du Plessis Mornay's son. If the States-General should be forced into the defensive he hoped that the time would soon come when he would be allowed more than the direction of strategy: the sovereignty that had once been offered to his predecessor.

If, then, relations with France were not altogether satisfactory, in spite of the increased subsidy, there was more trouble with England than Oldenbarnevelt had perhaps expected after the comparatively favourable results of his embassy.

Relations with the English ambassador Winwood, who was later to play a large part in Oldenbarnevelt's fall, were from the start less easy than with Gilpin. It was not due to Winwood's strong Calvinist sympathies, but to trade with the enemy, against which the Netherlands were scarcely less strict than England had been in years gone by. Under Philip II Netherlands ships were either openly allowed to sail to Spain and Belgium or quietly ignored; trade with the enemy had been a main source of income for Netherlands merchants and admiralties, while the English, dreading new Armadas, were doing everything in their power to put a stop to the trade, at any rate with Spain. But now Philip III and Albert had either strictly forbidden Netherlands trade with their territory or imposed such duties on it that it was no longer profitable; moreover, the new East and West Indies trade, and the *straatvaart* had made the Netherlands less dependent on such trade. Since the Peace of London England, on the contrary, had the greatest interest in expanding trade relations with Spanish and Belgian harbours. Such traffic was naturally not encouraged by the Netherlands: in fact, the Belgian harbours were blockaded more stringently than ever and shipping to Spain was assailed by an ever-growing number of privateers.

Caron had spoken to Oldenbarnevelt about the blockade, especially the closing of the Scheldt, when he crossed to Holland after the Peace of London to discuss its effects on Anglo-Netherlands relations. Winwood constantly brought the matter up for a year, but, as he wrote after one of his talks with Oldenbarnevelt, 'I find him (as them all) peremptory in this point, not to yield to the opening of these ports, whereupon the preservation of their estate doth depend.'

James eventually realized this with regard to Antwerp and relaxed his pressure, but he was more indignant about Dunkirk. English ships sailing to that port were held up and set on fire, while Netherlands ships were allowed past the blockade. Winwood had various unpleasant talks about it with Oldenbarnevelt, who 'insists peremptorily upon these blocked havens of Flanders'.

This was one more example of Oldenbarnevelt's 'peremptory' behaviour, offensive to so many. He blandly denied that Netherlands shipping was allowed into Dunkirk. But when Winwood, incensed at such brazenness, threatened to air his grievances publicly in the States-General, Oldenbarnevelt hastily offered compensation. The admiralties of Holland could not afford investigation into the passage allowed to Holland's ships, as not all the provinces would agree to this officially tolerated smuggling.

Privateering also caused trouble for Oldenbarnevelt. At first he watched the phenomenal increase of near-piracy with interest. The draft still exists, in Oldenbarnevelt's handwriting, of a placard calling on merchants to arm themselves to recoup losses as freebooters, according to orders given by the admiralty. It sounds like the sorcerer's apprentice conjuring up what he could not stop. Once they had become freebooters the more or less honest merchants disregarded admiralty orders, which in any case often gave a distorted version of maritime law. When letters of marque were issued no great heed was given to the actual loss suffered by the applicant. Early in 1606 almost anyone could obtain such a letter of marque; by the middle of March of that year no fewer than 130 freebooters are said to have sailed out of Netherlands harbours, greater in number than ever the Sea Beggars had been, a real scourge of God upon the seas. The losers, sometimes of their lives, always of their property, were from Dunkirk, Spain or Portugal, but mostly neutrals, among whom the hard-hit English protested the loudest, without reflecting that they were getting back the treatment they had themselves given the Netherlanders in the 1580s and 1590s. General rules for the issue of letters of marque had been laid down in 1604, but more far-reaching restriction appeared necessary; the States of Holland proposed in 1606 to impose three: renewal of the letters annually; payment of sureties from which any compensation could be paid; granting letters of marque 'with discretion'. The first and the third stipulations did

347

not go far enough: only the second was of any use, provided the surety was high enough. On 10 July all letters of marque were withdrawn and the surety for renewal or issue of new letters was set so high that adventurers no longer applied for them. A considerable proportion of the existing privateers became stateless pirates, the others adapted themselves gradually to legal activities.

A marginal result of the wild privateering fever, which in fact had been caught from the Dunkirkers and Spinola themselves, was the attempt to set up a French East Indies Company. Oldenbarnevelt treated his French friends with just as peremptory a refusal as he had the English in the matter of entering the Scheldt. A Baptist director of the East Indies Company, Pieter Lijntgens, had conscientious objections when this company, seizing more and more rich cargoes, also began to develop into a privateering concern. Perhaps he also thought that there would be greater profit in plying the trade with the East Indies under a neutral flag, not plundering, but then not being plundered by the Portuguese either. He applied for support to Henry IV, who was all in favour and flooded the States-General with requests for cooperation in obtaining pilots and crews for the newly formed company. Naturally Oldenbarnevelt could not permit this so soon after granting a monopoly to the Netherlands company. He tried to make it clear to the King in letters and via Aerssen, but only succeeded when, after the judicious presentation of gifts from captured vessels, he had succeeded in convincing the minister for economic affairs, Rosny, that there was something attractive about prize law and that peaceful trade had little to offer France.

Foreign policy with regard to Germany was making quite other demands than those of defending privateering against the English and the East Indies Company against France. There it was a matter of integrating the Protestant princes in joint anti-Spanish action. Dillenburg and Heidelberg were the starting points of Pieter Brederode's unwearying efforts: since 1602 he had been exerting them under Oldenbarnevelt's direction but in his own characteristically sanctimonious tone to win over all, or as many as possible, of the other princes to Holland's cause. Backed by Oldenbarnevelt, he was the spiritual father of the loose organization now and then exerting some influence abroad at this time under the name of 'Korrespondierende'. Nothing further came of it for a time because its leader, the Elector Palatine, was on bad terms with Henry IV owing to the Bouillon affair.[1] It was not till Netherlands mediation had put this matter right in 1606 that the way was clear for vigorous support by France of Brederode's plans. This resulted in the foundation of the well-known though somewhat inefficient *Union* in 1608. Brederode also managed to extract some money from a few German princes. Though

[1] See p. 324.

the amount was small in relation to the total war budget it made a great difference, in the States-General's straitened circumstances, to the preparation of the campaign in 1605. A considerable number of troops could be levied in Germany, in addition to those now permitted by James to be raised in England.

The danger was now acute. Spinola returned from Spain in 1605 as commander-in-chief with the title of 'maestro de campo general' and promoted to the order of the Golden Fleece, an exceptional distinction for a banker. More effective was the fact that there had been considerable recruiting, not only in Spain but also in Belgium and in England, where James was dividing his favours between the two sides. It was important to anticipate his attack by prompt aggressive measures. Maurice however, could not take the field till May for the usual reason: the grants had come in late. He attacked Antwerp with a fairly large force. The plans were, however, betrayed by indiscretions, for which Oldenbarnevelt was later blamed.[1] Maurice was then sent across the Scheldt to reinforce Fort IJzendijke and from there to prepare an invasion of Flanders. The manoeuvre was a mistake. Maurice and Oldenbarnevelt both credited themselves with having realized the threat of Spinola's superior army in the east. The two assumptions are, on the face of it, incompatible. The truth is probably that at first Maurice would have preferred to march eastwards. Once he had crossed to Zeeland–Flanders, however, and was near Spinola's camp at Boeckhout, where there seemed to be no movement, he thought it unlikely that the Spanish forces would be transferred along the outer lines; he offered passive resistance when in June the States-General regretted their original decision and directed him eastwards. It had become most urgent when Spinola's main forces, having left Boeckhout unobserved, crossed the Rhine at Kaiserswerth. It is not known why Maurice stayed another month in Zeeland–Flanders, still arguing with the States-General, who finally countered that he was not 'best informed of the whole situation'. When he eventually moved with his main force it was too late to prevent the fall of Oldenzaal and Lingen.

After capturing Lingen Spinola moved back southwards on his tracks. Maurice followed him to Wesel, again falling out with the States-General. Disturbed by alarming reports from Brabant and Flanders they ordered Maurice to send reinforcements to that quarter, which he refused with forceful arguments. After Wachtendonck and Cracau had also fallen into enemy hands – Rheinberg, now entirely isolated, was saved up for a later campaign –

[1] It was alleged in a pamphlet that he had one of his favourites warn his friends in Antwerp to be on their guard, as His Excellency and the States-General were to attack the town. There is no substance whatsoever in this accusation.

Maurice returned to The Hague on 2 December, irritated at the opposition that he considered he had been shown again during the year by the States and Oldenbarnevelt himself.

December was, as usual, mainly devoted to the discussion of ways and means. Things were deteriorating and Oldenbarnevelt met with hardly less opposition to his efforts to improve the financial position than Alva had to his imposition of the Tenth Penny.

All kinds of circumstances had increased war expenditure since the Peace of Vervins, while regular revenue had diminished. This was largely due to the almost complete evaporation of convoy taxes and *licenten*, so that the admiralties could no longer be self-supporting and needed heavy subsidies from the exchequer.

The greatest expenditure had been on the expedition to Dunkirk and the three years' defence of Ostend, which swallowed up a fortune. In addition the capture of territory in the east and later of Zeeland–Flanders had lengthened the frontiers, requiring considerable fortification. Higher contributions by Gelderland and Overijsel did not counterbalance it. The severe outbreak of plague in 1602 had caused great economic damage. This and other factors made it extremely difficult for Friesland and Zeeland to raise their quota of the mounting war expenditure, of which interest on former loans and annuities amounted to 350,000 guilders annually. After long negotiations Zeeland's quota was reduced from 16% to 14%, mainly at the expense of Holland's share. Tax increases were therefore needed in this province and a great deal of Oldenbarnevelt's energy was absorbed in the first few years of the seventeenth century to achieving the necessary unanimity among the nineteen voting members, with their different interests. Again and again he proposed suspension of the unanimity ruling for financial matters, as had been done before in emergencies. It was refused: each time the deputies returned home full of good intentions to induce their towns to fall in with the majority. But their choice had to remain free and was usually adverse. Time and again the States of Holland rose after rejecting all, or practically all Oldenbarnevelt's tax proposals. The result was of course that the burden of debt mounted, notwithstanding warnings from the nobility, whose spokesman Oldenbarnevelt was. In 1606 the States-General were in debt to the tune of three and a half million and the States of Holland probably still further.

Matters were made worse by an evil for which Oldenbarnevelt was largely responsible: an inadequate check on the collectors of taxes. The sureties these men had to deposit, already low in proportion to the enormous sums passing through their hands, were sometimes inadequately enforced. The old-boy network, later to injure the reputation of Holland's oligarchs, was already in evidence. The failure of the Rotterdam receiver, Oldenbarnevelt's old friend Esaias de Lint, in 1602, was preceded or followed by that of the collectors of Dordrecht, Leiden, Gouda and Gorcum, and the crowning disgrace was the bankruptcy of the receiver-general of Holland, Cornelis van Mierop, in 1612.

At the beginning of 1604 Oldenbarnevelt decided to ask three bodies – The Hoge Raad, the Hof van Holland and the Audit Office of Holland, for advice on the financial situation. In their recommendation, issued on 8 March 1604, they strongly condemned irresponsible loans. The unanimity rule on this subject would have to be strictly obeyed; expenditure had to be cut down level to the means for covering it. The best means of achieving this was offensive warfare; in case of need and the demand of greater expenditure on defence it was not to be voted till the necessary cover had been found.

Oldenbarnevelt wrote later in his autobiography that the nobles had considered this a good plan, but most of the towns had no relish for it, and His Excellency still less.

It cannot be said that these opponents were wrong. The recommendations by the three bodies were academic counsels of perfection. They regarded the burden of debt as the chief obstacle to sound financing. An attempt – by means naturally not stated – could be made to reduce war expenditure, but the redemption of debt was the whole of their remedy for monetary ills. How could this be done? First of all by the sale of annuities and the issue of instantly redeemable debentures, if necessary to be made obligatory for wealthier citizens. Then the revenue from ground-tax, which had been mortgaged to the towns, should be made available by ceding to the towns the yield of other taxes. A tax on annuities was recommended. Finally no new loans should be entered into. There was no room for mild measures, the recommendation concluded: 'they did not know where to find any buried treasure'.

François Francken, a judge in the Hoge Raad and a great theoretician, drafted this advice. When it was submitted to the States of Holland, Oldenbarnevelt pointed out that the country's troubles did not by any means all spring from the payment of interest; there were many others. Everyone knew that action should be adjusted to means, but the way things worked out in war on the one hand, and the constitution on the other, made it impossible in practice. With regard to taking the offensive, which Oldenbarnevelt was clearly pressing for, Maurice would not attempt it for good strategic reasons, either during the siege of Ostend or later, when Spinola's credit enabled the Spaniards steadily to put superior forces into the field.

This was all very fine, but if it was impossible to economize or collect higher taxes, and floating new loans was disastrous for state credit and the interest level, how was a sound financial situation to be attained? Oldenbarne-velt complained in July 1606 to Winwood that it was no longer possible to borrow or raise the interest, so that it was necessary 'to seek all artifices & to use sophistries and fallacies to keep them from despair . . . their wants being so great that they live from day to day'.[1] Oldenbarnevelt himself was often near the despair from which he kept others. The inland provinces had not been paying their grants for years. Their arrears had risen in 1606 to seven million in eight years. Drastic measures like those taken with Groningen[2] did not invite a repetition and national bankruptcy, with catastrophic results for the conduct of the war, seemed imminent.

The only consolation was that things did not seem any easier for the enemy from a financial point of view. Spinola left again for Spain at the end of the 1605 campaign to arrange the financial basis of the next one. At first his trip was not very successful. English sources informed Oldenbarnevelt that the English ambassador in Spain, Sir Charles Cornwallis, was greatly struck by the poor state not only of Spanish finances, but of their navy and adminis-tration in general. Nor were things any better in Belgium. Ostend had been more of a financial drain on the besiegers than on the besieged. The only hope was the arrival of the yearly treasure fleet. It would be Philip III's last chance of indirectly recapturing his paternal inheritance. Spinola realized during his second stay that the spirit had gone out of the King and his ministers, espe-cially his principal minister, Lerma, and although Spinola did everything to make the 1606 campaign a success, the cause of his leanings towards peace, soon to become apparent, can be traced to his disappointments from January to May 1606. For that was the time it took him to complete the financial acrobatics which involved him in so much personal risk. It only left time for half a summer of fighting. This benefited the defenders who, if driven into a corner, could rely on the approach of winter putting an end to fighting.

Owing to Spanish superiority in the field and the precarious financial situation, the Netherlands came to depend more and more on support from abroad, especially from France, which had been making itself responsible for the English subsidy for two and a half years. In the autumn of 1605 Henry calculated that he had nearly cleaned his slate with England by payment of the *tiers*. This meant a reduction of one-third in the subsidy from France. Both Aerssen and Buzanval were giving warnings about this and the latter complained that Oldenbarnevelt was now less candid with him. He wondered if it meant some secret understanding with Spain. Henry wanted an oral report on this subject from an unprejudiced diplomat. He thought Buzanval

---

[1] Salisbury Papers, 84/65/222.
[2] See pp. 239 ff.

had become too Dutchified, so he sent St-Aubin, the brother of his former minister Sancy, to the Netherlands to act as his informant.

The report made by this St-Aubin towards the end of December was unsatisfactory as far as a possible offensive in Flanders was concerned. After the fall of Oldenzaal and Lingen an attack by superior forces under Spinola might be directed at Friesland. It would have to be resisted, thus moving the theatre of war as far as possible from France. Henry was furious at the prospect, summoned Aerssen and gave him a good dressing-down. But he left the next year's subsidy standing at two million, being afraid of a possible capitulation, a subject on which Oldenbarnevelt had spoken evasively; he made it clear though that his wishes and interests must then be taken into account. Aerssen promised this with a great display of subservience, but in private he was jubilant: after all he had neatly avoided a reduction in the subsidy. Oldenbarnevelt was however to write eight years later, after a rupture between Aerssen and himself, that it was not Aerssen who had scored this gain but St-Aubin and Buzanval, both put up to it by Oldenbarnevelt in person. Aerssen clearly boasted too much, but Oldenbarnevelt was less than fair to him. Of course it was in fact the constant pressure to which Henry was subjected by all those *au fait* with conditions in the Netherlands that forced him to take the decision.

But how could Oldenbarnevelt give any guarantee that Aerssen's submissiveness was not a pretence and that the war was really going to be conducted according to Henry's ideas?

Bouillon had fortified the town of Sedan, on the Belgian frontier. He was obviously in league with the other side. If Henry found himself obliged to subdue him by force it might lead to a renewal of war with Spain. In that case the King had to be sure of his Netherlands ally, both with regard to possible peace and the use made of his subsidies. He therefore decided on another move in the direction of a kind of sovereignty, but changed circumstances since 1584 had made this idea chimerical. The provinces, and in particular Maurice and Oldenbarnevelt, would never bargain away the fruits of such a long struggle towards independence for a few millions from a Catholic monarch; his interests were running parallel with those of the Netherlands merchants now, but they certainly would not do so in the future. Aerssen knew this quite well, when the King and his advisers approached him on the subject. But he realized the prime necessity of keeping Henry in a good frame of mind and not discouraging him. It was after all Oldenbarnevelt, not his young representative, who had to deal with the matter, and it would take time. Meanwhile Henry might have cooled down and the matter could be dropped without giving him offence.

When therefore the French King proposed that Aerssen should go to the Netherlands and cautiously broach the subject of an offer of sovereignty, he did not refuse. At the dictation of Henry and his ministers he lent himself to the composition of a very curious memorandum to be shown to the leaders of the Republic. Actually in the form of a questionnaire to be filled in by Oldenbarnevelt, the memorandum by no means laid all the emphasis on sovereignty for Henry. Only five of the twenty-three questions were unambiguously addressed to it. Two others, concerning freedom of worship for Catholics and payment for Catholic clergy, could be considered in the Netherlands as an interference incompatible with their independence. The other questions related to the possibility of continuing the war without an increase of subsidy; that of open declaration of war by France or, on the contrary, of a peace through French mediation; and finally the question of Netherlands intervention in the dispute between the King and his subject, the Duke of Bouillon. This last request was the ostensible reason for Aerssen's journey, and it is the only subject mentioned in the States-General's resolution, passed at his proposal on 6 March 1606.

The memorandum was not seen except by Oldenbarnevelt, Maurice and two States-General deputies. They appear to have conferred only on the objectionable questions of sovereignty and religion, which were answered with a firm negative. Oldenbarnevelt wrote later that he had been very displeased at Aerssen's coming and had given him a severe reprimand. He accused the ambassador of having given Henry a taste for sovereignty, of consenting to freedom of worship and payment of papist clergy, and of having promised that even after an eventual conquest of Belgium, the Netherlands would maintain war taxation at the same level. Oldenbarnevelt obviously wrote these accusations with the memorandum Aerssen had brought with him by his side; writing eight years later in bitterness of spirit, Oldenbarnevelt must have thought that it was Aerssen's own work. In fact he had made no promises at all. He had used the tones of good diplomacy by flattering Henry with the assurance that the States would study his proposals (sympathetically). Oldenbarnevelt may have warned the young man of the dangers of raising hopes in such a way. He was certainly not seriously displeased. Aerssen's salary was raised on this occasion by 1,000 guilders a year; at the beginning of 1607 he repeated his tactics, as will be shown later, which he would never have dared to do if Oldenbarnevelt had taken a strong line with him in 1606.

When Aerssen returned to France, Henry had already forgotten his list of questions, just as Aerssen must have expected, only rather sooner. The campaign against Sedan was in full swing and Aerssen was just in time to carry out successfully, and with the help of Louise de Coligny, the order given him by the States to mediate. Spanish support for the rebellion had been neither sought nor given. It was therefore easy for the King to decide on a general pardon for Bouillon, in return for which the Duke had to allow the Sedan fortress to be occupied by the King's troops. In these circumstances the King did not desire a breach with Spain. On the other hand he realized the Hollanders were obliged to conduct a defensive war, in which Spinola and not Maurice would determine the battleground. Defensive war in particular needed a great deal of money, so the King decided to leave the questions of the subsidy and the sovereignty as they were. There were indeed some difficulties about payment in 1606, first because the short campaign against Sedan had used up all the available funds, and later because the King and his ministers could not refrain from expressing every grievance they nursed against their ally in terms of withholding the subsidy.

Meanwhile the summer campaign of 1606 had begun. Both sides were very late starters, to the annoyance of Henry, still dreaming of offensives and not grasping that it was the piecemeal payment of his assistance that caused the States' delay. On the enemy side it was caused by the late return of Spinola, who did not get back to Brussels till the end of May, so that it was July before he got under way by crossing the Rhine at Ruhrort, leaving the strongly defended Rheinberg in his rear.

His plan was to cross the IJsel with his main forces, while a strong detachment under Bucquoy was to force a crossing of the river Waal in the neighbourhood of Nijmegen. Maurice had the advantage of the inside lines and hoped to manage with much lesser numbers, even when Oldenbarnevelt urged him to concentrate all the troops available from Rheinberg and Flanders between Arnhem and Zutfen. Made nervous by the unfortunate campaign in the previous year, Oldenbarnevelt concerned himself with military detail[1] this summer more than ever before. Maurice took no more notice than was strictly necessary to avoid disputes, thus returning in this, his last campaign before the Truce, to the theme on which all his previous campaigns had been variations. Bucquoy was prevented from crossing the Waal and Spinola from crossing the IJsel, so that the first part of the campaign ended in August with the meagre gain for Spinola of two little towns in the eastern corner, Groenlo and Lochem. Spinola again transferred the theatre of war to the south, as in 1605, and Maurice followed him to Wesel to keep an eye on the siege of Rheinberg. The situation in Flanders in 1604 now repeated itself. Maurice remained idle at Wesel, which led to great 'scandal' in the States of

---

[1] The Resolutions on this subject for July and August 1606 cover no fewer than twenty-five pages of the printed edition.

Holland, the more so as the relief of Groenlo was foiled by Maurice's lethargy; he claimed that he wanted to wait for orders from The Hague.

The States-General resolved to send Oldenbarnevelt at the head of a committee of their deputies to Wesel in order to spur Maurice on to greater activity. The members took the necessary money with them. Oldenbarnevelt, whose mind was much occupied with the possibility of a revision of relations with Spain and France, would have been glad to be excused this mission; he said it did not accord with the promise made him in 1604, after one of his many threats to resign, that he was not to be sent on journeys abroad. The States-General must have held that the front where Maurice was engaged could not be regarded as 'abroad'. The mission was especially needed as Maurice's officers were spreading the tale that it was the States-General who had stopped an attempt to relieve Rheinberg.

Such rumours had to be suppressed, though there may have been something in them. Rheinberg was a distant outpost, devouring soldiers and money, and lines of communcation were difficult to maintain. The Netherlands could not risk a battle in the field owing to the inequality of numbers. There may also have been a more Machiavellian motive which Oldenbarnevelt hardly admitted even to himself. By this time he had come to the conclusion that peace was necessary for the Netherlands, if it could be obtained on the basis of the status quo; according to reliable sources this was what the Spaniards were about to offer. Naturally there would be much opposition to peace negotiations so much at variance with the views held during the last twenty years, and it would be all the stronger if the 1606 campaign ended with a victorious relief of Rheinberg. Such an idea may be regarded as treasonous and Oldenbarnevelt would have stoutly denied that he had ever entertained it. Let us say that he did not entertain it, but he had a look at it. The ultimate objective was certainly not treasonous, as in the event of peace the occupation of this town, in Cologne territory, was not a Netherlands interest.

However this may be, Oldenbarnevelt made no serious attempt to drive the unwilling Maurice into an offensive along the Rhine. Rheinberg capitulated on 1 October. Afterwards Spinola's troops began to mutiny as an indirect consequence of Netherlands naval action under Haultain, delaying the arrival of the treasure fleet and destroying Spinola's credit. Maurice thought he had a good chance of recapturing Groenlo. The States-General had left it entirely to Maurice whether he would undertake anything, a proof that mutual confidence had not been shaken by the fall of Rheinberg. Spinola managed to pacify his men, however, and advanced on Groenlo, whereupon Maurice abandoned the siege in the middle of November and returned to The Hague.

This was the end of the last campaign in the Eighty Years War with which Oldenbarnevelt was to be concerned, except for Maurice's and Spinola's bloodless manoeuvres in 1614, half-way through the Truce. Immediately after the conclusion of the 1606 campaign negotiations began leading to the arrangement of an armistice before the end of the winter interval. It is in these negotiations and those that followed, up till 1609, first about peace and then about a long truce, that Oldenbarnevelt reached the zenith of his career and the highest level of his genius.